lonely planet

Budapest

Steve Fallon

LONELY PLANET PUBLICATIONS
Melbourne • Oakland • London • Paris

Budapest
1st edition – August 2000

Published by
Lonely Planet Publications Pty Ltd A.C.N. 005 607 983
192 Burwood Rd, Hawthorn, Victoria 3122, Australia

Lonely Planet Offices
Australia PO Box 617, Hawthorn, Victoria 3122
USA 150 Linden St, Oakland, CA 94607
UK 10a Spring Place, London NW5 3BH
France 1 rue du Dahomey, 75011 Paris

Photographs
Many of the images in this guide are available for licensing from
Lonely Planet Images.
email: lpi@lonelyplanet.com.au

Front cover photograph
Heroes' Square (Tomas Muscionico, PNI Images)

ISBN 1 86450 118 9

Printed by Colorcraft Ltd, Hong Kong

Contents – Text

PLACES TO EAT 127

ENTERTAINMENT 146

SHOPPING 153

EXCURSIONS 159

LANGUAGE 169

GLOSSARY 175

ALTERNATIVE PLACE NAMES 178

INDEX 189

METRIC CONVERSION inside back cover

Contents – Maps

FACTS ABOUT BUDAPEST

PLACES TO EAT

COLOUR MAP SECTION   see back pages

The Author

Steve Fallon

Born in Boston, Massachusetts, Steve worked an assortment of menial but character-building – so his parents told him – jobs as a youngster to finance trips to Europe and South America. He graduated from Georgetown University in 1975 with a Bachelor of Science in modern languages and then taught English at the University of Silesia near Katowice in Poland. After he had worked for several years for a Gannett newspaper and obtained a master's degree in journalism, his fascination with the 'new' Asia took him to Hong Kong, where he lived and worked for 13 years for a variety of publications and in television and owned and ran a travel bookshop. Steve lived in Budapest for 2½ years from where he wrote *Hungary* and *Slovenia* before moving to London in 1994. He has written or contributed to a number of other Lonely Planet titles.

FROM THE AUTHOR

Once again this one is for Michael Rothschild, still the point on any map of any scale, physical and political. Friends in Budapest who were helpful included Ildikó Nagy Moran and Csaba & Jackie Lengyel de Bagota. Special thanks to Jane Leuenberger for her hospitality, warmth and good chat. Much appreciated. Tourinform remains the most authoritative and knowledgable source of information on Budapest; *köszönöm szépen* to staff on Sütő utca. Péter Lengyel pointed out the correct wine roads to follow and I am very grateful (though a bit worse for wear). Dr Zsuzsa Medgyes of M&G Marketing in Budapest showed me the way again and again. Thanks to Judy Finn for assisting with some of the research.

This Book

Some of the text and illustrative material from the third edition of *Hungary* has been used in this book.

From the Publisher
This first edition of *Budapest* was produced in Lonely Planet's Melbourne office and coordinated by Carolyn Bain (editorial) and Csanád Csutoros (mapping and design).

Editing and proofing assistance was provided by Susie Ashworth, Yvonne Byron and Darren O'Connell; mapping and design assistance by Birgit Jordan and Mark Griffiths.

Thanks to Quentin Frayne for laying out the language chapter, Fiona Croyden from LPI Images for assistance with images, Matt King for coordinating the illustrations, Tim Uden for assistance and Maria Vallianos for the cover.

Foreword

ABOUT LONELY PLANET GUIDEBOOKS

The story begins with a classic travel adventure: Tony and Maureen Wheeler's 1972 journey across Europe and Asia to Australia. Useful information about the overland trail did not exist at that time, so Tony and Maureen published the first Lonely Planet guidebook to meet a growing need.

From a kitchen table, then from a tiny office in Melbourne (Australia), Lonely Planet has become the largest independent travel publisher in the world, an international company with offices in Melbourne, Oakland (USA), London (UK) and Paris (France).

Today Lonely Planet guidebooks cover the globe. There is an ever-growing list of books and there's information in a variety of forms and media. Some things haven't changed. The main aim is still to help make it possible for adventurous travellers to get out there – to explore and better understand the world.

At Lonely Planet we believe travellers can make a positive contribution to the countries they visit – if they respect their host communities and spend their money wisely. Since 1986 a percentage of the income from each book has been donated to aid projects and human rights campaigns.

Updates Lonely Planet thoroughly updates each guidebook as often as possible. This usually means there are around two years between editions, although for more unusual or more stable destinations the gap can be longer. Check the imprint page (following the colour map at the beginning of the book) for publication dates.

Between editions up-to-date information is available in two free newsletters – the paper *Planet Talk* and email *Comet* (to subscribe, contact any Lonely Planet office) – and on our Web site at www.lonelyplanet.com. The *Upgrades* section of the Web site covers a number of important and volatile destinations and is regularly updated by Lonely Planet authors. *Scoop* covers news and current affairs relevant to travellers. And, lastly, the *Thorn Tree* bulletin board and *Postcards* section of the site carry unverified, but fascinating, reports from travellers.

Correspondence The process of creating new editions begins with the letters, postcards and emails received from travellers. This correspondence often includes suggestions, criticisms and comments about the current editions. Interesting excerpts are immediately passed on via newsletters and the Web site, and everything goes to our authors to be verified when they're researching on the road. We're keen to get more feedback from organisations or individuals who represent communities visited by travellers.

> Lonely Planet gathers information for everyone who's curious about the planet – and especially for those who explore it first-hand. Through guidebooks, phrasebooks, activity guides, maps, literature, newsletters, image library, TV series and Web site we act as an information exchange for a worldwide community of travellers.

6

Research Authors aim to gather sufficient practical information to enable travellers to make informed choices and to make the mechanics of a journey run smoothly. They also research historical and cultural background to help enrich the travel experience and allow travellers to understand and respond appropriately to cultural and environmental issues.

Authors don't stay in every hotel because that would mean spending a couple of months in each medium-sized city and, no, they don't eat at every restaurant because that would mean stretching belts beyond capacity. They do visit hotels and restaurants to check standards and prices, but feedback based on readers' direct experiences can be very helpful.

Many of our authors work undercover, others aren't so secretive. None of them accept freebies in exchange for positive write-ups. And none of our guidebooks contain any advertising.

Production Authors submit their raw manuscripts and maps to offices in Australia, USA, UK or France. Editors and cartographers – all experienced travellers themselves – then begin the process of assembling the pieces. When the book finally hits the shops, some things are already out of date, we start getting feedback from readers and the process begins again …

WARNING & REQUEST

Things change – prices go up, schedules change, good places go bad and bad places go bankrupt – nothing stays the same. So, if you find things better or worse, recently opened or long since closed, please tell us and help make the next edition even more accurate and useful. We genuinely value all the feedback we receive. Julie Young coordinates a well travelled team that reads and acknowledges every letter, postcard and email and ensures that every morsel of information finds its way to the appropriate authors, editors and cartographers for verification.

Everyone who writes to us will find their name in the next edition of the appropriate guidebook. They will also receive the latest issue of *Planet Talk*, our quarterly printed newsletter, or *Comet*, our monthly email newsletter. Subscriptions to both newsletters are free. The very best contributions will be rewarded with a free guidebook.

Excerpts from your correspondence may appear in new editions of Lonely Planet guidebooks, the Lonely Planet Web site, *Planet Talk* or *Comet*, so please let us know if you *don't* want your letter published or your name acknowledged.

Send all correspondence to the Lonely Planet office closest to you:

Australia: PO Box 617, Hawthorn, Victoria 3122
USA: 150 Linden St, Oakland, CA 94607
UK: 10A Spring Place, London NW5 3BH
France: 1 rue du Dahomey, 75011 Paris

Or email us at: talk2us@lonelyplanet.com.au

For news, views and updates see our Web site: www.lonelyplanet.com

HOW TO USE A LONELY PLANET GUIDEBOOK

The best way to use a Lonely Planet guidebook is any way you choose. At Lonely Planet we believe the most memorable travel experiences are often those that are unexpected, and the finest discoveries are those you make yourself. Guidebooks are not intended to be used as if they provide a detailed set of infallible instructions!

Contents All Lonely Planet guidebooks follow roughly the same format. The Facts about the Destination chapters or sections give background information ranging from history to weather. Facts for the Visitor gives practical information on issues like visas and health. Getting There & Away gives a brief starting point for researching travel to and from the destination. Getting Around gives an overview of the transport options when you arrive.

The peculiar demands of each destination determine how subsequent chapters are broken up, but some things remain constant. We always start with background, then proceed to sights, places to stay, places to eat, entertainment, getting there and away, and getting around information – in that order.

Heading Hierarchy Lonely Planet headings are used in a strict hierarchical structure that can be visualised as a set of Russian dolls. Each heading (and its following text) is encompassed by any preceding heading that is higher on the hierarchical ladder.

Entry Points We do not assume guidebooks will be read from beginning to end, but that people will dip into them. The traditional entry points are the list of contents and the index. In addition, however, some books have a complete list of maps and an index map illustrating map coverage.

There may also be a colour map that shows highlights. These highlights are dealt with in greater detail in the Facts for the Visitor chapter, along with planning questions and suggested itineraries. Each chapter covering a geographical region usually begins with a locator map and another list of highlights. Once you find something of interest in a list of highlights, turn to the index.

Maps Maps play a crucial role in Lonely Planet guidebooks and include a huge amount of information. A legend is printed on the back page. We seek to have complete consistency between maps and text, and to have every important place in the text captured on a map. Map key numbers usually start in the top left corner.

Although inclusion in a guidebook usually implies a recommendation we cannot list every good place. Exclusion does not necessarily imply criticism. In fact there are a number of reasons why we might exclude a place – sometimes it is simply inappropriate to encourage an influx of travellers.

Introduction

There is no other city in Hungary like Budapest. With upwards of two million inhabitants, the metropolis is home to one-fifth of the country's total population. Budapest is what urban planners call a hypertrophic city – the over-enlarged 'head' of a nation-state's 'body' – and the next biggest city (Debrecen) is barely a tenth of its size. As Hungary's *főváros* (main city or capital), Budapest is the administrative, business and cultural centre; virtually everything in Hungary starts, finishes or is currently taking place here.

But it's the beauty of Budapest that sets it apart from other cities in Hungary and many others in Eastern and Western Europe as well. Straddling a gentle curve in the mighty Danube River, the city is flanked by the Buda Hills on the west bank and what is essentially the start of the Great Plain to the east. Architecturally, it is a gem. Though the city may lack the Gothic and other medieval buildings so ubiquitous in, say, Prague, there is enough baroque, neoclassical and Art Nouveau architecture here to satisfy anyone.

Overall Budapest has a *fin-de-siècle* feel to it, for it was then, during the industrial boom and the capital's 'golden age', that most of what you see today was built. In some places, particularly along the Nagykörút (Big Ring Road) and up broad Andrássy út to the sprawling Városliget (City Park), Budapest's sobriquet – 'the Paris of Central Europe' – is well deserved. Nearly every building has some interesting or unusual detail, from Art Nouveau glazed tiles and neoclassical bas-reliefs to bullet holes and shrapnel scorings left over from WWII and the 1956 Uprising that still cry out in silent fury.

In fact, Budapest's scars are not very well hidden. Industrial and automobile pollution has exacerbated the decay, but in recent years the rebuilding and renovations have been nothing short of astonishing. Indeed, some people think the city is tidying itself up a bit too quickly. When I first moved to the city in the early 1990s a locally produced guidebook advised potential visitors to 'hurry up and come before Budapest turns into just another capital of just another nice social democratic European country' (or words to that effect). 'As if', I remember thinking in those 'Wild East' days of change and disappointment. 'As if…'

It's true that, in the process of reclaiming its well-deserved title of *világváros* (world-class city), Budapest has taken on all the baggage that such a process usually demands: organised crime, faceless modern architecture, a mobile phone at the ear of every 'suit', a McDonald's on every corner. Yet Budapest remains – and will always remain – Hungarian: exotic, sometimes inscrutable, often passionate, with its two feet firmly planted in Europe but with a glance every now and then eastward to the spawning grounds of its citizens.

Budapest is at its best in the spring and summer just after dusk when Castle Hill is bathed in a warm yellow light. Stroll along the Duna korzó (Danube Embankment) on the Pest side or across any of the bridges, past young couples embracing passionately. It's then that you'll feel the romance of a city that, despite all attempts both from within and without to destroy it, has never died.

It's a city that has given me much since our first chance meeting and when I sing a song of Budapest today it may be in a beautiful and expressive language that I once considered impenetrable, of a people I thought I'd never know, of an often sad but confident nation whose history seemed too complex ever to comprehend. There's no doubt that the 'Queen of the Danube' will offer you just as much as she has me.

Facts about Budapest

HISTORY

Strictly speaking, the story of Budapest begins in 1873 when hilly, residential Buda and historic Óbuda on the western bank of the Danube River merged with flat, industrial Pest on the east to form what was at first called Pest-Buda. But like everything here, it's not that simple.

Early Inhabitants

The Carpathian Basin, in the centre of which lies Budapest, has been populated for hundreds of thousands – perhaps millions – of years. Archaeological excavations carried out in 1999 at Rudabánya, some 220km north-east of Budapest, unearthed the skull of a female Rudapithecus, a prehistoric ancestor of humans who lived here some 10 million years ago. Bone fragments found at Vértesszőlős, some 70km to the northwest of the capital, in the 1960s and believed to be half a million years old suggest that Palaeolithic and later Neanderthal humans were attracted to the area by the warm-water springs and the abundance of reindeer, bears and mammoths.

During the Neolithic period (around 5000 BC), changes in the climate forced much of the indigenous wildlife to migrate northward. The domestication of animals and the first forms of agriculture appeared, as indeed they did in much of Europe.

Indo-European tribes from the Balkans stormed the Carpathian Basin from the south in horse-drawn wheeled carts in about 2000 BC, bringing with them copper tools and weapons. After the introduction of more durable bronze, forts were built and a military elite developed.

Over the next millennium, invaders from the west (Illyrians, Thracians) and east (Scythians) brought iron, but the metal was not in common use until the Celts arrived in the Carpathian Basin in about the 3rd century BC. They introduced glass and crafted some of the fine gold jewellery that can still be seen in the Hungarian National Museum.

They also built a settlement at Óbuda, which they called Ak Ink (Ample Water).

Around the beginning of the Christian era, the Romans conquered the area west of the Danube River and established the province of Pannonia, later divided into Pannonia Superior and Pannonia Inferior. Subsequent victories over the Celts extended their domination across the Tisza River as far as Dacia (now Romania). The Romans brought writing, viticulture and stone architecture, and at the end of the 1st century AD established Aquincum, a key military garrison and civilian town in today's Óbuda. Aquincum became the administrative seat of Pannonia Inferior in 106 AD and a fully fledged colony in 194. The proconsul's palace was built at Contra Aquincum, on a secure island in the Danube (today's Óbudai hajógyári-sziget).

The Great Migrations

The first of the so-called Great Migrations of nomadic peoples from Asia reached the eastern outposts of the Roman Empire in Dacia late in the 2nd century AD. Within two centuries, they were forced to flee Aquincum and the rest of Pannonia by the Huns, whose short-lived empire was established by Attila.

Following the death of Attila in 453, Germanic tribes such as the Ostrogoths, Longobards and Gepids occupied the region for the next century and a half until the Avars, a powerful Turkic people, gained control of the Carpathian Basin in the 6th century. They in turn were subdued by Charlemagne in 796 and converted to Christianity. By that time, the Carpathian Basin was virtually unpopulated except for scattered groups of Turkic and Germanic tribes on the plains and Slavs in the northern hills.

The Magyars & the Conquest

The origin of the Magyars, as the Hungarians call themselves, is a complicated issue, not in the least helped by the similarity – in

English at least – of the words 'Hun' and 'Hungary', which are *not* related. One thing is certain: Magyars are part of the Finno-Ugric group of peoples, who inhabited the forests somewhere between the middle Volga River and the Ural Mountains in western Siberia as early as 4000 BC.

By about 2000 BC, population growth had forced the Finnish-Estonian branch to move westward, ultimately reaching the Baltic Sea. The Ugrians moved from the south-eastern slopes of the Urals into the valleys of the region, and switched from hunting and fishing to farming and raising livestock, especially horses. Their equestrian skills proved useful half a millennium later when climatic changes brought drought, forcing them to move northward onto the steppes.

On the grasslands, the Ugrians turned to nomadic herding. After 500 BC, by which time the use of iron had become common among the tribes, a group moved westward to the area of Bashkiria in Central Asia. Here they lived among Persians and Bulgars and began referring to themselves as Magyars (from the Finno-Ugric words *mon*, 'to speak', and *er*, 'man').

After several centuries, another group split away and moved south to the Don River under the control of the Khazars. Here they lived among different groups under a tribal alliance called *onogur* (or '10 peoples'). This is the derivation of the word 'Hungary' in English and 'Ungarn' in German. Their last migration before the conquest of the Carpathian Basin brought them to what modern Hungarians call the Etelköz, the region between the Dnieper and lower Danube Rivers above the Black Sea.

Nomadic groups of Magyars probably reached the Carpathian Basin as early as the mid-8th century, acting as mercenaries for various armies. It is believed that while the men were away during one such campaign in about 889, a fierce people from the Asiatic steppe called the Pechenegs attacked the Etelköz settlements. Fearing a repeat attack, seven tribes under the leadership of Árpád – the *gyula* or chief military commander – struck out for the Carpathian

Basin. They crossed the Verecke Pass in today's Ukraine some time between 893 and 895. Within five years Árpád had established his seat on today's Csepel Island while his brother Kurszán was based in Óbuda; Buda and Pest were no more than small villages.

The Magyars met almost no resistance and, being very adroit at riding and shooting (a common Christian prayer during the Dark Ages was 'Save us, O Lord, from the arrows of the Hungarians'), they began plundering and pillaging, taking slaves and amassing booty. Their raids took them as far as Spain, northern Germany and southern Italy, but they were stopped by the German king Otto I at the battle of Augsburg in 955.

The defeat left the Magyar tribes in disarray and, like the Bohemian, Polish and Russian princes of the time, they had to choose between their more powerful neighbours – Byzantium to the south and east or the Holy Roman Empire to the west – to form an alliance. Individual Magyar chieftains began acting independently but, in 973, Prince Géza, the great-grandson of Árpád, asked the Holy Roman emperor Otto II to send Catholic missionaries to Hungary. Géza was baptised at his capital, Esztergom, some 46km upriver from Budapest, as was his son Vajk, who took the Christian name Stephen (István). When Géza died, Stephen ruled as prince, but three years later, on Christmas Day in 1000, he was crowned 'Christian King' Stephen I with a crown sent from Rome by Pope Sylvester II. Hungary the kingdom – and the nation – was born.

King Stephen I & the Árpád Dynasty

Stephen ruthlessly set about consolidating royal authority by expropriating the land of the clan chieftains and establishing a system of counties (*megye*) protected by fortified castles (*vár*) from his seat at Székesfehérvár, 66km south-west of Budapest. Much land was transferred to loyal (mostly Germanic) knights, and the crown began minting coins.

Shrewdly, Stephen sought the support of the church throughout and, to hasten the conversion of the populace, he ordered one in every 10 villages to build a church. He also established 10 episcopates, two of which were made archbishoprics (Kalocsa and Esztergom). Monasteries staffed by foreign scholars were set up around the country. By the time of Stephen's death in 1038 (he was later canonised St Stephen), Hungary was a nascent Christian nation, increasingly multiethnic and westward-looking.

The next two and a half centuries – the reign of the House of Árpád – would test the new kingdom to the limit. The period was one of relentless struggles between rival pretenders to the throne, which weakened the young nation's defences against its powerful neighbours. There was a brief hiatus under King Ladislas I (László; ruled 1077-95), who fended off attacks from Byzantium, and under his successor Koloman the Bookish (Könyves Kálmán), who encouraged literature, art and the writing of chronicles until his death in 1116.

Tension flared again when the Byzantine emperor made a grab for Hungary's provinces in Dalmatia and Croatia, which it had attached by the early 12th century. But he was stopped by Béla III, a powerful ruler from 1173 to 1196 who had a permanent residence built at Esztergom (then an alternative royal seat to Székesfehérvár) but was headquartered at Óbuda. Béla's son, Andrew II (András; ruled 1205-35), however, weakened the crown when he gave in to local barons' demands for more land in order to fund his crusades. This led to the Golden Bull, a kind of Magna Carta signed at Székesfehérvár in 1222, which limited some of the king's powers in favour of the nobility.

When Béla IV (ruled 1235-70) tried to regain the estates, the barons were able to oppose him on equal terms. Fearing Mongol expansion and realising he could not count on local help, Béla looked to the west and brought in German and Slovak settlers. His efforts were in vain. In 1241 the Mongols raced through the country, plundering and burning Pest to the ground and occupying Óbuda.

To rebuild the country as quickly as possible after the Mongol retreat, Béla again invited Germans and Saxons to settle here. He also built a castle at Buda and proclaimed Pest a municipality by royal charter, bestowing civic rights on the citizens of both towns in 1244 and 1255; another century would go by before Óbuda's citizens won the same rights. All three began to develop into major towns.

But Béla did not always play his cards right. In a bid to appease the lesser nobility, he handed over large tracts of land to the barons. This enhanced their position and bids for more independence even further. At the time of Béla's death in the late 13th century, anarchy ruled. The Árpád line died out with the death of the heirless Andrew III in 1301.

Medieval Budapest

The struggle for the Hungarian throne after the death of Andrew III involved several European dynasties, but it was Charles

Robert (Károly Róbert) of the French House of Anjou who finally won out (with the pope's blessing) in 1307 and ruled until 1342 from a palace he had built at Visegrád. Buda would not play a leading role in Hungarian history for another 50 years, but after that it would never look back.

Under Charles Robert's son and successor, Louis the Great (Nagy Lajos; ruled 1342-82), Hungary returned to a policy of conquest. A brilliant military strategist, Louis acquired territory in the Balkans as far as Dalmatia and, through an alliance, as far north as Poland. But his successes were short-lived and the menace of the Ottoman Turks had begun.

As Louis had sired no sons, one of his daughters, Mary, succeeded him. This was deemed unacceptable by the barons, who rose up against the 'petticoat throne'. Within a short time, Mary's husband, Sigismund (Zsigmond; ruled 1387-1437) of Luxembourg, was crowned king. Sigismund's long reign brought peace at home, and there was a great flowering of Gothic art and architecture. Sigismund enlarged the Royal Palace, founded a university at Óbuda (1389) and oversaw the construction of the first pontoon bridge over the Danube. But despite these advances and his enthronement as Holy Roman emperor in 1433, he was unable to stop the march of the Turks up through the Balkans.

A Transylvanian general of Romanian origin, János Hunyadi began his career at the court of Sigismund. When Sigismund's successor, Vladislav I (Úlászló) of the Polish Jagiellon dynasty, was killed fighting the Turks at Varna in 1444, Hunyadi acted as regent. His victory over the Turks at Belgrade in 1456 checked the Ottoman advance into Hungary for 70 years and assured the coronation of his son Matthias (Mátyás), the greatest ruler of medieval Hungary.

Matthias, called 'the Raven' (Corvinus) from his coat of arms, ruled from 1458 to 1490. Wisely, he maintained a mercenary force through taxation of the nobility, and this 'Black Army' conquered Moravia, Bohemia and even parts of Austria. Not only did Matthias Corvinus make Hungary one of

Central Europe's leading powers, but under his rule Buda enjoyed something of a golden age and for the first time became the focus of the nation. His second wife, the Neapolitan queen Beatrice, brought artisans from Italy who completely rebuilt and extended the palace; the beauty and sheer size of the residence astonished visitors and the palace's royal library became a major cultural and artistic centre of Renaissance Europe.

But while Matthias busied himself with centralising power for the crown, he ignored the growing Turkish threat. His successor Vladislav II (Úlászló) was unable to maintain even royal authority as the members of the diet (assembly), which met to approve royal decrees, squandered royal funds, sold off the royal library and expropriated land. In 1514, what had begun as a crusade organised by the power-hungry archbishop of Esztergom, Tamás Bakócz, turned into uprising against the landlords by peasants who rallied under their leader, György Dózsa, near Pest.

The revolt was brutally repressed, some 70,000 peasants were tortured and executed, and Dózsa himself was fried alive on a red-hot iron throne. The retrograde Tripartitum Law that followed in 1522 codified the rights and privileges of the barons and nobles and reduced the peasants to perpetual serfdom. By the time Louis II (Lajos) took the throne in 1516 at the tender age of nine, he couldn't rely on either side.

The Battle of Mohács & Turkish Occupation

The defeat of Louis' ragtag army by the Ottoman Turks at Mohács in 1526 is a watershed in Hungarian history. On the battlefield near this small town in Southern Transdanubia, some 195km south of Budapest, a relatively prosperous and independent medieval Hungary died, sending the nation into a tailspin of partition, foreign domination and despair that can still be felt today.

It would be unfair to put all the blame on the weak and indecisive boy-king Louis or on his commander-in-chief Pál Tomori, the archbishop of Kalocsa. Bickering among the nobility and the brutal crackdown of the

Kings, Saints, Strong Men & Premiers

The following is a list of the most important monarchs, rulers, dictators and leaders in Hungarian history. Names are given in English, with the Magyar equivalents in brackets. The dates refer to their reigns or terms of office.

Árpád Dynasty

Árpád	886-907
Géza	972-997
Stephen I (István)	1000-38
Ladislas I (László)	1077-95
Koloman (Könyves Kálmán)	1095-1116
Béla III	1173-96
Andrew II (András or Endre)	1205-35
Béla IV	1235-70
Andrew III	1290-1301

Mixed Dynasties

Charles Robert (Károly Róbert)	1307-42
Louis the Great (Nagy Lajos)	1342-82
Mary (Mária)	1383-87
Sigismund (Zsigmond)	1387-1437
János Hunyadi (regent)	1445-56
Matthias (Mátyás) Corvinus	1458-90
Vladislav II (Úlászló)	1490-1516
Louis II (Lajos)	1516-26
John Szapolyai (Zápolyai János)	1526-40

Habsburg Dynasty

Ferdinand I (Ferdinánd)	1526-64
Maximilian II (Miksa)	1564-76
Leopold I (Lipót)	1655-1705
Maria Theresa (Mária Terézia)	1740-80
Joseph II (József)	1780-90
Ferdinand V	1835-48
Franz Joseph (Ferenc József)	1848-1916
Charles IV (Károly)	1916-18

Political Leaders

Mihály Károlyi	1919
Béla Kun	1919
Miklós Horthy (regent)	1920-44
Ferenc Szálasi	1944-45
Mátyás Rákosi	1947-56
János Kádár	1956-88
Károly Grósz	1988-90
József Antall	1990-93
Péter Boross	1993-94
Gyula Horn	1994-98
Viktor Orbán	1998-

Dózsa uprising more than a decade earlier had severely weakened Hungary's military power, and there was virtually nothing left in the royal coffers. By 1526, the Ottoman sultan Suleiman the Magnificent had taken much of the Balkans, including Belgrade, and was poised to march on Buda with a force of 80,000 men.

Unable – or unwilling – to wait for reinforcements from Transylvania under the command of his rival John Szapolyai (Zápolyai János), Louis rushed from Buda with a motley army of 25,000 men of mixed nationalities to battle the Turks and was soundly thrashed in less than two hours. Along with bishops, nobles and an estimated 20,000 soldiers, the king himself was killed – crushed by his horse while trying to retreat across a stream.

The Turks then turned north, sacking and burning Buda before retreating. John Szapolyai, who had sat out the battle in the castle at Tokaj, was crowned king three months later but, despite grovelling before the Turks, he was never able to exploit the power he had sought so madly. Greed, self-interest and ambition had led Hungary to defeat itself.

After the Turks returned and took Buda for good in 1541, Hungary was divided into three parts. The central part, with Buda as its capital, went to the Turks while parts of Transdanubia and what is now Slovakia were governed by the Austrian House of Habsburg and assisted by the Hungarian nobility based at Bratislava (Pozsony in Hungarian). The principality of Transylvania east of the Tisza River prospered as a vassal state of the Ottoman Empire. It was a division that would remain in place for more than 150 years.

The Turkish occupation was marked by constant fighting among the three divisions: Catholic 'Royal Hungary' was pitted against not only the Turks but the Protestant Transylvanian princes. Although Habsburg Hungary enjoyed something of a cultural renaissance during this period, the Turkish-occupied central part and Buda itself suffered greatly, with many people fleeing the town to Pest, where some churches remained. The Turks did little building in Buda apart from a few bathhouses, dervish monasteries and tombs; for the most part, they converted churches into mosques and used existing public buildings for administration.

Turkish power began to wane in the 17th century, and with the help of the Polish army, Austrian and Hungarian forces liberated Buda in 1686. An imperial army under Eugene of Savoy wiped out the last Turkish army in Hungary at the Battle of Zenta (now Senta in Yugoslavia) 13 years later.

Habsburg Rule

The expulsion of the Turks did not result in a free and independent Hungary. Buda and the rest of the country were under military occupation and governed from Bratislava, and the policies of the Catholic Habsburgs' Counter-Reformation and heavy taxation further alienated the nobility. In 1703, the Transylvanian prince Ferenc Rákóczi II assembled an army of *kuruc* forces (anti-Habsburg mercenaries) against the Austrians. The war dragged on for eight years, during which time the rebels 'deposed' the Habsburgs as the rulers of Hungary. But superior imperial forces and lack of funds forced the kuruc forces to negotiate a separate peace with Vienna behind Rákóczi's back. The 1703-11 War of Independence had failed, but Rákóczi was the first leader to unite Hungarians against the Habsburgs.

Though the compromise had brought the fighting to an end, Hungary was now a mere province of the Habsburg Empire. Its main cities – Buda, Óbuda and Pest – counted a total of some 12,200 people. With the ascension of Maria Theresa to the throne in 1740, the Hungarian nobility pledged their 'lives and blood' to her at the diet in Bratislava in exchange for concessions. Thus began the period of enlightened absolutism that would continue under the rule of

her son, the 'hatted king' (so-called as he was never crowned in Hungary) Joseph II, who ruled for a decade from 1780.

Under the reigns of Maria Theresa and Joseph, Hungary took great steps forward economically and culturally but, at the same time, the first real steps toward integration with Austria began. The depopulated areas in the east and south were settled by Romanians and Serbs while German Swabians went to Transdanubia. Buda effectively became the German-speaking town of Ofen and the first German newspaper was published there in 1730. Pest, fuelled by the grain and livestock trades, began to develop outside the city walls. In 1749 the foundations for a new palace were laid in Buda, the university was moved from Nagyszombat (now Trnava in Slovakia) to Buda in 1777 and six years later Joseph made Buda the nation's administrative centre.

Joseph's attempts to modernise society by dissolving the all-powerful (and corrupt) religious orders, abolishing serfdom and replacing 'neutral' Latin with German as the official language of state administration were opposed by the Hungarian nobility, and the king rescinded most of these orders on his deathbed.

Dissenting voices could still be heard, and the ideals of the French Revolution of 1789 began to take root in certain intellectual circles in Hungary. In 1795 Ignác Martonovics, a former Franciscan priest, and six other pro-republican Jacobins were beheaded at Vérmező (Blood Meadow) in Buda for plotting against the crown.

By 1800, Pest (population 30,000) was the nation's most important commercial centre while Buda, with 24,000 people, remained a royal garrison town and developed under the eye of the monarch. But 90% of the national population worked the land, and it was primarily through agriculture that modernisation would come to Hungary.

Liberalism and social reform found their greatest supporters among certain members of the aristocracy in Pest. A prime example was Count István Széchenyi (1791-1860), a true Renaissance man (see the boxed text 'The Greatest Hungarian') who advocated

The Greatest Hungarian

The contributions Count István Széchenyi made to Hungary were enormous and extremely varied. In his seminal 1830 work *Hitel* (meaning 'credit' and based on *hit*, or 'trust'), he advocated sweeping economic reforms and the abolition of serfdom (he himself had distributed the bulk of his property to landless peasants two years earlier). The Chain Bridge, the design of which Széchenyi helped push through Parliament, was the first link between Buda and Pest and for the first time everyone, nobles included, had to pay a toll.

Széchenyi was instrumental in straightening the serpentine Tisza River, which rescued half of Hungary's arable land from flooding and erosion, and his work made the Danube navigable as far as the Iron Gates in Romania. He arranged the financing for Hungary's first railway lines (from Budapest north and east to Vác and Szolnok and west to what is now Wiener Neustadt in Austria) and launched the first steam transport on the Danube and Lake Balaton. A lover of all things English, Széchenyi got the upper classes interested in horse racing with the express purpose of improving breeding stock for farming. A large financial contribution made by Széchenyi led to the establishment of the prestigious Academy of Sciences.

Széchenyi joined Lajos Batthyány's revolutionary government in 1848, but political squabbling and open conflict with Vienna caused him to lose control and he suffered a nervous breakdown. Despite a decade of convalescence in an asylum, Széchenyi never fully recovered and tragically he took his own life in 1860.

For all his accomplishments, Széchenyi's contemporary and fellow reformer, Lajos Kossuth, called him 'the greatest Hungarian'. The dynamic but troubled visionary retains that accolade to this day.

regulation of the Tisza and Danube Rivers as much for commerce and irrigation as for safety; the devastating Danube flood of 1838 had taken a heavy toll, with more than half the homes in Pest washed away.

The proponents of gradual reform were quickly superseded, however, by a more radical faction demanding more immediate action. The group included such men as Miklós Wesselényi, Ferenc Deák and the poet Ferenc Kölcsey, but the predominant figure was Lajos Kossuth (1802-94). It was this dynamic lawyer and journalist who would lead Hungary to its greatest ever confrontation with the Habsburgs.

The 1848-49 War of Independence

The Habsburg Empire began to weaken as Hungarian nationalism increased early in the 19th century. The Hungarians, suspicious of Napoleon's policies, ignored French appeals to revolt against Vienna, and certain reforms were introduced: the replacement of Latin, the official language of administration, with Magyar; a law allowing serfs alternative means of discharging their feudal obligations of service; and increased Hungarian representation in the Council of State.

The reforms carried out were too limited and far too late, however, and the diet became more defiant in its dealings with the crown. At the same time, the wave of revolution sweeping Europe spurred on the more radical faction. On 3 March 1848, Kossuth made a fiery speech in parliament demanding an end to feudalism. On 15 March, a group calling itself the Youth of March led by the poet Sándor Petőfi, who read out his poem *Nemzeti Dal* (National Song) on the steps of the national museum, took to the streets of Pest to press for radical reforms and even revolution. The event is still commemorated as National Day.

The frightened government in Vienna quickly approved plans for a new Hungarian ministry responsible to the diet to be led by the liberal count Lajos Batthyány and to include Deák, Kossuth and Széchenyi. The Habsburgs also reluctantly agreed to abolish

the abolition of serfdom and returned much of his own land to the peasantry, cleverly promoted horse racing among the upper classes in order to improve breeding stock for use in agriculture and oversaw the serfdom and proclaim equality under the law. But the diet voted to raise a local army and Habsburg patience began to wear very thin.

In September, Habsburg forces under the governor of Croatia, Josip Jelačić, launched an attack on Hungary and Batthyány's government was dissolved. Pest and Buda fell to the Austrian army; the Hungarians hastily formed a national defence commission and moved the government seat to Debrecen, where Kossuth was elected leader. In April 1849, the parliament declared Hungary's full independence and the 'dethronement' of the Habsburgs for the second time. Rebel forces besieged Buda in May.

The new Habsburg emperor, Franz Joseph (1848-1916), was nothing like his feeble-minded predecessor, Ferdinand V, and quickly took action. He sought the assistance of Russian Tsar Nicholas I, who obliged with 200,000 troops. Support for the revolution was already crumbling, however, particularly in areas of mixed population where the Magyars were seen as oppressors. Weak and outnumbered, the rebel troops had been defeated by the summer of 1849.

A series of brutal reprisals ensued. Batthyány and 13 of his generals were executed (the so-called Martyrs of Arad), and Kossuth went into exile in Turkey. (Petőfi had been killed in battle.) Habsburg troops then went around the country systematically blowing up castles and fortifications lest they be used by resurgent rebels. What little of medieval Buda and Pest that had remained after the Turks and the 1703-11 War of Independence was now reduced to rubble.

The Dual Monarchy

Hungary was again merged into the Habsburg Empire as a conquered province and 'neo-absolutism' was the order of the day. Hungarian prisoners were forced to build the Citadella atop Gellért Hill to 'defend' the city from further insurrection, but by the time it was ready in 1851 the political climate had changed. Passive resistance among Hungarians and disastrous military defeats for the Habsburgs in 1859 and 1865 pushed Franz Joseph to the negotiating table with liberal Hungarians under Deák's leadership.

The result was the Compromise of 1867 (*Ausgleich* in German, which actually means 'balance' or 'reconciliation'), which created the Dual Monarchy of Austria (the empire) and Hungary (the kingdom). It was a federated state of two parliaments and two capitals – Vienna and Budapest (the city that would be incorporated six years later when Buda, Pest and Óbuda united). Only defence, foreign relations and customs were shared. Hungary was even allowed to raise a small army.

This 'Age of Dualism' would carry on until 1918 and spark an economic, cultural and intellectual rebirth in Budapest – a 'golden age' that the city has yet to see again. Trade and industry boomed, factories were established and the composers Franz (Ferenc) Liszt and Ferenc Erkel were making beautiful music. The middle class, dominated by Germans and Jews in Pest, burgeoned, and the capital entered into a frenzy of building.

Much of what you see in Budapest today – from the grand boulevards and their Eclectic-style apartment blocks to the Parliament building, Műcsarnok and Matthias Church in the Castle District – was built at this time. The apex of this *belle époque* was the six-month exhibition in 1896 in City Park celebrating the millennium of the Magyar conquest (*honfoglalás*) of the Carpathian Basin. A small replica of Vajdahunyad Castle in Transylvania, but with Gothic, Romanesque and baroque wings and additions to reflect architectural styles from all over Hungary, was built to house the exhibits (it now houses the Agricultural Museum). Some four million visitors from Hungary and abroad were transported to the fairground on Continental Europe's first underground railway (now the M1 or little yellow line). By the turn of the 20th century the population of the 'new' capital jumped from about 280,000 at the time of the Compromise to three-quarters of a million, and Budapest was Europe's sixth-largest city.

But all was not well in the capital. The city-based working class had almost no rights – and the situation in the countryside remained as dire as it was in the Middle

Ages. Minorities under Hungarian control – Czechs, Slovaks, Croatians and Romanians – were under increased pressure to 'Magyarise' and viewed their new rulers as oppressors. Increasingly they worked to dismember the empire.

WWI & the Republic of Councils

In July 1914, a month to the day after the assassination of Archduke Franz Ferdinand, the heir to the Habsburg throne, by a Bosnian Serb in Sarajevo, the Dual Monarchy entered WWI allied with the German Empire. The result was disastrous, with heavy destruction and hundreds of thousands killed on the Russian and Italian fronts. At the Armistice in 1918 the fate of the Dual Monarchy (and Hungary as a multinational kingdom) was sealed.

A republic under the leadership of Count Mihály Károlyi was set up in Budapest immediately after the war, and the Habsburg monarchy was dethroned for the third and final time. But the fledgling republic would not last long. Widespread destitution, the occupation of Hungary by the Allies, and the success of the Bolshevik Revolution in Russia had radicalised much of the Budapest working class.

In March 1919 a group of Hungarian communists under Béla Kun seized power. The so-called Republic of Councils (*Tanácsköztársaság*) set out to nationalise industry and private property and build a fairer society, but mass opposition to the regime unleashed a reign of 'red terror' in Budapest and around the country. In August Romanian troops occupied the capital and Kun and his comrades (including Minister of Culture Béla Lugosi) fled to Vienna. The Romanians camped out at Oktogon, taking whatever they wanted when they wanted it, and left the city in November – just ahead of Admiral Miklós Horthy, the hero of the Battle of Rijeka, mounted on a white stallion and leading 25,000 Hungarian troops into what he called the *bűnös város* (sinful city).

The Horthy Years & WWII

In Hungary's first-ever secret-ballot election (January 1920), parliament chose a kingdom as the form of state and – lacking a king – elected Admiral Horthy as its regent, who would remain so until the latter days of WWII. The arrangement confused even US President Franklin D Roosevelt in the early days of the war. After being briefed by an aide on the government and leadership of Hungary, he reportedly said: 'Let me see if I understand you right: Hungary is a kingdom without a king run by a regent who's an admiral without a navy?'

Horthy embarked on a 'white terror' – every bit as brutal as the red one of Béla Kun – that attacked communists, social democrats and Jews for their roles in supporting the Republic of Councils. As the regime was consolidated, it showed itself to be extremely rightist and conservative, advocating the status quo and 'traditional values' – family, state, religion. Though the country had the remnants of a parliamentary system, Horthy was all-powerful, and very few reforms were enacted. On the contrary, the lot of the working class and the peasantry worsened.

One thing everyone agreed on was that the return of the territories lost in the Treaty of Trianon (see the boxed text 'Trianon: A Seven-Letter Word') was essential for national development. Budapest was swollen with ethnic Hungarian refugees from Romania, Czechoslovakia and the Kingdom of Serbs, Croats and Slovenes, unemployment raged and the economy was at a standstill. Hungary obviously could not count on the victors – France, Britain and the USA – to help recoup its land; instead, it sought help from the fascist governments of Germany and Italy. Hungary's move to the right intensified throughout the 1930s, though it remained silent when WWII broke out in September 1939.

Horthy hoped an alliance would not mean actually having to enter the war but, after recovering northern Transylvania and part of Croatia with Germany's assistance, he was forced to join the Axis in June 1941. The war was as disastrous for Hungary as the 1914-18 one had been, and hundreds of thousands of Hungarian troops died while retreating from Stalingrad, where they'd been used as cannon fodder. Realising too

Trianon: A Seven-Letter Word

In June 1920, scarcely a year and a half after the Armistice was signed ending WWI, the victorious Allies drew up a postwar settlement under the Treaty of Trianon that enlarged some countries, truncated others and created several 'successor states'. As one of the defeated enemy nations and with large numbers of minorities clamouring for independence within its borders, Hungary stood to lose more than most. And it certainly did. Hungary was reduced to 40% of its historical size and, while it was now largely a uniform, homogeneous nation-state, for millions of ethnic Hungarians in Romania, Yugoslavia and Czechoslovakia, the tables had been turned: they were now in the minority.

'Trianon' became the singularly most hated word in Hungary, and the *diktátum* is often reviled today as if it were imposed on the nation yesterday. Many of the problems it created remain to this day, and it has coloured Hungary's relations with its neighbours for four score years.

late that his country was again on the losing side, Horthy began negotiating a separate peace with the Allies.

The result was the total occupation of Hungary by the German army in March 1944, with Adolf Eichmann based in the Buda Hills and the Wehrmacht billeted in the Astoria hotel. Horthy was kidnapped and deported to Germany and Ferenc Szálasi, the deranged leader of the pro-Nazi Arrow Cross Party, was installed as leader. (Horthy would later find exile in Portugal, where he died in 1957. Despite some public outcry, his body was returned to Hungary in September 1993 and reburied in the family plot at Kenderes, east of Szolnok.)

The Arrow Cross moved quickly to quash any opposition, and thousands of liberal politicians and labour leaders were arrested. At the same time, its puppet government introduced anti-Jewish legislation similar to that in Germany, and Jews, relatively safe under Horthy, were rounded up into ghettos by Hungarian Nazis. In the summer of 1944,

less than a year before the war's end, some 400,000 Jewish men, women and children were deported to Auschwitz and other labour camps, where they succumbed to disease, starved or were savagely murdered by the German fascists and their henchmen. Those Jews who did survive owed their lives to Raoul Wallenberg, a Budapest-based Swedish diplomat (see the boxed text 'Raoul Wallenberg, Righteous Gentile' in the Things to See & Do chapter).

Budapest now became an international battleground for the first time since the Turkish occupation, and bombs began falling everywhere but particularly in Angyalföld and Zugló, where there were munitions factories. The resistance movement drew support from many sides, including the communists, and by Christmas 1944 the Soviet army had surrounded Budapest. When the Germans and Hungarian Nazis rejected a settlement, the siege of the capital began. By the time the German war machine had surrendered in April 1945, many of Budapest's homes, historical buildings and churches had been destroyed. The vindictive Germans even blew up Buda Castle and every bridge spanning the Danube while retreating.

The People's Republic

When free elections were held in November 1945, the Independent Smallholders Party received 57% of the vote. But Soviet political officers, backed by the occupying Soviet army, forced three other parties – including the Social Democrats and Communists – into a coalition. Limited democracy prevailed, and land-reform laws, sponsored by the Communist minister of agriculture, Imre Nagy, were enacted, wiping away the prewar feudal structure. Budapest experienced the worst hyperinflation the world has ever known at this time, with notes worth up to 10,000 trillion pengő issued before the new currency (the forint) was introduced.

Within a couple of years, the Communists were ready to take complete control. After a rigged election held under a complicated new electoral law in 1947, they declared their candidate, Mátyás Rákosi, victorious. The Social Democrats were forced to merge with the Communists into the Hungarian Socialist Workers Party.

In 1948 Rákosi, a big fan of Stalin, began a process of nationalisation and unfeasibly fast industrialisation at the expense of agriculture. Peasants were forced into collective farms, and all produce had to be delivered to state warehouses. A network of spies and informers exposed 'class enemies' (like Cardinal József Mindszenty – see the boxed text in the Things to See & Do chapter) to the secret police (the ÁVO, or ÁVH after 1949), who interrogated them at their headquarters on Andrássy út in Pest and sent them to trial at the Military Court of Justice on Fő utca in Buda. Some were executed; many more were sent into internal exile or condemned to labour camps like the notorious one at Recsk in the Mátra Hills. It is estimated that during this period a quarter of the adult population faced police or judicial proceedings.

Bitter feuding within the party began, and purges and Stalinesque show trials became the norm. László Rajk, the Communist minister of the interior (which also controlled the ÁVO), was executed for 'Titoism'; his successor János Kádár was tortured and jailed. In August 1949, the nation was proclaimed the 'People's Republic of Hungary'; in the ensuing years apartment blocks, small businesses and retail outlets in Budapest were expropriated by the state and new cultural and sports facilities – including the People's Stadium (Népstadion) – were built.

With Krushchev's denunciation of Stalin in 1956 just three years after the dictator's death, Rákosi's tenure was up and the terror began to abate. Under pressure from within the party, Rákosi's successor, Ernő Gerő, rehabilitated Rajk posthumously and readmitted Imre Nagy, who had been expelled from the party a year earlier for suggesting reforms. But Gerő was ultimately as much a hardliner as Rákosi had been, and by October 1956, during Rajk's reburial, murmured calls for a real reform of the system – 'communism with a human face' – could already be heard.

The 1956 Uprising

The nation's greatest tragedy – an event that for a while shook the world, rocked communism and pitted Hungarian against Hungarian – began in Budapest on 23 October when some 50,000 university students assembled at Bem tér in Buda, shouting anti-Soviet slogans and demanding that the reformist Nagy be named prime minister. That night a crowd pulled down the colossal statue of Stalin near Heroes' Square and shots were fired by ÁVH agents on another group gathering outside the headquarters of Hungarian Radio on Bródy Sándor utca in Pest. Budapest was in revolution.

Two days later Nagy formed a government (which included János Kádár), and for a short time it appeared that he might be successful in transforming Hungary into a neutral, multiparty state. But on 1 November Soviet tanks and troops crossed into Hungary and within 72 hours began attacking Budapest and other centres. Kádár, who had slipped away from Budapest to join the Russian invaders, was installed as leader.

Fierce street fighting continued for several days – fighting was especially heavy at the Corvin Cinema and the nearby Kilián army barracks on József körút in Pest and Szena tér in Buda – and was spurred on by Radio Free Europe broadcasts and disingenuous promises of support from the West, embroiled in the Suez Canal crisis at the time. When the fighting was over, 25,000 people were dead. Then the reprisals – the worst in the city's history – began. An estimated 20,000 people were arrested and 2000 – including Nagy and his associates – were executed. Another 250,000 refugees fled to Austria. The government lost what little credibility it had enjoyed and the city some of its most competent and talented citizens. As for the physical scars, look around you at so many buildings in Pest: those holes and pockmarks you see on the exterior walls were caused by bullets and shrapnel.

Hungary under Kádár

The transformation of János Kádár from traitor and most hated man in the land to respected reformer is one of the most astonishing *tours de force* of the 20th century.

After the reprisals and the consolidation of his regime, Kádár began a program to liberalise the social and economic structure based on compromise. (His most quoted line is 'Whoever is not against us is with us' – a reversal of the Stalinist adage that 'Those not with us are against us'.) In 1968, he and the economist Rezső Nyers unveiled the New Economic Mechanism (NEM) to introduce elements of a market to the planned economy. But even this proved too daring for many party conservatives. Nyers was ousted and the NEM whittled away.

Kádár managed to survive that power struggle and went on to introduce greater consumerism and market socialism. By the mid-1970s Hungary was light years ahead of any other Soviet bloc country in its standard of living, freedom of movement and opportunities to criticise the government. People may have had to wait seven years for a Lada car or 12 for a telephone, but most Hungarians could at least enjoy access to a second house in the countryside and a decent material life. The 'Hungarian model' attracted much Western attention – and investment.

But things began to sour in the 1980s. The Kádár system of 'goulash socialism', which had seemed 'timeless and everlasting' as one Hungarian writer has put it, was incapable of dealing with such 'unsocialist' problems as unemployment, soaring inflation and the largest per-capita foreign debt in the region. Kádár and the 'old guard' refused to hear talk about party reforms and the government was dismissed in May 1988.

Renewal & Change

Three reformers – Nyers, Károly Grósz and Imre Pozsgay – took control. Party conservatives at first put a lid on real change by demanding a retreat from political liberalisation in exchange for their support of the new regime's economic policies. But the tide had already turned. Throughout the summer and autumn of 1988, pro-democracy demonstrations were held in Budapest as new political parties were formed and old ones revived. In February 1989 Pozsgay, seeing the writing on the wall as Mikhail Gorbachev kissed babies and launched his reforms in the Soviet Union, announced in parliament that the events of 1956 had been a 'popular uprising', not the 'counter-revolution' that the regime had always said it was. Four months later hundreds of thousands of people attended the reburial of Imre Nagy and other victims of 1956 at Kerepesi Cemetery in Budapest.

In September 1989, again at Pozsgay's instigation, Hungary cut away the electrified wire fence separating it from Austria. The move released a wave of East Germans holidaying in Hungary into the West and the opening attracted thousands more. The collapse of the communist regimes around the region was now unstoppable. What Hungarians now call *az átkos 40 év* ('the accursed 40 years') had come to a withering, almost feeble, end.

The Republic of Hungary Again

In October 1989, on the 33rd anniversary of the 1956 Uprising, the nation once again became the Republic of Hungary. At their party congress in Budapest the communists surrendered their monopoly on power, paving the way for free elections in March 1990. The party's name was changed from the Hungarian Socialist Workers' Party to the Hungarian Socialist Party (MSZP).

The MSZP's new program advocated social democracy and a free market economy, but this was not enough to shake off the stigma of its four decades of autocratic rule. The 1990 vote was won by the centrist Hungarian Democratic Forum (MDF), which advocated a gradual transition to capitalism. The social-democratic Alliance of Free Democrats (SZDSZ), which had called for much faster change, came second and the socialists trailed far behind. As Gorbachev looked on, Hungary changed political systems with scarcely a murmur. The last Soviet troops left Hungary in June 1991, place names like Lenin utca and Marx tér ended up on the stinking trash heap of history and monuments to 'glorious workers' and 'esteemed leaders' were packed off to a socialist-realist zoo called Statue Park (see the Things to See & Do chapter for details).

In coalition with two smaller parties – the Independent Smallholders (FKgP) and the Christian Democrats (KDNP) – the MDF provided Hungary with sound government during its painful transition to a full market economy. Those years saw Hungary's northern (Czechoslovakia) and southern (Yugoslavia) neighbours split apart along ethnic lines. Prime Minister József Antall did little to improve relations with Slovakia, Romania and Yugoslavia by claiming to be the 'emotional and spiritual' prime minister of the large Hungarian minorities in those countries. In mid-1993 the MDF was forced to expel István Csurka, a party vice president, after he made ultra-nationalistic and anti-Semitic statements that tarnished Hungary's image as a bastion of moderation and stability in a volatile region. Antall died after a long fight with cancer in December 1993 and was replaced by Interior Minister Péter Boross.

Despite initial successes in curbing inflation and lowering interest rates, a host of economic problems slowed the pace of development, and the government's laissez-faire policies did not help. Like most people in the region, Hungarians had unrealistically expected a much faster improvement in their living standards. Most of them – 76% according to a poll in mid-1993 – were 'very disappointed'.

In the elections of May 1994 the Socialist Party, led by Gyula Horn, won an absolute majority in parliament. This in no way implied a return to the past, and Horn was quick to point out that it was in fact his party that had initiated the whole reform process in the first place. (As foreign minister in 1989 Horn had played a key role in opening the border with Austria.) Árpád Göncz of the SZDSZ was elected for a second five-year term as president of the republic in 1995.

After its dire showing in the 1994 elections, the Federation of Young Democrats (FIDESZ), which until 1993 limited membership to those aged under 35 in order to

emphasise a past untainted by communism, privilege and corruption, moved to the right and added the extension 'MPP' (Hungarian Civic Party) to its name to attract the support of the burgeoning middle class. The socialist government's renewed support of the Nagymáros project on the Danube (see the boxed text 'Dam Nations' in the Excursions chapter) caused an outcry, something FIDESZ-MPP leader Viktor Orbán milked for everything it was worth.

In the May 1998 parliamentary elections, FIDESZ-MPP won 148 of the 386 seats. Against the wishes of many supporters, it quickly entered into a coalition with the very conservative Independent Smallholders Party (FKgP) and the Hungarian Democratic Forum (MDF) to form a government. Orbán was named prime minister and remains so – but, from the looks of it, only just. He engages in an almost daily squaring off with the FKgP's wily leader, József Torgyán, and is regularly outmanoeuvred, much to the amusement – or despair – of most Hungarians.

GEOGRAPHY

Budapest lies in the north-central part of Hungary, some 250km south-east of Vienna. It is by far Hungary's largest city and has for its borders Csepel Island in the Danube River to the south, the Danube Bend to the north (24km), the Buda Hills to the west and the start of the Great Plain to the east (29km).

The focal point is the Danube River, which divides the city into two quite distinct halves: Buda, mostly residential and built on the hills and high river terraces of the western side, and commercial Pest on a large, sandy plain across to the east. It is a large, sprawling city measuring 525 sq km and, with few exceptions (eg, Buda Hills, City Park, some excursions), the areas beyond the Nagykörút (literally the 'Big Ring Road') in Pest and west of Moszkva tér in Buda are residential or industrial and of little interest to visitors.

Budapest is a well laid-out city in which it is almost difficult to get lost. It is divided into 23 kerület, or districts, which usually have traditional names like Lipótváros (Leopold Town) or Víziváros (Watertown). For more information see Orientation in the Facts for the Visitor chapter.

National Regions

Although Hungary is divided into 19 administrative counties (*megye*), these will mean little to outsiders. But it will be helpful to at least know the names of the eight main regions: Budapest and its environs; the Danube Bend to the north; Western Transdanubia to the west and north-west; Lake Balaton and Central Transdanubia to the south-west; Southern Transdanubia to the south and south-west; the Great Plain to the east and south-east; the Northern Uplands to the north and north-east; and the North-East itself.

CLIMATE

Budapest has a temperate, transitional climate – somewhere between the mild, rainy weather of Transdanubia protected by the Alps to the west and the harsh, variable climate of the flat and open Great Plain to the east.

Spring arrives early in April in Budapest and usually ends in showers. Summer can be very hot and humid. It rains for most of November and doesn't usually get cold until mid-December. Winter is relatively short, often cloudy and damp but sometimes brilliantly sunny. What little snow the city gets usually disappears after a few days.

January is the coldest month (with temperatures between -4° and 0°C) and July the hottest (18° to 23°C). The number of hours of sunshine a year averages about 2000 – among the highest in Europe; from April to

the end of September, you can expect the sun to shine for about 10 hours a day. Mean annual precipitation is about 600mm. The climate chart on this page shows you what to expect and when to expect it.

For information on weather conditions in Budapest, ring the national weather forecast service from 8 am to 8 pm daily on ☎ 212 2070 or mobile ☎ 06-90 304 621. You can also check out their Web site at www.met.hu.

ECOLOGY & ENVIRONMENT

As in the rest of Hungary, pollution is – and will remain for some time to come – a large and costly problem in Budapest. Low-grade coal that continues to fuel some industry and heat homes creates sulphur dioxide and acid rain that threatens the flora and fauna of the Buda Hills to the west and the Börzsöny and Pilis ranges to the north and north-west.

Automobiles manufactured in the former Soviet bloc, especially the two-stroke East

Cyanide Spill

The greatest threat to Hungary's environment in recent years came shortly after the start of the new century. A reservoir containing water contaminated with cyanide at a gold mine near Baia Mare in north-western Romania overflowed its banks and spilled into the Someş (Szamos in Hungarian) River. Within days cyanide levels in the Tisza, into which the Szamos flows, were 700 times above acceptable levels, poisoning the drinking water of some two million people and causing ecological havoc. Less than a month after the mishap some 300 tonnes of dead fish had been collected and, while the cyanide was believed to have been diluted once the Tisza joined the much wider Danube near Novi Sad in Yugoslavia, it was feared that the entire food chain of the Hungarian Tisza had been destroyed. The World Wide Fund for Nature in Budapest said at the time that the Tisza would be affected for at least a decade. Other environmentalists have likened the devastation to that caused by the Chernobyl nuclear reactor meltdown of 1986.

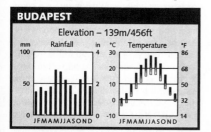

BUDAPEST

Elevation – 139m/456ft

Rainfall (mm / in)

Temperature (°C / °F)

JFMAMJJASOND

German Trabants still seen trawling the streets of the capital, have raised nitrogen oxide levels to among the highest in Europe, reducing the life span of both its citizens and cultural monuments. Waste created by the Soviet military, particularly buried toxic chemicals and routinely dumped jet fuel, threatens the soil, the ground-water supply, rivers and nearby lakes as does the overuse of nitrate fertilisers in the hinterland.

There are bright spots, however. Government funding for the environment has been increased and some work has been carried out in the areas worst hit. Brown coal, once the main energy source, now accounts for only one-third of energy production. Yet even at an accelerated rate the total clean-up is expected to take at least another decade.

FLORA & FAUNA

Budapest and vicinity counts a total of eight protected areas of national importance. The largest area within the city proper encompasses the Buda Hills, the lungs of the city and a 10,500-hectare protected area of dolomite and limestone rocks, steep ravines, rocky grasslands and more than 150 caves. Sashegy (Eagle Hill), a 30-hectare conservation area in south Buda, harbours both cold-resistant and heat-seeking dolomitic flora as well as snake-eyed skinks.

The most impressive natural area near the capital, however, is the new 51,500-hectare Danube-Ipoly National Park taking in the Börzsöny and Pilis Hills on opposite sides of the Danube to the north and north-east. Among some of the Pilis' botanical attractions are the endangered Pannonian fennels and the dolomitic flax, with its waxy yellow flowers. The flora and fauna of the Börzsöny Hills is more diverse; some 70 protected plant species and 117 bird species have been recorded here.

GOVERNMENT & POLITICS
National Government

Hungary's 1989 constitution provides for a parliamentary system of government. The unicameral assembly consists of 386 members chosen for four years in a complex, two-round system that balances direct and proportional representation. The head of state, the president, is elected by the house for five years. The prime minister is head of government.

Hungary has six parties represented in the parliament elected in 1998: FIDESZ-MPP (148 seats), the MSZP (134), FKgP (48), the SZDSZ (24), the MDF (17) and MIÉP (13) as well as two independent members. The Christian Democrats (KDNP) have no representation in the 1998 parliament.

The party in charge of the ruling coalition is – in theory – FIDESZ-MPP (see The Republic of Hungary Again in the previous History section). The party furthest to the left is the MSZP, the opposition Hungarian Socialist Party. The most right-wing is the conservative and nationalist MIÉP (Hungarian Party for Justice and Life), led by the controversial István Csurka.

In foreign policy, Hungary has taken a more assertive role in recent years as it looks to full integration into Western Europe. It became a fully fledged member of NATO in March 1999, and the government is expected to increase defence spending by some 45% in 2000 as it upgrades its military to meet NATO standards.

One of the biggest thorns in the country's side in the 1990s was Slovakia's work on the Danube dam at Gabčikovo, north-west of Budapest (see the boxed text 'Dam Nations' in the Excursions chapter). Though Hungary signed an agreement with Slovakia – home to some 600,000 ethnic Hungarians – in March 1995, it took the Slovakian government a full year to ratify it. Relations between the two countries remain strained.

Local Government

Budapest is governed by a municipal council (*fővárosi önkormánzat*), whose members are elected to four-year terms and whose leader is the lord mayor (*főpolgármester*). The current mayor, the youthful SZDSZ liberal Gábor Demszky, won his third term in office in October 1998 after joining forces with the MSZP socialists to gain 37 of the assembly's 66 seats. The opposition is the FIDESZ-MPP coalition with 22 seats. The ultra-rightist MIÉP holds seven seats.

Demszky ran his campaign under the slogan *Világvárost építünk* (Let's Build a World-Class City), which carried both metaphysical and quite concrete meanings. Two of his grand projects – the M4 metro line from Pest to south Buda and a new National Theatre in the centre of Erzsébet tér, whose foundations had already been laid – looked like going forward after he resumed office but the parliament axed both plans for financial reasons. The City of Budapest has now begun a lawsuit against the Orbán government.

ECONOMY

Hungary, with Budapest as its true economic centre, today has the most developed economy in Eastern Europe and is on the fast-track to EU membership by 2004 at the latest.

Memories of the transition from a state-controlled economy to market-driven capitalism have dimmed as inflation and unemployment levels approach those of Western Europe. Hungary's 4% growth in gross domestic product is among the highest in Europe as consumers increase purchases of household appliances, cars and television sets made in the country. By comparison, the average growth rate in the EU was 2.2% in 1999.

Hungary is poorly endowed with natural resources but this has proved a blessing, for it means the country isn't saddled with the number of rusting industrial plants processing iron or coal that still plague Poland and neighbouring Slovakia. Instead, manufacturing and brainpower have led to jobs that have reduced unemployment to about 9% and inflation to just over 10% (from 31% in 1995). Over the next few years, inflation is targeted to fall to about 6%.

Economic growth has been driven by foreign exporters like Royal Philips Electronics, Europe's largest producer of consumer electronics products, and automobile manufacturer General Motors, both of which have factories in Hungary. They've helped pump about $21 billion in foreign direct investment into the country since 1989, the highest level of foreign money of all the former communist countries.

These foreign companies have set up in Hungary because the workforce is considered flexible, skilled, highly educated and, well, cheap. A 'good' monthly salary for a young university graduate starting a job at a company like the telecommunications conglomerate Matáv is about 150,000Ft (approximately US$575), while the average monthly income nationwide is only about 68,000Ft (US$260). Also the American Chamber of Commerce in Budapest figures that office operations in the Hungarian capital cost about one-third less than in Western European cities.

It's not just the sale of light industrial goods to Germany and Austria, which consume almost half of all Hungarian exports, that is powering the economy. Budapest has developed a mini-Silicon Valley of high-tech Internet and software companies. The capital is home to Uproar, for example, which produces internationally accessed Internet game shows. Graphisoft is one of the world's largest makers of computer-aided design software for architects. And in a sign of the times, shares in both companies can be traded on European stock exchanges.

POPULATION & PEOPLE

With almost two million inhabitants, Budapest is home to about 20% of Hungary's total population. Most are Magyars, an Asiatic people of obscure origins who do not speak an Indo-European language and make up the vast majority of Hungary's 10.1 million people. Another five million Magyars live outside the national borders, notably the estimated two million in Transylvania (now Romania), who constitute the largest ethnic minority in Europe. There are 600,000 in Slovakia, 650,000 in Yugoslavia and Croatia and 200,000 in Ukraine.

No exact breakdown exists but the ethnic make-up in the capital reflects the national one. Magyars constitute more than 97% of the population while non-Magyar minorities making their home here include Roma (1.5% to 2.5% of the population), Germans (0.3%), Romanians (0.25%), Slovaks (0.1%) and Croatians and Serbs (0.1%).

The Roma

The origins of the Gypsies (Hungarian: *cigány*), who call themselves the Roma (singular: Rom) and speak Romany, a language closely related to several tongues still spoken in northern India, remain a mystery. It is generally accepted, however, that they began migrating to Persia from India sometime in the 10th century and had reached the Balkans by the 14th century. They have been in Hungary for at least 500 years, and their numbers today are estimated at anywhere between 150,000 and 250,000 people.

Though traditionally a travelling people, in modern times the Roma have by and large settled down in Hungary and work as smiths and tinkers, livestock and horse traders and as musicians (see Music & Dance under Arts in this chapter). As a group, however, they are chronically underemployed and have been the hardest hit by economic recession. Statistically, Roma families are twice the size of *gadje*, or non-Roma, ones.

Unsettled people have always been persecuted in one form or another by those who stay put and Hungarian Roma are no exception. They are widely despised and remain the scapegoats for everything that goes wrong, from the rise in petty theft and prostitution to the loss of jobs. Though their rights are inscribed in the 1989 constitution along with other ethnic minorities, their housing ranks among the worst in the nation, police are regularly accused of harassing them and, more than any other group, they fear a revival of right-wing nationalism. You will probably be shocked at what even educated, well-travelled Budapesters say about Roma and their way of life.

Life expectancy in Hungary is relatively low by European standards: 68 years for men, 75 for women. The nation also has one of Europe's lowest rates of natural population increase: -3.2 per 1000 population. Sadly, it also claims the dubious distinction of having the highest suicide rate in the world (see the boxed text on the following page).

The population density of Budapest is 3549 people per sq km against a national average of 109 per sq km.

EDUCATION

Hungary is a well-educated society with a literacy rate of about 98%. School is compulsory for children aged six to 16.

The education system generally follows the German model. Primary or elementary school (*általános iskola*) is followed by four years of secondary education, which can be in grammar (*gimnázium*) or vocational/trade schools (*szakiskola*). About 30% of those aged over 18 have secondary-school certificates. College and university matriculation is very competitive – places are few and entrance requirements pretty stiff. Still, about 10% of the population holds university degrees, a quarter of which are in engineering and economics.

Most of Hungary's most prestigious universities are based in Budapest, including: the Loránd Eötvös University of Science (ELTE), which was founded in 1635 and moved to Budapest in 1777 from what is now Trnava in Slovakia; the 200-year-old Semmelweis University of Medicine (SOTE); the Budapest Technical University (BME) established in 1782; and the Budapest University of Economic Sciences (known as 'Közgáz').

Hungary has an international reputation in certain areas of specialised education. A unique method of music education with preliminary emphasis on voice instruction devised by the composer Zoltán Kodály (1882-1967) is widespread. The Pető Institute in Budapest has a very high success rate in teaching children with cerebral palsy to walk.

SCIENCE

Hungarians have made great contributions to the sciences and related fields. Albert Szent-Györgyi won the Nobel Prize for Physiology or Medicine in 1937 for his discovery of vitamin C, Georg von Békésy the same prize in 1961 for his research on the inner ear and Eugene Paul Wigner received his Nobel Prize in 1963 for his research in

A Dubious Distinction

Psychologists are still out to lunch on why Hungary should have Europe's highest suicide rate – 38.6 per 100,000 people. Some say that the Magyar propensity for gloom leads to the ultimate act of despair (see Social Life in the Society & Conduct section of this chapter). Others link it to a phenomenon not uncommon late in the 19th century. As the Hungarian aristocracy withered away, the *kisnemesség* (lower nobility – some of them no better off than the local peasantry) would do themselves in to 'save their name and honour'. As a result, suicide was – and is – not looked upon dishonourably here. The church allows victims to be buried in hallowed ground and the euphemistic sentence used in obituaries is: 'Kovács János died suddenly and tragically.' About 60% of suicides are by hanging.

And, who, you may ask, comes next in the suicide sweepstakes? Believe it or not, it's the Finns, the Magyars' closest linguistic cousins, who rank second with 26.6 suicide deaths per 100,000. Forget genes; apparently we're all tied by tongues.

nuclear physics. Both Edward Teller and Leo Szilard worked on the so-called Manhattan Project, which led to the development of the atomic bomb, under the Nobel Prize-winning Italian-American physicist Enrico Fermi.

ARTS

Hungarian art has been both stunted and spurred on by the pivotal events in the nation's history. King Stephen's conversion to Catholicism brought Romanesque and Gothic art and architecture to Hungary, while the Turkish occupation nipped most of Hungary's Renaissance in the bud and left much of its Gothic legacy in ruins. The Habsburgs opened the doors to baroque influences. The arts thrived under the Dual Monarchy, then through truncation and even under fascism. The early days of communism brought art celebrating wheat sheaves and muscle-bound steelworkers to less-than-impressed Budapest urbanites, but much money was spent on music and 'correct art' like classical theatre.

While the artistic, cultural and literary hypertrophy of Budapest is indisputable, it would be foolish – if not impossible – to ignore folk art when discussing urban (and urbane) fine art in Hungary. The two have been inextricably linked for several centuries and have greatly influenced one another. The music of Béla Bartók and the ceramic sculptures of Margit Kovács are deeply rooted in traditional Hungarian culture. Even the architecture of the Secession (see the special section 'Budapest's *Fin-de-Siècle* Architecture' in this chapter) incorporated many folk elements.

Music & Dance

Hungary has made many contributions to the music world, but one person stands head and shoulders above all: Franz – or Ferenc – Liszt. Liszt (1811-86), who established the Academy of Music in Budapest, liked to describe himself as 'part Gypsy', and some of his works, notably *Hungarian Rhapsodies*, echo traditional Roma music.

Ferenc Erkel (1810-93) is the father of Hungarian opera and two of his works – the stirringly nationalist *Bánk Bán*, based on József Katona's play, and *László Hunyadi* – are standards at the State Opera House. Erkel also composed the music for the Hungarian national anthem.

Imre Kálmán (1882-1953) was Hungary's most celebrated composer of operettas. *The Queen of the Csárdás* is his most popular – and campiest – work. Try to catch it at the Budapest Operetta Theatre on VI Nagymező utca in Pest.

Béla Bartók (1881-1945) and Zoltán Kodály (1882-1967) made the first systematic study of Hungarian folk music together, travelling and recording throughout the Magyar linguistic region in 1906. Both integrated some of their findings into their own compositions – Bartók in *Bluebeard's Castle*, for example, and Kodály in his *Peacock Variations*.

Hungarian folk musicians play violins, zithers, hurdy-gurdies, bagpipes and lutes on a five-note scale. There is a variety of different groups but ones to watch out for are Méta and Muzsikás (especially when Marta Sebestyén sings). Anyone playing the haunting music of the Csángó region in eastern Transylvania is also a good bet.

Traditional Yiddish music is less known than Gypsy and Roma music but is of similar origin, having once been closely associated with Central European folk music. Until WWI so-called *klezmer* dance bands were led by the violin and cymbalom, but the influence of Yiddish theatre and the first wax recordings inspired a switch to the clarinet, which is the predominant instrument today. Klezmer music is currently going through a great renaissance in Budapest and the Budapest Klezmer Band is world class.

There are two ballet companies based at the Opera House in Budapest though the best in the country is the Győr Ballet (from Western Transdanubia). Groups like the State Folk Ensemble perform dances essentially for tourists throughout the year; visit a *táncház* (literally 'dance house' but more like a folk-music workshop) if you prefer authentic folk dance and not touristy two-stepping.

There are several symphony orchestras based in the capital, including Budapest Festival Orchestra and the Hungarian Radio & Television Orchestra.

Literature

No-one could have put it better than the poet Gyula Illyés (1902-83): 'The Hungarian language,' he wrote, 'is at one and the same time our softest cradle and our most solid coffin.' The difficulty and subtlety of the Magyar tongue has excluded most outsiders from Hungarian literature and, though it would be wonderful to be able to read the swashbuckling odes and love poems of Bálint Balassi (1554-94) or Miklós Zrínyi's *Peril of Sziget* in the original, most people will have to make do with what they can find in English translation.

Sándor Petőfi (1823-49) is Hungary's most celebrated and accessible poet, and a line from his work *National Song* became the rallying cry for the 1848-49 War of Independence, in which Petőfi fought and

died. A deeply philosophical play called *The Tragedy of Man* by Imre Madách (1823-64), published a decade after Hungary's defeat in the War of Independence, is still considered to be the country's greatest classical drama. It is available in English from the Corvinus publishing house.

The defeat in 1849 led many writers to look to romanticism for inspiration and solace: heroes, winners and knights in shining armour. Petőfi's comrade-in-arms, János Arany (1817-82), whose name is synonymous with impeccable Hungarian, wrote epic poetry (*Toldi Trilogy*) and ballads.

Another friend of Petőfi, the prolific novelist Mór Jókai (1825-1904), wrote of heroism and honesty in such wonderful works as *The Man with the Golden Touch* and *Black Diamonds*. This 'Hungarian Dickens' still enjoys widespread popularity. Another perennial favourite, Kálmán Mikszáth (1847-1910), wrote satirical tales like *St Peter's Umbrella* in which he poked fun at the declining gentry. Apparently the former US president Theodore Roosevelt enjoyed the latter work so much that he insisted on visiting the ageing novelist during a European tour in 1910.

Zsigmond Móricz (1879-1942) was a very different type of writer. His works, very much in the tradition of the French naturalist Émile Zola (1840-1902), examined the harsh reality of peasant life in late-19th-century Hungary. Corvinus publishes his *Relations* in English. His contemporary, Mihály Babits (1883-1941), poet and the editor of the influential literary magazine *Nyugat* (West), made the rejuvenation of Hungarian literature his lifelong work.

Two other important names of this period are the poet and short-story writer Dezső Kosztolányi (1885-1936), some of whose stories are collected in *April Fool* (Noran Books), and the novelist Gyula Krúdy (1878-1933), whose *Sunflower* (Corvinus) and *The Adventures of Sindbad* (Central European University Press) are now available in English.

Two 20th-century poets are unsurpassed in Hungarian letters. Endre Ady (1877-1919), who is sometimes described as a

Rubik Cubes, Vitamin C & Zsa Zsa

It is not enough to be Hungarian – one must also have talent.'

Slogan spotted in a Toronto employment office in the early 1960s

The contributions made by Hungarians to any number of fields – from films and toys to science and fine art – both at home and abroad have been enormous, especially when you consider the nation's relatively small population. The following is a list of people whom you may not have known were Hungarian or of Hungarian ancestry:

Brassaï (born Halász Gyula; 1899-1984). French poet, draftsman, sculptor and photographer, known for his dramatic photographs of Paris at night.

Capa, Robert (Friedmann Endre; 1913-54). One of the greatest war photographers and photo-journalists of the 20th century.

Cukor, George (1899-1983), legendary American film producer/director (*The Philadelphia Story*).

Curtis, Tony (Bernard Schwartz; 1925-). Evergreen American actor (*Spartacus*).

Eszterhas, Joe (1944-). American scriptwriter (*Basic Instinct*).

Gabor, Eva (1921-95). American actress chiefly remembered for her starring role as a New York City socialite making her comical life on a farm in the 1960s TV series *Green Acres*; younger sister of Zsa Zsa.

Gabor, Zsa Zsa (?-). Ageless-ish American starlet of grade BBB films and older sister of Eva.

Houdini, Harry (Weisz Erich; 1874-1926). American magician and celebrated escape artist.

Lauder, Estée (1910?-). American fragrance and cosmetics baroness.

Liszt, Franz (Liszt Ferenc; 1811-86). Piano virtuoso and composer.

Lugosi, Béla (Blasko Béla; 1884-1956). The film world's only true Dracula, and Minister of Culture under the Béla Kun regime (see the History section).

Rubik, Ernő (1944-). Inventor of the hottest toy of the 1980 Christmas season – an infuriating plastic cube with 54 small squares that when twisted out of its original arrangement has 43 quintillion variations.

Soros, George (Soros György; 1930-). Billionaire financier and philanthropist.

Szent-Györgyi, Dr Albert (1893-1986). Nobel Prize-winning biochemist who discovered vitamin C.

Vasarely, Victor (Vásárhelyi Győző; 1908-97). French painter of geometric abstractions and father of the op art movement.

Wilder, Billy (Wilder Samuel; 1906-). American film director and producer (*Some Like It Hot*).

~~~~~~~~~~~~~~~~~~~~~~~~~~~~~~~

successor to Petőfi, was a reformer who ruthlessly attacked the complacency and materialism of Hungary at that time. The socialist Attila József (1905-1937) wrote of alienation and turmoil in a technological age; *By the Danube* is brilliant even in English translation (included in *Winter Night*, an anthology of his poems from Corvinus). József fell afoul of both the underground communist movement and the Horthy regime. Tragically, he threw himself under a train at the age of 32.

György Konrád (1933-), Péter Nádas (1942-) and Péter Esterházy (1950-) are three of Hungary's most important contemporary writers. Konrád's *A Feast in the Garden* (1985) is an almost autobiographical account of the fate of the Jewish community in a small eastern Hungarian town. *A Book of Memoirs* by Nádas concerns the decline of communism in the style of Thomas Mann. In *The End of a Family Story*, he uses a child narrator as a filter for the adult experience of 1950s communist Hungary.

Esterházy's *A Little Hungarian Pornography* is a difficult but enjoyable read.

Painting & Architecture

You won't find as much Romanesque and Gothic art and architecture in Budapest as you would in Slovakia or the Czech Republic – the Mongols, Turks and Habsburgs destroyed most of it – but the Royal Palace incorporates many Gothic features and the sedile (niches with seats) in the Castle District, most notably on I Úri utca (Nos 32 and 36) and Országház utca 9, are pure Gothic. The chapels in the Inner Town Parish Church have some fine Gothic and Renaissance tabernacles and you can't miss the Renaissance stonework, the Gothic wooden sculptures and panel paintings and late-Gothic triptychs at the Hungarian National Gallery.

Baroque abounds in Budapest as it does in the rest of Hungary; you'll see architectural examples of it everywhere. The Church of St Anne on I Batthyány tér in Buda and the Óbuda Parish Church on III Flórián tér are fine examples of ecclesiastical baroque while the Citadella on Gellért Hill in Buda and the municipal council office on V Váráosház utca in Pest are baroque in its secular form.

Distinctly Hungarian art and architecture didn't come into its own until the mid-19th century when Mihály Pollack, József Hild and Miklós Ybl began changing the face of Budapest. The romantic nationalist school of heroic paintings, best exemplified by Bertalan Székely (1835-1910) and Gyula Benczúr (1844-1920), gratefully gave way to the realism of Mihály Munkácsy (1844-1900). But the greatest painters from this period were Kosztka Tivadar Csontváry (1853-1919) and József Rippl-Rónai (1861-1927), whose works are on display at the National Gallery and the Municipal Gallery of the Kiscelli Museum.

The 20th-century painter Victor Vasarely (1908-97), the so-called father of op art, has his own museum in Óbuda, as does the contemporary sculptor Imre Varga.

The romantic Eclectic and Secessionist styles of architects like Ödön Lechner (Buda-

pest Museum of Applied Art, former Post Office Savings Bank) and the Hungarian Art Nouveau of Aladár Arkay (Városligeti Calvinist Church) brought unique architecture to Hungary at the end of the 19th century and the start of the 20th (see the special section 'Budapest's *Fin-de-Siècle* Architecture' in this chapter). Fans of Art Nouveau will find in Budapest some of the best examples of that style outside Vienna and Brussels.

Postwar architecture in Hungary is almost completely forgettable. One exception is the work of Imre Makovecz, who has developed his own 'organic' style (not always popular locally) using unusual materials like tree trunks and turf. His work is everywhere in the rest of Hungary but it's hard to find in Budapest. Two fine examples include the Hungarian Art Academy at III Kesske utca 25 in Óbuda and the spectacular funerary chapel with its reverse vaulted ceiling at Farkasréti Cemetery in district XII.

Folk Art

Hungary has one of the richest folk traditions in Europe and, quite apart from its music, this is where the country often has come to the fore in art. Many urban Hungarians probably wouldn't want to hear that, considering folk art a bit *déclassé* and its elevation the work of the communist regime, but it's true.

From the beginning of the 18th century, as segments of the Hungarian peasantry became more prosperous, ordinary people tried to make their world more beautiful by painting and decorating objects and clothing. It's important to remember two things when looking at folk art. First, with very few exceptions only practical objects used daily were decorated. Second, this is not 'court art' or the work of artisans making Chinese cloisonné or Fabergé eggs. It is the work of ordinary people trying to express the simple world around them in a new and different way. Some of it is excellent and occasionally you will spot the work of a true genius who probably never ventured beyond their village or farm.

[Continued on page 35]

BUDAPEST'S FIN-DE-SIÈCLE ARCHITECTURE

Art Nouveau architecture and its local variation, Secessionism, abound in Budapest, and examples can be seen throughout the city. Their sinuous curves, flowing, asymmetrical forms, and colourful tiles and other decorative elements stand out like beacons in a sea of refined and elegant baroque and mannered, geometric neoclassical buildings. And it's not uncommon to hear visitors to the city gasp in surprise as they round a corner and spot yet another fine example.

Some people – myself included – go out of their way for another glimpse of such 'concealed' favourites as the Geology Institute at XIV Stefánia út 14 (designed by Ödön Lechner, 1899) and the National Association for the Blind on XIV Hermina utca 47 (Lechner, 1907) near the City Park or the Philanthia flower shop (Albert Körössy, 1907) at V Váci utca 9, with its exquisite Art Nouveau interior. It's almost as if we are all afraid that these wonderful structures – built at a time when all was right with the world in affluent, cosmopolitan Budapest – will wither and disappear unless they are bathed regularly in admiring glances.

Art Nouveau was both an architectural style and an art form that flourished in Europe and the USA from about 1890 to 1910. It began in Britain as the Arts and Crafts Movement, an attempt to create a new organic style in direct opposition to the imitative banalities spawned by the Industrial Revolution. It soon spread to Europe, where it took on distinctly local characteristics. In France it became known as Art Nouveau or Style 1900, in Germany Jugendstil and in Italy Stile Liberty.

In Austria-Hungary, a group of artists in Vienna called the Secessionists lent its name to the more geometric local style of architecture: Sezessionstil (szecesszió in Hungarian). In Budapest, the use of traditional facades with allegorical and historical figures and scenes, folk motifs and Zsolnay ceramics and other local materials led to an Eclectic style. Though working within an Art Nouveau/Secessionist framework, this style emerged as something uniquely Hungarian.

Fashion and styles changed as rapidly and whimsically at the start of the 20th century as they do today, and by the end of the first decade Art Nouveau and its variations were considered limited, old-fashioned and even tacky. Fortunately for us and the good citizens of Budapest, the economic and political torpor of the prewar period and the 40-year 'big sleep' after WWII left many Art Nouveau/Secessionist buildings weathered but intact – many more, in fact, than remain in such important centres as Paris, Vienna and Brussels. Some are now getting face-lifts and being used for different purposes, including such gems as the Gresham Palace (Zsigmond Quittner, 1907) at V Roosevelt tér 5-6, now being converted into a hotel.

The first Hungarian architect to look to Art Nouveau for inspiration was Frigyes Spiegel, and his exotic and symbolic ornamentation (birds, shells, flowers, fish etc) can still be seen on apartment blocks

Previous page: Extravagant ornamentation at VI Bajcsy-Zsilinszky út 63. (Photo by David Greedy)

Top: A wide shot of the Gellért Hotel with the Petőfi Bridge in the background. This hotel features examples of Art Nouveau, such as the entrance hall of its thermal spa.

Middle: Exterior detail of the Geology Institute. On the left are the front doors of the building. The photo on the right shows the locally developed multicoloured tiles in the background. These tiles are common in Budapest but are subject to damage from the environment.

Bottom: The main entrance hall of the Geology Institute, featuring symbols of geological elements.

Top Left: Statues placed atop buildings are a common sight in Budapest. This one is at VI Bajcsy-Zsilinszky út across the street from the Arany János metro stop.

Top Right: The National Association for the Blind is located near City Park. Built in 1907, it is another of the city's best-kept architectural jewels.

Middle Left: Detail of Gresham Palace, also dating from 1907.

Middle Right: The performance hall of the Liszt Academy of Music is an impressive example of early 1900s architecture. It is one of Budapest's top concert venues.

Bottom Left: On the 2nd floor of the Applied Arts Museum, visitors seem very small compared to the huge, ornate archways that date from the early 1900s.

Bottom Right: The Elephant House at the City Zoo is another example of early 1900s design.

at VI Bajcsy-Zsilinszky út 63 and (barely) at VI Izabella utca 94. But for a better idea of how the principles of the new style were applied with a distinctly Magyar twist, have a look at some of the large civic buildings designed by Ödön Lechner.

The most ambitious of this master builder's works in the capital is undoubtedly the Applied Arts Museum at IX Üllői út 33-37, which will likely be on your itinerary (see Walking Tour 11 in the Things to See & Do chapter). Purpose-built as a museum and completed in time for the millenary exhibition in 1896, it was faced and roofed in a variety of Zsolnay ceramic tiles, and its turrets, domes and ornamental figures lend it an 'Eastern' or 'Indian' feel. In Lipótváros, V Szabadság tér boasts Lechner's crowning glory, the delightful Post Office Savings Bank, a Secessionist extravaganza of floral mosaics, folk motifs and ceramic figures. The bull's head atop the central tower symbolises the nomadic past of the Magyars while the ceramic bees scurrying up the semi-pillars towards their hives represent industry and economy.

The Liszt Academy of Music (Flóris Korb & Kálmán Giergl, 1907) at VI Liszt Ferenc tér 8 is not so interesting for its exterior as for its decorative elements within. There's the Art Nouveau frescoes by Aladár Kőrösfői Kriesch, a leader of the seminal Gödöllő Artists' Colony, and the stained glass by Miksa Róth. Also note the grid of laurel leaves below the ceiling, which mimics the ironwork dome of the Secessionists' own building (1897) in Vienna, and the large blue Zsolnay ceramic orbs on the staircase landings.

Other buildings worth a detour are the former Török Bank House (Ármin Hegedűs & Henrik Böhm, 1906) at V Szervita tér 3, with its wonderful Secessionist mosaic in the upper gable; the primary school (Ármin Hegedűs, 1906) at VII Dob utca 85, with its mosaics depicting contemporary children's games; and the Calvinist church (Aladár Arkay, 1913) at VII Városligeti fasor 7, a stunning example of late Art Nouveau architecture with carved wooden gates, stained glass and ceramic tiles on the facade. The apartment block (Emil Vidor, 1903) at V Honvéd utca 3 is one of the most intact Art Nouveau structures in the city. It contains some lovely interior features and the exterior has recently been renovated.

The Art Nouveau/Secessionist style was hardly restricted to public buildings, and the affluent districts to the west of City Park are happy hunting grounds for some of the best examples of residences built in this style. Many of these structures were funded by wealthy industrialists who demanded that the architects include a personal statement beyond the pattern in vogue. The cream-coloured Egger Villa (Emil Vidor, 1902) at VII Városligeti fasor 24 is among the purest – and most extravagant – examples of Art Nouveau in the city. Across the road the green villa with the curious turret at No 33 was designed by Vidor for his father in 1905 and incorporates any number of European styles in vogue at the time, including French Art Nouveau. It is now a college. Other interesting buildings in this area are the apartment block with lovely stained glass and grillwork at VI Bajza utca 42, built by Zoltán

Bálint and Lajos Jámbor in 1902, and the flats at VI Munkácsy Mihály 23 (Albert Körössy, 1904).

One of the joys of this city is that you'll find elements of Art Nouveau and Secessionism in the oddest places, not just in grandiose public buildings or pompous residences; keep your eyes open and you'll spot bits and pieces everywhere. The City Zoo's main entrance and the Elephant House (Kornél Neuschloss-Knüsli, 1911) are extravagant examples influenced by the Islamic architecture in vogue in Europe at the time. The Gellért Hotel, designed by Ármin Hegedűs in 1909 and completed in 1918, contains examples of late Art Nouveau, notably the thermal spa with its enormous arched glass entrance hall and Zsolnay ceramic fountains in the bathing pools. And embellishment in the new style was not even reserved for the living. The Schmidl family tomb (Béla Lajta, 1903) in the Jewish section of the New Municipal Cemetery (Új köztemető) on X Kozma utca is a masterpiece of Art Nouveau, with Jewish and folk elements ornamented with ceramics and mosaics.

DAVID GREEDY

Left: Ornamentation at VI Bajcsy-Zsilinszky út 35

[Continued from page 30]

In Budapest the best place to see this type of art is the Museum of Ethnography on V Kossuth Lajos tér 12 (see the Things to See & Do chapter). Keep an eye out for the distinctive black and red fabric woven in the marshy Sárköz region of Southern Transdanubia; the embroidery of the Palóc people of the Northern Uplands, especially around the village of Hollókő, the Mátyó folk from Mezőkövesd and the women of Kalocsa; the folk pottery of Hódmezővásárhely, Karcag and Tiszafüred on the Great Plain and the Őrség region of Western Transdanubia; the wooden or bone mangling boards, honey-cake moulds, mirror cases, tobacco holders, saltcellars etc carved by the shepherds and swineherds of Somogy County south of Lake Balaton and the cowherds of the Hortobágy; and the trousseau chests with tulips painted on them (*tulipán láda*) traditionally made and decorated everywhere.

Cinema

The scarcity of government grants has limited the production of quality Hungarian films recently, but a handful of good (and even great) ones still get produced every year. For classics, look out for anything by Oscar-winning István Szabó (*Sweet Emma, Dear Böbe, The Taste of Sunshine*), Miklós Jancsó (*The Red and the White*) and Péter Bacsó (*The Witness, Live Show*). György Szomjas' *Junk Film* and more recent *Gangster Movie*, Lívia Gyarmathy's *The Joy of Cheating*, Gábor Dettre's *Diary of the Hurdy-Gurdy Man*, György Molnár's *Anna's Film* and Marcell Iványi's award-winning *Wind* are more recent films showing the great talent of their directors.

Other favourites are *Simon Mágus*, the epic tale of two magicians and a young woman directed by Ildikó Enyedi, and many of the films of comic director Péter Timár. His *Csinibaba* is a satirical look at life – and film production quality – during the communist regime. Timár's *Zimmer Feri* (sic), set on Lake Balaton, pits a young practical joker against a bunch of loud German tourists. *6:3* takes viewers back to

1953 to that glorious moment when Hungary defeated England in football by that score at Ferencváros stadium (see Spectator Sports in the Entertainment chapter).

SOCIETY & CONDUCT
Traditional Culture

Apart from the Busójárás festival at Mohács in Southern Transdanubia, Farsang and other pre-Lenten carnivals are celebrated in Budapest and other urban centres at balls and private parties and some people go in costume. The sprinkling of water or perfume on young girls on Easter Monday is now rare, though the Christmas tradition of *Betlehemzés*, where young men and boys carry model churches containing a manger from door to door, can still be seen in some parts of the countryside. A popular event for Budapesters with tenuous ties to the countryside is the *disznótor*, the slaughtering of a pig followed by an orgy of feasting and drinking. (The butchering, gratefully, is done somewhere out the back by an able-bodied peasant.) Wine harvest festivals occur throughout the wine-growing regions in September and October, and there's a massive wine festival held in venues throughout Budapest in early September.

Social Life

In general Hungarians – and people from Budapest in particular – are not uninhibited like the Romanians or sentimental Slavs who will laugh or cry at the drop of a hat (or a drink). They are reserved, very formal people. Forget the impassioned, devil-may-care Gypsy-fiddling stereotype – it doesn't exist. The national anthem calls Hungarians 'a people torn by fate' and the overall mood is one of *honfibú* (literally 'patriotic sorrow', but really a penchant for the blues with a sufficient amount of hope to keep most people going).

This mood certainly predates communism. To illustrate what she calls the 'dark streak in the Hungarian temperament', the veteran US foreign correspondent Flora Lewis recounts a story from the 1930s in *Europe: A Tapestry of Nations*. 'It was said,' she writes, 'that a song called *Gloomy*

Sunday so deeply moved otherwise normal people (in Budapest) that whenever it was played, they would rush to commit suicide by jumping off a Danube bridge.' The song has been covered in English by several artists, including Billie Holiday and Sinéad O'Connor.

Hungarians are almost always extremely polite in social interaction, and the language can be very courtly – even when doing business with the butcher or having your hair cut. The standard greeting for a man to a woman (or youngsters to their elders, regardless of the sex) is *Csókolom* ('I kiss it' – 'it' being the hand, of course). People of all ages – even close friends – shake hands profusely when meeting up.

But while all this gentility certainly oils the wheels that turn a sometimes difficult society, it can be used to keep 'outsiders' (foreigners and other Hungarians) at a distance. Perhaps as an extension of this desire to keep everything running as smoothly as possible, Hungarians are always extremely helpful in an emergency – be it an accident, a pick-pocketing or simply helping someone who's lost their way.

Like Spaniards, Poles and many others with a Catholic background, Hungarians celebrate name days rather than birthdays. Name days are usually the Catholic feast day of their patron saint, but less holy names have a date too. All Hungarian calendars list them as do newspapers; there's even a telephone number to call that tells Hungarians which name is being remembered that day. Flowers, cakes or a bottle of wine are the usual gifts, and tradition dictates that you can present them up to eight days after the event.

Drinking is an important part of social life in a country that has produced wine and fruit brandies for thousands of years. Consumption is high; only France and Germany drink more alcohol per capita. Alcoholism in Hungary is not as visible to the outsider as it is, say, in Poland, but it's there nonetheless: in the smoky *borozó* (wine bar) that opens at dawn and does a brisk business all day, or in the kitchen as the working mother downs another half-litre of

vodka while trying to cope with her job, household chores and family. Official figures suggest that as many as 6% of the population are fully fledged alcoholics, but some experts say that between 40% and 50% of all males drink 'problematically'. There is little pressure for others (particularly women) to drink, and if you really don't want that glass of apricot brandy your host hands you, refuse politely.

Hungarians let their hair – and most of their clothes – down in summer at lake and riverside resorts and even in city parks and along the Danube Embankment. In warm weather you'll see more public displays of affection on the streets than perhaps anywhere else in the world. It's all very romantic, but beware: in the remoter corners of Budapest's parks you may stumble upon more passionate displays (which always seems to embarrass the stumbler more than the active participants).

Dos & Don'ts

If you're invited to someone's home, bring a bunch of flowers (available in profusion all year and very inexpensive) or a bottle of good local wine. You can talk about anything, but money is a touchy subject. Traditionally, the discussion or manifestation of wealth – wearing flashy jewellery, for example – was considered gauche here (as it was throughout Eastern Europe). Nowadays no-one thinks they have enough money, and those still in the low-paying public sector are often jealous of people who have made the leap to better jobs in the private sector. Your salary – piddling as you may think it is back home – will astonish most Hungarians.

Though it's almost impossible to calculate (the 'black economy' being so widespread and important), the average monthly salary in Hungary at the time of writing was just under 68,000Ft (US$260/£164/A$418).

Treatment of Animals

Hungarians as a whole are extremely fond of animals and Budapest has scores of *állat-díszhal bolt*, pet shops selling everything from puppies and hamsters to tropical fish. They are especially fond of dogs (you can't miss the mop-like *puli*, the sleek *vizsla* or the giant white *komondor* breeds indigenous to Hungary), and people of all ages go gaga over a particularly friendly or attractive one. I should know; I was at the other end of the lead for 2½ years.

RELIGION

Throughout history, religion in Hungary has often been a question of expediency. Under King Stephen, Catholicism won the battle for dominance over Orthodoxy and, while the majority of Hungarians were quite happily Protestants by the end of the 16th century, many donned a new mantle during the Counter-Reformation under the Habsburgs. During the Turkish occupation thousands of Hungarians converted to Islam – though not always willingly.

As a result of all this, Hungarians tend to have a more pragmatic approach to religion than most of their neighbours, and almost none of the bigotry. It has even been suggested that this generally sceptical view of matters of faith has led to Hungarians' high rate of success in science and mathematics. Except in villages and on the most important holy days (Easter, the Assumption of Mary, Christmas), churches are never full. The Jewish community in Budapest, though, has seen a great revitalisation in recent years.

Of those Hungarians declaring religious affiliation, about 68% say they are Roman Catholic, 21% Reformed (Calvinist) Protestant and 6% Evangelical (Lutheran) Protestant. There are also small Greek Catholic and Orthodox congregations. Hungary's Jews number about 80,000, down from a prewar population of almost 10 times that size. Some 400,000 died during deportation under the fascist Arrow Cross in 1944 or were murdered in Nazi concentration camps. Many others emigrated after 1956.

LANGUAGE

The national language is Hungarian (Magyar), and Hungarians like to boast that it ranks with Japanese and Arabic as among the world's most difficult. All languages are hard for non-native speakers to master, but it's true, Hungarian is a bitch to learn. Don't let this put you off attempting a few words and phrases, however. Partly as a reaction to the compulsory study of Russian in all schools until the late 1980s, Hungarians prefer to speak only Hungarian – attempt a few words in Magyar and they'll be impressed, take it as a compliment and be extremely encouraging.

The second most useful language for getting around in Budapest is German. Historical ties, geographical proximity and the fact that it was the preferred language of the literati up until the turn of the 20th century have given it almost semi-official status. However, outside Budapest and Transdanubia, the frequency and quality of spoken German is low.

English is slowly becoming more common in Budapest; if you're desperate, look for someone young, preferably under the age of 25. Familiarity with Italian is increasing due to tourism, but French and Spanish will be of little use.

For more on what to say and how to say it *Magyarul* (in Hungarian – literally 'Hungarian-ly'), see the Language chapter at the back of this book.

Facts for the Visitor

WHEN TO GO

Every season has its attractions – and its limitations – in Budapest. Though it can be pretty wet in May and early June, spring is just glorious here. The summer is warm, sunny and unusually long but, as elsewhere in Europe, Budapest comes to a grinding halt in August, which Hungarians traditionally call 'the cucumber-growing season' because that's about the only thing happening (although lots more festivals are now scheduled in that month).

Autumn is beautiful, particularly in the Buda Hills, though the foliage is more colourful in the Mátra or Bükk Hills of the Northern Uplands. Winter can be wonderful, with bright blue skies, a light dusting of snow on church spires, ice floes in the Danube and ice skating in City Park. But it can also be cold and bleak, with museums and other tourist sights closed or their hours sharply curtailed.

For more information, see the Climate section in the Facts about Budapest chapter.

ORIENTATION

Budapest lies in the north-central part of Hungary, some 250km south-east of Vienna. It is a large, sprawling city measuring 525 sq km and, with few exceptions (eg, Buda Hills, City Park, some excursions), the areas beyond the Nagykörút (literally the 'Big Ring Road') in Pest and west of Moszkva tér in Buda are residential or industrial and of little interest to visitors. It is a well laid-out city and it is almost difficult to get lost here.

If you look at a map of the city you'll see that two ring roads – the big one and the semicircular Kiskörút (Little Ring Road) – link three of the bridges across the Danube and essentially define central Pest. The Nagykörút consists of Szent István körút, Teréz körút, Erzsébet körút, József körút and Ferenc körút. The Kiskörút comprises Károly körút, Múzeum körút and Vámház körút. Important boulevards like Bajcsy-Zsilinszky út, leafy Andrássy út, Rákóczi út

and Üllői út fan out from the ring roads, creating large squares and circles.

Buda is dominated by Castle and Gellért Hills. The main roads here are Margit körút (the only part of either ring road that crosses the river), Fő utca and Attila út on either side of Castle Hill, and Hegyalja út and Bartók Béla út running west and south-west.

Many visitors will arrive at one of the three train stations: Keleti (Eastern), Nyugati (Western) and Déli (Southern); see Train in the Getting There & Away chapter for details. All three stations are on one of the three metro lines, which converge at Deák tér, a busy square a few minutes' walk north-east of the Inner Town (Belváros).

Budapest is divided into 23 *kerület*, or districts, which usually have traditional names like Lipótváros (Leopold Town) or Víziváros (Watertown). While these can sometimes help visitors negotiate their way around (all of Castle Hill is in district I, for example, and the Inner Town is district V), we've divided the city into a dozen walks for easy touring. The Roman numeral appearing before each street address signifies the district.

MAPS

Lonely Planet's *Budapest City Map* has a street and sights index and covers the more popular parts of town in detail.

The best folding maps to the city are Cartographia's 1:20,000 (350Ft) and 1:28,000 (300Ft) *Budapest City* ones available everywhere. If you plan to see the city thoroughly or stay more than just a few days, the *Budapest Atlas*, also from Cartographia, is indispensable for long-term stayers. It comes in two scales: 1:25,000 (1000Ft) and the larger-sized 1:20,000 (1300Ft). Both have indexes with all the new street names and some descriptive information in English. There is also a 1:25,000 pocket atlas of the Inner Town available for 390Ft.

Cartographia has its own outlet at VI Bajcsy-Zsilinszky út 37 (Map 5; ☎ 312 6001, metro Arany János utca), but it's not

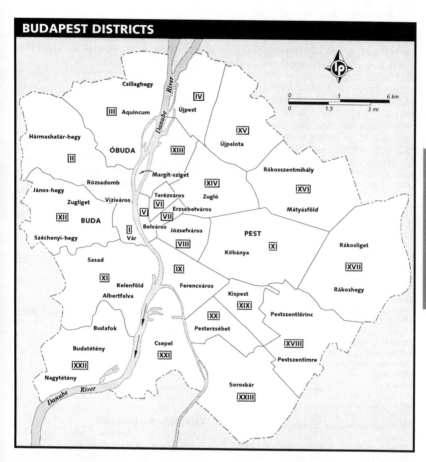

BUDAPEST DISTRICTS

(Map showing Budapest districts, including: Csillaghegy, IV, III Aquincum, Újpest, Hármashatár-hegy, II, XV, Újpalota, ÓBUDA, XIII, Rákosszentmihály, Margit-sziget, XIV, XVI, Rózsadomb, Terézváros, Zugló, János-hegy, Víziváros, VI, Mátyásföld, Zugliget, V, Erzsébetváros, XII, BUDA, VII, Belváros, Józsefváros, PEST, I Vár, VIII, Széchenyi-hegy, Kőbánya, X, Rákosliget, Sasad, IX, XVII, XI, Kelenföld, Ferencváros, Rákoshegy, Albertfalva, Kispest, XIX, Pestszentlőrinc, XX, Budafok, Pesterzsébet, XVIII, Budatétény, Csepel, Pestszentimre, XXII, XXI, Nagytétény, Soroskár, XXIII, Danube River)

Scale: 0 – 3 – 6 km / 0 – 1.5 – 3 mi

self-service, which can be annoying. A better bet is the small Párisi udvari könyvesbolt (Párisi Udvar bookshop) in the Párisi Udvar at V Petőfi Sándor utca 2 (Map 5; ☎ 318 3136, metro Ferenciek tere), the larger Libri map shop at VII Nyár utca 1 (Map 5; ☎ 322 0438, metro Blaha Lujza tér), open from 9.30 am to 5.30 pm weekdays, or the Lira & Lánt map shop (Map 5; ☎ 317 3130) at V Sas utca 1.

TOURIST OFFICES
Local Tourist Offices

The best single source of information is the Hungarian National Tourist Office's main Tourinform branch (Map 5; ☎ 317 9800, fax 317 9656, @ hungary@tourinform.hu) at V Sütő utca 2, just off Deák tér (metro Deák tér) in Pest. It's open from 9 am to 7 pm weekdays and to 4 pm at the weekend. Though the staff can't book you accommodation, they'll send you somewhere that does and will help with anything else – from maps and ferry schedules to where to find vegetarian food.

Among other Tourinform offices is the one at Nyugati train station (Map 5; ☎/fax 302 8580, @ budapest2@tourinform.hu) next to platform No 10, which is open from

7 am to 8 pm daily (metro Nyugati pálya-udvar), and the office (Map 5; ☎ 352 1433, fax 352 9804, ✆ budapest3@tourinform.hu) at VII Király utca 93 (metro Vörösmarty utca), which is open from 9 am to 6 pm daily.

The Budapest Tourist Office (BTO; Map 4; ☎ 488 0453, fax 488 0474) at I Tár-nok utca 9-11 in the Castle District can point you in the right direction, organise tours and change money from 8 am to 8 pm daily from April to October, and from 9 am to 6 pm the rest of the year. There's a Pest branch (Map 5; ☎ 322 4098, fax 342 2541) at VI Liszt Ferenc tér 11 (metro Oktogon).

Many of the offices listed under Travel Agencies later and those under Private Rooms in the Places to Stay chapter also provide information and often brochures and maps.

Tourist Offices Abroad

The national tourist office has branches in some 16 countries, including the following:

Austria
(☎ 0222-585 201210, fax 585 201221,
✆ htvienna@hungarytourism.hu)
Opernring 3-5, A-1010 Vienna
Czech Republic
(☎ 02-2109 0135, fax 2109 0139, ✆ htprague@hungarytourism.hu) Rumunská 22, 22537 Prague 2
France
(☎ 01 53 70 67 17, fax 01 47 04 83 57,
✆ htparis@hungarytourism.hu) 140 Avenue Victor Hugo, 75116 Paris
Web site: www.office-de-tourisme.com
Germany
Frankfurt: (☎ 069-9291 190, fax 9291 1918,
✆ htfrankfurt@hungarytourism.hu) Berliner Strasse 72, D-60311 Frankfurt-am-Main
Berlin: (☎ 030-243 146 0, fax 243 146 13,
✆ htberlin@hungarytourism.hu) Karl Liebknecht Strasse 34, D-10178 Berlin
Netherlands
(☎ 070-320 9092, fax 327 2833, ✆ htden haga@hungarytourism.hu) Postbus 91644, 2509 EE The Hague
Romania
(☎/fax 064-414 520, ✆ htcluj@hungary tourism.hu) Consulate of Hungary, Piata Unirii, CP 352, 3400 Cluj-Napoca
UK
(☎/fax 020-7823 1032, fax 7823 1459,
✆ htlondon@hungarytourism.hu), 46 Eaton Place, London SW1X 8AL

Ukraine
(☎ 044-229 9628, fax 229 9661, ✆ htkiev@hungarytourism.hu) vul Striletska 16, 252034 Kiev 34
USA
(☎ 212-355 0240, fax 207 4103, ✆ htnew york@hungarytourism.hu) 150 East 58th St, 33/F, New York, NY 10155-3398
Web site: www.gotohungary.com

In countries without a national tourist office branch, contact the Hungarian national airlines, Malév, which has offices or associated agencies in some four dozen countries worldwide, including the following:

Australia
(☎ 02-9244 2111, fax 9290 3306, ✆ wassyd@worldaviation.com.au) World Aviation Systems, 403 George St, Sydney 2000 NSW
Canada
(☎ 416-944 0093, fax 944 0095, ✆ toronto@malev.hu) 175 Bloor St East, Suite 909, Toronto, Ont M4W 3R8
Ireland
(☎ 1-844 6127, fax 844 6092, ✆ dublin@malev.hu) South Apron, Gategourmet Building, Dublin Airport
New Zealand
(☎ 09-379 4455, fax 377 5648) World Aviation Systems, Trustbank Building, 6/F, 229 Queen St, Auckland 1
Yugoslavia
(☎ 011-323 9673, fax 323 0224)
Ul Nusiceva 4, 3/F, Belgrade

TRAVEL AGENCIES

Unless noted otherwise, travel agencies in Budapest are open from 8 or 8.30 am to 5 pm weekdays, and in summer till noon or 1 pm Saturday.

An outfit called Vista has the most comprehensive array of services of any travel agency in Budapest – it's one of only three such outfits in the world. It's an amazing place and they do everything – from room bookings and chauffeured Trabant service to adventure sport and discounted student air fares (but *not* domestic train tickets). For all your outgoing needs (air tickets, package tours etc) go to the Vista Travel Centre (Map 5; ☎ 269 6032, fax 267 5568, ✆ info@vista.hu) at VI Andrássy út 1 (enter from VI Paulay Ede utca), which is open from 9 am to 6.30 pm weekdays and to 2.30 pm Saturday. The nearby Vista Visitor Centre (Map 5; ☎ 268 0888, fax 267 5568) at VI Paulay Ede utca 7 does all the incoming stuff – tourist information, study and eco tours etc – and has a popular cafe, a bookshop called Bamako and a call centre. It's open 24 hours a day seven days a week. Visit its Web site at www.vista.hu.

In Pest, the main Ibusz office (Map 5; ☎ 317 1806 or 318 1763, ✉ reservation@ ibusz.hu), V Ferenciek tere 10, supplies travel brochures, and the staff are usually very good about answering general questions. It also changes money, books all forms of accommodation and accepts credit card payments. Another Ibusz office (Map 5; ☎ 321 2932 or 322 2452) is at VII Dob utca 1 (metro Astoria).

Express (Map 5; ☎ 317 6634, fax 317 6823) at V Semmelweis utca 4 (metro Astoria), open from 8.30 am to 4 pm weekdays (to 5 pm Thursday and, from June to September, from 9 am to noon Saturday), sells BIJ train tickets with discounts of up to 35% on international trains to those under the age of 26. There's another Express office (Map 5; ☎ 331 7777, fax 331 6393) at V Szabadság tér 16 (metro Kossuth tér).

The Wasteels agency (☎ 210 2802) on platform No 9 at Keleti train station (Map 3; metro Keleti pályaudvar) also sells BIJ tickets. You must have an ISIC or GO25 card (available from Express or Vista for 900Ft) to get the student fare. The office is open from 8 am to 7 pm weekdays and to 1 pm Saturday.

Other helpful agencies in Pest are Budapest Tourist (Map 5; ☎ 318 6167, fax 318 6062), V Roosevelt tér 5, and Cooptourist (Map 5; ☎ 374 6229 or 332 6387) at Kossuth Lajos tér 13-15. In Buda, aside from the agencies at Déli train station mentioned in the Places to Stay chapter, there's a Cooptourist (Map 6; ☎ 209 6667) at XI Bartók Béla út 4.

DOCUMENTS
Passport
Almost everyone entering Hungary must have a valid passport, though citizens of Austria, Belgium, France, Italy, Liechtenstein, Luxembourg, Germany, Slovenia, Spain and Switzerland need only produce their national identity card. It's a good idea to carry your passport or other identification at all times.

Visas
Citizens of the USA, Canada, all European countries (except Albania and Turkey) and South Africa do not require visas to visit Hungary for stays of up to 90 days. Nationals of Australia, Hong Kong, Singapore, Taiwan and New Zealand (among others) still do need them. If you hold a passport from one of these countries, check current visa requirements at an embassy or consulate or any Malév or national tourist office branch.

A single-entry visa can be purchased at a Hungarian consulate or foreign mission in your country of residence upon receipt of US$40 and three photos (it costs US$65 if purchased at a foreign mission outside your country of residence or at the border). A double-entry tourist visa costs US$75/100, and you must have five photos. A multiple-entry visa is US$180/200. Some consulates charge US$15 extra for express service (10 minutes as opposed to overnight). Single and double-entry visas are valid for six months prior to use. Multiple entries are good for a year.

Be sure to get a tourist rather than a transit visa; the latter – available for single (US$38/50), double (US$65/90) and multiple (US$150/180) crossings – is only good for a stay of 48 hours and cannot be extended. On a transit visa you must enter and leave through different border crossings and have a visa (if required) for the next country you visit. A tourist visa can be extended (3000Ft) at the central police station (*rendőrkapitánység*) of any city or town, provided you do so 48 hours before it expires. Rather than face the bureaucracy, most travellers just go to a neighbouring country like Austria and then re-enter.

Visas are issued at most international highway border crossings (see Car & Motorcycle in the Getting There & Away chapter) and the airport, but this usually involves a wait and there are not always photo booths nearby if you've forgotten your mug shots. Visas are never issued on trains and seldom to passengers on international buses.

You are supposed to register with the police if staying in one place for more than 30 days, and your hotel, hostel, camping ground or private room booked through an agency will do it for you. In other situations (eg, if you're staying with friends or relatives), you have to take care of this yourself within 72 hours of your arrival. The office in Budapest dealing with foreigners' registrations is KEOKH (Map 3; ☎ 343 0034) at VI Városligeti fasor 46-48 (metro Bajza utca or trolleybus No 75 or 79). Don't worry if you haven't got round to it; it's a hangover from the old regime, and enforcement has been fairly lax. Address registration forms for foreigners (*lakcímbejelentő lap külföldiek részére*) are available at main post offices.

Travel Insurance

You should seriously consider taking out travel insurance. This not only covers you for medical expenses and luggage theft or loss but also for cancellation or delays in your travel arrangements. (You could fall seriously ill two days before departure, for example.) Cover depends on your insurance and type of airline ticket, so ask both your insurer and your ticket-issuing agency to explain where you stand. Ticket loss is also covered by travel insurance.

Paying for your airline ticket with a credit card often provides limited travel accident insurance, and you may be able to reclaim the payment if the operator doesn't deliver. In the UK, for instance, institutions issuing credit cards are required by law to reimburse consumers if a company goes into liquidation and the amount in contention is more than UK£100. Ask your credit card company what it's prepared to cover.

Driving Licence & Permits

If you don't hold a European driving licence and plan to drive while in Budapest, obtain an International Driving Permit from your local automobile association before

you leave – you'll need a passport photo and a valid local licence. They are usually inexpensive and valid for one year only.

Hostel Cards

A hostel card is sometimes useful here. Though no hostels in Budapest actually require you to be a Hostelling International (or associated) member, they sometimes charge less if you have a card. Express, with several offices in Budapest (see Travel Agencies earlier), will issue you an HI card for 1250Ft.

Student, Youth & Teacher Cards

The International Student Identity Card (ISIC), a plastic ID-style card, provides discounts on some forms of transport and cheap admission to museums, sights and even films. If you're aged under 26 but not a student, you can apply for a GO25 card issued by the Federation of International Youth Travel Organisations (FIYTO), which gives much the same discounts and benefits. An ITIC identifies the holder as a teacher and offers similar deals. Express sells all these cards for 900Ft each.

Seniors Cards

Many attractions offer reduced-price admission for people over 60 or 65 (sometimes as low as 55 for women) but this is usually just for Hungarian *nyugdíjasok* (pensioners). For a fee of around €15, European residents aged over 60 can get a Rail Europe Senior (RES) card as an add-on to their national rail senior pass. It entitles the holder to reduced European fares of about 30%.

Discount Cards

Budapest Card One of the best deals around for short-term visitors, the Budapest Card offers holders unlimited travel on public transport; free admission to some 55 museums and other sights, including the City Zoo and the caves of the Buda Hills; discounts in shops, restaurants, entertainment venues, sports facilities and the medicinal baths as well as on cultural, folklore and tour programs, the airport bus and car hire and pleasure flights. The card, which costs

2800/3400Ft for an adult and one child under 14 years of age for two/three days, is available at Tourinform offices, major train stations and the Hotelinfo travel agency (Map 5; ☎ 267 0896) at V Váci utca 78-80 in Budapest and at Malév offices and travel agencies overseas.

Hungary Card This discount card (3920Ft), valid for 13 months, offers savings of between 5% and 25% on hotels, pensions, camp sites and restaurants throughout Hungary (including the capital), up to 50% on train, bus and boat travel, and some museums and cultural events are free to card holders. It even gives you a 15% discount on the Budapest Card described above. It is available at the same outlets as the Budapest Card.

Copies

The hassles brought on by losing your passport can be considerably reduced if you have a record of its number and issue date, or even better, photocopies of the relevant data pages. A photocopy of your birth certificate can also be useful. Also add the serial numbers of your travellers cheques (cross them off as you cash them) and photocopies of your credit cards, airline ticket and other travel documents.

It's also a good idea to store details of your vital travel documents in Lonely Planet's free online Travel Vault in case you lose the photocopies or can't be bothered with them. Your password-protected Travel Vault is accessible online anywhere in the world – create it at www.ekno. lonelyplanet.com.

EMBASSIES & CONSULATES
Hungarian Embassies & Consulates

Hungarian embassies and consulates abroad include the following:

Australia
(☎ 02-6282 3226) 17 Beale Crescent, Deakin, ACT 2600
(☎ 02-9328 7859) Edgecliff Centre, Suite 405, 203-233 New South Head Road, Edgecliff, NSW 2027

Austria
(☎ 0222-533 2631) 1 Bankgasse 4-6, 1010 Vienna
Canada
(☎ 613-230 9614) 299 Waverley St, Ottawa, Ont K2P 0V9
(☎ 416-923 8981) 121 Bloor St East, Suite 1115, Toronto, Ont M4W 3M5
Croatia
(☎ 01-422 296) Ul Krlezin Gvozd 11/a, 41000 Zagreb
Czech Republic
(☎ 02-365 041) Ul Badeniho 1, 12537 Prague 6
France
(☎ 01 43 54 66 96) 92 Rue Bonaparte, 75006 Paris
Germany
(☎ 030-220 2561) Unter den Linden 72, 10177 Berlin
(☎ 0228-371 112) Turmstrasse 30, 53175 Bonn
(☎ 089-911 032) Vollmannstrasse 2, 81927 Munich 8
Ireland
(☎ 01-661 2902) 2 Fitzwilliam Place, Dublin 2
Netherlands
(☎ 070-350 0404) Hogeweg 14, 2585 JD The Hague
New Zealand
(☎ 04-938 0427, fax 938 0428) 151 Orangi Kaupapa Rd, Wellington 6005
Romania
(☎ 01-311 0062) Strada Jean-Louis Calderon 63-65, Bucharest
Slovakia
(☎ 07-533 0541) Sedlarska ul 3, 81425 Bratislava
Slovenia
(☎ 061-152 1882) Ul Konrada Babnika 5, Ljubljana-Sentvid 1210
South Africa
(☎ 012-433 030) 959 Arcadia St, 0132 Pretoria
(☎ 021-641 547) 14 Fernwood Ave, Rondebosch, 7701 Cape Town
UK
(☎ 020-7235 5218) 35 Eaton Place, London SW1X 8BY
Ukraine
(☎ 044-212 4134) Ul Rejterskaya 33, 252901 Kiev
USA
(☎ 202-362 6730) 3910 Shoemaker St NW, Washington, DC 20008
(☎ 212-752 0661) 223 East 52nd St, New York, NY 10022
Yugoslavia
(☎ 011-444 0472) Ul Ivana Milutinovica 74, Belgrade 11000

Embassies in Budapest

Selected countries with representation in Budapest follow.

Australia (☎ 201 8899) XII Királyhágó tér 8-9 (open 9 am to noon weekdays)
Austria (☎ 352 6913) VI Benczúr utca 16 (open 9 to 11 am weekdays)
Canada (☎ 275 1200) XII Budakeszi út 32 (open 8 am to noon weekdays)
Croatia (☎ 249 2215) XII Arató utca 22/b (open 10 am to 2 pm weekdays)
Czech Republic (☎ 351 0539) VI Székely Bertalan utca 4 (open 8.30 am to 12.30 pm weekdays)
France (☎ 332 4980) VI Lendvay utca 27 (open 9 am to 12.30 pm weekdays)
Germany (☎ 467 3500) XIV Stefánia út 101-103 (open 9 am to noon weekdays)
Ireland (☎ 302 9600) V Szabadság tér 7 (open 9.30 am to 12.30 pm and 2.30 to 4.30 pm weekdays)
Netherlands (☎ 326 5301) II Füge utca 5-7 (open 10 am to noon weekdays)
Romania (☎ 352 0271) XIV Thököly út 72 (open 8.30 am to noon Monday to Wednesday, to 11.30 am Friday)
Slovakia (☎ 251 7973) XIV Gervay utca 44 (open 8.30 to 11.30 am and 2 to 3.30 pm weekdays)
Slovenia (☎ 335 6694) II Cseppkő utca 68 (open 9 am to noon weekdays)
South Africa (☎ 392 0999) II Gárdonyi Géza út 17 (open 9 am to 12.30 pm weekdays)
UK (☎ 266 2888) V Harmincad utca 6 (open 9.30 am to noon and 2 to 4 pm weekdays)
Ukraine (☎ 355 9609) XII Nógrádi utca 8 (open 9 am to noon weekdays)
USA (☎ 475 4400 or 475 4703 after hours) V Szabadság tér 12 (open 8.15 am to 5 pm weekdays)
Yugoslavia (☎ 322 9838) VI Dózsa György út 92/b (open 10 am to 1 pm weekdays)

CUSTOMS

You can bring in the usual personal effects as well as 250 cigarettes, 2L of wine and 1L of spirits duty-free.

When leaving Budapest, you are not supposed to take out valuable antiques without a special permit (see the boxed text 'Permission Granted' in the Shopping chapter).

Restrictions on the import/export of forint won't affect most travellers; the ceiling is now 350,000Ft.

MONEY
Currency

The Hungarian forint (Ft) was once divided into 100 fillér, worthless little aluminium coins that have now been withdrawn from circulation. There are coins of one, two, five, 10, 20, 50 and 100Ft.

Notes come in six denominations: 200, 500, 1000, 2000, 5000 and 10,000Ft.

The green 200Ft features King Charles Robert (Károly Róbert) and his castle at Diósgyőr near Miskolc. The hero of the independence wars, Ferenc Rákóczi II, and Sárospatak Castle are on the burgundy-coloured 500Ft note.

The 1000Ft note is blue and bears a portrait of King Matthias Corvinus, with Hercules Well at Visegrád Castle on the other side. The 17th-century prince of Transylvania, Gábor Bethlen, is shown alone on one side of the 2000Ft bill and meeting with advisers on the other.

The 'greatest Hungarian', Count István Széchenyi and his family home at Nagycenk is on the purplish 5000Ft note. The highest-denominated bill (10,000Ft) is reserved for King Stephen, naturally enough, with Esztergom appearing on the other side.

Exchange Rates

Exchange rates at the time of going to press were:

country	unit		forint
Australia	A$1	=	156Ft
Austria	AS1	=	19Ft
Canada	C$1	=	180Ft
European Union	€1	=	257Ft
France	1FF	=	39Ft
Germany	DM1	=	132Ft
Ireland	IR£1	=	327Ft
Japan	¥100	=	247Ft
Netherlands	fl	=	117Ft
New Zealand	NZ$1	=	130Ft
South Africa	R1	=	41Ft
UK	£1	=	420Ft
USA	US$1	=	265Ft

Exchanging Money

Cash & Travellers Cheques Nothing beats cash for convenience – or risk. However, it's always prudent to carry a little foreign cash – US$50 or DM100, say – in case you can't find an automatic teller machine (ATM) nearby or there's no bank or travel office open to cash your travellers cheques.

You can exchange cash and travellers cheques – American Express, Visa and Thomas Cook are the most recognisable brands in Budapest – at most banks and post offices; the National Savings Bank (Országos Takarékpénztár or OTP) has branches everywhere and charges no commission on travellers cheques. Travel agents usually take a commission of 1% to 2%. Using private money-change bureaus can be convenient but expensive. Shops never accept travellers cheques.

Though the forint is now a totally convertible currency, you should avoid changing too much. You are allowed to change leftover forint back into foreign currency without limit, but you must have official receipts for anything over 20,0000Ft. It might be difficult exchanging forint beyond the borders of Hungary's neighbours.

ATMs & Credit Cards The hassle of trying to change travellers cheques at the weekend, rip-off bureaux de change and the allure of the black market have all gone the way of the dodo in Budapest, with the arrival of ATMs that accept most credit and cash cards.

Credit cards are still not as commonly used as payment as in Western European cities but they're gaining ground, especially American Express, Visa and MasterCard. You'll be able to use them at upmarket restaurants, shops, hotels, car-rental firms, travel agencies and petrol stations.

K&H banks and post offices will give you a cash advance on most major credit cards; American Express (Map 5) is at V Deák Ferenc utca 10.

International Transfers Having money wired to Budapest through Thomas Cook or American Express is fairly straightforward; for the latter you don't need to be a cardholder and it takes less than a day. You should know the sender's full name, the exact amount and the reference number when you're picking up the cash. With a passport or other ID you'll be given the amount in US dollars or forint. The sender pays the service fee (eg, US$20 for $100, US$40 for $500, US$60 for $1000 etc).

Guaranteed Cheques Many banks, including OTP branches, as well as post offices in Budapest will cash up to three Eurocheques worth 35,000Ft per transaction.

Black Market It's senseless to make use of the black market to change money. The advantage – 5% to 10% on the outside – is not worth the bother, it's illegal and you are almost sure to be ripped off anyway.

Costs

Relatively high inflation and the systematic devaluation of the forint has made life very difficult for Hungarians earning local salaries, but for foreign travellers Budapest remains a bargain destination for food, lodging and transport. If you stay in private rooms, eat at medium-priced restaurants and travel by public transport, you should get by easily on less than US$25 a day without scrimping. Those putting up in hostels, dormitories or camping grounds and eating at self-service restaurants or food stalls will cut costs substantially.

Because of the rapidly changing value of the forint, many hotels quote their rates in Deutschmarks – at least until June 2002 when that currency ceases to exist in favour of the euro. Also the national rail company MÁV has begun to list its prices in euros. In such cases, we have had to follow suit. For restaurants, all other forms of transport, articles in shops etc we always quote prices in forint.

Tipping & Bargaining

In general Hungary is a very tip-conscious society and virtually everyone routinely tips waiters, hairdressers and taxi drivers. Doctors and dentists accept 'gratitude money' (see Health later in this chapter), and even

FACTS FOR THE VISITOR

The Euro

On 1 January 1999 a new currency, the euro (denoted with the symbol €), was introduced in 11 EU countries, including Germany and Austria. Euro banknotes and coins will be introduced on 1 January 2002, ushering in a period of dual use of euros and local currency. By July 2002 local currency in the 11 countries will be withdrawn and only euros will remain. The effect of the euro's introduction on travel in Hungary will mainly be restricted to the replacement of the Deutschmark by the euro. Many places to stay and travel agencies may also show prices in euros (the MÁV rail network already does), while the euro may well replace the US dollar as the best hard currency to travel with in Europe. The full effect of the euro's introduction on travel in Hungary, and Europe for that matter, is hard to predict, and you should check with your travel agent before you leave.

petrol station and thermal spa attendants expect 50Ft to 100Ft. If you were less than impressed with the service at the restaurant, the joyride in the taxi or the way someone cut your hair, leave next to nothing or nothing at all. He or she will get the message.

The way you tip in restaurants is unusual. You never leave the money on the table – this is considered both rude and stupid here – but tell the waiter how much you're paying in total. If the bill is 1540Ft, you're paying with a 2000Ft note and you think the waiter deserves the extra 10%, first ask if service is included (some restaurants add it to the bill automatically). If it isn't, say you're paying 1700Ft or that you want 300Ft back.

Bargaining was never the done thing under the old regime; except for the privileged class, everyone paid the same amount by weight and volume for items freely available, including a scoop of ice cream. Though you'll never be able to do it in shops, you may haggle in flea markets or with individuals selling folk crafts. But even this is not as commonplace as it is in other parts of Eastern Europe.

Taxes & Refunds

ÁFA, a value-added tax (VAT) of between 12% and 25%, covers the purchase of all new goods in Hungary. It is almost always included in the quoted price but sometimes it is on top, so be wary. Visitors are not exempt, but they can claim refunds for total purchases of more than 50,000Ft on one invoice. However, claiming your money is a bit complicated. You must take the goods out of the country within 90 days, the ÁFA receipts (available from the shops where you made the purchases) should be stamped by customs at the border and the claim has to be made within six months of the purchase. No ÁFA is refunded on the purchase of works of art and antiques. Cash refunds are made at the following points before departure: Ferihegy Airport, the Mahart International Landing Stage on Belgrád rakpart in Budapest, Keleti train station and Ibusz branch offices at international border crossings.

Two outfits in Budapest that can help with refunds are Global Refund Tax Free Shopping (☎/fax 212 4906) at II Bég utca 3-5 and Inteltrade (☎ 356 9800, fax 375 0616) at I Csalogány utca 6-10.

Like most other municipalities in Hungary, Budapest levies a tourist tax on most forms of accommodation of about 3%. This may or may not be included in the rate you are quoted.

POST & COMMUNICATIONS

The Hungarian Postal Service (Magyar Posta) has improved somewhat in recent years; perhaps its jaunty logo of a stylised St Stephen's crown has helped kick-start it into the 21st century. But post offices are usually still crowded, service is slow and the exclusively Magyar-speaking staff would put the fear in Margaret Thatcher herself.

Postal Rates

Letters sent within Budapest costs 27Ft; for the rest of Hungary and neighbouring countries it's 32Ft (add 79/160Ft if you want to send it registered/express). Postcards within/outside the city and to neighbouring countries are 24/27Ft. Foreign air mail is 100Ft to 110Ft for up to 20g and 190Ft to 210Ft for 20 to 100g base rate plus 15Ft per 10g for air mail charge. Thus a standard 20g letter to most of Western Europe costs 130Ft and to the rest of the world 140Ft. Postcards are 130Ft and 140Ft respectively.

Sending & Receiving Mail

To beat the crowds at the post office, ask at kiosks, newsagents or stationery shops if they sell stamps. If you must deal with the post office, you'll be relieved to learn that most people are there to pay electric, gas and telephone bills or parking fines. To get in and out with a minimum of fuss (and tears), look for the window marked with the symbol of an envelope. Make sure the destination of your letter is written clearly, and simply hand it over to the clerk. He or she will apply the stamps for you, postmark it and send it on its way.

If you are trying to send a parcel, look for the sign 'Csomagfeladás' or 'Csomagfelvétel'. Packages must not weigh more than 2kg or else you'll face a Kafkaesque nightmare of permits and queues; try to send small packages. Books and printed matter are exceptions. You can send up to 2kg in one box for between 2200Ft and 2800Ft and up to 5kg for 5500Ft to 6900Ft.

Hungarian addresses start with the name of the recipient, followed on the next line by the postal code and city or town and then the street name and number. The postal code consists of four digits. The first indicates the city or town, the second and third the district and the last the neighbourhood.

Budapest's main post office (open from 8 am to 8 pm weekdays and to 2 pm Saturday) is in Pest at V Petőfi Sándor utca 13-15 (Map 5; metro Deák tér). It sells boxes of varying sizes for 300Ft to 600Ft. All post marked 'Poste Restante, Budapest' also arrives here but pick it up from the entrance at V Városháza utca 18; look for the sign 'Postán maradó', and make sure you have identification. Since the family name always comes first in Hungarian usage, have the sender underline your last name, as letters are often misfiled under foreigners' first names. You can have your mail delivered to American Express (1052 Budapest,

Deák Ferenc utca 10) if you have an AmEx credit card or travellers cheques.

The post office next to Nyugati train station (Map 5), VI Teréz körút 51, is open from 8 am to 8 pm daily while the one at Keleti station (Map 3), VIII Baross tér 11, keeps even longer hours: from 7 am to 9 pm but Monday to Saturday only.

Telephone

You can make domestic and international calls from public telephones, which are usually in good working order. To avoid having to carry a purse or pocket full of change, buy a telephone card from any post office or newsagent. These come in message units of 50/120Ft and cost 800/1800Ft. Telephone boxes with a black and white arrow and red target on the door and the word 'Visszahívható' display a telephone number, which can be phoned back.

The Belvárosi (Inner Town) Telephone Centre (Map 5; ☎ 317 5500) run by Matáv at V Petőfi Sándor utca 17-19 is open from 8 am to 8 pm weekdays, 9 am to 3 pm Saturday. There's also a call centre at the Vista Visitor Centre (see Travel Agencies earlier).

All localities in Hungary have a two-digit telephone area code, except for Budapest, which simply has a '1'. To make a local call in Budapest, pick up the receiver and listen for the neutral and continuous dial tone, then dial the seven-digit number. For a trunk call in Hungary, dial ☎ 06 and wait for the second, brrrring, tone. Then dial the six-digit number preceded by the two-digit area code. You must *always* dial ☎ 06 if ringing a mobile telephone (these mobile area codes are usually ☎ 209, 309 or 609).

The procedure for making an international call is the same except that you dial ☎ 00, followed by the country and area codes and then the number. International phone charges are: 132/99Ft per minute to neighbouring countries from a public/private telephone; 180/135Ft to most of Europe; 185/139Ft to North America, Australia and New Zealand; 450/338Ft to much of East Asia and the Pacific; 524/393Ft to the Middle East; and 625/469Ft to south Asia. The country code for Hungary is ☎ 36.

FACTS FOR THE VISITOR

There's a wide range of local and international phonecards. Lonely Planet's eKno Communication Card is aimed specifically at independent travellers and provides budget international calls, a range of messaging services, free email and travel information – for local calls, you're usually better off with a local card. You can join online at www. ekno.lonelyplanet.com, or by phone from Budapest by dialling ☎ 00-800 13572. Once you have joined, to use eKno from Hungary, dial ☎ 00-800 13568. Check the eKno Web site for joining and access numbers from other countries and updates on budget local access numbers and new features.

The AmCard (☎ 00-800 01213), a smart card with a face value of 3000Ft, will save you between 17% and 43% on phone calls to Europe, the USA and Asia. You can also get straight through to an operator based in your home country by dialling the 'country direct' number from a public phone (charges are reversed), but you need a coin or phone card for the initial connection and these services can be very expensive.

Australia Direct	☎ 00-800 11573
Australia (Telstra)	☎ 00-800 06111
Britain Direct (BT)	☎ 00-800 04411
Britain (Mercury)	☎ 00-800 04412
Canada Direct	☎ 00-800 01211
New Zealand Direct	☎ 00-800 06411
South Africa Direct	☎ 00-800 02711
USA Direct (AT&T)	☎ 00-800 01111
USA MCI	☎ 00-800 01411
USA Sprint Express	☎ 00-800 01877

Other numbers you may find useful include:

Domestic operator (English spoken)
   ☎ 198
International operator (English spoken)
   ☎ 199
Mobile phone directory assistance
   ☎ 464 6020 for area code 209
   ☎ 265 8585 for 309
   ☎ 265 8585 for 609
Time (in Hungarian)
   ☎ 080
Wake-up call (in Hungarian)
   ☎ 193

For emergency numbers see Emergencies later in this chapter.

Fax
The Belvárosi Telephone Centre (see under Telephone earlier) has fax and email as well as international telephone services. You can also send or receive faxes at hotel business centres like the one at the Kempinski Corvinus hotel (Map 5; ☎ 429 3777), V Erzsébet tér 7-8.

Email & Internet Access
Budapest counts up to a dozen cybercafes, but they are often crowded and reservations are not just advisable but essential at some. Many hostels also have at least one terminal. See that section in the Places to Stay chapter.

Budapest Net (Map 5; ☎ 328 0292, fax 328 0294, ✉ info@budapestnet.hu) V Kecskeméti utca 5 (metro Kálvin tér). With more than 30 terminals, this is the largest Internet cafe in Central Europe. It costs 700Ft to log on for the first hour, 500Ft thereafter. It's open from 10 am to 10 pm daily.

C3 (Centre for Culture & Communication; Map 4; ☎ 214 6856, fax 214 6872, ✉ info@c3.hu) I Országház utca 9 (bus No 16 from Erzsébet tér). Eight terminals available for free use for up to two hours but book ahead. Open 9 am to between 5 and 9 pm weekdays, from 10 am to 6 pm Sunday.

Café Eckermann (Map 5; ☎ 374 4076, fax 374 4080) Goethe Institute, VI Andrássy út 24 (metro Opera). Free access to one of three terminals limited to one hour a week. Open from 2 to 10 pm weekdays, from 10 am to 10 pm Saturday.

Cyber Sushi (Map 3; ☎ 391 5871, ✉ info@cyber-sushi.net) Rózsakert Shopping Centre, 3/F, II Gábor Áron utca 74-78 (bus No 11 from Batthyány tér). With its mega-fast machines, this place is a good bet if the more central cafes are booked up. We don't understand the sushi connection though; it doesn't seem to be on the menu. Open from 10 to 2 am daily.

Matáv Internet Café (☎ 267 6618, fax 485 6616, ✉ tanczos@lm.matav.hu) V Petőfi Sándor 17-19 (inside the Belvárosi Telephone Centre, Map 5; metro Deák tér). Some 16 terminals available for use from 9 am to 8 pm weekdays and from 10 am to 3 pm at the weekend and costing 300/500Ft per half-hour/hour use.

Teleport Internet Café (Map 5; ☎ 267 6361, ✆ teleport@skylab.net) VIII Vas utca 7 (metro Blaha Lujza tér). A dozen terminals available for use (500Ft per hour) from noon to 10 pm Monday to Saturday.

Vista Internet Café (☎ 267 8603, fax 267 5568, ✆ incoming@vista.hu) VII Paulay Ede utca 7 (inside the Vista Visitor Centre, Map 5; metro Deák tér). Six terminals available from 8 am to 10 pm weekdays and from 10 am to 10 pm at the weekend (11/660Ft per minute/hour).

INTERNET RESOURCES

The World Wide Web is a rich resource for travellers. You can research your trip, hunt down bargain air fares, book hotels, check the weather or chat with locals and other travellers about the best places to visit (or avoid!).

There's no better place to start your Web explorations than the Lonely Planet Web site (www.lonelyplanet.com). Here you'll find succinct summaries on travelling to most places on earth, postcards from other travellers and the Thorn Tree bulletin board, where you can ask questions before you go or dispense advice when you get back. You can also find travel news and updates to many of our most popular guidebooks, and the subWWWay section links you to the most useful travel resources elsewhere on the Web.

Other useful Web sites include:

Budapest Week Online Events, music and movie listings
www.budapestweek.com
Businessweb A wealth of information on business and economics
www.businessweb.hu
Hotels Information on hotels throughout Hungary
www.miwo.hu
www.hotels.hu
www.hotelshungary.com
www.hotelinfo.hu
Hungary.com A broad range of topics – from links to government offices to hotels
www.hungary.com
Hungary-Info Basic information on Hungary with business and travel links
www.hungary-info.com.
HVG Weekly magazine *HVG* (see Newspapers & Magazines) with summaries of lead stories
www.hvg.hu

Inside Hungary National news
www.insidehungary.com
Tourinform Tourist information and links
www.tourinform.hu
www.hungarytourism.hu

BOOKS

There's no shortage of books on Budapest and things Hungarian – from travel guides and histories to travelogues and cookery books. Once one of Budapest's biggest bargains, books have become more expensive, though they haven't yet reached prices comparable with the West.

Lonely Planet

Hungary takes a detailed look at the country, for those exploring beyond the capital.
Eastern Europe, Central Europe and *Europe on a shoestring* all contain chapters on Hungary, including sections on Budapest.
Eastern Europe phrasebook contains lengthy sections of useful words and expressions in Hungarian.

Guidebooks

Budapest: A Critical Guide by András Török. If you want a very personal look at one man's home town – without much practical help, however – pick up a copy. It's basically five walking tours and a lot of esoteric ruminations written by a 'thinking dandy' born and raised in the capital.
Budapest: A Cultural Guide by Michael Jacobs. Another good walking guide from a very solid historical (at times almost academic) perspective.
Jewish Heritage Travel: A Guide to Central and Eastern Europe by Ruth Gruber. Contains a comprehensive chapter on Hungary with lots on Budapest.
Jewish Budapest: Monuments, Rites, History by Kinga Frojimovics et al. A much more exhaustive study.
The Expatriate's Guide to Budapest & Hungary (Budapest Week Publishing), edited by Elysia Gallo and David Landry. A book offering much of interest for those who plan to stay a while in Hungary.
Budapest Architectural Guide (6 BT Publishing) edited by Zsuzsa Lőrinczi and Mihály Vargha. The most serious guide to Budapest's 20th-century cityscape is this bilingual guide which takes a detailed look at almost 300 buildings from 1896 to the present.

Travel

Travellers writing diary accounts usually treat Hungary and Budapest rather cursorily as they make tracks for 'more exotic' cities and countries farther east.

Between the Woods and the Water by Patrick Leigh Fermor. Fermor describes his 1933 walk through Hungary en route to Constantinople and, in doing so, he wrote the classic account of the country.

Stealing from a Deep Place by Brian Hall. Sensitive but never cloying, the author describes his tempered love affair with the still-communist Budapest of the 1980s.

The Double Eagle: Vienna, Budapest and Prague by Stephen Brook. A cultural and political commentary on the three major Habsburg cities through the eyes of a modern traveller. It has just gone out of print but can often be found at second-hand bookshops.

The City of the Magyar by Miss Julia Pardoe. One of the best sources for contemporary views of early-19th century Hungary, published in 1840. You'll only find this three-volume set (almost an entire volume is devoted to Budapest) in a library or antiquarian bookshop.

History & Politics

An Illustrated History of Budapest (Corvina) by Géza Buzinkay. An oversized and illustrated easy entry to the complicated history of the capital.

Hungary: A Brief History by István Lázár. A light, almost silly, history by geologist-cum-journalist

The Magyars: Their Life & Civilisation by Gyula László. A dense anthology of the beliefs, traditions and culture of the Hungarians at the time of the conquest.

A History of Modern Hungary by Jörg K Hoensch. Covers the period from 1867 to 1994 in a balanced, though somewhat dry, way.

A History of Hungary edited by Peter F Sugar. Arguably the best single-volume history of Hungary in English by one of the most incisive historians of Central and Eastern Europe.

Budapest 1900 by John Lukacs. For a closer look at *fin-de-siècle* Budapest pick up a copy of this illustrated social history of the capital at the height of its glory.

A Golden Age: Art & Society in Hungary 1896-1914 (Corvina) edited by Gyöngyi Éri and Zsuzsa Jobbágyi. This glossy book also covers the late 19th and early 20th centuries.

General

Budapest Then & Now by Imre Móra. A lightweight collection of essays by a columnist for the *Budapest Business Journal* which offers the occasional bit of esoteric information about the capital.

Homage to the Eighth District by Giorgio & Nicola Pressburger. The poignant account of life in what was a Jewish working-class section of Budapest during and after WWII. The twin brothers emigrated to Italy in 1956.

Under the Frog by Tibor Fischer. An amusing account of a basketball team's antics in the Hungary of the early 1950s.

The Wines & Vines of Hungary (New World Publishing) by Stephen Kirkland. Positively the best guide to Hungarian wine, leaving no leaf – or bottle – unturned.

Hungarian Folk Art (Corvina) by Tamás Hofer & Edit Fél. Oversized picture book that offers a good introduction to the subject.

Hungarian Ethnography and Folklore by Iván Balassa & Gyula Ortutay. This real gem is an 800-page opus that weighs in at 3kg and leaves no question on traditional culture unanswered. It's out of print but can still be found in Budapest and some provincial bookshops. Highly recommended.

NEWSPAPERS & MAGAZINES

As in most European countries, printed news has strong political affiliations in Hungary. The two main exceptions are the highly respected weekly news magazine *Heti Világgazdaság* (World Economy Weekly), better known as *HVG*, and the former Communist Party mouthpiece *Népszabadság* (People's Freedom), which is now completely independent (though socialist-orientated) and has the highest paid circulation of any newspaper. (The daily commuter freebie *Metro* counts more readers, however.)

Since the demise of *Budapest Week* in print in favour of its Web site (see Internet Resources earlier) the capital counts only two English-language weeklies: the fluffy *Budapest Sun* (158Ft) tabloid, with a particularly useful Style supplement of entertainment listings, and the *Budapest Business Journal* (see Doing Business in this chapter). The monthly *Budapest Style* magazine has features, interviews etc.

A number of Western newspapers are available on the day of publication at many large kiosks, newsagents and hotels in Budapest. They include the *International Herald Tribune*, the European edition of the *Wall Street Journal*, the *Financial Times* and the weekly *Guardian International*.

Another useful English-language periodical is the erudite *Hungarian Quarterly* (US$8), which examines a wide variety of issues in great depth and is a valuable source of current Hungarian thinking in translation.

Convenient places for foreign-language newspapers and magazines are the small bookshop in the Kempinski Corvinus hotel at V Erzsébet tér 7-8; the outdoor kiosk on V Deák Ferenc utca as you enter Vörösmarty tér; the Hírker newsstand in the subway below Nyugati tér, and the Világsajtó háza (World Press House; Map 5) at V Városház utca 3-5 (open 7 am to 7 pm weekdays, to 6 pm Saturday and from 8 am to 4 pm Sunday).

RADIO & TV

With the sale of state-owned TV2, Magyar Televízió (MTV) controls only one channel (MTV1) though there's a host of cable and satellite ones (Duna Televízió, RTL Klub, M Sat, ZTV etc) broadcasting everything from game shows and Top 40 hits to the Flintstones – all in (or dubbed into) Hungarian. Most larger hotels and pensions now subscribe to satellite channels that receive stations like Sky News, CNN, Eurosport and MTV (the music – not the Magyar – one).

Hungarian Radio has stations named after Lajos Kossuth (news; 98.6 FM), Sándor Petőfi (1960s to 80s music, news; 94.8 FM) and Béla Bartók (classical music, news; 105.3 FM) and there's a whole range of stations playing trashy pop and mixes. The one exception is Rádió Tilos (98 FM), a former pirate station that has the best music line-up in Budapest.

VIDEO SYSTEMS

If you want to record or buy video tapes to play back home, you won't get the picture if the image registration systems are different.

Like most of Australia and Europe, Hungary uses PAL, which is incompatible with the North American and Japanese NTSC system or the SECAM system used in France.

PHOTOGRAPHY & VIDEO

All major brands of film are readily available here and you can have your film developed in one hour at many locations in Budapest, including any of the dozen or so Fotex outlets (VII Rákóczi út 2, V Váci utca 9 etc).

Film prices vary, but basically 24 exposures of 100 ASA Kodacolor II, Agfa or Fujifilm will cost from 690Ft to 799Ft and 36 exposures between 880Ft and 1090Ft. Ektachrome 100 is 1490Ft. Developing print film costs about 699Ft a roll; for the prints themselves, you choose the size and pay accordingly (10cm x 15cm prints cost 79Ft each). Slide film costs 799Ft to process. Video film like TDK EHG 30/45 minutes costs 990/1310Ft.

TIME

Hungary lies in the Central European Time Zone. Winter time is GMT plus one hour and in summer it's GMT plus two hours. Clocks are advanced at 2 am on the last Sunday in March and set back at the same time on the last Sunday in October. Without taking daylight-saving times into account, when it's noon in Budapest, it's:

1 pm in Athens
11 pm in Auckland
noon in Belgrade
noon in Berlin
noon in Bratislava
1 pm in Bucharest
7 pm in Hong Kong
11 am in London
2 pm in Moscow
6 am in New York
noon in Paris
noon in Prague
3 am in San Francisco
9 pm in Sydney
8 pm in Tokyo
6 am in Toronto
noon in Vienna
noon in Warsaw
noon in Zagreb

ELECTRICITY

The electric current here is 220V, 50Hz AC. Plugs are the European type with two round pins.

WEIGHTS & MEASURES

Hungary uses the metric system – there's a conversion table at the back of this book. In supermarkets and outdoor markets, fresh food is sold by weight or by piece (*darab*). When ordering by weight, you specify by kilos or *deka* (decagrams – 50dg is equal to 0.5kg or a little more than 1lb).

Beer at a *söröző* (pub) is served in a *pohár* (0.3L) or a *korsó* (0.4L or 0.5L). Wine in an old-fashioned *borozó* (wine bar) is ladled out by the *deci* (decilitre, 0.1L), but in more modern places it comes by the ill-defined 'glass'.

LAUNDRY

There are no self-service laundries (*patyolat*) in Budapest though some of the hostels (see the Places to Stay chapter) have washing machines and dryers. Generally you select to have your laundry done in one or six hours or the following day and pay accordingly (from about 1100Ft).

The Top Clean chain (☎ 227 5648) does a fairly reliable and affordable job on both laundry and dry cleaning and has some 40 locations around the city, including ones at V Arany János utca 34 (Map 5; metro Arany János utca) and at the new West End City Centre shopping mall, VI Váci út 3 (metro Nyugati pályaudvar). In general they're open from 7 am to 6.30 pm weekdays, from 8 am to 1 pm Saturday.

Central full-service laundries include the Nádor Szalon (Map 5; ☎ 317 1542) at V József nádor tér 9 (metro Vörösmarty tér) and Irisz Szalon (Map 5; ☎ 269 6840) at VII Rákóczi út 8/b (metro Astoria) or a branch (☎ 317 2092) near Ferenciek tere at V Városház utca 3-5. Anila (☎ 331 7189), VI Zichy Jenő 44, has an expensive pickup/drop-off service and charges by the piece: 550Ft for jeans, 60Ft for socks etc. The best (and most expensive) dry-cleaning services are available at the Kempinski Corvinus and Budapest Marriott hotels.

TOILETS

Public toilets in Budapest are invariably staffed by an old *néné* (auntie), who mops the floor continuously, hands out sheets of grade AAA sandpaper and has seen it all. The usual charge is 50Ft a go and even restaurants and cafes sometimes charge their patrons.

LEFT LUGGAGE

There's a left-luggage office inside Erzsébet tér bus station open from 6 am to 7 pm daily (to 8 pm on Monday and Friday). The left-luggage office at Népstadion bus station is open from 6 am to 6 pm daily.

Keleti and Nyugati train stations have left-luggage sections open round the clock and from 5 am to midnight respectively (140Ft to 280Ft). Déli train station has coin-operated lockers (200Ft). The left-luggage facility at Ferihegy Airport's Terminal 2B is open round the clock (250/800/5000Ft per hour/day/week).

HEALTH

Budapest poses no health risks though mosquitoes can be a real scourge around pools, ponds and the Danube in summer, so be armed with insect repellent (*rovarírtó*). One insect that can bring on more than just an itch, though, is the forest tick (*kullancs*), which burrows under the skin causing inflammation and even encephalitis. It has become a common problem in parts of Central and Eastern Europe, especially eastern Austria, Germany, the Czech Republic and Hungary. You might consider getting an FSME (meningo-encephalitis) vaccination if you plan to do extensive hiking and camping in other parts of Hungary such as Transdanubia or the Northern Uplands between May and September.

First-aid and ambulance services are free of charge for citizens of the UK as well as Scandinavian and most Eastern European countries and former republics of the USSR, though follow-up treatment and medicine must be paid for. Treatment at a public outpatient clinic (*rendelő intézet*) costs little, but doctors working privately sometimes charge much more. A consultation in a

Shiver Me Timbers: Malaria in Hungary

Though it could hardly be called typical, my only experience with a Hungarian hospital was an unqualified success. I had been living in Hungary for six months by then, enjoying things I'd scarcely dreamed about during a dozen or so years in Hong Kong, like attending organ concerts in 18th-century baroque churches and buying raspberries by the kilogram. And at last my partner and I had found a flat with character – a large one perched on the side of Gellért Hill, within neck-craning view of the lovely bronze lady proclaiming liberty throughout the city.

Then I began to feel sick. Really sick. It came fast, as these things often do, and in a matter of days I was running fevers of almost 41°C (that's a delirium-inducing 105.8°F) that would then plummet, throwing me into chilling spasms and sweats. My doctor was phlegmatic as I dripped great puddles onto the floor of his surgery. 'These summer flus are hard to shake,' he said, cautioning me to rest, take vitamins, drink plenty of fluids etc.

After one particularly severe bout of fever, I found myself flipping through an Asian guidebook and reminiscing about a 'farewell' trip we'd made to a remote part of Indonesia the previous winter. I read the health section and the penny dropped. Sure the symptoms were familiar, but aren't they always when you're sick? And it had been over half a year...

Still, I sought advice by telephone from staff at the Hospital for Tropical Diseases in London, who told me to be tested immediately, and the US embassy directed me to the only hospital in Budapest – in Hungary for that matter – dealing with tropical illnesses. Three hours after arriving at the Szent László Hospital in central Pest I had the positive results in hand: two types of malaria contracted in the swamps of south-western Irian Jaya.

It was a speedy, well-nursed recovery and with a half-dozen Lariam tablets in me and a prescribed follow-up course of primaquine to zap the *plasmodium vivax* and *plasmodium falciparum* in their deepest lairs, I was up in no time. My ward mates – a Cambodian student called Sowan suffering from appendicitis and 91-year-old Péter with jaundice – and I would stroll through the old gardens dressed only in our dressing gowns, looking like characters from a Thomas Mann novel.

So a *maláriás beteg* (the malaria patient) – a rare breed indeed in Hungary – became the resident 'talking dog' and an odd mix of doctors and nurses would stop me for a look, a quick examination and a lot of free advice. 'You are *sure* you took all of the prophylactics faithfully – the chloroquine and the Paludrine?' one asked with doubt in her eyes. Did I know about resistant strains, that malaria could lie dormant for up to a year, that a cold shower directly on the kidneys could 'coax' it out? (That last one made me wince as I remembered the ice-cold plunge pool at my favourite Turkish bath.)

The head physician examined me after three days and told me to get dressed. Once I'd paid the relatively modest fee for the private room, board, care and drugs, he said I could return to Gellért Hill and start rearranging the furniture.

FACTS FOR THE VISITOR

Hungarian doctor's surgery (*orvosi rendelő*) costs roughly 3000Ft to 5000Ft while a home visit is 8000Ft to 10,000Ft. Consultations and treatment are much more expensive in the new Western-style clinics.

Medical Services

The huge MÁV hospital (MÁV kórház; Map 3; ☎ 269 5656), occupying an entire city block at VI Podmaniczky utca 111-110 (metro Hősök tere) delivers round-the-clock care (enter from Rippl-Rónai utca 35 after hours) and can bill foreigners but is not really equipped to do so. In most cases you should seek out a private clinic for medical services.

International Medical Services (Map 2; ☎/fax 329 9349, @ imskekes@euroweb .hu), XIII Váci út 202 (metro Gyöngyösi utca) in Pest, is a flash private medical clinic, the first but not necessarily the best in Hungary, where consultations start at 6700Ft and home visits at 11,700Ft. It is open from 7.30 am to 8 pm. There's another branch (Map 2; ☎/fax 250 3829) open 24 hours in Óbuda at III Vihar utca 29.

The American Clinic (Map 3; ☎ 224 9090, ✉ budapest@americanclinics.com) on the 5th floor at I Hattyú utca 14 (metro Moszkva tér) offers 24-hour medical care primarily to corporate clients as prices for non-members are very much at American levels: 20,000Ft for a basic consultation. The clinic is open from 8.30 am to 6.30 pm weekdays (to 5.30 pm Friday), 8 am till noon Saturday and 10 am to 2 pm Sunday.

Dental Services
Dental work is usually of a high standard in Budapest and cheap by Western standards. Some Budapest dentists advertise in the English-language press.

The Interako Dental Co-op (☎ 175 1455 or 349 2243), XII Zugligeti út 60 (bus No 158 from Moszkva tér) deals with all things dental, as well as offering a whole range of medical services and specialises in treating foreigners. Consultations cost 2000Ft to 3000Ft though treatment by a specialist can be higher (eg, to see a gynaecologist costs 6000Ft). It is open from 8 am to 8 pm weekdays and 9 am to 3 pm Saturday. A more conveniently located clinic and open 24 hours to boot is the SOS Dental Service (Map 5; ☎ 267 9602) at VI Király utca 14 (metro Deák tér).

Pharmacies
All of Budapest's 23 districts have a rotating all-night pharmacy; a sign on the door of any pharmacy will help you locate the closest 24-hour one.

The Teréz Patika (Map 5; ☎ 311 4439) at VI Teréz körút 41 (metro Nyugati pályaudvar) has a 24-hour window (ring for service) as does the Csillag Gyógyszertár (Map 5; ☎ 314 3694) at VIII Rákóczi út 39 (metro Blaha Lujza tér).

HIV/AIDS Organisations
The numbers of registered AIDS cases and those who are HIV-positive are relatively low – 210 and 600 respectively – though epidemiologists here estimate the actual number of those infected with HIV to be over 3500. Those could multiply quickly, particularly as Budapest has become the sex-industry capital of Eastern and Central Europe.

Two AIDS lines operate in the capital: a 24-hour information line at ☎ 338 4555 and a help line (some English spoken) on ☎ 338 2419, available from 8 am to 4 pm weekdays (to 1 pm Friday).

WOMEN TRAVELLERS
Hungarian men can be very sexist in their thinking, but women in Budapest do not suffer any particular form of harassment (though rape and domestic violence get little media coverage here). Most men – even drunks – are effusively polite with women. Women may not be made to feel especially welcome when eating or drinking alone, but it's really no different here than in many other countries in Europe.

Try calling the Women's Line (Nővonal) on ☎ 06-80 505 303 or contact one of the following organisations dealing with women's issues:

Women for Women against Violence (NANE; help line ☎ 267 4900 open from 6 to 10 pm daily) PO Box 660, Budapest 1462
Feminist Network PO Box 701, Budapest 1399

GAY & LESBIAN TRAVELLERS
There are magazines for both gay men (*Mások*) and lesbians (*Labrisz*) published sporadically. A couple of help lines will provide further information. Visit the gay Web site at www.gayguide.net/europe/Hungary/budapest or call the following:

Háttér Gay & Lesbian Association help line ☎ 329 3380, open from 6 to 11 pm daily
Gay Switchboard help line mobile ☎ 06-309 323 334, fax 351 2015, open from 4 to 8 pm weekdays

See also Gay & Lesbian Venues in the Entertainment chapter for information.

DISABLED TRAVELLERS
Budapest has a very long way to go before it becomes accessible to the physically

challenged (one positive step: the 5000Ft and 10,000Ft notes have markings in Braille). Wheelchair ramps, toilets fitted for the disabled and so on are virtually nonexistent though audible traffic signals for the blind are becoming increasingly commonplace.

For more information, contact:

Hungarian Disabled Association (MEOSZ; ☎ 368 1758) San Marco utca 76, Budapest 1035

SENIOR TRAVELLERS

Seniors are sometimes entitled to discounts on things such as public transport and museum admission fees, provided they show proof of their age. See Seniors Cards under Documents earlier in the chapter for more information.

BUDAPEST FOR CHILDREN

Successful travel with young children requires planning and effort. Don't try to overdo things; even for adults, packing too much into the time available can cause problems. Make sure the activities include the kids as well – balance that morning at Budapest's Museum of Fine Arts with an afternoon at the nearby Grand Circus or a performance at the Budapest Puppet Theatre. Include children in the trip planning; if they've helped to work out where you will be going, they will be much more interested when they get there. Lonely Planet's *Travel with Children* by Maureen Wheeler is a good resource.

Most car-rental firms in Budapest have children's safety seats for hire at a nominal cost, but it is essential that you book them in advance. The same goes for highchairs and cots (cribs); they're standard in many restaurants and hotels but numbers are limited. The choice of baby food, infant formulas, soy and cow's milk, disposable nappies (diapers) and the like can be as great in Hungarian supermarkets these days as it is back home, but the opening hours may be quite different. Don't get caught out at the weekend.

The Fővárosi Nagycirkusz (Municipal Grand Circus; Map 3; ☎ 343 9630), XIV

Állatkerti körút 7 (metro Széchenyi fürdő), has performances at 7.30 pm Wednesday; 3.30 and 7.30 pm Thursday and Friday; 10 am, 3.30 and 7.30 pm Saturday and 10 am and 3.30 pm Sunday from mid-April to August. Although the matinees are occasionally booked out by school groups, there's almost always space in the evening. Advance tickets (400Ft to 800Ft) are sold at the circus itself.

The Budapest Bábszínház (Budapest Puppet Theatre; Map 5; ☎ 321 5200), VI Andrássy út 69 (metro Vörösmarty utca), presents shows designed for children during the day and occasional evening programs for adults.

Vidám Park (Amusement Park; Map 3; ☎ 343 9810), XIV Állatkerti körút 14-16 (metro Széchenyi fürdő), on 2½ hectares in City Park, is a 150-year-old fun fair with a couple of dozen new rides as well as a vintage wooden roller coaster, go-karts and dodgem cars (100/50Ft per ride). It is open from 10 am to 8 pm daily between April and September and to 7 pm the rest of the year.

LIBRARIES

Libraries in Budapest offeribng foreign-language publications include:

The Foreign Language Library (Map 5; ☎ 318 3188) V Molnár utca 11 (metro Ferenciek tere). You can join for 700Ft a year, but you'll need a Hungarian address and identification to do so. It's open from 10 am to 8 pm weekdays (from noon on Wednesday).

The British Council (Map 3; ☎ 321 4039) VI Benczúr utca 26 (metro Bajza utca). It charges 1500Ft for a one-year membership, allowing the card holder to borrow books, audio cassettes and magazines (videos cost extra). It's open from 11 am to 6 pm weekdays (to 5 pm Friday).

The America House Library (Map 3; ☎ 343 0148 ext 4435) on the campus of Loránd Eötvös Science University (ELTE) at XIV Ajtósi Dürer sor 19-21, just below the university's English-language library. America House will issue a library card valid for a year for 3000Ft. It is open from 9 am to 6 pm Monday, Tuesday and Thursday, noon to 6 pm Wednesday and 9 am to 5 pm Friday. The university library (☎ 343 0148 ext 4439) is open to the public, but for reading only.

CULTURAL CENTRES

Cultural centres in Budapest include:

Institut Français (Map 4; ☎ 202 1133) I Fő utca 17. Open from 1 to 7 pm Tuesday to Friday and from 10 am to 1 pm Saturday.

Italian Institute of Culture (Map 5; ☎ 318 8144) VIII Bródy Sándor utca 8. Open from 10 am to 6 pm weekdays.

Goethe Institute (Map 5; ☎ 374 4076, fax 374 4080) VI Andrássy út 24 (metro Opera). Eckermann Café (see Email & Internet Access earlier in the chapter) is the place for German culture and periodicals as well as sending emails and surfing the Internet. Open from 2 to 10 pm weekdays, from 10 am to 10 pm Saturday.

DANGERS & ANNOYANCES

No parts of Budapest are 'off-limits' to visitors, although some locals now avoid Margaret Island after dark and you may want to give the dodgier parts of the 8th and 9th districts (areas of prostitution) a wide berth – unless you're in the market. The tit-for-tat gangland bombings in Budapest, one of which killed four people in July 1998, have not affected foreigners.

As elsewhere when travelling, you are most vulnerable to car thieves, pickpockets, scammers, taxi louts and dishonest waiters. To avoid having your car ripped off, follow the usual security procedures. Don't park it in a darkened street, make sure the burglar alarm is armed and have a steering-wheel lock in place.

Pickpocketing is most common in markets, the Castle District, Váci utca and Hősök tere, and on certain buses (eg, No 7) and trams (Nos 2, 4, 6, 47 & 49); in the past, metro No 1 (the little yellow line) has been plagued by thieves who work in pairs and even well-dressed gangs in casual sports gear. Though this has decreased with the presence of police officers on board metro trains and on the platforms, the buses are still a hazard; I had my mobile phone (and buried in a bottomless shoulder bag, it was) pinched on bus No 112 the last time I was in Budapest. Clever thief.

Scams involving attractive young women, gullible guys, expensive drinks in nightclubs and a frog-marching to the nearest ATM by gorillas in residence are all the rage these days – we get letters from male readers complaining they've been ripped off all the time. Guys, please: if it seems too good to be true, it is – trust me and the mirror – and the tab in these cases has run into hundreds and even thousands of dollars for such vanity. A list of these rip-off cafes and restaurants (they change all the time) is available at tourist offices and the US embassy, which circulates the information to hotels and hostels. The police will not (and actually cannot) be of much help in these matters. Caveat emptor.

Taking a taxi in Budapest can be an expensive – even violent – experience. Always call a taxi from a phone and give the number (almost always somewhere in the phone box) to the dispatcher. For more information, see Taxi in the Getting Around chapter.

It is not unknown for waiters to try to rip you off once they see you are a foreigner. They may try to bring you an unordered dish or make a 'mistake' when tallying the bill. If you think there's a discrepancy, ask for the menu and check the bill carefully. The most common ruse is to bring you the most expensive beer or wine when you order a draught or a glass. Ask the price first. If you've been taken for more than 15% or 20% of the bill, call for the manager. Otherwise just don't leave a tip (see the Tipping & Bargaining section earlier in this chapter). There have been some reports of unscrupulous waiters and/or shop assistants making quick and very high-tech duplicates of credit or debit card information with a machine. If your cards leave your possession for a longer period than is normal, consider cancelling them.

If you've left something on any form of public transport in Budapest contact the BKV lost and found office (Map 5; ☎ 267 5299), VII Akácfa utca 18, between 7 am and 3 pm weekdays.

Cigarette smoking is rampant among both sexes and all ages in Budapest, which some visitors find extremely annoying. Equally irksome is the amount of dog shit on the pavements nowadays. As in Paris, watch your step.

EMERGENCIES

In the event of an emergency, the following are the most important telephone numbers:

Police   ☎ 107
Fire   ☎ 105
Ambulance   ☎ 104 or ☎ 311 1666
24-hour car assistance ☎ 188 (nationwide) or
  ☎ 212 2821 or 212 2938 (Hungarian Automobile Club) in Budapest

LEGAL MATTERS

If you need to report a crime or a lost or stolen passport or credit card, first call the emergency police help number at ☎ 107 or go to the police station of the district you're in. In the Inner Town that would be the station (Map 5; ☎ 302 5935) at V Szalay utca 11-13 (metro Kossuth tér). If possible, ask a Hungarian speaker to accompany you. In the high season, police officers pair up with university students who act as translators, and patrol the busiest areas.

The main city and national police station (Map 2) is housed in a futuristic landmark building on XIII Teve utca near the Árpád híd metro station. There are plans afoot to add a country-wide police help number (☎ 117), possibly by mid-2000, which will have English and German-speaking staff available round the clock.

There is a 100% ban on alcohol when you are driving in Budapest, and this rule is *very* strictly enforced. Do not think you will get away with even a few glasses of wine at lunch; if caught with any alcohol in the blood, you will be fined up to 60,000Ft. If the level is high, you will be arrested and your licence taken away. In the event of an accident, the drinking party is automatically regarded as guilty. It's not much fun while on holiday, but you'll have to follow the lead of Hungarians and elect a designated driver who will abstain from alcohol at a party or a meal. Those who don't believe this warning will learn the hard way. I know I did.

The office in Budapest dealing with foreigners' visa registrations is KEOKH (Map 3; ☎ 343 0034) at VI Városligeti fasor 46-48 (metro Bajza utca or trolleybus No 75 or 79).

BUSINESS HOURS

With rare exceptions, the opening hours (*nyitvatartás*) of a business, museum or government office are posted on the front door (*nyitva* is 'open' and *zárva* is 'closed'). Grocery stores and supermarkets are usually open from 7 am to 7 pm weekdays and to 1 pm Saturday, but a few big supermarkets now open to 1 or 2 pm on Sunday. There's always at least one 'nonstop' around – convenience stores, open round the clock and selling basic food items, bottled drinks and cigarettes, have sprung up all over the country.

Department stores, clothiers and bookshops keep shorter hours: roughly from 10 am to 6 pm weekdays (though some stay open until 7 or 8 pm on Thursday) and 9 am to 1 pm Saturday. Many private shops close early on Friday and during most of August. Restaurants can stay open till midnight or even later, but many more traditional ones close as early as 10.30 pm.

Bank hours vary but generally they're open from 8 am to 3 or 4 pm Monday to Thursday and to 1 pm Friday. The main post office in any Budapest district is open from 8 am to 7 or 8 pm weekdays and till noon or even 2 pm Saturday. Branch offices close much earlier – usually at 4 pm – and are never open at the weekend.

PUBLIC HOLIDAYS & SPECIAL EVENTS

Hungary celebrates nine public holidays (*ünnep*) a year:

New Year's Day – 1 January
1848 Revolution/National Day – 15 March
Easter Monday – March/April
Labour Day – 1 May
Whit Monday – May/June
St Stephen's/Constitution Day – 20 August
1956 Remembrance/Republic Day – 23 October
Christmas holidays – 25-26 December

Countless festivals and events are held in and around Budapest each year; look out for the tourist board's annual *Events in Hungary from January to December* for a complete listing.

Among the most important annual events are the following:

January
New Year Operetta Gala at the Vigadó on 1 January

February
Opera Ball at the Opera House

March
Budapest Spring Festival

April
Welcome Marathon

June
World Music Festival
Búcsú (Farewell) Festival of rock and pop music
Duna Carnival Folklore Festival

June-July
Ferencváros Summer Festival (in late June and July)
Jewish Summer Festival (in late June/early July)

August
BudaFest Summer Opera & Ballet Festival
Pepsi Island (Pepsi-sziget) Festival of Music and Culture on Óbuda Island
Hungarian Formula-1 Grand Prix in Magyoród near Budapest

September
International Wine Festival
European Heritage Days

October
Budapest Marathon
Autumn Festival

December
New Year's Eve Masked Ball at the Opera House

DOING BUSINESS

Budapest means business nowadays and the city has never been so well geared up for welcoming investors.

The main source of information in English for businesspeople in Budapest is the *Budapest Business Journal* (450Ft; ☎ 374 3344, ✆ circulation@bbj.hu), an almost archival publication of financial news and business stories. *Business Hungary*, published by the American Chamber of Commerce (see the following list) and available free to members or by subscription (US$250 per annum) is more feature-orientated but very useful for contacts.

The *Central European Business Weekly* (200Ft) and the *Central European Economic Review* (330Ft), published monthly by the *Wall Street Journal*, look at the region as a whole.

For basic information on business, try www.hungary-info.com. There's a wealth of information on business and economics at www.businessweb.hu. The Budapest Business Journal's Hungary AM service (✆ HunAM@pc.bbj.hu) offers a three-page synopsis of Budapest's five major dailies. Hungary around the Clock (☎ 351 7142, ✆ info@kingfish.hu) provides a daily summary of business and political news before 9 am.

Important addresses and/or useful sources of information include the following:

American Chamber of Commerce in Hungary (Map 5; ☎ 266 9880, ✆ amcham@hungary .com) V Deák Ferenc utca 10, Rm 404. Open 9 am to 5 pm.
British Chamber of Commerce in Hungary (Map 5; ☎ 302 5200, ✆ bcch@bcch.hu) V Bank utca 6, 2/F. Open 9 am to noon to nonmembers.
Budapest Chamber of Commerce & Industry (Budapesti Kereskedelmi és Iparkamra; ☎ 214 1827) I Krisztina körút 99
Canadian Chamber of Commerce in Hungary (☎/fax 318 4712) V Aranykéz utca 2. Open 9 am to 5 pm.
Economy Ministry (Gazdasági Minisztérium; Map 5; ☎ 312 2355) V Honvéd utca 13-15 Web site: www.gm.hu
Finance Ministry (Pénzügy Minisztérium; Map 5; ☎ 318 2066, fax 318 2570) V József nádor tér 2-4
Hungarian Chamber of Commerce & Industry (Magyar Kereskedelmi és Iparkamra; ☎ 474 5140, ✆ mkik@mail.mkik.hu) V Kossuth Lajos tér 6-8 Web site: www.mkik.hu
Investment & Trade Development Agency of Hungary (ITDH; Magyar Befektetési és Kereskedelmfejlesztési Iroda; ☎ 318 0051, ✆ itdh@itd.hu) V Dorottya utca 4
National Bank of Hungary (Magyar Nemzeti Bank; Map 5; ☎ 302 3000, fax 332 3913, V Szabadság tér 8-9)

For photocopying, digital printing and computer services like scanning, visit one of six outlets of Copy General (www.copygeneral .hu), including the main branch (Map 5; ☎ 302 3206) at V Kálmán Imre utca 22. You can rent a mobile phone from Creditel (mobile ☎ 06-209 365 000, ✉ office@ creditel.hu), II Frankel Leó út 20.

All the major courier companies are represented here including DHL (Map 5; ☎ 266 555), VIII Rákóczi út 1-3, and Fedex (☎ 216 3606), IX Nádasdy utca 2-4.

Among the most reliable translation services is METAford (☎ 375 1976, mobile ☎ 06-309 891 947, ✉ lengyelp@mail.data net.hu), II Lupény utca 3/b. Others include Forduna (☎ 209 2482, ✉ forduna@mail .datanet.hu), XI Bartók Béla út 86 and Reflex (☎ 268 9561), VI Andrássy út 13. The latter has a Web site at www.reflex.hu.

WORK

Travellers on tourist visas in Budapest are not supposed to accept employment, but many end up teaching, doing a little writing for the English-language press or even working for foreign firms without permits. Check the English-language telephone book or advertisements for English-language schools in the *Budapest Sun*, which also has job listings, but the pay is generally pretty low. You can do much better teaching privately (1000Ft to 2000Ft per 45-minute 'hour') once you've built up the contacts.

Obtaining an official work permit involves a Byzantine paper chase with Hungarian bureaucracy and, at the end of it all, you'll have to pay local income tax. First you'll need a letter of support from your prospective employer to get a one-year renewable residency. You'll need copies of your birth certificate and school transcript or academic record officially translated into Hungarian (3000Ft per page). A medical exam and AIDS test (12,000Ft) is also mandatory. The office in Budapest dealing with foreigners' registrations is KEOKH (Map 3; ☎ 343 0034) at VI Városligeti fasor 46-48.

FACTS FOR THE VISITOR

Getting There & Away

AIR

Malév Hungarian Airlines (www.malev
.hu), the national carrier, flies nonstop to
Budapest's Ferihegy International Airport
from North America, the Middle East, Asia
and more than three dozen cities in Continental Europe and the British Isles. Some
three dozen other airlines also serve the
Hungarian capital.

Malév flights arrive and depart from Ferihegy Terminal 2A; all other international
airlines use the new Terminal 2B. (The old
Terminal 1, about 5km to the west, is now
used only for cargo or special flights.) The
general information number for both terminals at Ferihegy is ☎ 296 9696. Otherwise,
call ☎ 296 7000 or 296 6578 for departures
and ☎ 296 8000 or 296 8268 for arrivals at
Terminal 2A. For Terminal 2B call ☎ 296
5882/83/84 for departures and ☎ 296
5052/53/54 for arrivals.

Departure Tax

An air passenger duty (*illeték*) of normally
between 3000Ft and 6500Ft is levied on all
air tickets written in Hungary. The one exception to these amounts is JFK Airport in
New York, which attracts a tax of 12,000Ft.
There are no other departure or port taxes.

Other Parts of Hungary

There are no scheduled flights within Hungary. The cost of domestic air taxis is pro-
hibitive (eg, 87,000Ft/DM680 from Budapest
to Szeged on the Southern Plain and back),
and the trips can take almost as long as the
train when you add the time required to get
to/from the airports. Several better-known
air-taxi firms with offices in Budapest are In-
dicator (☎ 202 6284), XII Városmajor utca
30; Air Service Hungary (☎ 385 1344), XI
Kőérberki út 36; and Avia-Express (☎ 296
7092 or 296 6383) at Ferihegy Terminal 1.

The UK & Continental Europe

Malév flies nonstop to Budapest from the following destinations: Amsterdam, Athens,

Barcelona, Berlin, Brussels, Bucharest,
Cologne, Copenhagen, Dublin, Düsseldorf,
Frankfurt, Hamburg, Helsinki, Istanbul, Kau-
nas, Kiev, Larnaca, London, Madrid, Milan,
Moscow, Munich, Oslo, Paris, Prague, Riga,
Rome, St Petersburg, Sarajevo, Skopje,
Sofia, Stockholm, Stuttgart, Thessaloniki,
Tirana, Vienna, Warsaw, Zagreb and Zürich.

Airlines serving Budapest from European
gateways include: Aeroflot (Moscow), Air
Baltic (Riga), Air France (Paris), Air Lithua-
nia (Vilnius), Air Malta (Malta), Air Ukraine
(Kiev), Alitalia (Rome, Milan), Austrian
Airlines (Vienna), Balkan Airlines (Sofia),
British Airways and British Midland (Lon-
don), Czech Airlines (Prague), Finnair
(Helsinki), Iberia (Madrid), KLM-Royal
Dutch Airlines (Amsterdam), LOT Polish
Airlines (Warsaw), Lufthansa (Düsseldorf,
Frankfurt, Hamburg, Munich, Stuttgart),
Olympic Airways (Athens), Sabena (Brus-
sels), SAS (Copenhagen), Swissair (Geneva,

Zürich), Tarom Romanian (Bucharest) and Turkish Airlines (Istanbul).

At the time of writing, British Airways was offering basic return excursion tickets with fixed dates (and heavy penalties if you change them) from London to Budapest for about UK£235 to UK£280, depending on whether you wanted to travel on a weekend; those under 26 paid £20 less. British Midland had a discount fare for UK£170. Of course you could always fly to Prague on BA's budget airline, Go (☎ 0845 605 4321), or to Vienna with KLM's Buzz (☎ 0870 240 7070) for UK£100 and then cover the last leg by bus or train. For details, check out their Web sites: www.go-fly.com and www.buzzaway.com.

From Budapest, most destinations in Europe on Malév cost from 40,000Ft to 55,000Ft return, including Warsaw and Prague (46,000Ft each). A return flight to Moscow is 64,000Ft.

The USA & Canada
Malév and Delta Air Lines run a daily joint service to/from New York (JFK Airport); Malév runs a direct flight to/from Toronto twice a week. From New York with Malév, the standard return fare hovers around US$900 though a discounted one with the usual restrictions costs about US$420.

From Budapest you should be able to fly return to New York for 109,000Ft (75,000Ft for those under 26).

Australia
The easiest way to get to Hungary from Australia is to fly Qantas from Sydney or Melbourne to London and connect with a Malév or British Airways flight to Budapest. Another option is Sydney to Frankfurt and then Malév or Lufthansa to Budapest. A less frequently served routing is Sydney or Melbourne to Bangkok and then the thrice-weekly nonstop Malév flight to Budapest. A return flight to Sydney or Melbourne from Budapest costs about 168,000Ft.

Africa & the Middle East
Malév flies nonstop four times a week to Tel Aviv while El Al Israel Airlines has a thrice-weekly service. Malév and EgyptAir serve Cairo three times a week. Malév also flies nonstop twice a week to Beirut. There are two Malév flights a week to Damascus and one to Tripoli. Tunis Air flies nonstop once a week to Budapest.

Asia
Malév flies nonstop to/from Bangkok (145,000Ft return, 104,000Ft under 26) three times a week and runs a direct flight six times weekly to Beijing with Air China (via Helsinki) and Swissair (via Zürich). From Hong Kong there are two weekly flights on Lauda Air to Vienna and three a week from Bangkok. Lufthansa (via Frankfurt) and British Airways (via London) also offer good deals to Budapest from Asia.

A return excursion ticket valid for six months on Lauda Air from Bangkok to Vienna is US$1200. From the same gateway BA flies to Budapest via London and Lufthansa via Frankfurt for about US$1600. From Bombay to Budapest on Swissair (via Zürich) costs from US$1000.

Airline Offices
Malév's main ticket office (Map 5; ☎ 235 3565 or 266 5616) is near Vörösmarty tér at V Dorottya utca 2. There's another office (☎ 235 3535) at V Roosevelt tér 2. In addition, Malév has a ticketing desk at Terminal 2A (☎ 296 7179 or 296 7211) and one at Terminal 2B (☎ 296 7544 or 296 5767).

Other major carriers with offices in Budapest include:

Aeroflot (☎ 318 5955) V Váci utca 4
Air Canada (☎ 317 9109) V Vörösmarty tér 6
Air France (☎ 318 0441) V Kristóf tér 6
Air India (☎ 318 4804) V Vörösmarty tér 6
Alitalia (☎ 373 7782) V Ferenciek tere 2
Austrian Airlines (☎ 327 9080) V Régiposta utca 5
Balkan Airlines (☎ 317 1818) V Párizsi utca 7
British Airways (☎ 318 4041) VIII Rákóczi út 1-3
Delta Air Lines (☎ 294 4400) V Apáczai Csere János utca 4
Iberia (☎ 317 1564) V Károlyi Mihály utca 19
KLM Royal Dutch Airlines (☎ 373 7737) VIII Rákóczi út 1-3
Lauda Air (☎ 266 3169) V Aranykéz utca 4-6

Air Travel Glossary

Cancellation Penalties If you have to cancel or change a discounted ticket, there are often heavy penalties involved; insurance can sometimes be taken out against these penalties. Some airlines impose penalties on regular tickets as well, particularly against 'no-show' passengers.

Courier Fares Businesses often need to send urgent documents or freight securely and quickly. Courier companies hire people to accompany the package through customs and, in return, offer a discount ticket which is sometimes a phenomenal bargain. However, you may have to surrender all your baggage allowance and take only carry-on luggage.

Full Fares Airlines traditionally offer 1st class (coded F), business class (coded J) and economy class (coded Y) tickets. These days there are so many promotional and discounted fares available that few passengers pay full economy fare.

Lost Tickets If you lose your airline ticket an airline will usually treat it like a travellers cheque and, after inquiries, issue you with another one. Legally, however, an airline is entitled to treat it like cash and if you lose it then it's gone forever. Take good care of your tickets.

Onward Tickets An entry requirement for many countries is that you have a ticket out of the country. If you're unsure of your next move, the easiest solution is to buy the cheapest onward ticket to a neighbouring country or a ticket from a reliable airline which can later be refunded if you do not use it.

Open-Jaw Tickets These are return tickets where you fly out to one place but return from another. If available, this can save you backtracking to your arrival point.

Overbooking Since every flight has some passengers who fail to show up, airlines often book more passengers than they have seats. Usually excess passengers make up for the no-shows, but occasionally somebody gets 'bumped' onto the next available flight. Guess who it is most likely to be? The passengers who check in late.

Promotional Fares These are officially discounted fares, available from travel agencies or direct from the airline.

Reconfirmation If you don't reconfirm your flight at least 72 hours prior to departure, the airline may delete your name from the passenger list. Ring to find out if your airline requires reconfirmation.

Restrictions Discounted tickets often have various restrictions on them – such as needing to be paid for in advance and incurring a penalty to be altered. Others are restrictions on the minimum and maximum period you must be away.

Round-the-World Tickets RTW tickets give you a limited period (usually a year) in which to circumnavigate the globe. You can go anywhere the carrying airlines go, as long as you don't backtrack. The number of stopovers or total number of separate flights is decided before you set off and they usually cost a bit more than a basic return flight.

Transferred Tickets Airline tickets cannot be transferred from one person to another. Travellers sometimes try to sell the return half of their ticket, but officials can ask you to prove that you are the person named on the ticket. On an international flight tickets are compared with passports.

Travel Periods Ticket prices vary with the time of year. There is a low (off-peak) season and a high (peak) season, and often a low-shoulder season and a high-shoulder season as well. Usually the fare depends on your outward flight – if you depart in the high season and return in the low season, you pay the high-season fare.

LOT Polish Airlines (☎ 317 2444) V Vigadó tér 3
Lufthansa (☎ 266 4511) V Váci utca 19-21
SAS (☎ 266 2633) V Bajcsy-Zsilinszky út 12
Sabena (☎ 318 4111) V Bajcsy-Zsilinszky út 12
Swissair (☎ 328 5000) V Kristóf tér 7-8

BUS

There are three important bus stations in Budapest. Most buses to/from Western and Central Europe as well as several neighbouring countries and destinations in Hungary south and west of Budapest leave from the station at V Erzsébet tér (Map 5; ☎ 317 2562 for international inquiries, ☎ 317 2345 for domestic ones, metro Deák tér). The international ticket office upstairs is open from 6 am to 7 pm weekdays and from 6.30 am to 4 pm Saturday from June to August, to 6 pm weekdays and 4 pm Saturday the rest of the year. There's a left-luggage office inside the station open from 6 am to 7 pm daily (to 8 pm on Monday and Friday).

In general, buses to/from Eastern Europe as well as Greece and Turkey and destinations in Hungary north and east of the capital leave from the bus station at Népstadion (Map 3; ☎ 252 1896 for international buses, ☎ 252 4498 for domestic ones, metro Népstadion), XIV Hungária körút 48-52. The international ticket office is open from 6 am to 6 pm weekdays, to 4 pm Saturday. The left-luggage office here is open from 6 am to 6 pm daily.

Most buses to the Danube Bend and parts of the Northern Uplands (eg, Balassagyarmat, Szécsény) arrive at and leave from the bus station (Map 2; ☎ 329 1682 or 329 1450, metro Árpád híd) just off XIII Róbert Károly körút on the Pest side of Árpád Bridge. A small bus station (Map 3; ☎ 201 3688, metro Moszkva tér) at I Széna tér 1/a in Buda handles some traffic to and from the Pilis Hills and towns north-west of the capital, including a few departures to Esztergom, as an alternative to the Árpád Bridge station.

Western & Central Europe

From Erzsébet tér there's a Volánbusz/ Eurolines service on Monday, Friday and Saturday throughout the year to Amsterdam via Frankfurt, Düsseldorf and Rotterdam (1615km, 22 hours) costing 28,500Ft (about US$121) one way and 44,000Ft (US$187) return, with a 10% discount for those under 26 or over 60 years of age. From early June to late September the Amsterdam bus runs four times a week and in July and early August it goes daily at slightly higher rates: 29,700Ft (US$125) one way, 46,700Ft (US$198) return. In summer this bus is often full, so try to book ahead.

The Budapest-Amsterdam bus goes through Austria, precluding the need for a Czech or Slovakian visa. In Amsterdam tickets are sold by Eurolines Nederland (☎ 020-560 87 87), Rokin 10, and at Amstel bus station, Julianaplein 5. In Budapest you can buy them upstairs at the Erzsébet tér bus station.

A similar service to Brussels (1395km, 19 hours, 18,900Ft/US$77 one way, 30,900Ft/$126 return) also operates three times a week (Wednesday, Thursday, Sunday) with an additional trip on Monday from July to mid-September. In Brussels, seek information and buy tickets from Eurolines' Belgian office (☎ 02-203 07 07) at 80 Rue du Progrès near the Gare du Nord.

Other buses departing from Erzsébet tér station between two and four times a week from May to September, and their one-way fares, are: Venice (770km, 12 hours, 12,800Ft/US$55); Bologna (945km, 16½ hours, 16,800Ft/US$72); Florence (1045km, 18½ hours, 19,400Ft/US$83); and Rome (1330km, 22½ hours, 23,300Ft/US$99). There are also buses to Hamburg via Berlin (two to four times a week, 1215km, 18½ hours, 24,570Ft/US$104); Milan (one or two a week, 1080km, 19 hours, 19,400Ft/ US$83); Munich (three to six a week, 700km, 10 hours, 19,400Ft/US$83); Paris (two to three times weekly, 1525km, 22½ hours, 29,250Ft/US$125); Zürich (twice a week, 1045km, 17½ hours, 20,670Ft/ US$88). A bus to Oslo with a transfer in Göteborg runs once a week (1915km, 34½ hours, 42,500Ft/US$180).

Buses run between Budapest and London via Vienna and Brussels on Wednesday,

Thursday and Sunday (1770km, 26 hours, 35,000Ft/US$149 one way, 50,600Ft/US$215 return). From June to October the bus also runs on Monday, and from July to early September it runs on Saturday too. In London check with Eurolines (☎ 020-7730 8235 for information, ☎ 0990-143219 for bookings), 52 Grosvenor Gardens SW1. In Paris inquire about Hungary-bound buses at Eurolines France (☎ 01 49 72 51 51) at the Gare Routière Internationale, 28 Avenue du Général de Gaulle.

Three daily buses make the run between Erzsébet tér and Vienna's Autobusbahnhof Wien-Mitte, departing from Budapest at 7 am, noon and 5 pm and from Vienna at 7 am and 5 and 7 pm (254km, 3½ hours, 6800Ft/US$29 one way, 8500Ft/US$36 return). From July to September an additional bus leaves Budapest at 9 am and Vienna at 3 pm daily and on Friday only the rest of the year. Still another bus departs Budapest at 7 pm and Vienna at 11 am Sunday to Friday during the same period. In Vienna, Eurolines (☎ 0222-712 0453) is at Autobusbahnhof Wien-Mitte, Landstrasser Hauptstrasse 1/b.

Czech Republic, Slovakia & Poland

From Erzsébet tér there are buses to Bratislava (daily, 207km, four hours, 2990Ft/US$13) and Prague (two to three times weekly, 535km, 8½ hours, 8500Ft/US$36). An extra night bus from Budapest to Prague runs on Sunday in summer, leaving Budapest at 10 pm and arriving at 6 am. From Népstadion buses head twice a week for Kraków via Zakopane (475km, 12 hours, 5200Ft/US$22).

Romania

By far the cheapest way to get to Romania is by bus from Népstadion, from where there are buses to Oradea (two a week, 260km, six hours, 2800Ft/US12), Arad (six a week, 282km, seven hours, 3100Ft/US$13), Timişoara (one a week, 334km, eight hours, 3800Ft/US$16) and Cluj-Napoca (two a week, 413km, 9½ hours, 4500Ft/US$19). A return ticket is about 50% more than a one-way ticket.

Yugoslavia & Greece

To reach Yugoslavia, you can catch a daily bus from Népstadion to Subotica (224km, 4½ hours, 2450Ft/US$11). There are also buses three times a week in summer from Népstadion to Athens (1570km, 26 hours, 23,500Ft/US$100).

Croatia & Slovenia

From June to mid-September a bus leaves Erzsébet tér on Friday for Rijeka (591km, 10 hours, 10,500Ft/US$45) on Croatia's Istrian Peninsula, calling also at Ljubljana, Koper and Piran in Slovenia.

TRAIN

Magyar Államvasutak, which translates as Hungarian State Railways and is universally known as MÁV (pronounced 'mahv'), links up with the European rail network in all directions, running trains as far as London (via Cologne and Brussels), Paris (via Frankfurt), Stockholm (via Hamburg and Copenhagen), Moscow, Rome and Istanbul (via Belgrade). The international trains listed below are expresses, and many – if not all – require seat reservations. On long hauls, sleepers are almost always available in both 1st and 2nd class, and couchettes are available in 2nd class. Surprisingly, not all express trains have dining or even buffet cars. Make sure you bring along some snacks and drinks as vendors can be few and far between. Hungarian trains are hardly luxurious but are generally clean and punctual.

Most international trains and domestic ones for the north and north-east arrive and depart from Budapest-Keleti (Eastern) train station (Map 3; ☎ 314 5010 or 313 6835); trains to some destinations in Romania as well as the Danube Bend and the Great Plain in Hungary leave from Budapest-Nyugati (Western) station (Map 5; ☎ 349 0115), while Budapest-Déli (Southern) station (Map 3; ☎ 375 6293 or 355 8657) handles trains to/from Zagreb and Rijeka in Croatia and destinations in Transdanubia and on and around Lake Balaton. But these are not hard-and-fast rules, so always make sure you check which station the train leaves from when you buy a ticket. The

Castle Hill offers monuments, museums and great views over the city.

The view along Akadémia utca to Parliament.

The Millenary Monument & Heroes' Square.

Széchenyi Chain Bridge (Széchenyi lánchíd), which opened in 1849.

The splendid Parliament interior.

Parliament and Danube by night.

The Rotunda, Parliament interior.

Elizabeth Bridge (Erzsébet híd), the first newly designed bridge to open after WWII.

central number for international train information is ☎ 461 5500.

To reduce confusion, specify your train by its name (these are listed in the following section and on the posted schedule) when requesting information or buying a ticket. You can get information and buy tickets directly at the three train stations, but it's easier to communicate with the information staff at MÁV's central ticket office (Map 5; ☎ 322 8082 or 322 9035) at VI Andrássy út 35. It's open from 9 am to 6 pm weekdays from April to September and to 5 pm the rest of the year. The office accepts credit cards though the train stations do not.

If you just want to get across the border, local trains are cheaper than international expresses, especially if you're on a one-way trip. Concession fares between cities of the former socialist countries are only available on return tickets.

Timetables for both domestic and international trains and buses use the 24-hour system. Remember that 0.05 means five minutes past midnight while 12.05 is five minutes past noon.

On many (though not all) bus and train timetables, Hungarians tend to use the Hungarian name for cities and towns in neighbouring countries. Many of these are in what once was Hungarian territory and the names are used by the Hungarian-speaking minorities who live there. You should at least be familiar with the more important ones to help decipher bus and (less so) train timetables. See the Alternative Place Names appendix at the back of this book.

Tickets & Discounts

Everyone gets a 30% to 55% discount on return fares to the Czech Republic, Croatia, Poland, Russia, Ukraine, Belarus, Lithuania and Latvia; it's a generous 55% to Slovakia and 70% to certain destinations in Romania. Also, there's a 40% concession on return fares from Budapest to six selected cities: Prague and Brno in the Czech Republic, and Warsaw, Kraków, Katowice and Gdynia in Poland. Sample 2nd-class return fares in euros/forint include the following:

Prague €54/13,959Ft; Moscow €93/24,154Ft; Warsaw €52/13,424Ft.

For tickets to destinations in Western Europe you'll pay the same as everywhere else unless you're aged under 26 and qualify for a BIJ (Billet International de Jeunesse) ticket, which cuts international fares by 25% to 35%; ask at MÁV, Express or the Wasteels office (☎ 210 2802) in Keleti train station. The following are sample return fares in euros/forint from Budapest: Amsterdam €199.50/51,870Ft; Berlin €183/47,643Ft; London €274/71,0986Ft; Munich €88/23,000Ft; Rome €152/39,395Ft; Vienna €54/14,040Ft. There's a 30% discounted return fare to Vienna of €41/10,608Ft if you come back to Budapest within four days. Three daily EuroCity (EC) trains to Vienna and points beyond charge a supplement of 1000Ft to 1500Ft. Seats in 1st class are always 50% more expensive than 2nd class.

An international seat reservation costs 650Ft. Fines are levied on passengers without tickets (400Ft) or seat reservations (1000Ft plus the reservation fee) where they are compulsory. Costs for sleepers depend on the destination, but a two-berth 2nd-class sleeper to Berlin/Prague/Venice/Moscow costs 5000/5460/7800/15,000Ft per person; 1st-class sleepers always cost 50% more than the ones in 2nd class. A 2nd-class couchette in a compartment for six people costs 4500Ft. Tickets are valid for 60 days from purchase and stopovers are permitted.

Budapest is no longer the bargain basement that it once was for tickets on the Trans-Siberian or the Trans-Mongolian railways. In fact, MÁV will only write you a ticket to Moscow; you have to buy the onward ticket from there (from about US$285, depending on the route). Of course, if you are coming back to Budapest from Moscow you get the 40% return discount.

When pricing train tickets from Western Europe remember that air fares (especially those out of London) often match or beat surface alternatives (especially trains) in terms of cost. For example, a return air fare from London to Budapest is available through discount travel agents off season

Border Crossings

The following is a list of border crossings between Hungary and its neighbouring countries that are open to all motorists (beginning in Austria and heading clockwise from there). The Hungarian checkpoint appears first, the foreign checkpoint (or closest town) follows, and references to cities or big towns are inserted in brackets after each.

Austria
Rábafüzes (5km north of Szentgotthárd)/Heiligenkreuz in Lafnitztal
Bucsu (13km west of Szombathely)/Schachendorf
Kőszeg/Rattersdorf
Kópháza (11km north of Sopron)/Deutschkreutz
Sopron (7km north-west of the city)/Klingenbach
Fertőrákos (open April to October to pedestrians & cyclists only)/Mörbisch
Fertőd/Pamhagen
Jánossomorja (14km south-west of Mosonmagyaróvár; open April to October to pedestrians & cyclists only)/Andau
Hegyeshalom (51km north-west of Győr)/Nickelsdorf

Slovakia
Rajka (18km north-west of Mosonmagyaróvár)/Rusovce
Vámosszabadi (13km north of Győr)/Medvedov
Komárom/Komárno
Parassapuszta (40km north of Vác)/Šahy
Balassagyarmat/Slovenské Darmoty
Somoskőújfalu (8km north of Salgótarján)/Filakovo
Bánréve (43km north-west of Miskolc)/Král
Tornyosnémeti (60km north-east of Miskolc)/Milhost
Sátoraljaújhely/Slovenské Nové Mesto

for around UK£170 or less. By comparison, a two-month return ticket by rail to Budapest available from Rail Europe (☎ 0990 848 848) costs UK£375/365 for adults/youths, though there are discounted fares of UK£240/230 available if the tickets are purchased a month in advance (Web site: www.raileurope.com).

Western & Central Europe
Some eight trains a day link Vienna with Budapest (three hours) via Hegyeshalom. Most of them leave from Vienna's Westbahnhof, including the *Orient Express* arriving from Paris (18 hours from Budapest) and Munich, the *Arrabona*, the EC *Bartók Béla* from Munich (eight hours) via Salzburg, the EC *Liszt Ferenc* from Cologne (11 hours) via

Frankfurt, the *Dacia Express* bound for Bucharest (13 hours) and the IC *Avala* bound for Belgrade (6½ hours). The early-morning EC *Lehár*, however, departs from Vienna's Südbahnhof and the *Beograd Express* arrives and departs in the wee hours from Budapest's 'fourth' station – Kelenföld in Buda. None requires a seat reservation, though they're highly recommended in summer.

Also, up to seven weekday trains (three at the weekend) leave Vienna's Südbahnhof for Sopron (75 minutes) via Ebenfurth; as many as 10 weekday (five at the weekend) trains also serve Sopron from Wiener Neustadt, which is easily accessible from Vienna. Some seven trains on weekdays (five at the weekend) make the three-hour trip from Graz to Szombathely.

Border Crossings

Ukraine
Záhony (23km north of Kisvárda)/Čop (23km south of Užgorod)
Beregsurány (21km north-east of Vásárosnamény)/Beregove)
Tiszabecs (27km north-east of Fehérgyarmat)/Vylok

Romania
Csengersima (40km south-east of Mátészalka)/Petea (11km north-west of Satu Mare)
Ártánd (25km south-east of Berettyóújfalu)/Borş (14km north-west of Oradea)
Méhkerék (24km north of Gyula)/Salonta
Gyula/Varşand (66km north of Arad)
Battonya (45km south-east of Orosháza)/Turnu
Nagylak (52km west of Szeged)/Nădlac (54km west of Arad)

Yugoslavia
Rözske (16km south-west of Szeged)/Horgoš (30km north-east of Subotica)
Tompa (30km south of Kiskunhalas)/Kelebija (11km north-west of Subotica)
Hercegszántó (32km south of Baja)/Bački Breg (28km north-west of Sombor)

Croatia
Udvar (12km south of Mohács)/Doboševica
Drávaszabolcs (9km south of Harkány)/Donji Miholjac (49km north-west of Osijek)
Barcs (32km south-west of Szigetvár)/Terezino Polje
Berzence (24km west of Nagyatád)/Gola
Letenye (26km west of Nagykanizsa)/Gorican

Slovenia
Rédics (9km south-west of Lenti)/Dolga Vas
Bajánsenye (60km west of Zalaegerszeg)/Hodoš

There are two or three trains a day from Berlin (Zoo, Ostbahnhof and Schnefeld stations) to Budapest (12½ hours) via Dresden, sometimes Prague and Bratislava: the *Spree-Donau Kurier*, the EC *Hungária* and the EC *Comenius*, which originates in Hamburg, a central point for trains from Malmö, Copenhagen and Amsterdam.

Czech Republic, Slovakia & Poland
In addition to being served by the EC *Hungária* and *Comenius* trains from Berlin, Prague (7½ to nine hours) also sees the IC *Csárdás*, the *Slovan* and the *Pannónia Express* from Bucharest daily. Each day two trains, the EC *Polonia* and the *Báthory*, leave Warsaw for Budapest (12 hours) passing through Katowice and Bratislava and/or

Štúrovo. The *Amicus* runs directly to/from Bratislava (three hours) every day.

The *Karpaty* from Warsaw bound for Bucharest passes through Kraków and Košice before reaching Miskolc, where you can change for Budapest. The *Cracovia* runs from Kraków to Budapest (13 hours) and Pécs via Košice. Another train, the *Rákóczi*, links Budapest (four hours) with Košice and Poprad Tatry, 100km to the north-west. The *Bem* connects Szczecin in north-western Poland with Budapest (17 hours) via Poznań, Wrocław and, in Slovakia, Lučenec.

Two additional local trains cover the 90km from Miskolc and Košice (two hours) every day. The 2km hop from Sátoraljaújhely to Slovenské Nové Mesto (three a day) is only a four-minute ride by train.

Ukraine & Russia

From Moscow to Budapest (38½ hours) there's only the *Tisza Express*, which travels via Kiev and Lvov in Ukraine. Most nationalities require a transit visa to travel through Ukraine.

Romania

From Bucharest to Budapest (12 to 14 hours) you can choose among four trains: the EC *Traianus*, the *Dacia*, the *Ister* the *Pannónia* and the *Muntenia*, all of which go via Arad and require seat reservations. The *Karpaty* goes to Bucharest from Miskolc.

There are three connections daily from Cluj-Napoca to Budapest (seven hours, via Oradea): the IC *Ady Endre*, the *Corona* (from Braşov) and the *Claudiopolis*. These trains require a seat reservation as does the *Partium*, which links Budapest and Oradea only.

There are two local trains a day linking Baia Mare in northern Romania with Budapest (eight hours) via Satu Mare and Debrecen. Otherwise you'll have to take one of two additional local trains from Debrecen across the border to Valea lui Mihai and catch a Romanian train there.

Bulgaria & Yugoslavia

The *Balkán Express*, originating in Istanbul (32 hours), links Budapest with Sofia (22 hours) via Belgrade. Other trains between Budapest and Belgrade via Subotica (seven to eight) include the *Beograd Express*, the *Ivo Andrić*, the IC *Avala* and the *Hellas*, which runs from Thessaloniki in Greece, via Skopje in Macedonia, and takes just over a day to arrive. Be warned that the *Beograd* arrives and departs from Kelenföld station in Buda. You must reserve your seats on some of these trains.

Two additional local trains (no reservations necessary) make the 1¾-hour, 45km journey between Subotica and Szeged every day.

Croatia & Slovenia

You can get to Budapest from Zagreb (six hours) on three trains, all of them via Siófok on Lake Balaton's southern shore: the *Maestral*, which originates in Split in summer (17¼ hours); the *Avas*; and the *Venezia Express* via Ljubljana (eight hours). The *Dráva*, which originates in Venice, also travels via Ljubljana but does not go via Zagreb. The *Kvarner* from Rijeka (nine hours) to Budapest via Zagreb follows the route to the north of the Balaton.

CAR & MOTORCYCLE

Hungary maintains 55 road crossings with its seven neighbours. Of these, about 20 (mostly in the north and north-east) are restricted to local citizens from both sides of the border (or, in the case of Austria, to Hungarian and EU citizens).

See the list of border crossings earlier in this chapter.

WALKING & HITCHING

To save the cost of an international ticket or just for fun, you may consider walking across the frontier into or out of Hungary. But many border guards frown on this practice, particularly in Romania, Yugoslavia and Ukraine; try hitching a ride instead.

There are three crossings to/from Slovakia where you won't have any problems. At Komárom, 88km north-west of Budapest, a bridge over the Danube connects the city with Komárno. At Sátoraljaújhely, northeast of Miskolc, another highway border crossing over the Ronyva River links the centre of town with Slovenské Nové Mesto. For information on the ferry from Esztergom to Štúrovo, see the Boat section later in this chapter.

To/from Romania, the easiest place to cross on foot is Nagylak/Nădlac between Szeged and Arad. There are eight local trains a day from the train station at Újszeged across the Tisza River from Szeged proper to Nagylak (47km, 1¼ hours) near the border. After crossing into Romania you must walk, cycle or hitch for 6km to Nădlac, where you can connect with up to four local trains a day to Arad (52km, 1½ hours).

If you're bound for Slovenia, take one of up to 10 trains a day from Zalaegerszeg to Rédics (49km, 1½ hours), which is only a couple of kilometres from the main highway border crossing into Slovenia. From the border it's a 5km walk south to the Lendava bus station, where you'll have a choice of five buses daily to Ljubljana (212km, four hours) and many more to Maribor (92km).

Ride-Share Agencies

There's a service in Budapest called Kenguru (Map 5; ☎ 266 5837 or 338 2019, ☻ kenguru@elender.hu), VIII Kőfaragó út 15 (metro Blaha Lujza tér), that matches up drivers and riders for a fee – mostly to points abroad. Kenguru gets 2Ft per kilometre and the driver 6Ft. Sample one-way costs are: Amsterdam 11,050Ft, London 12,900Ft, Munich 5750Ft, Paris 11,750Ft, Prague 4250Ft and Vienna 2150Ft. Kenguru is open from 8 am till 6 pm weekdays and from 10 am to 2 pm on weekends.

BICYCLE

Cyclists may have a problem crossing Hungarian border stations connected to main roads since bicycles are banned on motorways and national highways with single-digit route numbers.

See Cycling under Activities in the Things to See & Do chapter for more details on cycling in and around Budapest.

BOAT

Hungary's two main international river crossings involve – naturally – the Danube.

A hydrofoil service on the Danube from Budapest to Vienna (282km, 5½ hours) via Bratislava (on request) operates daily from early April to October with an extra sailing on certain days from early July to late August. Fares to Vienna are high: US$71/102 one way/return, but ISIC holders get a 20% discount and Eurail pass holders and children aged six to 15 get 50% off. Transporting a bicycle on the hydrofoil costs US$18. Adult one-way/return fares to Bratislava are US$64/91.

Ferries arrive and depart from the International Landing Stage (Nemzetközi hajó-állomás; Map 3) on Belgrád rakpart in Pest, just north of Szabadság Bridge. From early April to early July and from late August to October there's a daily sailing at

9 am from both Budapest and Vienna. From early July to late August boats leave both cities at 8 am. An additional one-departs from Budapest at 1 pm Thursday to Sunday and at the same time from Vienna from Friday to Monday. The boat docks in Vienna at the Reichsbrücke pier near Mexikoplatz.

Tickets are available in Budapest from Mahart Tours (☎ 318 1953) at the pier. The small office is open from 8 am to 4 pm on weekdays. At weekends the ticket window is open from 8 am to noon. In Vienna, get tickets from Mahart Tours (☎ 0222-729 2161) at Karlsplatz 2-8.

The second way of getting out of Hungary is much more 'pedestrian' – and cheaper. It's the year-round passenger and car ferry linking Esztergom with Štúrovo and is one of the easiest and most central ways to enter Hungary from Slovakia. The ferry crosses the Danube from Esztergom to Štúrovo 12 times a day from June to August with the first at 7.20 am and the last at 6.20 pm (from Štúrovo: on the hour from 8 am to 7 pm). During the rest of the year there are nine sailings starting at the same times. Adults/children pay 110/50Ft; it costs another 300Ft to take a car along, 200Ft for a motorcycle or bicycle.

ORGANISED TOURS

A number of agencies, including Vista, Ibusz and Cityrama (see Travel Agencies in the Facts for the Visitor chapter) offer excursions and special-interest guided tours (horse riding, cycling, bird-watching, Jewish culture etc) to every corner of Hungary. A 4½-hour tour by boat and bus to Szentendre or to Gödöllő by bus with Cityrama or Ibusz costs 9200Ft (children half-price) while a 10-hour tour of the Danube Bend by coach and boat with stops at Visegrád and Esztergom costs 15,000Ft.

These companies also offer day trips to Lake Balaton (Balatonfüred, Tihany and the southern shore), the Southern Plain (Lajosmizse or Bugacpuszta in Kiskunság National Park and Kecskemét), Eger and Hollókő for about 16,000Ft. Vista tours of the countryside start at DM57 per person.

Getting Around

THE AIRPORT
There are two terminals side by side at Budapest's Ferihegy International Airport, which is 24km south-east of the capital. Malév flights arrive and depart from Ferihegy Terminal 2A; all other international airlines use Terminal 2B, which opened in late 1998. (The old Terminal 1, about 5km to the west, is now used only for cargo or special flights.) Terminal 2B has an ATM, car rental and hotel booking desks, a post office open from 8 am to 3.30 pm weekdays and a left-luggage facility (see Left Luggage in the Facts for the Visitor chapter).

The general flight information phone number at the airport is ☎ 296 9696.

TO/FROM THE AIRPORT
With three much cheaper options for getting to/from Ferihegy (and a fourth on the way), it would be senseless to take a taxi and risk a major rip-off. If you do want to take a taxi, call one of the companies listed under Taxi later in the chapter with a mobile phone or from a phonebox at arrivals; you'll save between 1000Ft and 1500Ft on the posted airport fares (3900Ft to 4600Ft). The Tele 5 taxi company (☎ 355 5555) has a fare of 2555Ft to the airport from the city centre.

The Airport Minibus Service (☎ 296 8555 or 296 6283) picks up passengers wherever they're staying – be it a hotel, hostel or private home. But there are drawbacks: you have to book 24 hours in advance on departure and, as the van seats eight people, it can be a time-consuming process (and nerve-wracking if you're running late). The fare is 1500/2500Ft one way/return per person. Tickets into the city are available in the airport arrivals hall.

An easier way to go is with the airport-run Centrum Bus (☎ 296 8555), another minibus that links V Erzsébet tér (board it outside the Kempinski Corvinus) with both Ferihegy terminals every half-hour between 5.30 am and 9.30 pm (6 am to 10 pm from the airport). The fare is 600Ft (pay on the bus), and you're advised to count on 30 to 40 minutes' travel.

The cheapest way to go in either direction is to take the blue metro to the end of the line (Kőbánya-Kispest station) and board bus No 93 (the one with the red number). The total cost at the time of research was 180Ft.

A light rail connecting Ferihegy with central Pest is under construction.

PUBLIC TRANSPORT
Budapest has an ageing but safe, inexpensive and efficient transport system that will never have you waiting more than five or 10 minutes. There are five types of vehicles in use: metro trains, green HÉV trains, blue buses, yellow trams and red trolleybuses. They are all run by the BKV city transport company (☎ 342 2335).

Public transport in Budapest runs from 4.30 am till between 11.20 and 11.30 pm, depending on the station. There are also some 16 night buses (marked with an 'É' after the designated number) running every half-hour or so along the main routes. After 8 pm, you must board buses from the front entrance and show the driver your ticket or pass.

Fares & Passes
To travel on the metro, trams, trolleybuses, buses and the HÉV (as far as the city limits, which is the Békásmegyer stop) you must have a ticket, which you can buy at kiosks, newsstands or metro entrances. The basic fare at the time of writing was 90Ft, allowing you to travel as far as you want on the same metro line without changing; it drops to 60Ft if you are just going three stops within 30 minutes. For 95Ft you can travel five stops and make a change (transfer) at Deák tér to another metro line within one hour. Unlimited stations travelled with one change within one hour costs 135Ft. You must always travel in one continuous direction on a metro ticket; return trips are not allowed. Blocks of 10/20 single tickets cost 810/1500Ft.

A Street by Any Other Name

After WWII, most streets, squares and parks were renamed for people, political groups or anniversaries that have since become anathema to an independent, democratic Hungary. From April 1989, names were changed at a frantic pace and with a determination that some people felt was almost obsessive; at least 400 street names were changed in Budapest alone. Sometimes it has just been a case of returning a street or square to its original (perhaps medieval) name – from Lenin útja, say, to Szent korona útja (Street of the Holy Crown). Other times the name is new.

The new (or original) names are now pretty much in place all these years later, the old street signs with a red 'X' drawn across them have all but disappeared, and virtually no-one refers to Ferenciek tere (Square of the Franciscans) in Budapest, for example, as Felszabadulás tér (Liberation Square), which honoured the Soviet army's role in liberating Budapest in WWII.

Occasionally you'll come across an old signboard or map, particularly in the provinces, that may confuse. The following list includes the most common place names disposed of over the past decade. It's not necessary to know who the people were or what the dates signify; most Hungarians don't have a clue. Just remember that if you see any one of these names on an old map, it's almost certain to go by another name these days:

Április 4
Bacsó Béla
Béke (Peace)
Beloiannisz
Dimitrov
Engels (Frigyes)
Felszabadulás (Liberation)
Fürst Sándor
Hamburger Jenő
Kun Béla
Lenin
Magyar-Szovjet barátság (Hungarian-Soviet Friendship)
Marx (Károly)

Néphadsereg (People's Army)
Népköztársaság (People's Republic)
November 7
Rózsa Ferenc
Ságvári Endre
Sallai Imre
Schönherz Zoltán
Tanács (Council; see below)
Tanácsköztársaság (Council of the Republics)
Tolbuhin
Úttörő (Young Pioneer)
Vörös csillag (Red Star)
Vörös Hadsereg (Red Army)
Vörös október (Red October)

Where the streets have no (communist) name

You can get travelcards valid for transport on all metro lines, trams, buses, trolleybuses and the HÉV to the city limits for one day (700Ft) or three days (1400Ft). There's also a weekend family travelcard (covering two adults and two children under 14) for 1750Ft. None of these requires a photograph.

Seasonal passes good for a week (1650Ft), a fortnight (2250Ft) or a month (3400Ft) require a mug shot. All but the monthly passes are valid from midnight to midnight, so buy them in advance and specify the date(s) you want. The most central places to get them are at the Deák tér metro station and the Nyugati tér metro concourse.

Travelling 'black' (without a ticket or pass) is riskier than ever in Budapest; with increased surveillance (including a big crackdown in the metro), there's a good chance you'll get caught. Tickets are always checked on the HÉV. The on-the-spot fine is 1200Ft, which rises to 3000Ft if you pay later at the BKV office (Map 5), VII Akácfa utca 22. It's your call, but if you do get nabbed, do us all a favour: shut up and pay up. The inspectors – and your fellow passengers – hear the same boring (and false) stories every day of the year.

Metro

Budapest has three underground metro lines intersecting (only) at Deák tér: M1, the little yellow line from Vörösmarty tér to Mexikoi út; M2, the red line from Déli train station to Örs vezér tere; and M3, the blue line from Újpest-Központ to Kőbánya-Kispest. A possible source of confusion on the yellow line (nobody calls it the 'M1') is that one stop is called Vörösmarty tér and another is Vörösmarty utca. Plans to build a 7.3km line between Pest and south Buda (the M4) have been shelved by the national government, sparking a row with the municipal government (see Government & Politics in the Facts about Budapest chapter).

The metro is the fastest (but obviously the least scenic) way to go and the aboveground HÉV suburban railway functions almost like a fourth metro line. The HÉV itself has a total of four lines, but only one is of real use to most travellers: from Batthyány tér in Buda via Óbuda and Aquincum to Szentendre.

Bus, Tram & Trolleybus

There's an extensive network of trams, trolleybuses and buses, and you'll seldom wait more than a few minutes for any of them. On certain bus lines the same number bus may have a black or a red number. In this case, the red-numbered bus is the express, which makes limited stops and is faster. An invaluable transit map detailing all services is available for a nominal fee at most metro ticket booths.

Buses and trams are much of a muchness, though the latter are often faster and generally more pleasant for sightseeing. Trolleybuses go along cross streets in central Pest and are of little use to most visitors, with the sole exception of the ones to the City and Népliget Parks.

The most important tram lines (always marked with red lines on a Budapest map) are:

Nos 2 and 2/a, scenic trams that travel along the Pest side of the Danube as far as Jászai Mari tér

Nos 4 and 6, which start at Fehérvári út and Móricz Zsigmond körtér in district XI of south Buda respectively and follow the entire length of the Big Ring Road in Pest before terminating at Moszkva tér

No 18, which runs from southern Buda along Bartók Béla út through the Tabán to Moszkva tér

No 19, which covers part of the same route but then runs along the Buda side of the Danube to Batthyány tér

Nos 47 and 49, linking Deák tér in Pest with points in southern Buda

No 61, connecting Móricz Zsigmond körtér with Déli station and Moszkva tér

Some buses (always blue lines on a Budapest map) you might find useful include:

the black No 4, which runs from northern Pest via Heroes' Square to Deák tér (the red No 4 follows the same route but crosses over Chain Bridge into central Buda)

the 6É night bus, which follows the route of tram No 6 along the Big Ring Road

No 7, which cuts across a large swathe of central Pest and southern Buda from Bosnyák tér and down Rákóczi út to Kelenföld station in southern Buda

the No 14É night bus, which follows the blue metro line above ground

No 86, which runs the length of Buda from Kosztolányi Dezső tér to Óbuda

No 105, from Heroes' Square to Deák tér

CAR & MOTORCYCLE
Though it's not so bad at night, driving in Budapest during the day can be a nightmare: roadworks reduce traffic to a snail's crawl; there are more serious accidents than fender-benders; and parking spots are difficult to find. The public transport system is good and cheap. Use it.

Foreign driving licences are valid for one year after entering Hungary. Third-party liability insurance is compulsory. If your car is registered in the EU, it is assumed that you have it; all other motorists must be able to show a Green Card or will have to buy insurance at the border.

Road Rules
You must drive on the right. Speed limits for cars and motorcycles in Hungary are consistent everywhere and strictly enforced: 50km/h in built-up areas (from the town sign as you enter to the same sign with a red line through it as you leave); 80km/h on secondary and tertiary roads; 100km/h on most highways/dual carriageways; and 120km/h on motorways. Exceeding the limit will earn you a fine of between 5000Ft and 30,000Ft, which can no longer be paid for on the spot but at the post office or with a postal cheque.

The use of seat belts in the front (and in the back – if fitted – outside built-up areas) is compulsory, but this rule is often ignored. Motorcyclists must wear helmets, a law strictly enforced. Another law taken very seriously indeed is the one requiring *all* vehicles to use their headlights throughout the day outside built-up areas. Motorcycles must illuminate their headlights at all times. Using a mobile phone while driving is prohibited in Hungary.

Drink-driving is taken very seriously in Hungary, where there is a 100% ban on alcohol for anyone taking the wheel (see Legal Matters in the Facts for the Visitor chapter). There's a chauffeur service (mobile ☎ 06-30-9349 824) available in Budapest whereby a staff member will meet you and drive your car home should you have had too much (or anything at all, strictly speaking). Prices vary but the

'standard' seems to be double the taxi fare minus 20% (roughly 2000Ft for a trip across town). It takes about an hour for the driver to arrive on Friday or Saturday evening and at rush hour.

All accidents should be reported to the police (☎ 107) immediately. Several insurance companies handle auto liability, and minor claims can be settled without complications. Any claim on insurance policies bought in Hungary can also be made to Hungária Biztosító (Map 5; ☎ 301 6565), V Vadász utca 23-25. It is the largest insurance company in Hungary and deals with foreigners all the time.

For information on traffic and public road conditions in the capital call Főinform on ☎ 317 1173 (for the rest of the country call Útinform on ☎ 322 2238 or 322 7643). If you're trying to trace a towed vehicle, call ☎ 286 0163.

Motoring Organisations
The Yellow Angels (*Sárga Angyal*) of the Hungarian Automobile Club (Magyar Autóklub; Map 3; ☎ 212 2821) do basic car repairs free of charge in the event of a breakdown if you belong to an affiliated organisation such as AAA in the USA or AA in the UK. Towing, however, is still very expensive even with these reciprocal memberships. The Yellow Angels can be reached 24 hours a day at ☎ 188 (or ☎ 212 2938 in Budapest).

Petrol
Petrol (*benzin*) of 91 and unleaded (*ólommentes*) 95 and 98 octane is available everywhere and costs 195/199/207Ft per litre respectively. Most stations also have diesel fuel (*gáz-olaj*) costing 170Ft per litre. Payment by credit card is now standard at petrol stations in Budapest.

Parking
In Budapest parking now costs between 140Ft and 240Ft per hour on the street and in covered car parks. There are covered parking areas in Szervita tér and at the Kempinski Corvinus and Budapest Marriott hotels in the Inner Town.

Rental

In general, you must be at least 21 years of age and have had your licence for a year or longer to rent a car here. All the big international car-rental firms have offices in Budapest, but prices can be very high. An Opel Corsa from Avis (☎ 318 4158, fax 318 4859), V Szervita tér 8, for example, costs US$222 a week plus US$0.37 per kilometre and $20 a day insurance. The same car with unlimited kilometres and insurance costs US$131 a day or US$158 for a weekend. The 25% ÁFA (value-added tax) doesn't apply to nonresidents paying with foreign currency or credit card.

One of the cheapest outfits for renting cars is Inka (Map 5; ☎ 317 2150, fax 318 1843, @ inka@mail.hungary.net) at V Bajcsy-Zsilinszky út 16 or XIII Váci út 41 (☎ 350 1091, fax 349 4154). An Opel Corsa here costs US$155 a week plus US$0.26 per kilometre and US$8 a day for insurance (or US$80 a day with unlimited kilometres or US$100 for a weekend). Though more expensive than Inka, Americana Rent-a-Car (Map 3; ☎ 320 8287, @ americana@ mail.matav.hu), in the Ibis Volga hotel at XIII Dózsa György út 65, is reliable and has American cars with automatic transmissions. A Suzuki Swift with unlimited kilometres costs US$49 a day or $97 for a three-day weekend. Fox Autorent (☎ 457 1150), III Óbudai hajógyári-sziget 130, charges US$55 to $59 a day (US$324 a week) for a Suzuki Swift with unlimited mileage, insurance, home delivery and airport drop-off. Check out the Web site at www.fox-autorent.com.

TAXI

Taxis aren't as cheap as they once were in Budapest and, considering the excellent public transport network, you won't really have to use them much. We've heard from several readers who were grossly overcharged and even threatened by taxi drivers in Budapest, so taking a taxi in this city should be approached with caution. However, the reputable firms listed below have caught on to the concept of customer service and they now take complaints quite seriously.

Watch out for taxis with no name on the door and only a removable lighted taxi box on the roof; these are just guys with cars and the most likely to cheat you. Never get into a taxi that does not have a yellow licence plate and an identification badge displayed on the dashboard (required by law), the logo of one of the reputable taxi firms we list below on the side doors and a table of fares posted on the dashboard inside.

Not all taxi meters are set at the same rates, and some are much more expensive than others, but there are price ceilings within which cab companies are free to manoeuvre. From 6 am to 10 pm the highest flag-fall fee that can be legally charged is 200Ft, the per-kilometre charge 200Ft and the waiting fee 50Ft per minute; after that the fees are 280/280/70Ft. If you call a reputable cab company in advance, you'll probably pay something closer to 120/160/50Ft.

The following are the telephone numbers of reliable taxi firms in Budapest. You can call them from anywhere (the dispatchers usually speak English), and they'll arrive in a matter of minutes. Make sure you know the number of the phone you're using, as that's how they establish your address.

City	☎ 211 1111
Tele 5	☎ 355 5555
Fő	☎ 222 2222
Rádió	☎ 377 7777
Buda	☎ 233 3333

BOAT

BKV runs passenger ferries from IX Boráros tér (Map 6), beside Petőfi Bridge, to III Rómaifürdő and Pünkösdfürdő in Óbuda, a one-hour trip with many stops along the way, four times daily from Thursday to Sunday between late May and mid-September. Tickets (300/150Ft) are usually sold on board. The ferry stop closest to Castle Hill is I Batthyány tér, and V Petőfi tér is not far from Vörösmarty tér, a convenient place to pick up the boat on the Pest side.

See Boat in the following Organised Tours section for information about river cruises.

BICYCLE

More and more cyclists can be seen on the roads these days taking advantage of the excellent network of bike paths. The main roads in the city might be a bit too busy and nerve-wracking to allow enjoyable cycling, but the side streets are fine and there are some areas where biking is ideal. See Cycling under Activities in the Things to See & Do chapter for ideas on where to cycle and information on where to rent bikes.

ORGANISED TOURS
Bus

Many travel agencies, including Ibusz (☎ 317 8343) and Cityrama (☎ 302 4382), V Báthory utca 22, offer three-hour city tours from 5200/2600Ft. They also have excursions farther afield to the Danube Bend, Lake Balaton, the Southern Plain etc. See Organised Tours in the Getting There & Away chapter for details.

Budatours (Map 5; ☎ 331 1585), VI Andrássy út 2, runs seven tour buses a day in July and August (between two and three the rest of the year) from the Gresham Palace at V Roosevelt tér 5 (Map 5). It's a two-hour nonstop tour with taped commentary in 16 different languages and costs 4400/2200Ft. Queenybus (☎ 247 7159) departs twice daily (11 am and 2.20 pm) from St Stephen's Basilica (Map 5), V Bajcsy-Zsilinszky út, for three-hour city tours (4800/3600/2400Ft for adults/students/children). Both Budatours and Queenybus also have Parliament tours for 2800/1400Ft.

For those who prefer the hop-on, hop-off style of tour bus, N Bus (mobile ☎ 06-60 560 001) makes 1½-hour circuits (3500Ft) of the city from 9 am to 6 pm daily, stopping at 10 different sights.

Boat

From April to September Mahart (☎ 318 1704) has 1½-hour cruises on the Danube at noon and 7 pm daily for 800/400Ft. In April the cruise at noon operates on Sunday and holidays only, and in July and August the evening program begins at 7.45 pm and includes music and dance (900/450Ft). You can buy your ticket at the small ticket office by the river at Vigadó tér 3 (Map 5; metro Vörösmarty tér). Other more expensive cruises such as the ones on the *Legenda* (☎ 266 4190) for 2800/1400Ft for adults/children during the day and 3200/1600Ft in the evening are heavily promoted around town ('selection of 24 languages!'), but try to find the much cheaper Mahart boat. The night lights of the city rising to Buda Castle, Parliament, Gellért Hill and the Citadella make the evening trip far more attractive than the afternoon one. Budatours and Ibusz also offer themed cruises (folklore, dance etc) for from 10,900Ft and 12,900Ft.

Walking

Budapest Walks, organised by Robinson Travel (☎ 340 4232), offers a 2½-hour Gems of Buda Castle tour departing from Matthias Church (Map 5) in I Szentháromság tér at 2.30 pm Tuesday to Sunday from May to September and a Highlights of Pest one leaving from the Gerbeaud cafe in V Vörösmarty tér at 10.30 am on the same days. They cost 3200/1600Ft for adults/students and include museum entry fees.

IA Tours (mobile ☎ 06-30 211 8861) has a number of three-hour tours in English (2500/2000Ft) departing from in front of the Műcsarnok (Map 3) in XIV Hősök tere at 10 am to 2 pm daily from mid-June to September.

Castle Walks (☎ 488 0453 for information) will lead you through the winding ways and tortuous tales of the historic Castle District starting from Matthias Church (Map 5) for 1500Ft. Tours leave at 11 am daily from late June to September and at the weekend only from late September to late October.

Much more personal are Paul Street Tours (mobile ☎ 06-209 582 545, ✉ kfaurest@ hotmail.com), which cover the Castle District (1½ hours, DM38 per person or DM28 each for two or more people) as well as less-explored areas of Pest like the Jewish Quarter and Andrássy út (2½ hours, DM56 per person or DM38 per person for two or more), with lots of anecdotal background information on architecture and social history, especially life in and around the *udvar* (courtyards) of *fin-de-siècle* Pest. Tours are available year-round in English or Hungarian.

Specialised

Hungaria Koncert (☎ 317 2754) has a 2½-hour tour that focuses on Budapest's Jewish heritage, available at 11 am and 2 pm most weekdays from August to October (at 11.30 am on Sunday in October too). The tour includes a visit to the Great Synagogue, a walking tour of the ghetto, cantor music, and a nonkosher meal and a concert in the synagogue by the Budapest Klezmer Band for 6000/5400Ft adults/students (3900Ft for the concert alone). Tickets are available from locations throughout the city, including the Duna Palota (Map 5) at V Zrínyi utca and at the entrance to the synagogue (Map 5).

Things to See & Do

HIGHLIGHTS

Though it's all a matter of taste and interest, the highlights in the boxed text on this page lists what could be considered the top sights and activities in Budapest; at least a few of them should be included on every traveller's itinerary. For those with more time or an interest in seeing the city in greater depth, there are a dozen walking tours to follow.

WALKING TOURS

Budapest is an excellent city for walking, and there are sights around every corner – from a brightly tiled gem of an Art Nouveau building to peasant women fresh from the countryside hawking their home-made *barack lekvár* (apricot jam) or colourful embroidery at the markets.

The following 12 tours can easily be done individually or in tandem with the preceding or following ones; the dozen highlights listed here can be found along the way. Don't worry about doing every tour or even finishing one; linger as long as you like in a museum or market that takes your fancy, do a little shopping or even visit one of the city's fine thermal spas along the way.

Budapest's museums and other important sights are listed in alphabetical order and described in detail following this section for those of you who just want to visit a handful of places not close to one another and/or are not into walking. The 'Museums of Budapest' boxed text lists the city's collections by geographical area.

Budapest Highlights

The 'top 12' listed below (in no particular order) can also be found on the walking tours listed in this chapter.

- the **view of Pest** from Fishermen's Bastion on Castle Hill in district I (Walking Tour 1)
- the **view of Buda** from the waterfront tram No 2 on the Pest side (Walking Tour 6)
- a night at the **State Opera House**, VI Andrássy út 22 (Walking Tour 9)
- the period furniture and bric-a-brac at the **Applied Arts Museum**, IX Üllői út 33-37 (Walking Tour 11)
- a soak at any of the following **thermal baths**: Gellért, XI Kelenhegyi út 4; Rudas, I Döbrentei tér 9 (Walking Tour 2); Király, II Fő utca 84 (Walking Tour 3); or Széchenyi, XIV Állatkerti út 11, City Park (Walking Tour 9)
- the **two icons of Hungarian nationhood**: the Crown of St Stephen, now at the Parliament building (Walking Tour 7); and the saint-king's mortal remains in the Basilica of St Stephen, Bajcsy-Zsilinszky út (Walking Tour 6)
- the wonderfully restored **Central Market Hall** (Nagycsarnok) on IX Fővám tér (Walking Tour 11), or the more traditional outdoor market at VIII Rákóczi tér 34 (Walking Tour 11) or on XIII Lehel tér (Walking Tour 6)
- the Old Masters at the **Museum of Fine Arts**, XIV Hősök tere (Walking Tour 9)
- the descent (for better views) on the **Libegő (chairlift)** from János-hegy in the Buda Hills to Zugligeti út (Walking Tour 12)
- the Judaica collection at the **Jewish Museum**, VII Dohány utca 2 (Walking Tour 10)
- a slice of anything at any of the **traditional cafes** in the Places to Eat chapter, including the Művész, VI Andrássy út 29 (Walking Tour 9)
- a browse (and maybe a purchase) at the **Ecseri market**

Walking Tour 1: Castle Hill

Castle Hill, a 1km-long limestone plateau in Buda 170m above the Danube, contains Budapest's most important medieval monuments and some of its best museums. It is the premier sight for visitors to the city and, with its grand views and so many things to see, you should start your touring here. Castle Hill sits on a 28km network of caves formed by thermal springs. The caves were supposedly used by the Turks for military purposes and then as air-raid shelters during WWII. Castle Hill lies entirely in district I.

All the sights listed here can be found on the Castle Hill & Watertown Map 4.

The walled castle area consists of two distinct parts: the Old Town (Vár), where commoners lived in the Middle Ages (the current owners of the coveted burgher houses here are no longer so common) and the Royal Palace (Budavári palota), the original site of the castle built by Béla IV in the 13th century. To get to the former (where we'll start), take bus No 16 from Erzsébet tér in Pest, which terminates at Dísz tér. If you're already in Buda, find your way to Moszkva tér on the red metro line and up Várfok utca (south-east above the square) to Vienna Gate, the northern entrance to the Old Town. A small bus labelled 'Várbusz' follows the same route from the start of Várfok utca.

If you want to begin with all the museums in the Royal Palace, there are a number of transport options. The easiest is the **Sikló**, a funicular built in 1870 that takes passengers up in two minutes from Clark Ádám tér to Szent György tér between 7.30 am and 10.30 pm daily (closed on the Monday of every even-numbered week). It costs 300/150Ft for adults/children up to age 10 to ascend and is 250/100Ft to ride back down. Alternatively, you can walk up the **Király lépcső**, the 'Royal Steps' that lead from Hunyadi János út north-west of Clark Ádám tér, or the wide staircase that goes to the southern end of the Royal Palace from Szarvas tér.

The best way to see the **Old Town** is to stroll along the four medieval streets that more or less run parallel to one another and converge on Szentháromság tér. Poke your head into the attractive little courtyards (an acceptable activity) and visit the odd museum, but be selective; it would take you at least two full days to see everything on Castle Hill. A brief tour of the Old Town in one of the horse-drawn hackney cabs (*fiáker*) standing in Szentháromság tér will cost 1000Ft to 1500Ft per person.

You can start your tour by climbing to the top of **Vienna Gate** (Bécsi kapu), rebuilt in 1936 to mark the 250th anniversary of the retaking of the castle from the Turks. It's not all that huge, but when loquacious Hungarian children natter on, their parents tell them: 'Be quiet, your mouth is as big as the Vienna Gate!' The large building to the west with the superb tiled roof is the **National Archives** (Országos Levéltár; 1920); the rather podgy angel was installed in 1936 to commemorate the 250th anniversary of the liberation of Buda from the Turks. Across the square, which was a weekend market in the Middle Ages, a **Lutheran church** with the words 'A Mighty Fortress is Our God' written in Hungarian marks the start of Táncsics Mihály utca. On the west side of Bécsi kapu tér there's an attractive group of houses, especially No 7 with its medallions of classical poets and philosophers and the one with a round corner window at No 8. The serene woman holding a lamp, a symbol of art and enlightenment, is a memorial to Ferenc Kazinczy (1759-1831), poet and reformer of the Hungarian language.

Táncsics Mihály utca is a narrow street of little houses painted in lively hues and adorned with statues. Most have plaques with the word *műemlék* (memorial) attesting to their historical significance. The one at Táncsics Mihály utca 9, for example, cites that Lajos Kossuth was imprisoned here 'for his homeland' from 1837 to 1840. In the entrances to many of the courtyards, you'll notice lots of **sedilia** – stone niches dating as far back as the 13th century. Historians still debate their function. Some say they were merchant stalls, while others think servants cooled their heels here while their masters (or mistresses) paid a visit to the occupant.

Parts of the **medieval Jewish prayer house** (középkori zsidó imaház) at Táncsics Mihály utca 26 date from the 14th century; there's a small museum inside. Across the road to the south-east at No 7 is the **Museum of Music History** in an 18th-century palace with a lovely courtyard. Concerts are sometimes held in the Kodály Hall inside for a modest 400Ft. The controversial **Budapest Hilton** hotel, which incorporates parts of a 14th-century Dominican church and a baroque Jesuit college, is farther south at Hess András tér 1. Have a look at the little red hedgehog in the relief above the doorway at house No 3, which was an inn in the 14th century.

If you walk north along Fortuna utca, another street of decorated houses, you'll soon reach one of Budapest's most interesting small museums: the **Commerce & Catering Museum** at No 4. This street leads back into Bécsi kapu tér, but if you continue west along Petermann bíró utca you'll reach Kapisztrán tér. This square was named after John Capistranus (1386-1456), a charismatic Franciscan monk who raised an entire army for János Hunyadi in his campaign against the Turks. He was canonised in 1724 and is known as St John of Capistrano.

The large white building to the north of the square houses the **Military History Museum**. Around the corner, along the so-called **Anjou Bastion** (Anjou bástya), with displays detailing the development of the cannon, lies the turban-topped grave of Abdurrahman, the last Turkish governor of Budapest, who was killed here in 1686 on the day Buda was liberated. 'He was a heroic foe,' reads the tablet, 'may he rest in peace.' If you continue walking to the east you will reach the viewpoint atop the Vienna Gate. Below along Lovas utca is a small **exhibit of antique street lamps** maintained by the Electrotechnology Museum (see Walking Tour 10).

The large steeple on the south side of Kapisztrán tér, visible for kilometres to the west of Castle Hill, is the **Mary Magdalene Tower** (Magdolna torony), with a reconstructed window and a bit of foundation being all that is left of the church once

reserved for Hungarian-speakers in this district. It was used as a mosque during the Turkish occupation and was destroyed in an air raid during WWII. Travellers not worried about claustrophobia or nosebleeds can climb the 163 steps for a great view of Castle Hill and beyond.

From Kapisztrán tér, walk south on Országház utca, being careful not to miss the sedile (that's one of the sedilia described earlier) in the entrance to No 9 and the medieval houses painted white, lime and tangerine at Nos 18, 20 and 22.

The next street to the west running parallel, Úri utca, has some interesting courtyards, especially No 19 with a sundial and what looks like a tomb. There are more Gothic sedilia at Nos 32 and 36. The **Telephony Museum** at Úri utca 49 is housed in an old Clarist monastery. At No 9 of the same street is the entrance to the **Labyrinth** of Buda Castle.

Tree-lined Tóth Árpád sétány, the next 'street' (or walkway) over, follows the west wall from the Anjou Bastion to Dísz tér and has some great views of the Buda Hills.

On the corner of Úri utca and Szentháromság utca is a mounted **statue of András Hadik**, a Hussar field marshal in the wars against the Turks. If you're wondering – and I know you are – why the steed's brass testicles are so shiny, well, it's a student tradition in Budapest to give them a stroke before taking an exam. Szentháromság utca leads east into the square of the same name.

In the centre of the square there's a **Holy Trinity statue** (Szentháromság szobor), another one of the 'plague pillars' put up by grateful, healthy citizens in the early 18th century. Szentháromság tér is dominated by the Old Town's two most famous sights: Matthias Church, originally reserved for German-speakers, and beyond it the Fishermen's Bastion. If you'd like to break now there's a chance for a crash course on viticulture at the **House of Hungarian Wines** (☎ 212 1030), I Szentháromság tér 6, open from 11 am to 7 pm every day. It's the cheapest place in town to get wrecked. But with over 600 wines from all 22 of Hungary's wine regions and

80 to sample, 'crash' may soon become the operative word.

Bits of **Matthias Church** (Mátyás templom) – so named because the 15th-century Renaissance king Matthias Corvinus was married here – date back some 500 years, notably the carvings above the southern entrance. But basically the church is a neo-Gothic creation designed by the architect Frigyes Schulek in the late 19th century. The church has a colourful tile roof and a lovely tower; the interior is remarkable for its stained-glass windows and frescoes by the romantic painters Károly Lotz and Bertalan Székely. They also did the wall decorations, an unusual mixture of folk, Art Nouveau and Turkish designs.

Escape the crowds by walking down the steps to the right of the main altar to the crypt, which leads to the **Collection of Ecclesiastical Art**. There are organ concerts in the church on certain evenings, continuing a tradition that began in 1867 when Franz Liszt's *Hungarian Coronation Mass* was first played here for the crowning of Franz Joseph and Elizabeth as king and queen of Hungary.

The **Fishermen's Bastion** (Halász bástya) is another neo-Gothic masquerade that most visitors (and Hungarians) believe to be much older. But who cares? It looks medieval and still offers among the best views in Budapest. Built as a viewing platform in 1905 by Schulek, the bastion's name was taken from the guild of fishermen responsible for defending this stretch of the wall in the Middle Ages. The seven gleaming white turrets represent the Magyar tribes who entered the Carpathian Basin in the late 9th century. During the day you have to pay an entrance fee of 200/100Ft, which in theory goes towards preservation of the monument; in the evening, it is free and much more romantic.

Nearby is an equestrian **statue of St Stephen** (977-1038), Hungary's first king; the ornate detailing reflects sculptor Alajos Stróbl's deep leap into 11th-century art history.

The **Golden Eagle Pharmacy** (Aranysas patikaház), just north of Dísz tér at Tárnok utca 18, probably looks exactly the way it did in Buda Castle in the 16th century, though it was moved to its present site 100 years later. Today it houses a museum.

From Dísz tér, walk south along Színház utca to Szent György tér. Along the way you'll pass the **Castle Theatre** (Vár színház) on the left, built in 1736 as a Carmelite church and monastery, and across from it the bombed-out **Ministry of Defence**, another wartime casualty. During the Cold War, this site was NATO's nuclear target for Budapest, we're told. To the east is the **Sándor Palace** (Sándor palota), restored externally, while inside an important archaeological excavation continues. This has stalled somewhat impractical plans to turn the building into the prime minister's office. As the president's office, however, with a staff of only 45 or so, the building may see its future. It may also be the permanent home of the errant Crown of St Stephen (see the boxed text later in the chapter) when it leaves Parliament.

On the south-east side of Szent György tér is an enormous statue of the **Turul,** an eagle-like totem of the ancient Magyars (see the boxed text 'Blame It On the Bird'). The steps, beyond Corvinus Gate with its big black raven symbolising King Matthias Corvinus, lead to the Royal Palace.

The **Royal Palace** has been burned, bombed, razed, rebuilt and redesigned at least half a dozen times over the past seven centuries. What you see today clinging to the southern end of Castle Hill is an 18th and early 20th-century amalgam reconstructed after the last war, during which it was bombed to bits. Ironically, the palace was never used by the Habsburgs, though Admiral Horthy moved in during the interwar period.

The first part of the palace (Wing A) houses the **Ludwig Museum** of modern Hungarian and foreign (Andy Warhol, Roy Liechtenstein, Keith Haring etc) art. In the middle of the square facing the entrance, a Hortobágy *csikós* (cowboy) in full regalia tames a mighty *bábolna* steed, a sculpture that won international recognition for its creator, György Vastagh, at the Paris World Exhibitions of 1900 and 1901.

Blame It on the Bird

The ancient Magyars were strong believers in magic and celestial intervention, and the *táltos* (shaman) enjoyed an elevated position in their society. Certain animals – bears, stags and wolves, for example – were totemic, and it was taboo to mention them directly by name. Thus the wolf was 'the long-tailed one' and the stag the 'large-antlered one'. In other cases the original Magyar word for an animal deemed sacred was replaced with a foreign loan word: *medve* for 'bear' comes from the Slavic *medved*.

No other totemic animal is better known to modern Hungarians than the *turul*, an eagle or hawk-like bird that had supposedly impregnated Emese, the grandmother of Árpád. That legend can be viewed in many ways: as an attempt to foster a sense of common origin and group identity in the ethnically heterogeneous population of the time; as an effort to bestow a sacred origin on the House of Árpád and its rule; or just as a nice story – not entirely unlike the Virgin Mary begotten with child by the dove-like Holy Spirit.

Return to the square facing the Danube to get to Wing C or walk under the massive archway protected by snarling lions to Wing D to enter the National Gallery. Those choosing the former will enter what was once the palace terrace and gardens. In the centre stands a **statue of Eugene of Savoy**, who is credited with driving the Turks out of Hungary in 1686. It was designed by József Róna in 1897 and is considered to be the finest equestrian statue in the capital.

If you take the second route, you'll pass a Romantic-style fountain called **Matthias Well** with the young King Matthias Corvinus in his hunting garb. On the right is Szép Ilonka (Beautiful Helen), a protagonist of a Romantic ballad by Mihály Vörösmarty. The poor girl fell in love with the dashing 'hunter' and, upon learning his true identity and feeling unworthy, she died of a broken heart. Sad tale. The rather smuglooking fellow on the left is Galeotto

Marzio, an Italian chronicler at Matthias' court. The middle of the king's three dogs was blown up during the war; canine-loving Hungarians – and they all are – had an exact copy quickly made.

If you want to bail out of the tour now, there's a lift (elevator) to the right of the archway that will take you down to Dózsa tér and the bus stop (No 16) for Pest. The hallway leading to the lift has an interesting collection of historic photos of the palace, and there is an ATM – a rare breed in the Castle District – on the left side.

The **National Gallery** spreads out through Wings B, C and D and is devoted almost exclusively to Hungarian art from the Middle Ages onward, though there are a few German artists represented. Wing F of the palace on the west side of Lion Court contains the **Széchenyi National Library** (☎ 355 6967 or 375 7533), which has occasional exhibits. You can peruse the shelves and read the large collection of foreign newspapers by buying an annual membership of 2000Ft. The library is open from 1 to 9 pm Monday and from 9 am Tuesday to Saturday. The **Budapest History Museum** is in Wing E.

From the Budapest History Museum, exit through the rear doors, have a look around the castle walls and enter the palace gardens. **Ferdinand Gate** under the conical **Mace Tower** will bring you to a set of steps. These descend to Szarvas tér in the Tabán district via the Turkish cemetery dating from the decisive battle of 1686.

Walking Tour 2: Gellért Hill & the Tabán

Gellért hegy, a 235m rocky hill south-east of the castle, is crowned with a fortress of sorts and the Independence Monument, Budapest's unofficial symbol. From Gellért Hill, you can't beat the views of the Royal Palace or the Danube and its fine bridges, and Jubilee Park on the south side is an ideal spot for a picnic. The Tabán, the area between the two hills and stretching northwest as far as Déli train station, is associated with the Serbs, who settled here after fleeing from the Turks in the early 18th century.

Later it became known for its restaurants and wine gardens – a kind of Montmartre for Budapest – but it burned to the ground at the start of the 20th century. Today Gellért Hill and the Tabán are given over to private homes, parks and three public baths that make good use of the hot springs gushing from deep below Gellért Hill.

Unless indicated otherwise, the items listed in the following tour can be found on Map 3.

If you're starting the tour from Castle Hill, exit via Ferdinand Gate (Map 4) and walk south from Szarvas tér to **Elizabeth Bridge** (Erzsébet híd), the big white span rebuilt after the war and opened to great fanfare in 1964. To the west is a large gushing fountain and a **statue of St Gellért**, an Italian missionary invited to Hungary by King Stephen. The stairs lead to the top of the hill. Though bus No 27 runs from Móricz Zsigmond körtér almost to the top of the hill, we'll begin at Szent Gellért tér, which is accessible from Pest on bus No 7 or tram Nos 47 and 49 and from the Buda side on bus No 86 and tram Nos 18 and 19.

Bartók Béla út runs south-west from the square and leads to Móricz Zsigmond körtér, a busy 'circular square' or circus. Nearby, on Műegyetem rakpart along the river before Petőfi Bridge, stands **Budapest Technical University** (Budapesti Műszaki Egyetem; Map 6), whose students were the first to march during the Uprising on 23 October 1956.

Szent Gellért tér faces **Independence Bridge** (Szabadság híd), which opened for the millenary exhibition in 1896. It was destroyed by German bombs during WWII and rebuilt in 1946. The square is dominated by the **Gellért Hotel** (1918), an Art Nouveau pile and the city's favourite old-world hotel. If you don't want to fork out the US$100-plus to stay here (as every celebrity in the world seems to have done, judging from the guest book), you can take the waters in the impressive spa (once described as taking a bath in a cathedral) or use the indoor and outdoor swimming pools (see the special section 'Taking the Waters' later in this chapter). The entrance is on Kelenhegyi út.

Directly north on the small hill above the hotel is the **Cliff Chapel** (Sziklakápolna) built into a cave in 1926. It was the seat of the Paulite order until the late 1940s when the priests were arrested and the cave sealed off. It was reopened in the early 1990s and re-consecrated; the main altar with a symbolic fish is made partly of Zsolnay ceramic. Behind the church is the monastery, with its neo-Gothic turrets visible from Szabadság Bridge.

From the chapel, follow a small path called Verejték utca (Perspiration Street) and a walkway named after Dezső Szabó, a controversial writer killed in the last days of WWII. You'll pass a funny bust of this large and rather angry-looking man along the way as you ascend through what were once vineyards and are now the well-kept lawns and gardens of **Jubilee Park** (Jubileum park).

Another route to follow from Gellért tér is along Kelenhegyi út. At No 12-14 is the interesting Art Nouveau **studio building** (1903), which has enormous rooms with high ceilings in which huge socialist realist monuments were once constructed. Continue up Kelenhegyi út and turn north on Minerva utca. No 3a/b, the **Swedish embassy** during the war, is where the diplomat Raoul Wallenberg helped save the lives of thousands of Hungarian Jews (see the boxed text 'Raoul Wallenberg, Righteous Gentile' later in this chapter). The short flight of steps rejoins Verejték utca.

Towering above you is the **Citadella**, a fortress that never saw battle. Built by the Habsburgs after the 1848-49 War of Independence to 'defend' the city from further insurrection, by the time it was ready in 1851 the political climate had changed and the Citadella had become obsolete. It was given to the city in the 1890s and parts of it were symbolically blown to pieces. There's not much inside the Citadella today except for a hotel/hostel, a casino and restaurant, a pleasant outdoor cafe and about a dozen display cases reviewing the history of the city.

To the east along Citadella sétány stands the **Independence Monument** (Szabadság szobor), the lovely lady with the palm frond proclaiming freedom throughout the city and the land. It was erected in 1947 as a tribute to the Soviet soldiers who died liberating Budapest in 1945. But many Hungarians choose not to remember that fact any more and the victims' names in Cyrillic letters on the plinth and the statues of the Soviet soldiers were removed long ago. In fact, the independence monument had been designed by the politically 'flexible' sculptor Zsigmond Kisfaludi Strobl for the ultra-right government of Admiral Miklós Horthy. After the war, when pro-communist monuments were in short supply, Kisfaludi Strobl passed it off as a memorial to the Soviets.

If you walk west a few minutes, you'll come to what is the best vantage point in Budapest. The trail below leads to the **St Gellért Monument**, marking the spot where the bishop was hurled to his death in a spiked barrel in 1046 by pagan Hungarians resisting conversion. Directly across the street is the second of the area's three thermal spas, the **Rudas Bath** (Rudas gyógyfürdő; Map 4) at Döbrentei tér 9, and the most Turkish of them all in Budapest, with its octagonal pool, domed cupola with coloured glass and massive columns. It's reserved for men only except for groovy late-night parties – favourites of locals – known as Cinetrip Vízi-Mozi (see the Entertainment chapter), which take place here sporadically. If you're not male and/or don't have the inclination to visit, you can have a 'drinking cure' by visiting the **pump house** (ivócsarnok), which is below the bridge and within sight of the bath. A half-litre of the smelly hot water – meant to cure whatever ails you – costs just 20Ft; it is closed on weekends, however. To the north through the underpass is the **statue of Elizabeth**, Habsburg empress and Hungarian queen and the consort of Franz Joseph much beloved by Hungarians because, among other things, she learned to speak Hungarian. Sissi, as she was affectionately known, was assassinated by an Italian anarchist in Geneva.

As you walk north along Döbrentei utca (Map 4), have a look at the plaques at No 15. These mark the water level on the

Danube during two devastating floods in 1775 and 1838. What's interesting about them is that they are in German, Serbian and Hungarian, attesting to the mixed population that once lived here. The **Tabán Parish Church** (Tabáni plébániatemplom; Map 4) on the north side of Szarvas tér dates from the early 18th century. A short distance to the north-west, at I Apród utca 1-3, is the **Semmelweis Museum of Medical History** (Map 4), named in honour of the 19th-century physician known as 'the saviour of mothers'. He discovered the cause of life-threatening childbirth fever, which was caused by doctors not scrubbing up between the pathology and obstetrics departments.

To the east of the museum on Ybl Miklós tér (Map 4) is a lovely renovated building with a fountain known as the **Castle Garden Kiosk** (Várkert kioszk; Map 4). Once a pump house for Castle Hill, it was designed by Ybl in 1879 and is now a casino. The dilapidated steps and archways across the road, the **Castle Bazaar** (Várbazár; Map 4), once functioned as a pleasure park with shops that were later used as art studios.

Return to Szarvas tér and turn right on Attila út. In the park across the road you'll see a yellow block with a domed roof; this is the **Rác Bath** (Rác gyógyfürdő; Map 4). It's an Ybl design on the outside and a Turkish delight within.

There's not a heck of a lot to see along Attila út (though the neighbourhood seems to figure in Hungarian literature pretty often). The lift at the bottom of the Széchenyi National Library on Dózsa tér can whisk you back up to Castle Hill, but if you carry on you'll see the entrance to the **Alagút**, the tunnel under Castle Hill that links Chain Bridge with Attila, a main thoroughfare of Buda. But don't go under on foot; catch bus No 16 or 105.

The large park to the north as you emerge is the **Vérmező**, the 'Blood Field' where Ignác Martonovics and six other pro-republican intellectuals were beheaded in 1795 for plotting against the Habsburgs. Déli station, an eyesore completed in 1977, is across the Vérmező to the west.

Walking Tour 3: Víziváros

Víziváros (Watertown) is the narrow area between the Danube and Castle Hill that widens as it approaches Rózsadomb (Rose Hill) and Óbuda to the north-west and north, spreading as far west as Moszkva tér, one of the main transport hubs in Buda. In the Middle Ages, those involved in trades, crafts and fishing – the commoners who couldn't make the socio-economic ascent to the Old Town on Castle Hill – lived here. Under the Turks many of the district's churches were used as mosques, and baths were built, one of which is still functioning. Today Víziváros is an area of apartment blocks, shops and small businesses. It is the heart of urban Buda.

Unless otherwise indicated, sights in this section can be found initially on Map 4 and later on Map 3. Notice will be given when to make the switch.

Víziváros actually begins at Ybl Miklós tér, but the best place to begin a stroll is at **Clark Ádám tér**. You can reach it on foot from Batthyány tér by walking south along the river or via tram No 19, which links it with Szent Gellért tér. Bus No 16 from Deák tér stops here on its way to/from Castle Hill.

The square is named after the Scottish engineer who supervised the building of **Chain Bridge** (Lánchíd), leading from the square, and who designed the tunnel under Castle Hill, which took eight months to carve out of the limestone. The curious sculpture hidden in the bushes to the south is the **0km stone** (it looks like a elongated doughnut); all Hungarian roads to and from the capital are measured from this point.

Fő utca is the main street running through Víziváros and dates from Roman times. A French restaurant, popular with staff at the postmodern **Institut Français** across the road, is in the medieval house below street level at No 20 and has interesting Chinese reliefs above and below the windows. At the former **Capuchin church** at No 30, turned into a mosque by the Turks, you can see the remains of Islamic-style ogee-arched doors and windows on the south side. Around the corner there's the seal of King Matthias Corvinus – a raven and a ring – and the little square is called Corvin tér. The Eclectic building on the north side at No 8 is the **Budai Vigadó** (Buda Concert Hall), much less grand than its Pest counterpart and home to the State Folk Ensemble.

Lots of churches can be found along this route, but only one or two are worth a look inside. The neo-Gothic one on Szílagyi Dezső tér is the **Calvinist church** built at the end of the 19th century. The boat moored along the Danube is a hotel operated by North Koreans. The odd-looking tree trunk on the corner of Vám utca and Iskola utca is called the **Iron Stump** (Vastuskó), a log into which itinerant artisans and merchants would drive a nail to mark their visit.

From here on, most sights can be found on Map 3.

The next square is **Batthyány tér**, the centre of Víziváros and the best place to snap a picture of the Parliament building across the Danube River. In the centre of this rather shabby square is the entrance to both the red metro and the HÉV suburban line to Szentendre.

On the southern side of Batthyány tér is **St Anne's Church** (Szent Ana templom), whose completion in 1805 was the culmination of more than six decades' work because of the interruption caused by floods and an earthquake. It has one of the loveliest baroque interiors of any church in Budapest. The attached building at No 7 was an inn until 1724, then the church presbytery and now a fine cafe. Batthyány tér was called Upper Market Square in the Middle Ages, but the **market hall** (1902) to the west now contains just a supermarket and department store. Have a look at the double courtyard at No 4, which housed an elegant inn in the 18th century. The house at No 3 has friezes showing people gathering grapes and making wine.

A couple of streets north is Nagy Imre tér, with the enormous **Military Court of Justice** on the northern side. Here Imre Nagy and others were tried and sentenced to death in 1958. It was also the site of the notorious **Fő utca prison** where many lesser mortals (but victims nonetheless) were incarcerated and tortured. May they rest in peace.

The Bridges of Budapest

The bridges of Budapest, both landmarks and delightful vantage points over the Danube, are stitches that have bound Buda and Pest together since well before the two were linked politically. There are a total of nine spans, including two railroad bridges, but four stand head and shoulders above the rest. All were left in ruins by the retreating Nazis in 1945 but have since been rebuilt.

Margaret Bridge (Margit híd) introduces the Big Ring Road to the joys of Buda. It is unique in that it doglegs like a circumflex in order to stand at right angles to the Danube at its confluence at the southern tip of Margaret Island. It was originally built by the French engineer Ernest Gouin in 1876; the branch leading to the island was added in 1901.

The twin-towered bridge to the south, the city's oldest and arguably its most beautiful, is the **Széchenyi Chain Bridge** (Széchenyi lánchíd), which is named in honour of its initiator, István Széchenyi (see the boxed text 'The Greatest Hungarian' in the Facts about Budapest chapter). It was actually built by Scotsman Adam Clark, who enjoys one of the few places reserved for foreigners in the Hungarian panoply of heroes. When it opened in 1849, Chain Bridge was unique for two reasons: it was the first link between Buda and Pest; and the nobility – previously exempt from all taxation – had to pay up like everybody else to use it. At night it is illuminated with thousands of bulbs and is one of the city's most exquisite sights.

Elizabeth Bridge (Erzsébet híd) is the gleaming white though rather generic suspension bridge – it could almost appear on the back of a euro note – farther downstream. It enjoys a special place in the hearts of many Budapesters as it was the first newly designed bridge to reopen after the war. (The original span, erected in 1903, was too badly damaged to rebuild.) Boasting a higher arch than the others, it offers dramatic views of both Castle and Gellért Hills and, of course, the more attractive bridges to the north and south.

Independence Bridge (Szabadság híd) is a *fin-de-siècle* cantilevered span that many consider the world's most beautiful. Each post of the bridge, which was originally named after Habsburg Emperor Franz Joseph, is topped by a mythical *turul* bird ready to take flight.

Independence Bridge (Szabadság híd)

MARK AVELLINO

Király Bath (Király gyógyfürdő),parts of which date from 1580, is one block up at II Fő utca 84. Next to it across Ganz utca is the Greek Catholic **St Florian Chapel** (Szent Flórián kápolna), built in 1760 and dedicated to the patron saint of firefighters. The whole chapel was raised more than a metre in the 1930s after earlier flooding had washed up dirt and silt. Opposite is the new (and quite attractive) **Foreign Ministry building**.

The next square up is **Bem József tér**, named after the Pole József Bem who fought on the Hungarian side in the 1848-49 War of Independence. In 1956 students from the Technical University rallied in front of the statue here at the start of the uprising. Bem József utca leads westward from the square and at No 20 is the **Foundry Museum** – perhaps not to everyone's taste but a lot more interesting than it sounds.

Bem József utca joins Margit körút, Buda's only share of the Big Ring Road, a few streets to the west. If you were to follow it south-west for 10 minutes or so, you'd reach **Széna tér**. This square saw some of the heaviest fighting in Buda during the 1956 Uprising; today it is the site of **Mammut** (Mammoth), one of central Budapest's newest and biggest shopping malls. Moszkva tér, the large square to the south-west, is an important centre for transport connections.

At Bem József tér, Fő utca turns into Frankel Leó út, a tree-lined street of pricey antique shops. If you cross Margit körút and continue north, you'll reach Gül Baba utca on the left. This steep, narrow lane leads to the nicely renovated **tomb of Gül Baba**, named after a Muslim holy man who died in 1548.

Walking north along Frankel Leó út, you'll pass the **Lukács Bath** (Lukács gyógy-fürdő), one of the city's dirtier spas, at No 25-29. At No 49 and tucked away in an apartment block is the **Újlak Synagogue** built in 1888 on the site of an older prayer house. It is the only functioning synagogue left on the Buda side.

Walking Tour 4: Óbuda & Aquincum

Ó means ancient in Hungarian and, as its name suggests, Óbuda is the oldest part of Buda. The Romans established Aquincum, a key military garrison and civilian town near here at the end of the 1st century and it became the seat of the Roman province of Pannonia Inferior in 106 AD. When the Magyars arrived, they named it Buda, which became Óbuda when the Royal Palace was built on Castle Hill and turned into the real centre. Like the Tabán area to the south, Óbuda today is only a shadow of its former self.

Most visitors on their way to Szentendre are put off by what they see of Óbuda from the highway or the HÉV commuter train. Prefabricated housing blocks seem to go on forever, and the Árpád Bridge flyover splits the heart of the district (Flórián tér) in two. But behind all this are some of the most important Roman ruins in Hungary, noteworthy museums and small, quiet neighbourhoods that still recall *fin-de-siècle* Óbuda.

The listed items can be found on Map 2.

Flórián tér is the historic centre of Óbuda. You can reach it on the HÉV train from Batthyány tér (Árpád híd stop) or bus No 86 from many points along the Danube on the Buda side. Most people coming from Pest will catch the red metro line to Batthyány tér and board the HÉV. But if you're up near City Park (Városliget), walk south-east to the intersection of Hungária körút and Thököly

út and catch the No 1 tram, which avoids Buda and crosses Árpád Bridge into Óbuda.

Archaeology buffs taking the No 86 bus should descend at Nagyszombat utca (for HÉV passengers, it's the Timár utca stop), about 800m south of Flórián tér on Pacsirtamező utca, to explore the **Roman Military Amphitheatre** (Római katonai amfiteátrum) built in the 2nd century for the garrisons. It could accommodate up to 15,000 spectators and was larger than the Colosseum in Rome. The rest of the military camp extended from here north to Flórián tér

If you walk north-west along Bécsi út (the old road to Vienna) from here, you'll reach the **Kiscelli Museum** which towers above Kiscelli utca on the left at No 106.

The yellow baroque **Óbuda Parish Church** (Óbudai plébániatemplom; 1749) dominates the east side of Flórián tér. There's a massive rococo pulpit inside. The large neoclassical building beside the Aquincum hotel at III Lajos utca 163 is the former **Óbuda Synagogue** and now houses sound studios of Hungarian Television (MTV).

A branch of the **Budapest Gallery** directly opposite at Lajos utca 158 has some of the more interesting avant-garde exhibitions in Budapest.

In the subway below Flórián tér are Roman objects discovered in the area (many of them vandalised and covered in graffiti), including ancient **military baths**. Still more Roman ruins can be found in the park outside (including a reconstructed temple) and at the so-called **Hercules Villa** in the middle of a vast housing estate northwest of Flórián tér at Meggyfa utca 19-21.

Two squares north-east of Flórián tér and through the subway are Óbuda's most important museums. In the former Zichy Mansion at III Szentlélek tér 6 is the **Vasarely Museum** devoted to the works of the 'father of op art', Victor Vasarely (or Vásárhelyi Győző before he emigrated to Paris in 1930). In the back of the same building facing the courtyard (enter at Fő tér 1) is the unique **Kassák Museum**, a three-room art gallery with some real gems of early 20th-century avant-garde art.

Fő tér is a restored square of baroque houses, public buildings and restaurants. At No 4, the **Zsigmond Kun Collection** displays folk art amassed by a wealthy ethnographer in his 18th-century townhouse. Walking north-east from Fő tér, you'll see a group of odd metal sculptures of rather worried-looking women in the middle of the road. It is the work of the prolific Imre Varga, who seems to have sat on both sides of the fence politically for decades – sculpting Béla Kun and Lenin as easily as he did St Stephen and St Elizabeth. The **Imre Varga Collection** is housed in a charming townhouse nearby at III Laktanya utca 7.

The HÉV or bus Nos 34 and 43 from Szentlélek tér head north for a few stops to **Aquincum**, the most complete Roman civilian town in Hungary. A **Roman aqueduct** used to pass this way from a spring in the nearby park, and remains have been preserved in the central reservation (median strip) of the highway alongside the HÉV railway line. The prosperous town's heyday was in the 2nd and 3rd centuries, lasting until the Huns and assorted other hordes came and ruined everything. Who knows? Had the Romans stayed on, Hungarian might now be spoken with a lilting Italian accent.

Aquincum had paved streets and fairly sumptuous single-storey houses with courtyards, fountains and mosaic floors as well as sophisticated drainage and heating systems. Not all of this is easily apparent today as you walk among the ruins, but you can see their outlines as well as those of the big public baths, market, an early Christian church and a temple dedicated to Mithras, the chief deity of a religion that once rivalled Christianity in its number of believers (see the boxed text 'Mithras & the Great Sacrifice'). The **Aquincum Museum**, Szentendrei út 139, tries to put it all in perspective – unfortunately only in Hungarian.

Across Szentendrei út to the north-west is the **Civilian Amphitheatre** (Római polgári amfiteátrum), about half the size of the one reserved for the garrison. Much is left to the imagination, but you can still see the small cubicles where lions were kept and the

Mithras & the Great Sacrifice

Mithraism, the worship of the god Mithras, originated in Persia. As Roman rule extended into Asia, the religion became extremely popular with traders, imperial slaves and mercenaries of the Roman army and spread rapidly throughout the empire in the 2nd and 3rd centuries AD. It was the principal rival of Christianity until Constantine came to the throne in the 4th century.

Mithraism was a mysterious religion with devotees sworn to secrecy. What little is known of Mithras, the god of the sun, justice and social contract, has been deduced from reliefs and icons found in sanctuaries and temples like the one at Aquincum. Most of these portray Mithras clad in a Persian-style cap and tunic sacrificing a white bull. From the blood and semen of the bull sprout grain, grapes and living creatures. The bull is then transformed into the goddess Soma, the moon, who begins her cycle and time is born.

Mithraism and Christianity were close competitors partly because of the striking similarity in many of their rituals. Both involved the birth of a deity on 25 December, shepherds, death and resurrection and a form of baptism. Devotees knelt when they worshipped and a common meal – a 'communion' of bread and water – was a regular feature of both liturgies.

〰〰 〰〰 〰〰

'Gate of Death' to the west through which slain gladiators were carried.

North of Aquincum are the outer suburbs of **Rómaifürdő** and **Csillaghegy**, both of them on the HÉV line. The holiday area of Rómaifürdő (Roman Bath) has an open-air thermal pool in a big park, Budapest's largest camping ground and a collection of popular food kiosks and drink bars along the riverfront. The swimming pool and 'beach' in Csillaghegy is one of the most popular in the city. To reach them from the HÉV stop, walk west along Ürömi út for a few minutes to Pusztakúti út.

Walking Tour 5: Margaret Island

Neither Buda nor Pest, 2.5km-long Margaret Island (Margit sziget) in the middle of the Danube was always the domain of one religious order or another until the Turks came and turned what was then called the Island of Rabbits into – appropriately enough – a harem, from which all infidels were barred. It's been a public park open to everyone since the mid-19th century, though you may encounter some harem-like activity if you stray too far off the path in the twilight.

The items listed in this tour can be found on Maps 2 and 3.

With its large swimming complex, thermal spa, gardens and shaded walkways, the island is a lovely place to spend an afternoon away from the city. You can walk anywhere – on the paths, the shoreline, the grass – but don't try to camp: that's strictly *tilos* (forbidden).

Cross over to Margaret Island from Pest or Buda via tram No 4 or 6. Bus No 26 covers the length of the island as it makes the run between Nyugati station and Árpád Bridge. Cars are allowed on Margaret Island from Árpád Bridge only as far as the two big hotels at the north-eastern end. The rest is reserved for pedestrians and cyclists. If you follow the shoreline in winter, you'll see thermal water gushing from beneath the island into the river.

You can walk the length of Margaret Island in one direction and return on bus No 26. Or you can rent a bicycle from one of two stands. The first, open from March to October, is on the west side just past the stadium as you walk from Margaret Bridge. It charges 360/1300Ft per hour/day for a basic three-speed and a pedal coach is 1100Ft an hour. The other is Bringóhintó (☎ 329 2073) at the refreshment stand near the Japanese Garden in the north of the island and open all year. A bicycle/mountain bike costs 480/650Ft per hour and a pedal coach from 890 to 2090Ft, depending on how many adults and kids it seats. A twirl around the island in one of the horse-drawn coaches near the hotels costs from 1000Ft per person.

In the flower-bed roundabout at the end of the access road, the **Centennial Monument**, unveiled in 1973, marks the union of Buda, Pest and Óbuda 100 years earlier. A quarter of a century ago was an entirely different era, and the sculptor filled the strange cone with all sorts of socialist symbols. They remain – as if contained in a partially open time capsule.

Margaret Island boasts two popular swimming pools on its west side. The first is the indoor/outdoor **National Sports Pool** (Nemzeti sportuszoda), officially named after the Olympic swimming champion Alfréd Hajós, later an architect, who actually built the place. He won the 100m and 1200m races at the first modern Olympiad in 1896. Amateur water polo league play takes place here at the weekend. The **Palatinus**, a large complex of outdoor pools, huge water slides and strands to the north, is a madhouse on a hot summer afternoon, but a good place to watch Hungarians at play. If you want to take all your clothes off, there are single-sex sunbathing decks on the roof of the main building.

Just before you reach the Palatinus, you'll pass the ruins of the 13th-century **Franciscan church and monastery** (Ferences templom és kolostor) of which only the tower and a wall still stand. The Habsburg archduke Joseph built a summer residence here when he inherited the island in 1867. It was later converted into a hotel that operated until after WWII.

The octagonal **water tower** (víztorony; 1911) to the north-east rises above the **open-air theatre** (szabadtéri színpad), used for opera and plays in summer. Beyond the roundabout is the **Japanese Garden** with lily pads, carp and a small wooden bridge; one of the most romantic corners of Budapest, some say. The raised gazebo in front of you is called the **Musical Fountain**, a replica of one in Transylvania. A tape plays chimes and tinny snatches of a march on the hour.

The Romans used the thermal springs in the north-eastern part of the island and today the springs lie below the Thermal Margitsziget hotel (entrance on the south side). The **thermal spa** here is one of the cleanest and most modern in Budapest, but lacks atmosphere because of that.

South of the posh Grand hotel is the re-constructed Romanesque **Premonstraten-sian Church** (Premontre templom) dedicated to St Michael. Its 15th-century bell is real enough, though; it mysteriously appeared one night in 1914 under the roots of a walnut tree that had been knocked over in a storm. It was probably buried there by monks at the time of the Turkish invasion.

More ruins – but more important ones – lie a few steps south. These are the former **Dominican convent** (Domonkos kolostor) built by Béla IV whose scribes played an important role in the continuation of Hungarian scholarship. Its most famous resident was Béla's daughter, Margaret (1242-71). According to the story, the king promised to commit his daughter to a life of devotion in a nunnery if the Mongols were driven from the land. They were and she was – at nine years of age. Still, she seemed to enjoy it (if we're to believe the *Lives of the Saints*), especially the mortification-of-the-flesh parts. St Margaret, canonised only in 1943, commands something of a cult following in Hungary. A red marble sepulchre marks her original resting place, and there's a much-visited shrine with votives nearby.

Walking Tour 6: Szent István körút & Bajcsy-Zsilinszky út

This relatively brief walk crosses over into Pest and follows Szent István körút, the northernmost stretch of the Big Ring Road, to Nyugati tér and then south to Deák tér. You can reach Jászai Mari tér, the start of the walk, via tram No 4 or 6 from either side of the river or simply by walking over the bridge from Margaret Island. If you're coming from the Inner Town in Pest, hop on the waterfront tram No 2 to the terminus.

Unless indicated otherwise, the following items can be found on Map 5.

Two buildings of very different styles and functions face Jászai Mari tér, which is split in two by the foot of the bridge. To the north is an elegant 19th-century block of flats called **Palatinus House**. The modern building south of the square is the **White House**, the former headquarters of the Central Committee of the Hungarian Socialist Workers' Party. It now contains the offices of ministers of parliament. If you walk a bit farther north along the river to Szent István Park (Map 3) in the direction of the Calvinist church, with its tall, ugly belfry, you'll see a rarity in Budapest: a row of **Bauhaus apartments**. They may not look like much today after decades of bad copies, but they were the bee's knees when they were built in the late 1920s.

The area north of Szent István körút is called **Újlipótváros** (New Leopold Town) to distinguish it from Lipótváros around Parliament. (Archduke Leopold was the grandson of Habsburg Empress Maria Theresa.) It is a wonderful neighbourhood of tree-lined streets, boutiques and a few cafes and is vaguely reminiscent of uptown Manhattan. The area was upper-middle-class and Jewish before the war, and many of the 'safe houses' organised by the heroic Swedish diplomat Raoul Wallenberg during WWII were here (see the boxed text 'Raoul Wallenberg, Righteous Gentile'). Two blocks to the north is a street named after this great man (Map 3) bearing a commemorative plaque. In 1999 a statue of a man (Wallenberg) doing battle with a snake (evil) entitled *Kígyóölő* (Serpent Slayer) was erected in Szent István Park (Map 3), replacing one created by sculptor Pál Pátzay but mysteriously removed the night before its unveiling in 1949.

Szent István körút is an interesting street to stroll along; as elsewhere on the Big Ring Road, most of the Eclectic-style buildings, decorated with Atlases, reliefs and other details, were erected in the last part of the 19th century. Don't hesitate to explore the inner courtyards here and farther on – if Dublin is celebrated for its doors and London for its squares, Budapest is known for its lovely *udvar*.

This stretch of the boulevard is also good for shopping. The **Kárpáti és Szőnyi Antikvárium** at No 3, a second-hand and antiquarian bookshop, is excellent for browsing – it has old prints and maps in the chest of drawers at the back. Falk Miksa utca, the next street on the right and running south, is loaded with pricey antique shops (especially

Raoul Wallenberg, Righteous Gentile

Of all the 'righteous gentiles' honoured by Jews around the world, one of the best-known is Raoul Wallenberg, the Swedish diplomat and businessman who rescued as many as 35,000 Hungarian Jews during WWII.

Wallenberg, who came from a long line of bankers and diplomats, began working in 1936 for a trading firm whose president was a Hungarian Jew. In July 1944 the Swedish Foreign Ministry, at the request of Jewish and refugee organisations in the USA, sent the 32-year-old Wallenberg on a rescue mission to Budapest as an attaché to the embassy there. By that time, almost half a million Jews in Hungary had been sent to Nazi death camps.

Wallenberg immediately began issuing Swedish safe-conduct passes (called 'Wallenberg passports') and set up a series of 'safe houses' flying the flag of neutral countries where Jews could seek asylum. He even followed German 'death marches' and deportation trains, distributing food and clothing and actually pulling some 500 people off the cars along the way.

When the Soviet army entered Budapest in January 1945, Wallenberg went to Debrecen to report to the authorities, but in the wartime confusion was arrested for espionage and sent to Moscow. In the early 1950s, responding to reports that Wallenberg had been seen alive in a labour camp, the Soviet Union announced that he had in fact died of a heart attack in 1947. Several reports over the next two decades suggested Wallenberg was still alive, but none were ever confirmed.

TONY FANKHAUSER

Nos 10 and 32). You can get an idea of what Hungarians are off-loading these days from the second-hand **BÁV shop** on the corner of Szent István körút and Falk Miksa utca.

The attractive little theatre on your left as you continue along Szent István körút is the **Vígszínház** (Gaiety Theatre), a popular venue for comedies and musicals. When it was built in 1896, the new theatre's location was criticised for being too far out of the city.

You might recognise the large iron and glass structure on Nyugati tér (known as Marx tér until 1989) if you arrived by train from points east or Romania. It's the **Nyugati train station** (Nyugati pályaudvar) built in 1877 by the Paris-based Eiffel company. In the early 1970s a train actually crashed through the enormous glass screen on the main facade when its brakes failed, coming to rest at the tram line. The old restaurant room to the right now houses one of the world's most elegant McDonald's.

If you look north up Váci út from Nyugati tér, beyond the new West End City Centre shopping mall, you may catch sight of the twin spires of the **Lehel church** (Map 3), a 60-year-old copy of the 13th-century Romanesque church (now in ruins) at Zsámbék, 33km west of Budapest. The open-air **Lehel tér market** is one of the most colourful in the city.

From Nyugati tér, walk south on Bajcsy-Zsilinszky út for about 800m to the **Basilica of St Stephen** (Szent István bazilika), the main sight on this street. This neoclassical structure was built over the course of half a century and not completed until 1906. Much of the interruption had to do with the fiasco in 1868 when the dome collapsed. No-one was killed but it certainly must have frightened the horses. The basilica is rather dark and gloomy inside – disappointing for the city's largest and most important Catholic church, but a walk to the top of the dome offers one of the best views in the city. It is open from 10 am to 6 pm daily from April to October (300/200Ft).

To the right as you enter is a small **treasury** (kincstár) of ecclesiastical objects.

Behind the main altar in a small chapel rests the basilica's major draw card: the **Holy Right** (Szent Jobb), also known as the Holy Dexter. It is the mummified right hand of St Stephen (King Stephen I), an object of great devotion, returned to Hungary by Habsburg Empress Maria Theresa in 1771 after it was discovered in a monastery in Bosnia. Like the Crown of St Stephen, it too was snatched by the bad guys after WWII but was soon, er, handed back.

To view it, follow the signs for 'Szent Jobb' (yes, it's to the right). You have to put a coin into a little machine in front of it to light up the glass casket containing the Right. At almost 1000 years of age, it is – unsurprisingly – not a pretty sight. The treasury and chapel are open from 10 am to 5 pm (4 pm in winter) daily. Concerts are held here at 7 pm Monday from July to September.

Bajcsy-Zsilinszky út ends at Deák tér, a busy square and the only place where the three metro lines converge. In the subway below near the entrance to the metro is the **Underground Train Museum**, which gives the history of the three lines.

In the early part of the 20th century, big foreign insurance companies built their offices at Deák tér, with huge ones still standing. Madách Imre út, running east from the Little Ring Road, was originally designed to be as big and grand a boulevard as nearby Andrássy út. But WWII nipped the plan in the bud and it now ends abruptly after just two blocks. The cavernous hole near Erzsébet tér is supposed to be the site of a new National Theatre, but the project, embroiled in politics and larger-than-life egos, has been delayed.

Walking Tour 7: Northern Inner Town

This district, also called Lipótváros (Leopold Town), is full of offices, ministries and 19th-century apartment blocks.

The sights listed here can be found on Map 5.

From Deák tér, walk north-west through Erzsébet tér and west on József Attila utca toward the Danube. **Roosevelt tér**, named after the long-serving (1933-45) US president in

1947, is at the foot of Chain Bridge and offers the best view of Castle Hill.

In the middle of the square is a **statue of Ferenc Deák**, the Hungarian minister largely responsible for the Compromise in 1867, which brought about the Dual Monarchy of Austria and Hungary. The statues on the west side are of an Austrian and a Hungarian child holding hands in peaceful bliss. The Magyar kid's hair is tousled and he is naked; the Osztrák is demurely covered in a robe, his hair neatly coiffed.

The Art Nouveau building with the gold tiles to the east (Nos 5-6) is the **Gresham Palace**, built by an English insurance company in 1907. After much ado, plans to turn it into a 155-room, five-star hotel are under way, but first the developers had to dislodge the elderly tenants who refused to budge and then deal with the fact that the palace was structurally unsound.

The **Hungarian Academy of Sciences** (Magyar Tudományos Akadémia), founded by the late great Count István Széchenyi, is at the northern end of the square.

Szabadság tér (Independence Square), one of the largest squares in the city, is a few minutes' walk to the north-east. It has one of Budapest's few remaining monuments to the Soviets in its centre. On the east side at No 12 is the US embassy, where Cardinal József Mindszenty took refuge for 15 years until leaving for Vienna in 1971 (see the boxed text for details).

South of the embassy is the former **Post Office Savings Bank** building, now part of the **Hungarian National Bank** (Magyar Nemzeti Bank; MNB) next door. The former, a Secessionist extravaganza of colourful tiles and folk motifs built by Ödön Lechner in 1901, is completely restored; go around the corner for a better view from Hold utca. Have a look, too, at the reliefs on the MNB building that illustrate trade and commerce through history: Arab camel traders, African rug merchants, Chinese tea salesmen – and the inevitable attorney witnessing contracts.

The large white and yellow building on the west side of the square housed the Budapest Stock Exchange when it was built

Cardinal Mindszenty

Born József Pehm in the village of Csehimindszent near Szombathely in 1892, Mindszenty was politically active from the time of his ordination in 1915. Imprisoned under the short-lived regime of communist Béla Kun in 1919 and again when the fascist Arrow Cross came to power in 1944, Mindszenty was made archbishop of Esztergom (and thus primate of Hungary) in 1945 and cardinal the following year.

When the new cardinal refused to secularise Hungary's Roman Catholic schools under the new communist regime in 1948, he was arrested, tortured and sentenced to life imprisonment for treason. Released during the 1956 Uprising, Mindszenty took refuge in the US embassy on Szabadság tér when the communists returned to power. There he would remain until 1971.

As relations between the Kádár regime and the Holy See began to thaw in the late 1960s, the Vatican made several requests for the cardinal to leave Hungary, which he refused. Following the intervention of US President Richard Nixon, Mindszenty left for Vienna, where he continued to criticise the Vatican's relations with the regime in Hungary. He retired in 1974 and died the following year. But as he had vowed not to return to Esztergom until the last Soviet soldier had left Hungarian soil, Mindszenty's remains were not returned until May 1991 – in fact, several weeks before the last soldier had actually left.

in 1906. It is now the **headquarters of Magyar Televízió** (Hungarian Television; MTV).

North-west of Szabadság tér is Kossuth Lajos tér, the site of Budapest's most photographed building: the **Parliament**. This is where the national government sits and tourists are allowed in on certain days when Parliament is not in session. It is also the temporary home of the Crown of St Stephen (see the listing under Museums and Other Sights later in this chapter).

Opposite Parliament at V Kossuth Lajos tér 12 is the **Ethnography Museum**. As Hungary's largest indoor folk collection, it is somewhat disappointing, but it has some excellent rotating exhibits and the building itself, designed in 1893 to house the Supreme Court, is worth a look – especially the massive central hall with its marble columns and ceiling fresco of *Justice* by Károly Lotz. South of the museum and past the Ministry of Agriculture in Vértanúk tere is a **statue of Imre Nagy**, the reformist Communist prime minister executed in 1958 for his role in the Uprising two years before. It was unveiled to great ceremony in the summer of 1996.

Walking Tour 8: Inner Town

The Belváros (Inner Town) is the heart of Budapest and contains the most expensive property in the city, but it has something of a split personality. North of Ferenciek tere is the 'have' side with the flashiest boutiques, the biggest hotels, some expensive restaurants and the most tourists. You'll often hear more German, Italian and English spoken here than Hungarian. Until recently the south was the 'have not' section – studenty, quieter and more Hungarian. Now it too has been reserved for pedestrians and is full of trendy clubs, cafes and restaurants.

The sights listed here can be found on Map 5.

You can decide which part of the Belváros you want to explore first; we'll start with the latter. Busy Ferenciek tere, which divides the Inner Town at Szabadsajtó út (Free Press Avenue), is on the blue metro line and can be reached by bus No 7 from Buda or points east in Pest. To get here from the end of the last tour, take tram No 2 along the Danube and get off at Elizabeth Bridge.

The centre of this part of the Inner Town is Egyetem tér (University Square), a five-minute walk south along Károlyi Mihály utca from Ferenciek tere. The square's name refers to the branch of the prestigious **Loránd Eötvös Science University** (ELTE) at No 1-3. Next to the university building is the **University Church**, a lovely baroque structure built in 1748. Inside are a carved pulpit and pews, and over the altar is a copy of the Black Madonna of Częcstochowa so revered in Poland. The church is often full of young people – presumably those who haven't paid a visit to András Hadik's horse on Castle Hill (see Walking Tour 1).

Leafy Kecskeméti utca runs south-east from the square to Kálvin tér. At the end of it, near the Korona hotel on Kálvin tér, there's a plaque marking the location of the **Kecskemét Gate** (Kecskeméti kapu), part of the medieval city wall that was pulled down in the 1700s. Ráday utca, which leads south from Kálvin tér, is where university students entertain themselves. It is a pedestrian street full of cafes, clubs and restaurants.

Just north of Egyetem tér at V Károlyi Mihály utca 16, the **Hungarian Museum of Literature** has rooms devoted to Sándor Petőfi, Endre Ady, Mór Jókai and Attila József. The building to the north with the multicoloured dome at V Ferenciek tere 10 is the **University Library** (Egyetemi könyvtár).

South-west of Egyetem tér, at the corner of Szerb utca and Veres Pálné utca, stands the **Serbian Orthodox church** built by Serbs fleeing the Turks in the 17th century. The iconostasis is worth a look, but entry to the church is sometimes difficult; Saturday or Sunday morning is the best time to try.

There are a couple of interesting sights along **Veres Pálné utca**. The building at No 19 has bronze reliefs above the 2nd floor illustrating various stages of building in the capital. At the corner of the next street, Papnövelde utca, the enormous university building at No 4-10 is topped with little Greek temples on either side of the roof. A few steps north, Szivárvány köz (Rainbow Alley) is one of the narrowest and shortest streets in the city.

The best way to see the posher – the 'have' – side of the Inner Town is to walk up pedestrian **Váci utca**, the capital's premier – and most expensive – shopping street, with designer clothes, antique jewellery shops, pubs and bookshops for browsing. This was the total length of Pest in the Middle Ages. At V Ferenciek tere 5, walk through the **Párisi Udvar** (Parisian

Court) built in 1909, a decorated arcade with a domed ceiling, out onto tiny Kigyó utca. Váci utca is immediately to the west.

Make a little detour by turning east at Haris köz – once a privately owned street – and continue across Petőfi Sándor utca to Kamermayer Károly tér, a lovely little square with antique shops and boutiques, an old umbrella maker, artsy cafes and, in the centre, a statue of Károly Kamermayer, united Budapest's first mayor.

On the south-eastern corner of the square at V Városház utca 7 is the green **Pest county hall** (Pest Megyei Önkormánzat Hivatal) – the city of Budapest is in the county of Pest – a large neoclassical building with three courtyards that you can walk through during office hours. North of the square at V Városház utca 9-11 is the 18th-century **municipal council office** (Fővárosi Önkormánzat Hivatal), a rambling red and yellow structure that is the largest baroque building in the city.

Szervita tér is at the north-western end of Városház utca. Naturally there's the requisite **baroque church** (Szervita templom; 1732), but much more interesting are the buildings to the west. You'd probably never guess, but the **modern apartment block** at No 5 was built in 1912. Look up to the gable of the so-called **Török Bank House** (Török Bánkház at No 3); the Secessionist mosaic of *Patrona Hungariae* shows Hungarians paying homage to the Virgin Mary and dates from 1906. You can return to Váci utca via Régiposta utca.

Many of the buildings on Váci utca are worth a closer look, but as it's a narrow street you'll have to crane your neck or walk into one of the side lanes for a better view. **Thonet House** at 11/a is another masterpiece built by Ödön Lechner (1890), and the **Philanthia** flower shop at No 9 has an original Art Nouveau interior. The **Polgár Gallery** next door at No 11/b, in a building dating from 1912, has recently undergone a spectacular renovation and contains a stained glass domed ceiling. To the west, at Régiposta utca 13, there's a relief of an old postal coach by the ceramist Margit Kovács of Szentendre. The souvenir shop here always displays items of the same colour in its front window; originally the various shades of the same hue represented crafts from a particular region.

At the top of Váci utca, across from Kristóf tér with the little **Fishergirl Well**, is a brick outline of the foundations of the **Vác Gate** (Váci kapu), part of the old city wall. The street leads into **Vörösmarty tér**, a large square of smart shops, galleries, airline offices, cafes and an outdoor market of stalls selling tourist schlock and artists who will draw your portrait or caricature. Suitable for framing – maybe.

In the centre is a statue of the 19th-century poet after whom Vörösmarty tér was named. It is made of Italian marble and is protected in winter by a bizarre plastic 'iceberg' that kids love sliding on. The first – or last – stop of the little yellow metro line is also in the square, and at the northern end is **Gerbeaud**, Budapest's fanciest and most famous cafe and cake shop. Stop here for at least a cup of coffee and a *Dobos torta* (layered chocolate and cream cake). The Kisgerbeaud cake shop on the east side of the building does takeaway, and there's a new restaurant and pub as well.

The despised modern building on the west side of Vörösmarty tér (No 1) contains a large music shop and the main ticket office for concerts in the city. South of it at Deák utca 5 is the sumptuous **Bank Palace**, built in 1915 and completely renovated. It now houses the Budapest Stock Exchange.

The **Pesti Vigadó**, the Romantic-style concert hall built in 1865 but badly damaged during the war, faces the river on Vigadó tér to the west. But before proceeding, have a look in the foyer at Vigadó utca 6, which has one of those strange lifts called Pater Noster (see the boxed text 'Our Father Lifts').

A pleasant way to return to Ferenciek tere is along the **Duna korzó**, the riverside 'Danube Embankment' between the Chain and Elizabeth Bridges and above Belgrád rakpart, which is full of cafes, musicians and handicraft stalls by day and hookers and hustlers by night. The Duna korzó leads into Petőfi tér, named after the poet of the 1848-49 War of Independence and the

---

Our Father Lifts

Some of the strangest public conveyances you'll ever encounter can still be found in a few office and government buildings in Budapest. They're the strange *körfogó* (rotator) lifts or elevators, nicknamed 'Pater Nosters' for their resemblance to a large rosary. A Pater Noster is essentially a rotating series of individual cubicles that runs continuously. You don't push a button and wait for a door to open on a Pater Noster; you simply hop on just as a cubicle reaches the floor level and you jump out – quickly – when you reach your desired floor. If you were wondering what happens at the top, stay on and find out. And don't worry; you'll live. The lift simply descends to the ground floor in darkness to begin its next revolution again. The most central Pater Noster open to the public is at the Corvina bookshop, V Vörösmarty tér 1.

---

scene of political rallies (both legal and illegal) over subsequent years. Március 15 tér, which marks the date of the outbreak of the revolution, abuts it to the south.

On the east side of Március 15 tér, sitting uncomfortably close to the Elizabeth Bridge flyover, is the **Inner Town parish church** (Belvárosi plébániatemplom), where a Romanesque church was first built in the 12th century within a Roman fortress. You can see a few bits of the fort, **Contra Aquincum**, outside in the centre of the square. The church was rebuilt in the 14th and 18th centuries, and you can easily spot Gothic and baroque elements both inside and out. Two of the side chapels have 16th-century Renaissance tabernacles and the fifth one on the right is pure Gothic. There's a mihrab (Muslim prayer nook) in the chancel from the time when the Turks used the church as a mosque.

Behind the church is the arts faculty of ELTE. The two grand buildings flanking the western end of Ferenciek tere on Szabadsajtó út are the so-called **Klotild Palaces** built in 1902. They contain apartments on the upper floors, shops at street level and, at No 5, the **Budapest Exhibition Hall** (Budapesti Kiállítóterem) for temporary exhibits.

Walking Tour 9: Andrássy út & City Park

This is a rather long tour starting at Deák tér and following the most attractive boulevard in Budapest. The yellow metro runs just beneath Andrássy út from Deák tér to City Park (Városliget), so if you begin to lose your stamina, just go down and jump on.

The listed sights can first be found on Map 5. Later, where indicated, you should turn to Map 3.

Join Andrássy út a short way north of Deák tér as it splits away from Bajcsy-Zsilinszky út. This section of Andrássy út is lined with plane trees – cool and pleasant on a warm day. The **Postal Museum** at No 3.

The neo-Renaissance **Opera House** on the left at No 22 was designed by Miklós Ybl in 1884, and for many it is the city's most beautiful building. The interior is especially lovely and sparkles after a total overhaul in the 1980s. If you cannot attend a concert or an opera, join one of the guided tours (see the listing under the Museums and Other Sights section later in this chapter).

The building across from the Opera House, the so-called **Drechsler House**, was designed by the Art Nouveau master builder Ödön Lechner in 1882. Until recently it housed the State Ballet Institute but is now being redeveloped as a hotel and cafe. You can explore the interior courtyard from the west side (Dalszínház utca), but go around the corner for something even more magical: a Secessionist gem embellished with monkey faces, globes and geometric designs that is now the **New Theatre** (Új Színház) at VI Paulay Ede utca 35. It opened as the Parisiana music hall in 1909.

The old-world **Művész cafe** at Andrássy út 29 serves some of the best pastries in the city. Across the street is Nagymező utca, 'the Broadway of Budapest', counting a number of theatres, including the lovingly restored Thália (formerly the Arizona) at No 22-24. The **House of Hungarian Photographers**, VI Nagymező utca 20, has excellent exhibitions.

The **Fashion Gallery** (Divatcsarnok) at No 39, the fanciest emporium in town when it opened as the Grande Parisienne in 1912, contains the ornate **Ceremonial Hall** (Díszterem) on the mezzanine floor. The room is positively dripping with gilt, marquetry and frescoes by Károly Lotz. It is currently being redeveloped.

The Big Ring Road meets Andrássy út at **Oktogon**, a busy intersection full of fast-food places, shops, honking cars and pedestrians. Teréz körút runs to the north-west and for a block to the south-east where it becomes Erzsébet körút.

Beyond Oktogon, Andrássy út is lined with very grand buildings, housing such institutions as the **Budapest Puppet Theatre** at No 69, the **Academy of Fine Arts** at No 71 and **MÁV** headquarters at No 73-75. The former **secret police building** at No 60 has a ghastly history, for it was here that many activists of whatever political side was out of fashion before and after WWII were taken for interrogation and torture (including Cardinal Mindszenty). The walls were apparently double thickness to mute the screams. A plaque outside reads in part: 'We cannot forget the horror of terror, and the victims will always be remembered.' The **Franz Liszt Memorial Museum** is across the street at No 69 (but enter from VI Vörösmarty utca 35).

The next square (more accurately a circus) is Kodály körönd, one of the most beautiful in the city, though the four neo-Renaissance townhouses are in varying states of decay, including the former residence of the composer Zoltán Kodály at No 1. Just beyond the circus at VI Andrássy út 98 is the neo-Renaissance **Palavicini Palace**, the seat of a pro-fascist family who once owned most of the town of Szilvásvárad in the Bükk Hills.

From here on, listed items can be found on Map 3.

The last stretch of Andrássy út and the surrounding neighbourhoods are packed with stunning old mansions that are among the most desirable addresses in the city. It's no surprise to see that embassies, ministries, multinationals and even political parties (eg, Prime Minister Viktor Orbán's FIDESZ-MPP at VI Lendvay utca 28) have moved in.

The **Ferenc Hopp Museum of East Asian Art** is at VI Andrássy út 103 in the former villa of its collector and benefactor. Some of the collection is on exhibition at the nearby **György Ráth Museum** at VI Városligeti fasor 12, a few minutes' walk south on Bajza utca and then west. A short distance to the east and across the street at Városligeti fasor 7 is a stunning Art Nouveau **Calvinist church** (1913) designed by Aladár Arkay with carved wooden gates, stained glass and ceramic tiles on the facade. Other lovely buildings are at Nos 24 and 33 of the same street.

Andrássy út ends at **Hősök tere** (Heroes' Square), which has the nation's most solemn monument – an empty coffin representing one of the unknown insurgents from the 1956 Uprising beneath a stone tile – and a guard of honour.

The **Millenary Monument** (Ezeréves emlékmű), a 36m pillar backed by colonnades to the right and left, defines the square. About to take off from the top of the pillar is the Angel Gabriel, who is offering Vajk – the man who would become King Stephen – the Hungarian crown. At the base are Árpád and the six other Magyar chieftains who occupied the Carpathian Basin in the late 9th century. The statues and reliefs in and on the colonnades are of rulers and statesmen. The four allegorical figures atop are (from left to right): Work & Prosperity, War, Peace and Knowledge & Glory.

On the northern side of the square is the **Museum of Fine Arts** (1906), housing the city's outstanding collection of foreign works. To the south is the **Műcsarnok**, the ornate 'Art Gallery' or 'Palace of Art' built around the time of the millenary exhibition in 1896 and renovated a century later. It is used for temporary (usually modern) art exhibits. South of the hall, along the parade grounds of Dózsa György út, stood the 25m statue of Joseph Stalin pulled down by demonstrators on the first night of the 1956 Uprising.

Heroes' Square is in effect the entrance to **Városliget** (City Park), which hosted most of the events during Hungary's 1000th anniversary celebrations in 1896. Measuring almost a square kilometre in area, it is the largest park in Budapest and still has plenty to entertain visitors, including a ramshackle amusement park, a large thermal bath, a couple of museums and a large concert hall.

The **City Zoo** (Városi Állatkert) is a five-minute walk to the west along Állatkerti út, past **Gundel**, Budapest's – and Hungary's – most famous restaurant. A short distance to the east is the permanent **Grand Circus** and the **Amusement Park** (see Budapest for Children in the Facts for the Visitor chapter for details).

The gigantic 'wedding cake' building south of the circus just off XIV Kós Károly sétány is the **Széchenyi Bath**, which has indoor and outdoor thermal pools open year-round. For more information see the special section 'Taking the Waters'.

Due south, the large castle on the little island in the lake, which is transformed into a skating rink in winter, is **Vajdahunyad Castle** (Vajdahunyad vára), partly modelled after a fortress in Transylvania, but with Gothic, Romanesque and baroque wings and additions to reflect architectural styles from all over Hungary. The castle was erected as a temporary canvas structure for the millenary exhibition in 1896 but proved so popular that the same architect was commissioned to build it in stone. The stunning baroque wing, incorporating designs from castles and mansions around the country, now houses the **Agricultural Museum**.

The little church opposite the castle is called **Ják Chapel** (Jáki kápolna), but only its portal is copied from the 13th-century Abbey Church in Ják in Western Transdanubia. The statue of the hooded scribe south of the chapel is that of **Anonymous**, the unknown chronicler at the court of King Béla III who wrote a history of the early Magyars. Writers (both real and aspirant) touch his pen for inspiration.

In the park south of the lake, Americans will spot a familiar face. The **statue of George Washington** was erected by Hungarian Americans in 1906. It's on Washington György sétány.

[Continued on page 100]

Taking the Waters

MARK AVELLINO

DAVID GREEDY

DAVID GREEDY

Previous page: Magnificent interior of the Gellért Bath. (Photo by David Greedy.)

Top: Exterior facade of the Széchenyi Bath.

Middle: With three outdoor, naturally heated pools, as well as several indoor pools, the Széchenyi Bath offers its guests year-round access to warm, relaxing waters.

Bottom: Older men gather for games of chess in the warm waters of the Széchenyi Bath.

 Budapest is blessed with an abundance of hot springs – some 123 thermal and more than 400 mineral springs come from 14 different sources. As a result, 'taking the waters' at one of the city's many spas or combination spa and swimming pools is a real Budapest experience, so try to go at least once. Some date from Turkish 'times, others are Art Nouveau wonders, while a few more are spick-and-span modern establishments.

THERMAL BATHS

Generally, entry to the baths (*gyógyfürdő*) starts at 500Ft, which usually allows you to stay for two hours on weekdays and an hour and a half at weekends, though this rule is not always enforced. They offer a full range of serious medical treatments as well as services like massage (750/1500Ft for 15/30 minutes) and pedicure. Specify what you want when buying your ticket(s). The baths may sometimes look a bit rough around the edges, but they are clean and the water is changed continuously. You may want to wear rubber sandals though.

NB: Please be aware that some of the baths become gay venues on male-only days – especially the Király and Rác and, to a lesser extent, the Gellért. Not much actually goes on except for some intensive cruising, but those not into it may feel uncomfortable.

Gellért (Map 3; ☎ 466 6166) XI Kelenhegyi út 2-4 (tram No 18, 19, 47 or 49, bus No 7 or 86). Soaking in this Art Nouveau palace has been likened to taking a bath in a cathedral. It's open to men and women (separate sections) from 6 am to 7 pm weekdays and to 5 pm at the weekend, or to 3 pm from October to April (1200Ft).

Király (Map 3; ☎ 202 3688) II Fő utca 84 (bus No 60 or 86). The four pools, including the main one with a fantastic skylit dome, date from 1570. It's open to men from 9 am to 9 pm Monday, Wednesday and Friday, and to women from 6.30 am to 7 pm Tuesday and Thursday and to 12.30 pm Saturday (500Ft).

Lukács (Map 3; ☎ 326 1695) II Frankel Leó út 25-29 (tram No 17 or bus No 60 or 86). This sprawling 19th-century establishment has everything from thermal and mud baths to a swimming pool. The thermal baths are open to both men and women from 6 am to 7 pm Monday to Saturday and to 5 pm Sunday (6 am to 5 pm on both Saturday and Sunday from October to April). The mud and weight baths are segregated: men are welcome on Tuesday, Thursday and Saturday, and women on Monday, Wednesday and Friday (500Ft).

Rác (Map 4; ☎ 356 1322) I Hadnagy utca 8-10 (tram No 18 or bus No 78). The 19th-century exterior of this spa in a lovely park in the Tabán hides a Turkish core. It's open to men from 6.30 am to 7 pm Tuesday, Thursday and Saturday and to women the same hours on Monday, Wednesday and Friday (500Ft).

Rudas (Map 4; ☎ 356 1322) I Döbrentei tér 9 (tram No 18 or 19 or bus No 7 or 86). This is the most Turkish of all the baths in Budapest. The thermal baths are open to men only from 6 am to 7 pm weekdays and to 1 pm at the weekend (500Ft).

Széchenyi (Map 3; ☎ 321 0310) XIV Állatkerti út 11 (metro Széchenyi fürdő). This bath is unusual for Budapest for three reasons: its immense size; its bright, clean look; and its water temperatures, which really are what the wall plaques say they are. It's open to men and women (separate sections) from 6 am to 7 pm weekdays and to 5 pm at the weekend (500Ft).

Thermal (Map 2; ☎ 329 2300) Danubius Thermal Margitsziget hotel, XIII Margit-sziget (bus No 26). This thermal bath on leafy Margaret Island is the most upmarket in town and, at 1800Ft on weekdays and 2300Ft on weekends, the most expensive bath in the city. It's open to men and women from 7 am to 8 pm daily.

SWIMMING POOLS

Every town of any size in Hungary has at least one indoor and outdoor swimming pool (*uszoda*), and Budapest boasts dozens. They're always excellent places to get in a few laps (if indoor), cool off on a hot summer's day (if outdoor) or watch all the posers strut their stuff.

The system inside is similar to that at the baths except that rather than a cabin or cubicle, there are sometimes just lockers. Get changed and call the attendant, who will lock it, write the time on a chalkboard and hand you a key. Many pools require the use of a bathing cap, so bring your own or wear the plastic one provided, rented or sold for a nominal fee.

The following is a list of the best outdoor and indoor pools in the city. The former are usually open from May to September unless specified. Addresses for the swimming pools attached to the thermal baths can be found in the previous Thermal Baths section.

Csillaghegyi (☎ 250 1533) III Pusztakúti út 3 (HÉV Csillaghegy). The outdoor pools, with a capacity for 3000 bathers, are open from 7 or 8 am to 7 pm daily from May to September. The indoor pool is open from 6 am to 7 pm weekdays, to 4 pm Saturday and to 1 pm Sunday. There's a nudist section on the southern slope in summer (400Ft).

Dagály (Map 2; ☎ 320 2203) XIII Népfürdő utca 36 (metro Árpád híd or tram No 1). This huge complex has a total of 12 pools, with plenty of grass and shade. The outdoor pools are open from 6 am to 7 pm daily from May to September, the indoor ones from 6 am to 7 pm weekdays and to 5 pm at the weekend the rest of the year (500Ft).

Gellért The indoor and outdoor pools, with a wave machine and nicely landscaped gardens, are open from 6 am to 7 pm. On Friday and Saturday in July and August the pools reopen from 8 pm to midnight. In winter the indoor pools close at 5 pm at the weekend. It costs 1800/750Ft for adults/children to use the pool and spa.

Alfréd Hajós (National Sports) (Map 3; ☎ 340 4946) XIII Margit-sziget (bus No 26). The pools, one indoor and two outdoor, are open from 6 am to 5 pm weekdays and to 6 pm at the weekend – provided no competitions are on (350Ft).

Hélia (Map 3; ☎ 350 3277) Hélia Thermal hotel, XIII Kárpát utca 62-64 (metro Dósza György út or trolleybus No 79). This ultra-modern four-star hotel boasts three pools, sauna and steam room and a health-food bar (1800Ft).

Palatinus (Map 2; ☎ 340 4505) XIII Margit-sziget (bus No 26). The largest series of pools in the capital, seven in all plus a wave pool, are open from 8 am to 7 pm daily from May to August and from 10 am to 6 pm the first half of September. There are separate-sex roof decks for nude sunbathing (500Ft).

Római (☎ 388 9740) III Rozgonyi Piroska utca 2 (HÉV Rómaifürdő or bus No 34). The outdoor cold-water thermal pools are open from 8 am to 7 pm daily in season (400Ft).

Széchenyi The enormous and recently renovated pools of the Széchenyi baths, the largest medicinal baths still existing in Europe, contain thermal water so are open year-round. Opening hours are 6 am to 7 pm from May to September and 6 am to 7 pm weekdays and to 5 pm at the weekend the rest of the year (500Ft).

Thermal The indoor pool at the spa complex is open from 7 am to 8 pm daily (1800Ft weekdays, 2300Ft on weekends).

Right: Ornamentation at the Széchenyi Baths.

TONY FANKHAUSER

[Continued from page 96]

OK, it doesn't sound like a crowd-pleaser, but the **Transport Museum** in the park to the south-east at XIV Városligeti körút 11 is one of the most enjoyable in Budapest and great for children. The museum's air and space-travel collection is housed in the **Aviation Museum** in the Petőfi Csarnok, a large hall nearby at XIV Zichy Mihály utca 14, better known for its rock and pop concerts (see the Entertainment chapter).

The surrounding streets on the south-eastern corner of City Park are loaded with gorgeous buildings, residences and embassies. Some of my favourites are on **Stefánia út** (eg, the Geology Institute at No 14), but for something close by, just walk across Hermina utca to the Art Nouveau masterpiece at No 47, which now houses the National Association for the Blind.

Walking Tour 10: Oktogon to Blaha Lujza tér

The Big Ring Road slices district VII (also called Erzsébetváros or Elizabeth Town) in half between these two busy squares. The eastern side is a rather poor area with little of interest to visitors except the Keleti train station on Baross tér (Map 3). The western side, bounded by the Little Ring Road, has always been predominantly Jewish, and this was the ghetto where Jews were forced to live behind wooden fences when the Nazis occupied Hungary in 1944. From an estimated 800,000 people nationwide before the war, the Jewish population has dwindled to about 80,000 through wartime executions, deportations and emigration.

The sights listed below can be found on Map 5 unless otherwise indicated.

Your starting point, Oktogon, is on the yellow metro line. It can also be reached via tram Nos 4 and 6 from both Buda and the rest of Pest.

The **Liszt Academy of Music** (Liszt Zeneakadémia) is one block south-east of Oktogon just off Király utca at Liszt Ferenc tér 8; and the small **Stamp Museum** is at VII Hársfa utca 47 to the south-east. The

academy, built in 1907, attracts students from all over the world and is one of the top venues in Budapest for concerts. The interior, richly embellished with Zsolnay porcelain and frescoes, is worth a look even if you're not attending a performance. But there are always cheap tickets available to something – perhaps a recital or an early Saturday morning rehearsal. The box office is at the end of the main hall from the entrance at Király utca 64.

If you walk west on Király utca you'll pass a lovely neo-Gothic house (No 47) built in 1847 and, almost opposite, the **Church of St Teresa** (Szent Teréz templom; 1811) with a massive neoclassical altar and chandelier. **Klauzál tér**, the heart of the old Jewish Quarter, is a couple of streets south down Csányi utca.

The square and surrounding streets retain a feeling of prewar Budapest. Signs of a continued Jewish presence are still evident – in a kosher bakery at Kazinczy utca 28, the Kővári delicatessen at Kazinczy utca 41 and the Fröhlich cake shop and cafe at No 22, which has old Jewish favourites.

There are about half a dozen synagogues and prayer houses in the district once reserved for conservatives, the orthodox, Poles, Sephardics etc. The **Orthodox Synagogue**, at VII Kazinczy utca 29-31 (or enter from Dob utca 35), has been given a face-lift as has the Moorish **Conservative Synagogue** (1872) at VII Rumbach Sebestyén utca 11.

But none compares with the **Great Synagogue** (Nagy zsinagóga) at VII Dohány utca 2-8, the largest in the world outside New York. Built in 1859 with romantic and Moorish elements, the copper-domed synagogue was renovated with funds raised by the Hungarian government and a New York-based charity headed by the actor Tony Curtis, whose parents emigrated from Hungary in the 1920s. The organ, dating from 1859, has been completely rebuilt and concerts are held here in summer. The **Jewish Museum** is in the annexe to the left, next to the plaque noting that Theodore Herzl, the father of modern Zionism, was born at this site in 1860.

The **Holocaust Memorial** (1989, designed by Imre Varga) on the Wesselényi utca side of the synagogue stands over the mass graves of those murdered by the Nazis in 1944-45. On the leaves of the metal 'tree of life' are the family names of some of the 400,000 victims.

Nearby, in front of Dob utca 12, there's an unusual antifascist **monument to Carl Lutz**, a Swiss consul who, like Raoul Wallenberg, provided Jews with false papers in 1944. It portrays an angel on high sending down a long bolt of cloth to a victim. The **Electrotechnology Museum** is a short distance to the north-east.

Rákóczi út, a busy shopping street, leads to **Blaha Lujza tér**, named after a leading 19th-century stage actress. The subway under the square is one of the most lively in the city, with hustlers, beggars, peasants selling their wares, Peruvian musicians and, of course, pickpockets. The 18th-century **St Rókus Chapel** (Szent Rókus kápolna), Rákóczi út 27/a, is a cool oasis away from all the chaos.

North of Blaha Lujza tér at Erzsébet körút 9-11 is the Art Nouveau **New York Palace** and its famous **New York Café**, scene of many a literary gathering over the years. Find your way through the scaffolding – it's been here since the 1956 Uprising – have a cup of coffee and enjoy the splendour (ignoring the naff chandeliers). Scenes from the recent film *Crime and Punishment* with Ben Kingsley were shot here.

The city's 'other' opera house, the **Erkel Theatre** (Erkel Színház; Map 3), is at VIII Köztársaság tér 30, south-east of this stretch of Rákóczi út. From the outside, you'd never guess it was built in 1911. The building at No 26-27 is the former **Communist Party headquarters** from which members of the secret police were dragged and shot by demonstrators on 30 October 1956.

Rákóczi út ends at Baross tér and **Keleti train station** (Map 3). It was built in 1884 and renovated a century later. About 500m south on Fiumei út (tram No 23 or 24) is the entrance to **Kerepesi Cemetery** (Kerepesi temető; Map 3), Budapest's Highgate or Père Lachaise and deathly quiet during the week. The flower shop at the entrance at

VIII Fiumei út 16 sometimes has maps for sale, but you can strike out on your own, looking at the graves of creative and courageous men and women whose names have now been given to streets, squares and bridges around the city.

Some of the mausoleums are worthy of a Pharaoh, especially those of statesmen and national heroes like Lajos Kossuth, Ferenc Deák and Lajos Batthyány, all of which are undergoing massive restorations. Other tombs are quite moving (eg, those of Lujza Blaha and Endre Ady). Plot 21 contains the graves of many who died in the 1956 Uprising. Near the huge mausoleum for party honchos, which is topped with the words 'I lived for Communism, for the people', is the simple grave of János Kádár, who died in 1989, and his wife Mária Tamáska. The cemetery is open from 8 am to 7 pm daily.

If you're really into necropolises, you can reach the huge **New Municipal Cemetery** (Új köztemető) on the far eastern side of town in district X via tram No 28 from Blaha Lujza tér. It would be just another huge city cemetery if Imre Nagy, prime minister during the 1956 Uprising, and 2000 others hadn't been buried here in unmarked graves (plot Nos 300-301) after executions in the late 1940s and 1950s.

Today, the area has been turned into a moving **National Pantheon**, which stipulates that 'Only with a Hungarian soul can you pass through the gate.' The posts with Transylvanian-style notches mark the graves of some of the victims. The area is about a 30-minute walk from the entrance; walk eastward on the main road till you reach the end (and a yellow building), then head north. There are some signs pointing the way to '300, 301 parcela'. At peak periods you can take a microbus marked *'temető járat'* around the cemetery or hire a taxi at the gate.

Walking Tour 11: Blaha Lujza tér to Petőfi Bridge

From Blaha Lujza tér, the Big Ring Road runs through district VIII, also called Józsefváros (Joseph Town). The western side transforms itself from a neighbour-hood of lovely 19th-century townhouses and villas around the Little Ring Road to a large student quarter. East of the boulevard is the rough-and-tumble district so poignantly described in the Pressburger brothers' *Homage to the Eighth District.* Dilapidated entrances give way to dark and foreboding courtyards with few traces left of the dignified comfort enjoyed by the bourgeois residents in the early part of the 20th century. It is also the area where much of the fighting in October 1956 took place.

The sights listed below can be found on Map 5 unless otherwise indicated.

Rákóczi tér, the only real square on the Big Ring Road, is as good a place as any to get a feel for this area. It is the site of a busy **market hall** (vásárcsarnok), erected in 1897 and renovated in the early 1990s after a bad fire. The square is also the unofficial headquarters of Budapest's low-rent prostitutes who you'll see calling out in Hungarian or German to anyone who'll listen as early as 8 am.

Across the boulevard, Bródy Sándor utca runs west from Gutenberg tér (with a lovely Art Nouveau building at No 4) to the old **Hungarian Radio** (Magyar Rádió) building at No 5-7, where shots were first fired on 23 October 1956. Beyond it, at VIII Múzeum körút 14-16, is the **Hungarian National Museum**, the largest historical collection in the country. Designed by Mihály Pollack, the purpose-built museum opened in 1847 and a year later was the scene of a momentous event (though, as always, not recognised as such at the time). On 15 March a crowd gathered to hear the poet Sándor Petőfi recite *Nemzeti Dal* (National Song), a prelude to the 1848-49 Revolution.

You may enjoy walking around the **Museum Gardens**, laid out in 1856. The column to the left of the museum entrance once stood at the Forum in Rome. Have a look at some of the villas and public buildings on Pollack Mihály tér behind the museum and the white wrought-iron gate in the centre.

You can wander back to the Big Ring Road through any of the small streets. If you follow Baross utca eastward from Kálvin tér, drop into the **Ervin Szabó Library**, VIII Reviczky utca 3, built in 1887. With its gypsum ornaments, faded gold tracery and enormous chandeliers, you'll never see another public reading room like this (open from 9 am to 9 pm Monday, Tuesday, Thursday and Friday and to 1 pm at the weekend).

Farther east, across the Big Ring Road, the old **Telephone Exchange** building (1910) at VIII Horváth Mihály tér 18 (Map 3) has reliefs of classical figures using the then newfangled invention. The Art Deco **Corvin Film Palace** (Corvin Filmpalota; Map 3), at the southern end of Kisfaludy utca in the middle of a square flanked by Regency-like houses, has been restored to its former glory.

Directly to the west at IX Üllői út 33-37 is Hungary's equivalent of London's Victoria & Albert: the **Applied Arts Museum** (Map 3). In fact, the London museum was the inspiration when this museum was founded in 1864. The building, designed by Ödön Lechner and decorated with Zsolnay ceramic tiles, was completed for the millenary exhibition but was badly damaged during WWII and again in 1956.

The neighbourhood south of Üllői út is **Ferencváros** (Francis Town), home of the city's most popular football team, Ferencvárosi Torna Club (FTC) and many of its rougher supporters wearing green and white. (Its stadium at IX Üllői út 129 (Map 6) is the only one in the city where booze is banned.) Most of the area was washed away in the Great Flood of 1838.

The area to the west toward the Little Ring Road is dominated by the **Budapest Economics University** (Budapesti Közgazdaságtodományos Egyetem; Map 3) on Fővám tér and is full of hostels, little clubs and inexpensive places to eat. Pop into the university (entrance on the west side facing the river) for a look at its beautiful central courtyard and glass atrium. Nearby is the imposing **Nagycsarnok** (Great Market Hall; Map 3). It was built for the millenary exhibition and reopened in 1996 after a major face-lift. It is now the nicest covered market in the city.

Walking Tour 12: Buda Hills

With 'peaks' reaching over 500m, a comprehensive system of trails and no lack of unusual transport, the Buda Hills are the city's true playground and a welcome respite from hot, dusty Pest in summer. This is not an area of sights – though there are one or two. Come here just to relax and enjoy yourself. If you're walking, take along a copy of Cartographia's 1:30,000 *A Budai-hegység* map (No 6; 500Ft) to complement the trail markers.

Heading for the hills is more than half the fun. From the Moszkva tér metro station in Buda, walk westward along Szilágyi Erzsébet fasor for 10 minutes (or take tram No 18 or bus No 56 for two stops) to the circular high-rise Budapest hotel at No 47. Opposite is the terminus of the **Cog Railway** (Fogaskerekű). Built in 1874, the cog climbs for 3.5km to **Széchenyi-hegy** (427m), one of the prettiest residential areas in the city. The railway runs all year from 5 am to 11 pm and costs the same as a tram or bus.

At Széchenyi-hegy, you can stop for a picnic in the park south of the station or board the narrow-gauge **Children's Railway** (Gyermekvasút), two minutes to the south on Hegyhát út. The railway was built in 1951 by Pioneers (socialist Scouts) and is staffed entirely by children aged 10 to 14 – the engineer excepted – who will sell you tickets (120/60Ft) and tell you where to get off.

The little train chugs along for 12km, terminating at **Hűvös-völgy** (Chilly Valley). There are walks fanning out from any of the stops along the way, or you can return to Moszkva tér on tram No 56 from Hűvös-völgy. The train operates about once an hour daily from mid-March to October but Tuesday to Sunday only the rest of the year.

A more interesting way down, though, is to get off at **János-hegy**, the fourth stop and the highest point (527m) in the hills. There's an old lookout tower (1910) here, with excellent views of the city, and some good walks. About 700m west of the station is the **chairlift** (libegő), which will take you down to Zugligeti út. From here bus

No 158 returns to Moszkva tér. The chairlift runs from 9 am to 5 pm between April and September and 9.30 am to 4 pm the rest of the year; it is closed on Monday of every odd-numbered week. The one-way fare is 250/150Ft for adults/children, return is 400/300Ft.

Hármashatár-hegy (Three Border Hill) is less crowded even in the peak season and is a great spot for a picnic, hiking or watching the gliders push off from the hillside. The view is 360° and worth the trip alone. There's also a lovely restaurant here with a large open terrace. You can reach this hill by taking bus No 86 or tram No 17 in Buda to III Kolosy tér, from where bus Nos 65 goes to the Fenyőgyöngy restaurant on Szépvölgyi út at the base of Hármashatár-hegyi út.

Returning from Hármashatár on bus No 65, you might want to stop at **Pál-völgy Cave** (Map 2) at II Szépvölgyi út 162 (get off at Pálvölgy utca) or the one at **Szemlő-hegy** (Map 2), about a kilometre south-east of Pál-völgy at II Pusztaszeri út 35. See Caving in the Activities section later in this chapter for details.

The only other sight in the vicinity is the **Béla Bartók Memorial House** at II Csalán út 29, which is also on the No 29 bus route. The house was the composer's residence from 1932 to 1940 before he emigrated to the USA.

MUSEUMS & OTHER SIGHTS

The museums and some other sights mentioned on the 12 walking tours are listed alphabetically (by their English names) and described in detail below. The 'Museums of Budapest' boxed text on the following page lists the city's collections by geographical area.

Agricultural Museum

The Hungarian Agricultural Museum (Magyar Mezőgazdasági Múzeum; Map 3; ☎ 343 0573) in the stunning baroque wing of Vajdahunyad Castle, XIV Vajdahunyad sétány (metro Hősök tere), Europe's largest such collection, has permanent exhibits on cattle breeding, wine making,

The Museums of Budapest

The general locations of the museums and other sights mentioned on the 12 walking tours and listed in more detailed fashion under Museums and Other Sights appear below.

Buda

Béla Bartók Memorial House
Budapest History Museum
Commerce & Catering Museum
Ecclesiastical Art Collection
Foundry Museum
Golden Eagle Pharmacy Museum
Gül Baba's Tomb
Labyrinth
Ludwig Museum (Museum of Contemporary Art)
Medieval Jewish Prayer House
Military History Museum
Music History Museum
National Gallery
Semmelweis Medical History Museum
Statue Park
Telephony Museum

Pest

Agricultural Museum
Applied Arts Museum
Aviation Museum
Dreher Brewery
Electrotechnology Museum
Ethnography Museum
Fine Arts Museum

Ferenc Hopp East Asian Art Museum
House of Hungarian Photographers
Jewish Museum
Franz Liszt Memorial Museum
Literature Museum
Műcsarnok (Art Gallery)
National Museum
Natural History Museum
Opera House
Parliament
Postal Museum
György Ráth Museum
Stamp Museum
Transport Museum
Underground Train Museum
Zoo

Óbuda

Aquincum Museum
Budapest Gallery
Hercules Villa
Kassák Museum
Kiscelli Museum & Municipal Gallery
Zsigmond Kun Folk Art Collection (Óbuda Museum)
Imre Varga Collection
Vasarely Museum

hunting and fishing. After a visit here there's not much you won't know about Hungarian fruit production, cereals, wool, poultry and pig slaughtering – if that's what you want. It's open from 10 am to 5 pm Tuesday to Saturday and to 6 pm Sunday from March to mid-November but closes one hour earlier on the same days the rest of the year (200/50Ft adults/students & children).

Applied Arts Museum

The galleries of the Museum of Applied Arts (Iparművészeti Múzeum; Map 3; ☎ 217 5222) at IX Üllői út 33-37 (metro Ferenc körút), which surround a white-on-white main hall supposedly modelled on the Alhambra in southern Spain, contain Hungarian furnishings and bric-a-brac from the 18th to 19th centuries and the history of trades and crafts (glass making, book binding, gold smithing, leatherwork etc).

Don't miss the collection of Art Nouveau and Secessionist artefacts, the painted 18th-century coffered ceiling in the room with the old printing presses, or the stained-glass skylight in the entrance hall. The museum is open from 10 am to 6 pm Tuesday to Sunday from mid-March to mid-December and to 4 pm the rest of the year (300/100Ft). English-language tours (2000Ft) can be arranged in advance.

Aquincum Museum

The Aquincum Museum (Aquincumi Múzeum; Map 2; ☎ 368 8241), III Szentendrei út 139 (HÉV Aquincum), in the centre of what remains of this Roman civil settlement, tries to put the ruins in perspective, but unfortunately only in Hungarian. Keep an eye open for the replica of a 3rd-century portable organ (and the mosaic illustrating how it was played), pottery moulds, and floor mosaics from the governor's palace across the river on Óbuda Island. Most of the big sculptures and stone sarcophagi are outside to the left of the museum or behind it along a covered walkway. The museum and complex are open from 9 am to 6 pm Tuesday to Sunday from May to September, to 5 pm in April and October (400/200Ft, family 600Ft). English-language tours (2000Ft) by arrangement.

Aviation Museum

The Aviation Museum (Repülési Múzeum; Map 3; ☎ 343 0565), part of the Transport Museum's collection, is housed in the Petőfi Csarnok in City Park at XIV Zichy Mihály utca 14 (metro Széchenyi fürdő or trolleybus No 72). It contains passenger planes and gliders as well as the space capsule in which Hungary's first astronaut travelled. It is open from 10 am to 5 pm Tuesday to Friday from May to September, to 6 pm at the weekend. In the first two weeks of October, it closes an hour earlier on the same days (150/50Ft).

Béla Bartók Memorial House

The Béla Bartók Memorial House (Bartók Béla Emlékház; ☎ 394 2100), II Csalán út 29 (bus No 29), is where the great composer resided from 1932 before emigrating to the USA in 1940. Among other things on display is the old Edison recorder (complete with wax cylinders) he used to record Hungarian folk music in Transylvania, as well as furniture and other objects he collected. Concerts are held in the music hall most Friday evenings, and outside in the garden in summer. The museum is open from 10 am to 5 pm Tuesday to Sunday (200/100Ft).

Budapest Gallery

The exhibition house (kiállítóháza) of the Budapest Gallery (Map 2; ☎ 388 6771), III Lajos utca 158 (HÉV Árpád híd or bus No 86), hosts some of the most interesting avant-garde exhibitions in Budapest. It also has a standing exhibit of works by Pál Pátzay, whose sculptures can be seen throughout the city (eg, the fountain on Tárnok utca in the Castle District and the *Serpent Slayer* in honour of Raoul Wallenberg in Szent István Park). The gallery is open from 10 am to 6 pm Tuesday to Sunday (usually 100/50Ft).

Budapest History Museum

The Budapest History Museum (Budapesti Történeti Múzeum; Map 4; ☎ 355 8849), in Wing E of the Royal Palace, I Szent György tér (bus No 16 or Várbusz), traces the 2000 years of the city on three floors of jumbled exhibits. Restored palace rooms dating from the 15th century can be entered from the basement, which contains an exhibit on the Royal Palace in medieval Buda. Three vaulted halls, one with a magnificent door frame in red marble bearing the seal of Queen Beatrice and tiles with a raven and a ring (the seal of her husband King Matthias Corvinus), lead to the Gothic Hall, the Royal Cellar and the 14th-century Tower Chapel.

On the ground floor is an exhibit entitled 'Budapest in the Middle Ages' as well as Gothic statues of courtiers, squires and saints discovered by chance in 1974 during excavations and now kept in a temperature-controlled room. The exhibit on the 1st floor traces the history of the city from the expulsion of the Turks in 1686 to the present day.

The museum, sometimes called the Castle Museum (Vár Múzeum) is open from 10 am to 6 pm daily from mid-May to mid-September, the same times Wednesday to Monday only from March to mid-May and mid-September to mid-October, and from 10 am to 4 pm Wednesday to Monday the rest of the year (300/150Ft, family 600Ft).

Commerce & Catering Museum

The catering section of the Museum of Commerce & Catering (Kereskedelmi és

Vendéglátóipari Múzeum; Map 4; ☎ 375 6249), I Fortuna utca 4 (bus No 16 or Várbusz), contains an entire 19th-century cake shop in one of its three rooms, complete with a pastry kitchen. There are moulds for every occasion, a marble-lined icebox and an antique ice-cream maker. Much is made of those great confectioners Emil Gerbeaud of *cukrászda* fame and József Dobos, who gave his name to Dobos torta, a layered chocolate and cream cake with caramelised brown sugar top. The commerce collection traces retail trade in the capital. The museum is open from 10 am to 5 pm Wednesday to Friday, to 6 pm at the weekend (100/50Ft).

Dreher Brewery
Budapest's – and Hungary's – largest beer maker Dreher (☎ 261 1111 ext 1623), X Maglódi út 117 (tram No 28 or 37 from Blaha Lujza tér or bus 62 or 168 from Örs Vezér tere), welcomes visitors from 10 am to 12.30 pm weekdays but unfortunately only in groups of 15 people minimum at present. You might get lucky and be able to join an existing group or try rounding up the no-doubt-thirsty denizens of your hostel.

Ecclesiastical Art Collection
The Ecclesiastical Art Collection (Egyházművészeti Gyűtemény; Map 4; ☎ 355 5657) of Matthias Church, I Szentháromság tér 2 (bus No 16 or Várbusz), contains the usual monstrances, reliquaries, chalices and a copy of the Coronation Jewels, but you'll get some interesting views of the chancel from high up in the Royal Oratory. The collection is open from 9.30 am to 5.30 pm Monday to Saturday, from 11.30 am to 5.30 pm Sunday year-round (150/50Ft).

Electrotechnology Museum
The Hungarian Electrotechnology Museum (Magyar Elektrotechnikai Múzeum; Map 5; ☎ 322 0472), VII Kazinczy utca 21 (metro Astoria), doesn't sound like everyone's cup of tea, but the staff are very enthusiastic and some of the exhibits are unusual enough to warrant a visit. Its collection of electricity-consumption meters, one of the largest in

the world, is not very inspiring, though it has one that was installed in the apartment of 'Rákosi Mátyás elvtárs' (Comrade Mátyás Rákosi), the Communist Party secretary, on his 60th birthday in 1952.

The staff will also show you how the alarm system of the barbed-wire fence between Hungary and Austria once worked, and there's an exhibit on the nesting platforms that the electric company kindly builds for storks throughout the country so they won't interfere with the wires and electrocute themselves. The museum is open from 11 am to 5 pm Tuesday to Saturday (free).

Ethnography Museum
As the nation's largest indoor folk display, the Hungarian collection of the Museum of Ethnography (Néprajzi Múzeum; Map 5; ☎ 312 4878), V Kossuth Lajos tér 12 (metro Kossuth tér), contained in more than a dozen rooms here, is somewhat disappointing, but it's an easy introduction to traditional Hungarian life, the labels are also in English, the mock-ups of peasant houses from the Őrség and Sárköz regions of Transdanubia are pretty well done and there are some excellent rotating exhibits. On the next floor are displays dealing with the other peoples of Europe and farther afield. The building itself, designed in 1893 to house the Supreme Court, is worth a look – especially the massive central hall with its marble columns and ceiling fresco of *Justice* by Károly Lotz. The museum is open from 10 am to 6 pm Tuesday to Sunday from March to October, to 4 pm the rest of the year (300/150Ft).

Fine Arts Museum
The Museum of Fine Arts (Szépművészeti Múzeum; Map 3; ☎ 343 9759), XIV Hősök tere (metro Hősök tere), houses the city's outstanding collection of foreign works in a renovated building dating from 1906. The Old Masters collection is the most complete, with thousands of works from the Dutch and Flemish, Spanish, Italian, German, French and British schools between the 13th and 18th centuries, including seven paintings by El Greco. Other sections

include Egyptian and Greco-Roman arte-facts and 19th and 20th-century paintings, watercolours, graphics and sculpture, including some important impressionist works. The museum is open from 10 am to 5.30 pm Tuesday to Sunday (500/200Ft).

Foundry Museum

The exhibits (cast-iron stoves, bells, street furniture) at the Foundry Museum (Öntödei Múzeum; Map 3; ☎ 202 5327), II Bem József utca 20 (metro Moszkva tér or tram No 4 or 6), are housed in a foundry that was in use until the 1960s, and the massive ladles and cranes still stand, anxiously awaiting use. It is open from 9 am to 5 pm Tuesday to Sunday (90/40Ft).

Golden Eagle Pharmacy Museum

The Golden Eagle Pharmacy Museum (Aranysas Patikamúzeum; Map 4; ☎ 375 9772), just north of Dísz tér at I Tárnok utca 18 (bus No 16 or Várbusz), contains an unusual miniature of Christ as a pharmacist; the mock-up of an alchemist's lab with dried bats, tiny crocodiles and what appears to be eye of newt in jars is straight out of *The Addams Family*. There's also a 2000-year-old mummy's head and a small 'spice rack' used by 17th-century travellers for their daily fixes of herbs and other elixirs. The pharmacy museum is open from 10.30 am to 5.30 pm Tuesday to Sunday (60/20Ft).

Gül Baba's Tomb

The reconstructed Tomb of Gül Baba (Gül Baba türbéje; Map 3; ☎ 355 8849), II Mecset utca 14 (HÉV Margit híd or tram No 4 or 6), contains the remains of Gül Baba, a Ottoman Dervish who took part in the capture of Buda in 1541 and is known in Hungary as the 'Father of Roses'. To reach it walk up Gül Baba utca to the set of steps just past No 14, which will lead to a small octagonal building and a lookout tower. The tomb is still a place of pilgrimage for Muslims, and you must remove your shoes. It contains Islamic furnishings and is open from 10 am to 5.30 pm Tuesday to Sunday from May to September and to 4 pm in October (150/50Ft).

Hercules Villa

Hercules Villa (Herkules villa; Map 2; ☎ 250 1650), in the middle of a vast housing estate north-west of Flórián tér at III Meggyfa utca 19-21 (HÉV Filagoriát), is the name given to some reconstructed Roman ruins. The name is derived from the astonishing 3rd-century floor mosaics found in what was a Roman villa. It is open from 10 am to 2 pm Tuesday to Friday and to 6 pm at the weekend from April to October (150Ft).

Ferenc Hopp East Asian Art Museum

The Ferenc Hopp Museum of East Asian Art (Hopp Ferenc Kelet-ázsiai Művészeti Múzeum; Map 3; ☎ 322 8476) is in the former villa of its benefactor and namesake at VI Andrássy út 103 (metro Bajza utca). Founded in 1919, the museum has a good collection of Indonesian *wayang* puppets, Indian statuary and lamaist sculpture and scroll paintings from Tibet. There's an 18th-century Chinese moon gate in the back garden, but most of the Chinese and Japanese collection of ceramics and porcelain, textiles and sculpture is housed in the György Ráth Museum (see later in this section). The museum is open from 10 am to 6 pm Tuesday to Sunday from mid-March to December (160/50Ft).

House of Hungarian Photographers

The House of Hungarian Photographers (Magyar Fotográfusok Háza; Map 5) at the Modern Devil Photo Gallery (Mai Manó Fotógaléria; ☎ 302 4398), VI Nagymező utca 20 (metro Opera), is an extraordinary venue in the city's theatre district with top-class photography exhibitions. It is open from 2 to 6 pm Monday to Saturday (150/100Ft).

Jewish Museum

The Jewish Museum (Zsidó Múzeum; Map 5; ☎ 342 8949), in an annexe of the Great Synagogue at VII Dohány utca 2 (metro Astoria), contains objects related to religious and everyday life, and an interesting handwritten book of the local Burial Society from the 18th century. The Holocaust

Memorial Room – dark and sombre – relates the events of 1944-45, including the infamous mass murder of doctors and patients at a hospital on Maros utca. The museum is open from 10 am to 3 pm Monday to Friday and to 1 pm Sunday (400/200Ft).

Kassák Museum

The unique Kassák Museum (Map 2; ☎ 368 7021), III Fő tér 1 (HÉV Árpád híd or bus No 86), is a three-room art gallery with some real gems of early 20th-century avant-garde art as well as the complete works of the artist and writer Lajos Kassák (1887-1967). It's open from 10 am to 6 pm Tuesday to Sunday (200/100Ft).

Kiscelli Museum & Municipal Gallery

Housed in an 18th-century monastery, later a barracks that was badly damaged during WWII and again in 1956, the exhibits at the Kiscelli Museum (Map 2; ☎ 388 8560), III Kiscelli utca 106 (tram No 17 or bus No 60), painlessly tell the story of Budapest since liberation from the Turks. The museum counts among its best exhibits a complete 19th-century apothecary moved here from Kálvin tér, but my favourites are the rooms furnished in Empire, Biedermeier and Art Nouveau furniture that give you a good idea of how the affluent merchant class lived in Budapest in the 19th century. The Municipal Gallery (Fővárosi Képtár), with an impressive art collection (József Rippl-Rónai, Lajos Tihanyi, István Csók, László Károly etc) is also here. The museum and gallery are open from 10 am to 6 pm Tuesday to Sunday from April to October and to 4 pm the rest of the year (200/100Ft).

Labyrinth

The Labyrinth (Labirintus; Map 4; ☎ 375 6858), I Úri utca 9 (bus No 16 or Várbusz), a 1200m-long cave system some 16m under the Castle District, is another one of those rip-off tourist sites you'll find from London to Los Angles and Lhasa – and everywhere in between. Ogle at the damp rooms masquerading as one-time dungeons. Marvel at how fake the wax models

of historical figures look. Wince at the entry fee: 800/700Ft. The Labyrinth is open from 9.30 am to 7.30 pm daily, with tours leaving every 30 minutes.

Franz Liszt Memorial Museum

The Franz Liszt Memorial Museum (Liszt Ferenc Emlékmúzeum; Map 5; ☎ 322 9804), VI Vörösmarty utca 35 (metro Vörösmarty utca), is in the house where the great composer lived in an apartment on the 1st floor from 1881 until his death in 1886. The four rooms are filled with his pianos (including a tiny glass one), composer's table, portraits and personal effects. It's open from 10 am to 6 pm weekdays and from 9 am to 5 pm Saturday with a 'free' piano recital daily at 11 am (150/80Ft).

Literature Museum

The Hungarian Literature Museum (Magyar Irodalmi Múzeum; Map 5; ☎ 317 3611), V Károlyi Mihály utca 16 (metro Ferenciek tere), focuses on the work of Sándor Petőfi, Endre Ady, Mór Jókai and Attila József (among other writers). But even these great authors' works are not easy to obtain in (or translate into) English and probably won't mean much to most travellers. The museum is currently being renovated and will soon have a new library, concert/lecture hall and terrace. It is open from 10 am to 6 pm Tuesday to Sunday from March to October and to 4 pm the rest of the year (60/20Ft).

Ludwig Museum

The Ludwig Museum, also known as the Museum of Contemporary Art (Kortárs Művészeti Múzeum; Map 4; ☎ 375 9175) is in Wing A of the Royal Palace, I Szent György tér (bus No 16 or Várbusz). It surveys American pop art as well as works by German, French and North American artists of the 1980s, and Hungarian contemporary art. It is open from 10 am to 6 pm Tuesday to Sunday (300/150Ft).

Medical History Museum

The Semmelweis Medical History Museum (Semmelweis Orvostörténeti Múzeum; Map 4; ☎ 375 3533), I Apród utca 1-3 (bus

No 86 or tram No 19), traces the history of medicine from Graeco-Roman times through medical tools and implements and photographs, and yet another antique pharmacy – a Hungarian obsession – makes an appearance. Ignác Semmelweis (1818-65), the 'saviour of mothers' who discovered the cause of puerperal fever, was born here. The museum is open from 10.30 am to 6 pm Tuesday to Sunday (120/50Ft).

Medieval Jewish Prayer House

This small museum at the medieval Jewish prayer house (középkori zsidó imaház; Map 4; ☎ 355 8849), I Táncsics Mihály utca 26 (bus No 16 or Várbusz), contains documents and items linked to the Jewish community of Buda as well as Gothic stone carvings and tombstones. It is open from 10 am to 6 pm Tuesday to Sunday from May to October (100/50Ft).

Military History Museum

The Museum of Military History (Hadtörténeti Múzeum; Map 4; ☎ 356 9586), I Tóth Árpád sétány 40 (bus No 16 or Várbusz), has more weapons inside than a Los Angeles crack house but also does a pretty good job with uniforms, medals, flags and battle-themed fine art. Exhibits focus on the 15th-century fall of Buda Castle, the Hungarian Royal Army up to the time of Admiral Miklós Horthy and the 1956 Uprising.

Museum staff would like to point out that Stalin's right finger, broken off from the enormous sculpture that once 'graced' VII Dózsa György út, is no longer on display here but has been returned to its rightful owner.

The museum is open from 10 am to 6 pm Tuesday to Sunday from April to September, to 4 pm from October to mid-December and also in February and March (250/80Ft).

Műcsarnok

The opulent Műcsarnok (Map 3; ☎ 343 740), XIV Hősök tere (metro Hősök tere), which simply means 'Art Gallery' but is usually called the 'Palace of Art' in English, is the country's largest exhibition hall and hosts temporary exhibits of works by Hungarian and foreign artists in fine and applied art, photography and design. It's open from 10 am to 6 pm Tuesday to Sunday (300/100Ft).

Music History Museum

The Museum of Music History (Zenetörténeti Múzeum; Map 4; ☎ 214 6770), I Táncsics Mihály utca 7 (bus No 16 or Várbusz), traces the development of music and musical instruments in Hungary; the violin maker's workbench and the unusual 18th-century sextet table are particularly interesting. The paintings on loan from the Museum of Fine Arts all have musical themes. A special room upstairs is devoted to the work of Béla Bartók, with lots of scores. The museum is open from 10 am to 6 pm Tuesday to Sunday from March to December (300/150Ft).

National Gallery

The Hungarian National Gallery (Magyar Nemzeti Galéria; Map 4; ☎ 375 7533), in Wings B, C & D of the Royal Palace, I Szent György tér (bus No 16 or Várbusz), is an overwhelmingly large collection and traces the development of Hungarian art from the 10th century to the present day. The largest collections include medieval and Renaissance stonework, Gothic wooden sculptures and panel paintings, late Gothic winged altars, late Renaissance and baroque art. On no account should you miss the restored altar of St John the Baptist from Kisszebes (a town now in Romania) and the 16th-century painted wooden ceiling in the next room.

The museum also has an important collection of Hungarian paintings and sculpture from the 9th and 20th centuries. You won't recognise many names, but keep an eye open for works by the Romantic painters József Borsos, Gyula Benczúr and Mihály Munkácsy and the impressionists Jenő Gyárfás and Pál Merse Szinyei. Personal favourites include the harrowing depictions of war and the dispossessed by László Mednyánszky, the unique portraits by József Rippl-Rónai, the mammoth canvases by Tivadar Csontváry and the paintings of carnivals by the modern artist

Vilmos Aba-Novák. The National Gallery is open from 10 am to 6 pm Tuesday to Sunday from March to November and to 4 pm the rest of the year (300/100Ft).

National Museum

The Hungarian National Museum (Magyar Nemzeti Múzeum; Map 5; ☎ 338 2122), VIII Múzeum körút 14-16 (metro Kálvin tér), is the nation's largest historical collection. Exhibits trace the history of the Carpathian Basin from earliest times, of the Magyar people to 1849 and of Hungary in the 19th and 20th centuries in 16 comprehensive rooms. Look out for the enormous 3rd-century Roman mosaic from Balácapuszta, near Veszprém, at the foot of the central staircase, the crimson silk coronation robe stitched by nuns at Veszprém in 1031, the reconstructed 3rd-century Roman villa from Pannonia, the treasury room with pre-Conquest gold jewellery, a second treasury room with later gold objects (including the 11th-century Monomachus crown), the Turkish tent, the stunning baroque library and Beethoven's Broadwood piano that toured world capitals in 1992.

The Ceremonial Hall (Dísz terem) on the 2nd floor has been reserved for temporary exhibitions in the past. The National Museum is open from 10 am to 6 pm Tuesday to Sunday from mid-March to mid-October and to 5 pm the rest of the year (300/150Ft).

Natural History Museum

The Hungarian Natural History Museum (Magyar Természettudományi Múzeum; Map 6 check; ☎ 333 0655), VIII Ludovika tér 6 (metro Klinikák), the city's newest museum, is not on any of the 12 walks described earlier but is worth a look. It has lots of hands-on interactive displays, the geological park in front of the museum is well designed and there's a new exhibit focusing on the natural resources of the Carpathian Basin and the flora and fauna of Hungarian legends and tales. The museum is open from 10 am to 6 pm Wednesday to Monday from April to September and to 5 pm the rest of the year (240/120Ft; free on Friday afternoon).

Óbuda Museum

The Zsigmond Kun Folk Art Collection (Kun Zsigmond Népművészeti Gyűtemény; Map 2; ☎ 250 1020), part of the Óbuda Museum at III Fő tér 4 (HÉV Árpád híd or bus No 86), displays folk art amassed by a wealthy ethnographer in his 18th-century townhouse. Most of the pottery and ceramics are from his home town, Mezőtúr, near the Tisza River, but there are some rare Moravian and Swabian pieces and Transylvanian furniture and textiles. The attendants are very proud of the collection, so be prepared for some lengthy explanations. And don't ask about the priceless tile stove that a workman knocked over a few years ago unless you want to see a grown woman cry. It's open from 2 to 6 pm Tuesday to Friday and from 10 am to 6 pm at the weekend (120/60Ft).

Opera House

The neo-Renaissance Hungarian State Opera House (Magyar Állami Operaház; Map 5; ☎ 332 8197), VI Andrássy út 22 (metro Opera), offers guided tours at 3 and 4 pm daily. Tickets (900/450Ft) are available from the office on the east side of the building (Hajós utca), and the tour includes a brief musical performance.

Parliament

The colossal Parliament building (Országház; Map 5; ☎ 317 9800 or 268 4904), V Kossuth Lajos tér (metro Kossuth tér), built in 1902, has almost 700 rooms and 18 courtyards. It is a blend of many architectural styles and in sum works very well. The ornate structure was surfaced with a porous form of limestone that does not resist pollution very well; renovations began almost immediately after it opened and will continue until the building crumbles. English-language guided tours (☎ 441 4904 or 441 4415 for information) lasting 45 minutes are available at 10 am and 2 pm Wednesday to Sunday from July to September and at 10 am only the rest of the year (800/500Ft). Buy your tickets at gate No 10 and expect a lot of airport-style security checks.

The Crown of St Stephen

Legend tells us that it was Asztrik, the first abbot of the Benedictine monastery at Pannonhalma in Western Transdanubia, who presented a crown to Stephen as a gift from Pope Sylvester II around the year 1000, thus legitimising the new king's rule and assuring his loyalty to Rome rather than Constantinople. It's a nice (and convenient) story, but has nothing to do with the object temporarily on display in the Parliament building. That two-part crown with its characteristic bent cross, pendants hanging on either side and enamelled plaques of the Apostles probably dates from the 12th century. Regardless, the Crown of St Stephen has become the very symbol of the Hungarian nation.

The crown has disappeared several times over the centuries, only to reappear later. During the 13th-century Mongol invasions, the crown was dropped while being transported to a safe-house, giving the crown its jaunty, skewed look. More recently in 1945 Hungarian fascists fleeing the Soviet army took it to Austria. Eventually the crown fell into the hands of the US Army, which transferred it to Fort Knox in Kentucky. In 1978 the crown was returned to Hungary with great ceremony – and relief. Because legal judgements had always been handed down 'in the name of St Stephen's Crown' it was considered a living symbol and had thus been 'kidnapped'. To mark the millennium of the Hungarian state, the crown was moved to Parliament for one year on 1 January 2000.

The Crown of St Stephen, the single most-important object in the nation's patrimony, is on display in Parliament's central Domed Hall until the end of 2000 when it will probably be moved to the Sándor Palace in the Castle District. Also here are the ceremonial sword, orb, and the oldest object among the coronation regalia, the 10th-century sceptre with a crystal head. The crown and coronation regalia can be visited from 8 am to 6 pm weekdays, to 4 pm Saturday and to 2 pm Sunday. Entry costs 1100/600Ft but is free for native Hungarian speakers.

Postal Museum

The exhibits at the Postal Museum (Postamúzeum; Map 5; ☎ 269 6838), VI Andrássy út 3 (metro Bajcsy-Zsilinszky út) – original 19th-century post offices, old uniforms and coaches, those big brass horns etc – probably won't do much for you. But the museum is housed in the seven-room apartment of a wealthy late-19th-century businessman and is among the best-preserved in the city.

Even the communal staircase and hallway are richly decorated with fantastic murals. The museum is open from 10 am to 6 pm Tuesday to Sunday from April to October and to 4 pm the rest of the year (50/30Ft).

György Ráth Museum

The György Ráth Museum (Map 3; ☎ 342 3916), housed in an incredibly beautiful Art Nouveau residence at VI Városligeti fasor 12 (metro Bajza utca), contains most of the Chinese and Japanese collection of ceramics and porcelain, textiles and sculptures belonging to the Ferenc Hopp Museum of East Asian Art (see earlier listing). To reach it from there walk south on Bajza utca and then west. It is open from 10 am to 6 pm Tuesday to Sunday from April to October and to 4 pm the rest of the year (160/50Ft).

Stamp Museum

Philatelists will want to make a beeline for the Stamp Museum (Bélyegmúzeum; Map 5; ☎ 341 5526), VII Hársfa utca 47 (metro Oktogon or tram No 4 or 6), which contains some 300,000 stamps from around the world and every Hungarian first-day cover issued. It is open from 10 am to 6 pm Tuesday to Sunday from April to October and to 4 pm the rest of the year (50/30Ft).

Statue Park

A truly mind-blowing experience is a visit to Statue Park (Szobor Park; ☎ 227 7446), XXII Szabadkai út, home to three dozen busts, statues and plaques of Lenin, Marx, Béla Kun and 'heroic' workers that have ended up on trash heaps in other former socialist countries. Ogle at the socialist realism and try to imagine that at least four of these monstrous monuments were erected as recently as the late 1980s; many were still in place when I first moved to Budapest in early 1992. You can reach the park on the bus to Érd, which can be boarded from bay No 6 at the little station on the south side of XI Kosztolányi Dezső tér in Buda; get there from Pest on bus No 7 (black number). The park is open from 10 am to dusk daily from March to December and at the weekend only in January and February (250/150Ft; family 400Ft). See also the Web site at www.szoborpark.hu.

Telephony Museum

The Museum of Telephony (Telefónia Múzeum; Map 4; ☎ 201 8188), I Úri utca 49 (bus No 16 or Várbusz), documents the history of the telephone in Hungary since 1881, when the world's first switchboard – still working and the centrepiece of the museum – was set up here. Other exhibits pay tribute to Tivadár Puskás, a Hungarian associate of Thomas Edison, and of the latter's fleeting visit to Budapest in 1891. The museum is open from 10 am to 6 pm Tuesday to Sunday from April to October and to 4 pm the rest of the year (50/30Ft).

Transport Museum

OK, it doesn't sound like a crowd-pleaser, but the Transport Museum (Közlekedési Múzeum; Map 3; ☎ 343 0565) at XIV Városligeti körút 11 in City Park (metro Széchenyi fürdő or trolleybus No 72) is one of the most enjoyable in Budapest and great for children. In an old and a new wing there are scale models of ancient trains (some of which run), classic late 19th-century automobiles and lots of those old wooden bicycles called 'bone-shakers'. There are a few hands-on exhibits and lots of show-and-tell from the attendants. Outside are pieces from the original Danube bridges that were retrieved after the bombings of WWII. The museum is open from 10 am to 5 pm Tuesday to Friday and to 6 pm at the weekend from May to September; it closes an hour earlier the rest of the year (150/50Ft).

Underground Train Museum

The Underground Train Museum (Földalatti Vasúti Múzeum; ☎ 461 6500), in the pedestrian subway beneath V Deák tér (Map 5; metro Deák tér), traces the history of the capital's three underground lines and plans for the future. Much emphasis is put on the little yellow metro – Continental Europe's first underground railway – which opened for the millenary celebrations in 1896 and was completely renovated for the millecentenary 100 years later. The best thing in the tiny museum, which costs a metro ticket to get in, are the two old coaches with curved wooden benches. The track they're sitting on and the platform were actually part of the system until some diversions were made in 1973. The museum is open from 10 am to 6 pm Tuesday to Sunday.

Imre Varga Collection

The Imre Varga Collection (Varga Imre Gyűtemény; Map 2; ☎ 250 0274 or 461 6500) of the Budapest Gallery, III Laktanya utca 7 (HÉV Árpád híd or bus No 86), includes sculptures, statues, medals and drawings by Hungary's foremost sculptors. It is open from 10 am to 6 pm Tuesday to Sunday (200/100Ft).

Vasarely Museum

The Vasarely Museum (Map 2; ☎ 250 1540), housed in the crumbling Zichy Mansion at III Szentlélek tér 6 (HÉV Árpád híd or bus No 86), is devoted to the works of

ings and knights carved into the wall at the Basilica of St Stephen.

Fun at Vörösmarty tér.

udapest's oldest train station, the Nyugati, built in 1877.

katers at Vajdahunyad Castle.

The Ethnography Museum in what was once the Supreme Court.

DAVID GREEDY

Interior of the PestiEst cafe.

VERONICA GARBUTT

Budapest offers something for the high rollers.

DAVID GREEDY

The Thália theatre on Nagymező utca.

VERONICA GARBUTT

Yum stuff at Gerbeaud cafe.

Victory Vasarely, the 'father of op art'. The works, especially ones like *Dirac* and *Tlinko-F*, are excellent and fun to watch as they swell and move around the canvas. On the 1st floor are some of the unusual advertisements Vasarely did for French firms before the war. The museum is open from 10 am to 6 pm Tuesday to Sunday from mid-March to October and to 5 pm the rest of the year (50/20Ft).

Zoo
The large and recently renovated City Zoo (Városi Állatkert; Map 3; ☎ 343 6882), XIV Állatkerti út, has a good collection of animals (big cats, rhinos, hippopotamuses), but some visitors come here just to look at the Secessionist animal houses built in the early 20th century, such as the Elephant House with pachyderm heads in beetle-green Zsolnay ceramic and the Palm House erected by the Eiffel company of Paris. The zoo is open from 9 am to 7 pm daily from May to August and to between 4 and 6 pm the rest of the year, depending on the season (700/500Ft).

ACTIVITIES
Cycling
Parts of Budapest, including City and Népliget Parks, Margaret, Óbudai and Csepel Islands and the Buda Hills, are excellent places for cycling. At present, bike paths in the city total about 100km, including the path along Andrássy út, which has little bicycle traffic signals. There are places to rent bicycles on Margaret Island (see Walking Tour 5) and in City Park. The Best hostel and Charles Tourist Service in Pest (see the Places to Stay chapter) rent bicycles. Bikes can be transported on the HÉV and Cog Railway but not on the metro, buses or trams.

The Friends of the City Cycling Group (☎ 280 0888), V Curia utca 3, publishes the useful four-sheet *Budapesti bringás térkép* (Budapest Map for Bikers; 580Ft). Frigoria publishes a number of useful guides and maps, including *By Bike in Budapest*. One map-guide that takes in the surrounding areas and describes 30 different routes is

Kerékparral Budapest környéken (1200Ft), also published by Frigoria and available in most bookshops.

Horse Riding
In a nation of equestrians, the chances for riding in the capital are surprisingly limited. Riding schools in Budapest include the Budapest Horse Riding Club (Budapesti Lovas Klub; Map 3; ☎ 313 5210), VIII Kerepesi út 7, and Petneházy Lovascentrum (☎ 397 5048), II Feketefej utca 2-4, near Budakeszi. The latter offers beginner's lessons (1200Ft per half-hour), paddock practice (2000Ft per hour), trail riding (2500Ft per hour) and carriage rides. Prices increase by 500Ft at the weekend. The riding school is open from 9 am to noon and 2 pm to 4 pm Tuesday to Sunday.

You can book riding holidays through the Hungarian Equestrian Tourism Association (☎ 317 1644), V Ferenciek tere 4, or Pegazus Tours (Map 5; ☎ 317 1644, fax 267 0171, ✉ pegazus@mail.datanet.hu) almost next door at V Ferenciek tere 5.

Thermal Baths & Swimming
For details, see the special section 'Taking the Waters' earlier in this chapter, which details the bathhouses and swimming pools of the city.

Boating
Kayaking and canoeing on the Danube is not as popular a pursuit as it once was but it's still possible. Most rowing clubs will rent you a boat without prior booking, including the Danubius National Boating Association (☎ 329 3142) at XIII Hajós Alfréd sétány 2 on Margaret Island (bus No 26) and the Technical University Rowing Club (☎ 284 2126) at XX Vízisport utca 44 opposite Csepel Island (HÉV Torontál utca).

Caving
Budapest has a number of caves, two of which are open for walk-through guided tours in Hungarian. Pál-völgy Cave (Map 2; ☎ 325 9505) at II Szépvölgyi út 162 (bus No 65 from Kolosy tér in Óbuda), the

third-largest in Hungary, is noted for its stalactites and bats. Unfortunately, visitors only get to see about 500m of it on half-hour guided tours (250/150Ft), which run every hour from 10 am to 4 pm Tuesday to Sunday.

A more beautiful cave, with stalactites, stalagmites and weird grape-like formations, is the one at Szemlő-hegy (Map 2; ☎ 325 6001), about 1km south-east of Pál-völgy at II Pusztaszeri út 35 (bus No 29 from Kolosy tér). It is open from 10 am to 3 pm weekdays (closed Tuesday) and to 4 pm at the weekend (250/150Ft). A pass to visit both caves costs 350/250Ft.

More adventurous caving possibilities can be booked through the adventure sports department of the Vista Visitor Centre (see Travel Agencies in the Facts for the Visitor chapter) as well as at various hostels (see the Places to Stay chapter), including Diák-sport, Yellow Submarine Lotus and the Backpack Guesthouse. The Best hostel has a 2½-hour excursion to a cave opposite the one at Pál-völgy at 11 am every Tuesday and Thursday for 1900Ft.

Bird-Watching

It may come as a surprise, but Hungary has some of the best bird-watching areas in Europe. Indeed, some 373 of the continent's estimated 395 species have been sighted in Hungary. The country's indigenous populations of great white egrets, spoonbills and red-footed falcons, as well as the endangered imperial eagles, white-tailed eagles, corncrakes, aquatic warblers, saker falcons and great bustards are among the most important in Europe. The arrival of the storks in the Northern Uplands and the North-East in spring is a wonderful sight to behold.

The best areas overall are the Hortobágy region, Lake Fertö, the Vertés Hills, Agg-telek, the Little Balaton (Kis-Balaton) and Lake Tisza, but the Pilis and Buda Hills and even small lakes like the ones at Tata and Feher-tó north of Szeged and the Kiskunság salt lakes attract a wide variety of bird life. Spring and autumn are always good for passage sightings, but the best month overall is May.

DAVID TIPLING

Hungarian stork – delivering a baby?

First of all you should try to get a copy of one of Gerard Gorman books on the birds of Hungary or at least Eastern Europe, which include *Where to Watch Birds in Eastern Europe* and *The Birds of Hungary*.

The Hungarian Ornithological Society (MME; ☎ 395 2605) at XII Költő utca 21 in Budapest may be able to help with general information. A Debrecen-based company called Aquila Nature Tours offers day and week-long bird-watching tours led by ornithologists in and around the Hortobágy. Another group offering tours of between three and nine hours in the Hortobágy, Bükk Hills and at Lake Tisza is the Great Bustard Protection Centre (☎/fax 36-441 020, ✉ imrefater@externet.hu) at the Fauna Hotel in Besenyőtelek, some 30km north-west of Tiszafüred. For bird-watching around Lake Fertő, contact Balázs Molnár (☎ 99-355 718, fax 99-334942) at Fő utca 91 in Fertőrákos.

Tennis & Squash

There are some three dozen tennis clubs in Budapest usually charging between 1000Ft and 1200Ft per hour for use of their courts (clay and/or green set). Among the best are the Városmajor Tennis Academy (☎ 202 5337), XII Városmajor utca 63-69, and the Hungarian Radio Tennis Club (☎ 392 0120), II Vadaskerti utca 1-3.

For squash, contact the Griff Squash & Fitness Club (☎ 206 4065) at XI Bartók Béla út 152 (open from 7 am to midnight daily).

LANGUAGE COURSES

Schools teaching Hungarian to foreigners have proliferated in Budapest recently, but they vary greatly in quality, approach and success rates. You should establish whether your teacher has a degree in the Hungarian language and whether they have ever taught foreigners. You should be following a text or at least a comprehensive series of photocopies produced by your teacher. Remember also that you'll never get anywhere by simply sitting in class and not studying at home or practising with native speakers. Expect to pay 1000Ft per hour in a classroom with six to 12 students, 2000Ft in one with three to six, and 3000Ft to 3800Ft for a private lesson.

Reliable schools in the capital include:

Arany János Language School (☎ 311 8870)
  VI Csengery utca 68
Danubius Language School (☎ 269 1537)
  VI Bajcsy-Zsilinszky köz 1
Hungarian Language School (☎ 351 1191)
  VI Rippl-Rónai utca 4

Places to Stay

Accommodation in Budapest runs the gamut from hostels in converted flats and private rooms to luxury pensions in the Buda Hills and five-star properties charging well over DM500 a night for a double. The low season for hotels runs roughly from mid-October or November to March (not including the Christmas/New Year holidays). The high season is obviously summer, when prices can increase substantially. Almost without exception a hotel room rate includes breakfast. If you're driving, parking at many of the central Pest hotels will be difficult.

Because of the rapidly changing value of the forint, many hotels quote their rates in Deutschmarks – at least until June 2002 when that currency ceases to exist in favour of the euro. In such cases, we have had to follow suit.

PLACES TO STAY – BUDGET
Camping
Buda The largest site in Budapest is ***Római Camping*** *(☎ 368 6260 or 242 1934, fax 250 0426, III Szentendrei út 189, HÉV Rómaifürdő)*, with space for more than 2500 happy (or otherwise) campers in a shady park north of the city. Though the facility is open all year, the 45 cabins are available only from mid-April to mid-October (3600Ft and 6000Ft per double, depending on the category). Pitching a tent costs 715/920/1220Ft per person/tent/caravan. Use of the adjacent swimming pool and strand is included.

Up in the Buda Hills, ***Niche Camping*** *(☎ 200 8346, XII Zugligeti út 101, bus No 158 from Moszkva tér)* at the bottom station of the chairlift charges 2200Ft for two people with a tent to camp on one of the small hillside terraces or 1700Ft for a caravan plus 850Ft extra per person. There's also one on-site caravan at 2400Ft for a double, one bungalow at 3800Ft for two people and two rooms at 3300Ft for a double or 4950Ft for four people. It costs 700Ft a day to park. The site is open all year.

There's also camping at the ***Csillebérc*** youth centre (see Summer Hostels – Buda) costing DM6/7 per person/tent and DM18 for a campervan.

Pest About the most central – but hardly attractive – site you'll find to pitch a tent is ***Haller Camping*** *(Map 6; ☎ 215 5741, fax 218 7909, IX Haller utca 27, metro Nagyvárad or tram No 24)*, in the back garden of a cultural centre in urban Pest. It charges 300/1500/200Ft per person/tent/car and is open from June to mid-September.

Hostels
Hostel beds are available year-round in Budapest, but during the university summer holidays (generally July to 20 August, sometimes stretching into early September) the numbers increase exponentially. During this time, private outfits rent vacant dormitories from the universities and turn them into hostels, which they do their best to fill in order to make a profit. Competition is fierce and there are several rival hostel operators, so you can afford to shop around a bit. Prices average 1300Ft to 2500Ft for dormitory accommodation in rooms with four to 12 beds and 2500/3000Ft for doubles/triples.

Hostel or student cards are not required at any hostels in Budapest, but they'll sometimes get you a discount of up to 10%. Most hostels have laundry facilities (about 700Ft to 1000Ft for a load), breakfast for around 300Ft or so and a few now have Internet access. There's almost always an eat-in kitchen, storage lockers, TV lounge and no curfew.

Though you can go directly to all the hostels mentioned in this section, the Travellers' Youth Hostels-Mellow Mood group, a member of Hostelling International (HI), runs eight different hostels for individual travellers and has an office (☎ 343 0748) at Keleti train station open daily from 7 am to 11 pm (to 10 pm in winter). Staff will make bookings or you can go to their flagship hostel Diáksport (see Year-Round Hostels – Pest); there's no difference in price.

The Vista Visitor Centre (see Travel Agencies in the Facts for the Visitor chapter) is open 24 hours a day and makes hostel bookings. The Express office (Map 5; ☎ 331 7777) responsible for booking hostel beds is at V Szabadság tér 16, a block from the Kossuth Lajos tér (metro Kossuth tér). You can also telephone the hostel the night before; there's generally a receptionist who speaks English.

Year-Round Hostels – Buda A very popular hostel in Buda but quite a way out is the brightly coloured *Backpack Guesthouse (Map 6;* ☎ *385 8946,* @ *backpackguest@ hotmail.com, XI Takács Menyhért utca 33, bus No 7 or 7/a – black number – from Keleti train station or Ferenciek tere),* with 50 beds. A place in a dorm with seven to 11 beds is 1300Ft, one with four or five beds is 1600Ft and a double is 1900Ft per person. There's Internet access, a lovely back garden with a gazebo and a very laid-back clientele who appreciate all the gifts of Mother Nature.

If you've always dreamed of staying in a castle on the Danube, the *Citadella (Map 3;* ☎ *466 5794, fax 386 0505, XI Citadella sétány, bus No 27 from XI Móricz Zsigmond körtér)* almost fits the bill; it's in the fortress on Gellért Hill. In addition to hotel rooms (see Budget Hotels – Buda), it has 24 dorm beds for 1400Ft per person. The dorms are usually booked by groups a week ahead – call in advance for a reservation. Also, this area is something of a tourist trap and you may feel more like a prisoner than a prince or princess; if you're travelling alone try something more central.

In addition to its 180 beds on offer in summer, the *Martos* (see Summer Hostels – Buda) usually has about 20 beds available during the university year.

Year-Round Hostels – Pest Earning high marks for atmosphere, though a tad off the beaten track, is the friendly *Station* guesthouse *(Map 3;* ☎ *221 8864,* @ *station@ mail.matav.hu, XIV Mexikói út 36/b, metro Mexikói út or bus No 7).* It's a party place

with a 24-hour bar, pool table and occasional live entertainment. Someone will pick you up from the station if you call. Accommodation costs 1600/2000/2400Ft, depending on whether you're in a room with eight/four/three or two beds.

There are several much more central places in Pest though none are as welcoming as the Station. The 38-bed *Yellow Submarine Lotus (Map 4;* ☎ *331 9896,* @ *yellowsubmarine@mail.imperware.hu, 3/F, VI Teréz körút 56, metro Nyugati pályaudvar)* is a very central place to stay almost opposite Nyugati train station. It has a lot of facilities (laundry, Internet access, TVs in some rooms etc), but it can be very noisy as it overlooks one of Pest's busiest boulevards. It costs 2500/2000/1800Ft per person in rooms with two/four/up to 10 beds. The nearby *Best* hostel *(Map 5;* ☎ *332 4934,* @ *bestyh@mail.datanet.hu, 1/F, VI Podmaniczky utca 27, metro Nyugati pályaudvar)* has rooms with two to nine beds (total: 30) costing between 1700Ft and 2300Ft per person in large airy rooms, some of which have balconies. It will do your laundry for 700Ft, rent you a bike for 900Ft and organise a caving excursion to the Buda Hills (see Caving under Activities in the Things to See & Do chapter).

The *Caterina* guesthouse *(Map 5;* ☎ *342 0804,* @ *caterina@mail.inext.hu, 3/F, VI Andrássy út 47, metro Oktogon),* run by an affable English-speaking woman, charges 2400/1500Ft per person in a double/dorm room.

The *Museum* youth guesthouse *(Map 5;* ☎ *318 9508,* @ *museumgh@freemail.c3.hu, 1/F, VIII Mikszáth Kálmán tér 4, metro Kálvin tér),* with 22 beds in a run-down building in the centre of town, charges 1800Ft per person in rooms with six to eight beds. It is a little cramped and grungy (in the not-so-cool sense) but certainly its proximity to the nightlife of VIII Krúdy utca and IX Ráday utca is a plus. It has a smaller, more salubrious sister-hostel called *Ananda (Map 3;* ☎ *322 0502,* @ *anandayh@freemail.c3.hu, 2/F, VII Alsó erdősor utca 12, metro Keleti pályaudvar)* north-west of Keleti train station, with accommodation in rooms with four/six or eight beds costing 2000/1800Ft per person.

The *Royal* guesthouse *(Map 3; ☎ 303 8302, @ royalh@freemail.hu, 2/F, VIII Német utca 13, tram No 4 or 6)*, in a large converted flat with a central courtyard, is another hostel where the nightlife is close by and the accommodation (in rooms with four or six beds) is cheap at 1600Ft per person.

The *Diáksport (Map 3; ☎ 340 8585, @ travellers@matavnet.hu, XIII Dózsa György út 152, metro Dózsa György út)* is the main hostel of the Travellers' Youth Hostels-Mellow Mood group and the only one of its properties open all year. Although this 140-bed hostel is impersonal and the most crowded of all (hordes of backpackers), it offers a free minibus transfer from Keleti train station and in summer will take you to any of its other hostels that still have beds available. The Diáksport charges 2500Ft per person in rooms with between six and 12 beds and 2600Ft per person in triples and quads. The singles (3500Ft) and doubles (2700Ft to 3400Ft per person) are almost always full in summer. There's a 24-hour pub here called the Travellers' Bar.

The powder-blue *Marco Polo (Map 5; ☎ 344 5367, fax 344 5368, @ universum hostels@mail.matav.hu, VII Nyár utca 6, metro Blaha Lujza tér)*, the swish flagship of the Universum hostel chain with five branches and the only one of its hotels open year-round, is the place to choose if you want to splurge on a hostel. It is clean, central, with a small restaurant, a stray pool table, an outdoor terrace, Internet access and telephones in the rooms. Even the 12-bed dorm rooms are spotless and 'private', with beds separated by lockers and curtains. Per-person prices in rooms with one/two/three/four/six/12 beds are DM78/52/43/36/32/28, including breakfast.

Summer Hostels – Buda The Universum chain has three summer-time hostels in Buda, all in the vicinity of the Technical University (tram No 18,19, 47 or 49 or bus No 7 or 7/a). The *Landler (Map 6; ☎ 463 3621, fax 275 7046, XI Bartók Béla út 17)*, at the base of Gellért Hill, has rooms with two, three and four beds for between 2900Ft and 2600Ft per person. Rooms with the same number of beds but with private showers at the *Vásárhelyi (Map 6; ☎ 463 4326, fax 275 7046, XI Kruspér utca 2-4)* cost 3500Ft to 3200Ft per person. The *Rózsa (Map 6; ☎ 463 4250, fax 275 7046, XI Bercsényi utca 28-30)* has only doubles with shared shower and toilet for 2900Ft per person.

The Travellers' Youth Hostels-Mellow Mood group (see the Diáksport under Year-Round Hostels – Pest for central contact numbers) has four hostels open to individual travellers on the Buda side of the Danube. *Schönherz (Map 6; XI Irinyi József utca 42, tram No 4 or 6)*, a 22-storey skyscraper not far from the river, has rooms with two, three or four beds with shower costing 3600Ft per person. The nearby *Universitas (Map 6; XI Irinyi József utca 9-11, tram No 4 or 6)* has basic doubles from 2900Ft per person. Despite the faceless, institutional look of the building, the *Summer Hill (Map 6; XI Ménesi út 5, tram No 18, 19, 47 or 49 or bus No 7 or 7/a)* on the way up leafy Gellért Hill is quite comfortable, with suites including shower and toilet from 4500Ft per person. The *Bakfark (Map 3; II Bakfark Bálint utca 1-3, metro Moszkva tér or tram No 4 or 6)* is in a great location just on Margit körút.

The independent *Martos (Map 6; ☎ 463 3651, @ reception@hotel.martos.bme.hu, XI Sztoczek József utca 7, tram No 4 or 6)* is a fun, accessible and large (though somewhat run-down) hostel with 180 beds available in summer and another 20 on offer during the university year (1600Ft per person). It has free Internet access and laundry.

One of Budapest's nicest yet least-known places to stay is the *Csillebérc (☎ 395 6537, @ csill@mail.datanet.hu, XII Konkoly Thege Miklós út 21)*, a hotel and youth centre in the Buda Hills. This huge complex was once a Pioneer camp, and it's in a quiet, wooded location. Dormitory accommodation here is available from May to September only (between 1300Ft and 2000Ft per person), but it also functions as a hotel year-round (see Budget Hotels – Buda for prices).

To reach here take bus No 21 (black number) from Moszkva tér to the end of the line, then bus No 90 to the first stop after the railway tracks (or a 10-minute downhill walk).

Summer Hostels – Pest In summer the István Széchenyi College becomes *Strawberry I (Map 3; ☎ 218 4766, fax 260 9499, IX Ráday utca 43-45, metro Ferenc körút)*, a hostel with 54 doubles (2900Ft per person), triples and quad rooms (2340Ft) and the popular Ráday Klub. The nearby *Strawberry II (Map 3; ☎ 217 3033, fax 260 9499, IX Kinizsi utca 2-6, metro Ferenc körút)* is another modern six-storey student residence, with beds in doubles/quads costing 2900/2600Ft per person. These two places are close to one of the hippest new nightlife areas in the city.

The Travellers' Youth Hostels-Mellow Mood group based at the Diáksport hostel (see Year-Round Hostels – Pest for contact numbers) has three hostels in Pest that operate in July and August only. They are all open 24 hours a day, and you can check in any time, but you must check out by 9 am or pay for another night. An HI card earns a 10% discount. They all accept Visa, MasterCard and American Express credit cards.

The most central of these hostels is the *Bánki (Map 5; VI Podmaniczky utca 8, metro Nyugati pályaudvar)* near Nyugati station, with accommodation in rooms with two/four/eight beds costing 2800/2600/2500Ft per person. Other hostels somewhat farther afield in this chain are *California (Map 3; XIII Angyalföldi út 2, metro Dózsa György út)* and the *Selye (Map 3; IX Üllői út 22, metro Ferenc körút)*, with dormitory accommodation from 2500Ft.

The Universum group's *Apáczai (Map 5; ☎ 267 0311, fax 344 5368, V Papnövelde utca 4-6, metro Ferenciek tere)* is in a great area just off Egyetem tér, which is another neighbourhood absolutely in the thick of things. It has 35 rooms with two, four and six beds costing 2900/2600/2200Ft per person.

The little-known *Orient (Map 3; ☎ 210 0800 ext 198, VIII Tömő utca 35-41, metro Klinikák)*, occupying two floors of a medical university dormitory, is just a few stops

from the centre of town and charges just 1800Ft per person in four-bed dorm room. A bonus is its close proximity to the SOTE disco events (see Discos & Clubs in the Entertainment chapter).

Neither fish nor fowl due to its location and season, the *Sirály (Map 3; ☎ 329 3952, fax 322 2205, XIII Margit-sziget, tram No 4 or 6)* on leafy green Margaret Island has three very basic rooms with 12 beds in each (1400Ft) and large terrace gardens for sitting outdoors by the river. It is open from April or May to October.

Tourist Hostels

The Eravis chain (☎/fax 204 0047, ✉ sales@eravishotels.hu) at XI Bartók Béla út 152 in Buda runs a chain of nine hotels in Budapest that were once low-standard and very cheap tourist hostels but now have been upgraded – a few to as high as three-star level. A handful still have rooms with between two and four beds plus washbasin (shower and toilet in the hall) for students and budget travellers. Some of the Eravis properties are quite far out, but others are fairly central.

Buda The *Junior Griff* hotel *(Map 6; ☎ 203 2398, ✉ griff@eravishotels.hu, XI Bartók Béla út 152, tram No 19 or 49 or red bus No 7)* next to the flagship Griff hotel has triples and quads with sink from as low as 750Ft per person and doubles with shower for 3500Ft. The *Touring (☎ 250 3184, ✉ touring@touring.hu, Pünkösdfürdő utca 38, HÉV Békásmegyer)*, much farther afield in Csillaghegy but close to the Danube and the southern end of Szentendre Island, has the same types of rooms for from 2000Ft and 3900Ft per person.

Pest The *Góliát (Map 3; ☎ 350 1456, ✉ goliat@eravishotels.hu, XIII Kerekes utca 12-20, bus No 4)* in Angyalföld, northeast of the Inner Town and the Lehel market, has accommodation in basic rooms with three or four beds for between 1000Ft and 2300Ft per person. The nearby *Flandria (Map 2; ☎ 350 3181, ✉ flandria@eravishotels.hu, XIII Szegedi út 27, bus No 4)* has doubles, triples and quads from between 1300Ft and 3200Ft per person.

Private Rooms

The private rooms assigned by travel agencies are reasonably good value in Budapest. They generally cost from about 3000/5000Ft per single/double but there's a 30% supplement if you stay less than four nights. To get a room in the centre of town, you may have to try several offices. There are lots of rooms available, and even in July and August you'll be able to find something. You'll probably need to buy an indexed city map to find your room though.

Individuals on the streets outside the train stations and travel agencies may offer you an unofficial private room, but their prices are usually higher than those asked by the agencies, and there is no quality control. They vary considerably and cases of travellers being promised an idyllic room in the centre of town, only to be taken to a dreary, cramped flat in some distant suburb are not unknown. On the other hand, we've received dozens of letters extolling the virtues of the landlords who readers have dealt with directly in this way. You really have to use your own judgement here.

Tourinform does not arrange private accommodation, but will send you to a travel agency such as the ones listed here. Most of these are open only during normal business hours, so if you arrive late or at the weekend, try the 24-hour Vista Visitor Centre (see Travel Agencies in the Facts for the Visitor chapter) or Tribus (Map 5; ☎ 318 5776, ✉ tribus.hotel.service@mail.datanet.hu), V Apáczai Csere János utca 1 near the Budapest Marriott hotel (metro Ferenciek tere), another accommodation office that never shuts its doors. Also, some of the agencies will refer you to their head offices so it's best to try those first. If you're looking for an apartment, Alfonz Minihotel (Map 5; ☎ 352 8006, fax 352 8907) at VII Dob utca 71 (tram No 4 or 6), has affordable ones, mainly in districts VI, VII and VIII though there are a few in Buda Hills and Óbuda as well, from DM40 to DM100 per night. The office is open from 10 am to 7 pm daily.

Near Keleti Train Station The Ibusz office (☎ 342 9572) in Keleti train station, VIII Baross tér 11 (open from 8 am to 6 pm weekdays and to 4 pm Saturday) has private rooms, but there are only a few singles. Express (☎ 342 1772) opposite Ibusz also has private rooms. Another place for booking accommodation you might try is Ger Mi Room Service (mobile ☎ 06-309 347 098) near track No 6 in Keleti station and open from 7 am to 11 pm daily.

Budapest Tourist (Map 3; ☎ 333 7399) at VII Baross tér 3, south-west of Keleti train station at the start of Rákóczi út, also arranges private rooms for an incredibly cheap 1500Ft to 1600Ft per person.

Near Nyugati Train Station Ibusz (Map 5; ☎ 269 0388), next to Nyugati train station at VI Teréz körút 55, arranges private rooms. Also try Cooptourist (☎ 332 7126), VI Nyugati tér 1-2, in the underground concourse below the Skála department store and Nyugati train station. The main Cooptourist office (Map 5; ☎ 332 6387) is at V Kossuth Lajos tér 13-15 across from Parliament (metro Kossuth tér).

Near Erzsébet tér Bus Station The Vista Visitor Centre (see Travel Agencies in the Facts for the Visitor chapter) is only a three-minute walk from the international bus station. Cooptourist (Map 5; ☎ 311 7034), behind St Stephen's Basilica at VI Bajcsy-Zsilinszky út 17, has reasonably priced rooms. Also nearby is Ibusz (☎ 317 0532) at V Vörösmarty tér 6. One of the largest offices in the city offering private rooms is the main Budapest Tourist office (Map 5; ☎ 317 3555) at V Roosevelt tér 5 (open from 8 am to 5.30 pm weekdays).

Near the Hydrofoil Terminal Some of Budapest's least expensive private rooms are available from Ibusz's main office (Map 5; ☎ 317 3500) at V Ferenciek tere 10 (metro Ferenciek tere). It's open from 8 am to 4 pm weekdays, to 1 pm Saturday, and it accepts Visa and MasterCard. The 24-hour Tribus accommodation office (see Private Rooms earlier) is also within walking distance of both the pier and the Erzsébet tér bus station. Charles Tourist Service (Map 5; ☎ 318 0677, ✉ infoserv@elender.hu) near Ferenciek tere at Szabadsajtó utca 6 has rooms and even bicycles for rent. It is open from 9 am to 9 pm daily.

Near Déli Train Station At Déli train station private rooms can be arranged at Budapest Tourist (☎ 355 7167) in the mall in front of the station (open from 9 am to 5 pm weekdays, to 1 pm Saturday) for from 2500Ft per person. The main office of MÁV Tours (☎ 213 0301) in the station concourse books rooms in pensions and hotels and shares an office with the GWK *bureau de change*. It is open from 8 am to 6 pm weekdays, from 9 am to 1 pm Saturday.

Pensions
Budapest has scores of *panziók*, but most of them are in the outskirts of Pest or in the Buda Hills and not very convenient unless you have your own transport (preferably motorised). Pensions are popular with Germans and Austrians who like the homey atmosphere and the better breakfasts. Often pensions can cost as much as a moderate hotel, although there are some worthwhile exceptions.

Buda The *Büro* (Map 3; ☎ 212 2929, fax 212 2928, II Dékán utca 3, metro Moszkva tér), just a block off the north side of Moszkva tér, looks basic from the outside but its 10 rooms (9840/12,300Ft for a single/double with bath) are comfortable and have TVs and telephones.

The friendly *Papillon* (Map 3; ☎ 212 4750, ✉ rozsahegy@mail.matav.hu, II Rózsahegy utca 3/b), one of Buda's best-kept accommodation secrets, has 20 rooms with bath costing 6000Ft to 10,000Ft for singles and 7000Ft to 13,000Ft for doubles, depending on the season, and there's quite a nice little restaurant attached.

The 10-room *Kis Gellért* (Map 3; ☎ 209 4211 or mobile ☎ 06-209 332 236, XI Otthon utca 14, bus No 8 or 112 or tram No 61), named after the 'Little Gellért' hill to the west of the more famous bigger one, has doubles/triples with bath for 7000/12,000Ft in the high season and 5000/7000Ft in the low season.

A comfortable, very friendly place in Óbuda is the small, family-run *San Marco* (Map 2; ☎/fax 388 9997, III San Marco utca 6, tram No 17). It has five spic-and-span rooms on the 2nd floor (three with private bath), a pleasant courtyard out the back and air conditioning. Singles/doubles are 9000/10,000Ft, including breakfast.

Pest The *Dominik* (Map 3; ☎ 343 4419, fax 343 7655, XIV Cházár András utca 3), beside a large church on Thököly út, is just two stops north-east of Keleti train station on bus No 7 (black number). The 36 rooms with shared bath are DM40/50 for a single/double. It also has a five-person apartment for DM100. This friendly pension includes an all-you-can eat breakfast buffet and is a convenient place to stay for a few nights.

Hotels
A one-star hotel room will cost more than a private room, though the management won't mind if you stay only one night.

Buda The 12-room *Citadella* on Gellért Hill (see Year-Round Hostels – Buda) charges 7400Ft for a double with shared bath, 8200Ft for one with shower and 9000Ft for a double with bath.

The *Csillebérc* complex in the Buda Hills (see Summer Hostels – Buda) has a 73-room hotel with basic doubles for DM22 to DM26 and triples for DM30 to DM36, depending on the season. Bungalows for two with private bath are more costly at DM64 (DM52 in the low season).

Several inexpensive places are accessible on the HÉV line to Szentendre from Batthyány tér in Buda. The two-star *Touring* (see Tourist Hotels – Buda) in Csillaghegy has basic singles/doubles/triples for 7000/9500/11,500Ft, including breakfast – good value for small groups.

Pest The old *Park* hotel (Map 3; ☎ 313 1420, fax 313 5619, VIII Baross tér 10, metro Keleti pályaudvar), with 170 rooms directly opposite Keleti train station, charges 5950/7500Ft for a single/double without bath, or 7500/14,000Ft with shower, but it is often full. Even better value is the friendly, 70-room *Medosz* (Map 5; ☎ 353 1700, fax 332 4316, VI Jókai tér 9, metro Oktogon). Singles/doubles/triples with bath are DM56/80/120. A much divier place but very central is the 15-room *Metro* (Map 5; ☎ 329 3830, fax 329 2049, XIII Kádár utca 7, metro Nyugati pályaudvar), with singles/doubles from 9400/11,900Ft.

A real find is the *Radio Inn* apartment hotel (Map 3; ☎ 342 8347, fax 322 8284, VI Benczúr utca 19, metro Bajza utca), with large suites with bath, kitchen and one bed for 7500Ft to 9500Ft, depending on the season, and two beds for 9000Ft to 14,000Ft. A two-room suite costs between 11,960Ft and 19,500Ft.

Somewhat farther afield, the *Flandria* has singles/doubles/triples in the high season for DM44/54/64, including breakfast. In the low season, rooms are about DM10 less. Rates at the enormous, 11-storey *Góliát*, two blocks away from the Flandria, are similar. See Tourist Hotels – Pest for contact details.

PLACES TO STAY – MID-RANGE
Buda

The Eravis chain is a good bet for medium-priced hotels. Again, they're not always so ideally situated, but that's the price you (don't) have to pay for a hotel in Budapest. The group's flagship property, the 108-room three-star *Griff* (Map 6; ☎ 204 0044, **@** griff@erevishotels.hu, XI Bartók Béla út 152, tram No 19 or 49 or red bus No 7), and the 148-room three-star *Ventura* (Map 6; ☎ 208 1232, **@** ventura@eravishotels.hu, XI Fehérvári út 179, tram No 47 or 18) are both in south Buda.

The Griff is easier to get to, with singles/doubles at DM75/91 in the low season and DM108/139 in summer, and it has a great squash club and gym (see Activities in the Things to See & Do chapter). But the Ventura – all faux Art Deco in various shades of blue and purple – is slightly cheaper and a much more fun place to stay. Singles/

doubles here are DM70/87 or DM106/129, depending on the season.

Situated on the top four floors of an office block, the 37-room *Buda Center* hotel (Map 3; ☎ 201 6333, **@** hotelbch@euro web.hu, II Csalogány utca 23, metro Batthyány tér) is not the most attractive place to stay in Buda but the location – halfway between the Danube and Moszkva tér – is good. It's affordable too, especially in low season, with singles from DM60 to DM100 and doubles DM80 to DM120. Its Grand Shanghai restaurant is quite good.

For location *and* price in the Castle District, you can't beat *Kulturinnov* (Map 4; ☎ 355 0122, **@** mka3@mail.matav.hu, I Szentháromság tér 6, bus No 16 or Várbusz), a 16-room hotel in the former Finance Ministry. Chandeliers, artwork and a sprawling marble staircase greet you on entry and the halls often host art exhibitions or concerts. The rooms, though clean and with private baths, are not so nice. Singles/doubles are DM100/130.

Your first choice in the Buda Hills should be the *Panoráma* (☎ 395 6121, fax 395 6245, XII Rege út 21, bus No 21), next to the terminus of the Cog and Children's Railways on Széchenyi-hegy. Built in the 19th century, this three-storey hotel with a strange tower still has an old-world feel to it despite renovations, and has all the mod cons. Singles are DM65 to DM115 and doubles are DM110 to DM150, all with bath. The 54 bungalows for four that ring the swimming pool out the back almost have a country feel to them.

The nearby *Normafa* (☎ 395 6505, fax 395 6504, XII Eötvös út 52-54), is a newer place with 70 rooms and for atmosphere should be a distant second choice to the Panoráma. It does, however, have an indoor swimming pool and sauna. Singles are DM98 to DM125, doubles DM110 to DM139, depending on the season. Also in the hills, the 15-room *Beatrix* pension (☎ 275 0550, **@** beatrix@pronet.hu, II Széher út 3, bus No 29) charges DM70 to DM90 for singles, DM80 to DM100 for doubles. It's an attractive, friendly place in a leafy neighbourhood with a lovely garden.

In Óbuda, the 82-room *Tusculanum* hotel *(Map 2; ☎ 388 7673, ✉ tusculanum@ mail.matav.hu, III Záhony utca 10, HÉV Aquincum)* just off Szentendrei út is packed with groups but singles/doubles/triples are an affordable DM80/95/110.

Pest

A very central medium-priced place in Pest is the 39-room *City Ring* pension *(Map 5; ☎ 340 5450, ✉ ring@taverna.hu, XIII Szent István körút 22, metro Nyugati pályaudvar)*, with singles ranging from DM81 to DM126, doubles from DM122 to DM162, depending on the season. Two other pensions in the same group, charging the same prices, are the *City Mátyás (Map 5; ☎ 338 4711, ✉ matyas@taverna.hu, Március 15 tér 8, metro Ferenciek tere or tram No 2)*, with 53 rooms near Elizabeth Bridge, and the 32-room *City Pilvax (Map 5; ☎ 266 7660, ✉ pilvax@taverna.hu, Pilvax köz 1-3, metro Ferenciek tere)*, just off Váci utca.

The 74-room *Emke (Map 5; ☎ 322 9230, ✉ emke@pannoniahotels.hu, VII Akácfa utca 1-3, metro Blaha Lujza tér)* has singles for DM80 to DM130 and doubles for DM100 to DM150, depending on the season. Nearby, the *Club Ambra* hotel *(Map 5; ☎/fax 321 1533, ✉ mabrahotel@mail .matav.hu, VII Kis Diófa utca 13, metro Opera)* doesn't look like much on the outside, but its 21 air-conditioned suites are spacious and nicely furnished. Singles are DM100 to DM120 and doubles DM150 to DM200, depending on the season.

The 50-room *Thomas* hotel *(Map 3; ☎/fax 218 5505, IX Liliom utca 44, metro Ferenc körút)* – all multinational flags, mirrored frontage and primary colours in the up-and-coming Ferencváros utca is a real bargain compared with its neighbour, the Páva Plaza (see Places to Stay – Luxury), with singles/doubles at DM120/160.

The *Délibáb (Map 3; ☎ 342 9301, VI Délibáb utca 35, metro Hősök tere)*, across from Heroes' Square and City Park, is housed in an old Jewish orphanage and its 34 rooms (all with showers) are 9245/10,900/14,830Ft for singles/doubles/triples. To the south-west is the *Benczúr* hotel *(Map 3; ☎ 342 7970, ✉ hotel@hotel benczur.hu, VI Benczúr utca 35, metro Bajza utca)* a reconditioned, rather soulless place with 93 serviceable rooms costing from DM109 to DM145 for a single and DM129 to DM175 for a double.

Eravis' three-star *Ében (☎ 383 8418, ✉ eben@eravishotels.hu, XIV Nagy Lajos király útja 15-17, metro Örs vezér tér)* is an attractively appointed hotel with cable TV and the odd bit of art on the walls. Singles/ doubles/triples are DM80/106/125, and the Ében's pub-restaurant is one of the better outlets in this category of hotel.

The 131-room *Platánus* hotel *(Map 6; ☎ 333 6505, ✉ platanus@eravishotels.hu, VIII Könyves Kálmán körút 44, metro Népliget)* is moderately priced in the low season (singles/doubles with shower are DM80/100), but room prices jump to DM119/139 in summer. The Platánus has a restaurant with Gypsy music nightly, a pub and a fitness centre with a well-equipped gym, sauna and aerobics room.

Should the untouristed Angyalföld district of northern Pest and the Chinese market attract, choose the 96-room *Oriental* hotel *(Map 2; ☎ 239 2399, ✉ hoteloriental@ euroweb, XIII Fáy utca 61, tram No 14)*, with singles for DM80 to DM120 and doubles for DM100 to DM150. There are some decent Chinese restaurants nearby.

King's hotel *(Map 5; ☎/fax 352 7675, VII Nagy Diófa utca 25-27, metro Blaha Lujza tér)*, Budapest's only kosher hotel, has a restaurant (see Places to Eat – Pest) supervised by the chief rabbi of Budapest and there's even a wig shop in the lobby. Singles/doubles are DM90/120.

PLACES TO STAY – TOP END
Buda

The friendly *Victoria (Map 4; ☎ 457 8080, ✉ victoria@victoria.hu, I Bem rakpart 11, tram No 19 or bus No 86)* has 27 rooms with larger-than-life views of Parliament and the Danube and gets high marks for service and facilities. Singles/doubles are DM144/154 in the low season and DM189/199 in summer – good value for a four-star hotel. In the same area, the *Alba (Map 4; ☎ 375 9244,*

PLACES TO STAY

albahotelbudapest@mail.matav.hu, I Apor Péter utca 3, bus No 86) is a spotless 95-room hotel in a quiet cul-de-sac. Prices for singles/doubles start at DM140/160.

The ***Orion*** *(Map 4; ☎ 356 8583, ✆ orion hot@mail.matav.hu, I Döbrentei utca 13, tram No 18 or 19 or bus No 7 or 7/a)*, hidden away in the Tabán district, is a cosy, 30-room hotel with a relaxed atmosphere and within walking distance of the castle. Most importantly, unlike most three-star hotels in Budapest, it has central air conditioning. Singles/doubles are DM145/185.

If you want to be near the Danube, you can't get any closer than the ***Dunapart*** *(Map 4; ☎ 355 9001, fax 355 3770, I Alsó rakpart, tram No 19 or bus No 86)*, a boat hotel moored just off Szilágyi Dezső tér. Understandably, the 30 rooms are rather cramped, but the teak and brass fittings in the public areas and the pleasant restaurant and back deck make this former Black Sea cruiser worth considering. Singles/doubles in high season are DM140/170.

Pest

The central, 126-room ***Ibis Centrum*** *(Map 5; ☎ 215 8585, fax 215 8787, IX Ráday utca 6, metro Kálvin tér)* may not be the most atmospheric hotel in town, but the price is right for the location, with singles/doubles DM140/160 from April to October and DM115/125 during the rest of the year, and there's an on-site parking garage.

The ***Nemzeti*** *(Map 5; ☎ 477 2000, ✆ nemzeti@pannoniahotels.hu, VIII József körút 4, metro Blaha Lujza tér)*, with a beautifully renovated Art Nouveau exterior and inner courtyard, has 76 rooms (all with shower or bath) with singles/doubles starting at DM159/199.

The 42-room ***Centrál*** hotel *(Map 3; ☎ 321 2000, ✆ central.hotel@mail.datanet.hu, VI Munkácsy Mihály utca 5-7, metro Hősök tere)* is overpriced for what it is, with singles/doubles/triples at DM140/156/171, but many of the rooms have balconies and the location just off Andrássy út is quite grand.

The 139-room ***Liget*** hotel *(Map 3; ☎ 269 5300, ✆ hotel@liget.hu, VI Dózsa György út 106, metro Hősök tere)* faces the won-

derful Museum of Fine Arts, City Park and a very busy road. Singles are DM110 to DM170 and doubles DM158 to DM220, depending on the season. Some 55 of the rooms are air-conditioned, and the hotel rents bicycles to its guests.

PLACES TO STAY – LUXURY
Buda

Budapest's *grande dame* of hotels, the 233-room ***Gellért*** *(Map 3; ☎ 385 2200, ✆ sales@gellert.hu, XI Szent Gellért tér 1, tram No 18, 19, 47 or 49)*, is looking less tattered these days as renovations progress; some rooms are now very attractive. It's a four-star hotel but with loads more personality than most. The thermal baths are free for guests, but with the exception of the terrace restaurant on the Kelenhegyi út side, its other facilities are forgettable. Prices change depending on which way your room faces and what sort of bathroom it has, but singles range from DM200 to DM260, doubles from DM352 to DM410. Lower-level rooms facing the river can be noisy.

The 322-room ***Budapest Hilton*** *(Map 4; ☎ 488 6600, ✆ hiltonhu@hungary.net, I Hess András tér 1, bus No 16 or Várbusz)* on Castle Hill was built carefully in and around a 14th-century church and baroque college (though it still has its detractors). It has great views of the city and the Danube and some good facilities, including a medieval wine cellar serving a good range of Hungarian vintages. Singles are a minimum DM360, doubles from DM410. A more central branch, the 260-room ***Hilton West End City Centre*** *(☎ 238 9000, fax 238 9005, VI Váci út 3, metro Nyugati pályaudvar)* was scheduled to open early in the first year of the new century at the massive new West End City Centre shopping mall (Map 5) near Nyugati station.

A rambling 358-room place, the ***Park Flamenco*** *(Map 6; ☎ 372 2000, ✆ budfla@hungary.net, XI Tas ve₂r utca 7, tram No 19 or 49)* has little to recommend itself (faceless block, smallish rooms) except for its leafy location overlooking a park and Buda's 'Bottomless Lake'. Singles are from DM191 to DM220, doubles DM226 to DM270.

Pest

If you plan to attend a lot of performances at the State Opera House, you won't find any top-class hotel closer than the **K+K Opera** *(Map 5; ☎ 269 0222, ✉ kk.hotel .opera@kkhotel.hu, VI Révay utca 24)*, a 205-room Austrian-owned place with all the amenities you'd expect when paying DM190 to DM240 for a single and DM240 to DM270 for a double.

Though a chain hotel, the 247-room **Radisson Béke** *(Map 5; ☎ 301 1600, ✉ sales@budzh.resas.com, VI Teréz körút 43, metro Nyugati pályaudvar)* has several pluses, including a very central location on the Big Ring Road, a lovely Eclectic building dating from 1914 and great health facilities, including a swimming pool. Standard rooms are DM250 to DM310.

The new 186-room **Páva Plaza** *(Map 3; ☎ 477 7282 or 459 0065, ✉ tomotel@ hotelgloria.hu, IX Tompa utca 30-34, metro Ferenc körút)*, on a newly pedestrianised street in unlikely Ferencváros, counts a number of distinctions. It's the first entirely new hotel built in the capital in almost a decade and has complete state-of-the art technology and philosophy, with ISDN lines to every room, full access for the handicapped, allergen-free rooms and a restaurant serving bio-cuisine. Doubles start at DM239.

The 164-room **Danubius Grand Margitsziget** *(Map 2; ☎ 329 2300, ✉ margotel@ hungary.net, XIII Margit-sziget, bus No 26)*, built in 1873 on Margaret Island, is posh, quiet, has all the mod cons and is connected to the Thermal spa via an underground corridor. Of course it ain't cheap: singles are from DM180 to DM280, doubles DM230 to DM330, depending on the season and the view. The views of this narrow stretch of the Danube and Pest from this hotel are hardly what you would call spectacular, however.

Its sister hotel, the 206-room **Danubius Thermal Margitsziget** *(Map 2; ☎ 329 2300, ✉ margotel@hungary.net, XIII Margit-sziget, bus No 26)*, a 1970s concrete block due north, is not as nice but has all the spa facilities and costs DM10 less.

The **Kempinski Corvinus** *(Map 5; ☎ 429 3777, ✉ hotel@kempinski.hu, V Erzsébet tér 7-8, metro Deák tér)* is Budapest's (and Hungary's) most expensive hotel, with singles/doubles from DM480/ 560 (or DM520/600 for a 'superior' room). Essentially for business travellers on hefty expense accounts, the hotel has European service, American efficiency and Hungarian charm.

LONG-TERM RENTALS
Serviced Apartments

Budapest is chock-a-block with serviced apartments and apartment hotels. On the Buda side, the **Charles Apartment House** *(Map 4; ☎ 212 9169, ✉ charles@mail .matav.hu, I Hegyalja út 23)* has large singles/doubles/triples with tiny kitchens for DM89/104/129 per night and two-room apartments for DM180. Another place in Buda with serviced apartments and studios with garage is **Garzonház** *(Map 3; ☎/fax 224 9061, I Batthyány utca 49)*. The minimum stay here is one week.

If you like your style and plan to stay in Budapest for at least a month, the central **Millennium Court** *(Map 5; ☎ 235 1800, ✉ marriott.budapest@pronet.hu, V Pesti Barnabás utca 4, metro Ferenciek tere)* in Pest has serviced studio apartments measuring about 60 sq metres from DM184 a night and two-bedroom ones from DM268.

Two booking agencies you might try include City Centre Apartments (☎ 351 8229, mobile ☎ 06-309 422 263, ✉ ccity@ mail.datanet.hu), VII Thököly út 16, 1/F, metro Keleti pályaudvar, and PGT Apartments (☎ 302 8250, mobile ☎ 06-309 822 355), V Arany János utca 9, metro Arany János utca.

Finding a Flat

After the changes of 1989, many families in Budapest were given the opportunity to buy – at very low rates – the flats they were renting from the state since the 1950s. As a result, Budapest is full of fully paid-up flats waiting to be let.

Your best source of information is the daily classifieds-only newspaper *Expressz*

(68Ft) available at newsstands everywhere, or the monthly property magazines *Képes Ingatlan* or *Ingatlan Magazin*; check out the latter's Web site at www.ingatlan .veritas.hu. Since all these ads are in Hungarian – and the landlord will almost certainly be monolingual – you'll have to get a native speaker to assist you.

Rental prices vary according to the district but expect to pay at least 2000Ft per sq metre in the leafy, sought-after neighbourhoods in Buda and from 1000Ft per sq metre in Pest, with such exceptions as the diplomatic quarter west of City Park. The most expensive areas are districts II and XII in Buda, the cheapest districts are VIII (Józsefváros) and XIV (Zugló) in Pest.

Anyone looking for an apartment or long-term accommodation should remember to ask the estate agent or landlord about extra-safety locks for doors and windows, even (or perhaps especially) in the leafier residential neighbourhoods. If they say everything is fine, don't believe them.

Places to Eat

FOOD

A lot has been written about Hungarian food – some of it silly, much of it downright false. Yes, it's true that Hungarian cuisine has had many outside influences and that it makes great use of paprika. But even the hottest variety (called *csípős*) of that spice is pretty mild going; a taco with salsa or a chicken vindaloo will taste a lot more 'fiery' to you. Paprika in its many varieties is used predominantly with sour cream or in *rántás*, a heavy roux of pork lard and flour added to cooked vegetables. Most meat dishes are breaded and fried or baked.

Hungary's reputation as a culinary centre dates partly from the last century and partly from the chilly era of communism. In the heady days following the advent of the Dual Monarchy and right up to WWII, food became a passion among well-to-do city folk, and writers and poets sang its praises. This was the 'gilded age' of the famous chefs and confectioners Károly Gundel and József Dobos and the world took note; Hungarian restaurants sprouted up in cities all over the world.

After the war, Hungary's gastronomic reputation lived on – most notably because everything else in the region was so very bad. Hungarian food was, as one observer noted, 'a bright spot in a culinary black hole'. But most of the best chefs, including Gundel himself, had voted with their feet and left the country in the 1950s, and restaurants were put under state control. The reputation and the reality of food in Hungary had diverged.

Although inexpensive by Western standards and served in huge portions, restaurant food in Hungary can still be heavy and, frankly, unhealthy. Meat, sour cream and fat abound and, except in season, *saláta* means a plate of pickled beets, cabbage and peppers. There are a few bright spots, though. Vegetarian restaurants are opening up, and ethnic food – from Middle Eastern and Italian to fast-food Thai and Chinese – is very popular. And even Hungarian food seems to be going through a transformation; a kind of 'New Hungarian' cuisine is all the rage at many middle-level and up-market restaurants.

Meals

On the whole, Hungarians are not big breakfast eaters, preferring a cup of tea or coffee with an unadorned bread roll at the kitchen table or on the way to work. (It is said that Hungarians will 'eat bread with bread'.) Lunch, eaten at 1 pm, is often the main meal and can consist of two or three courses, though this is changing in the cities. Dinner – supper, really – is less substantial when eaten at home, often just sliced meats, cheese and some pickled vegetables.

It is important to note the various sauces and cooking methods unique to Hungarian food. *Pörkölt* (stew) is what almost everyone calls 'goulash' abroad; the addition of sour cream makes the dish, whatever it may contain, *paprikás*. *Gulyás* or *gulyásleves* is a thick-ish soup of beef, usually eaten as a main course. *Halászlé*, fish soup with paprika and one of the spicier dishes around, is also a main dish. Things stuffed (*töltött*) with meat and rice, such as cabbage or peppers, are cooked in rántás, tomato sauce or sour cream. As a savoury dish, *palacsinta* (pancakes) can be prepared in a similar way, but they also appear as a dessert with chocolate and nuts. *Lecsó* is a tasty stewed sauce of peppers, tomatoes and onions served with meat.

Pork is the preferred meat, followed by beef. Chicken and goose legs and turkey breasts – though not much else of the birds – make it onto most menus. Freshwater fish from Lake Balaton (such as the indigenous *fogas*, or pike-perch) and the Tisza River are plentiful, but quite expensive and often overcooked. Lamb and mutton are rarely eaten in Hungary.

A main course usually comes with some sort of starch and a little garnish of pickles.

Vegetables and salads must be ordered separately. A typical menu will have up to 10 pork and beef dishes, a couple of fish ones and usually only one poultry dish.

Vegetarian Food Such a carnivorous country is suspicious of non-meat eaters. 'You don't want meat?' I once heard a waiter snarl at an optimistic vegetarian. 'Then go to Romania!' Outside Budapest's few vegetarian restaurants, you'll have to make do with what's on the regular menu or shop for ingredients in the markets. The selection of fresh vegetables and fruit is not great in the dead of winter, but come spring a cycle of bounty begins: from strawberries and raspberries and cherries through all the stone fruits to apples and pears and nuts.

In restaurants, vegetarians can usually order fried mushroom caps (*gombafejek rántva*), pasta dishes with cheese such as *túrós csusza* and *sztrapacska*, or plain little dumplings (*galuska*). Salad as it's usually known around the world is called *vitamin saláta* here and is usually available when in season; everything else is *savanyúság* (literally 'sourness') or pickled things. When they're boiled, vegetables (*zöldség*) are 'English-style' or *angolos zöldség*. The traditional way of preparing vegetables is *főzelék*, where they're fried or boiled and then mixed into a roux with cream.

Lángos, a deep-fried dough with various toppings, is a cheap, meatless snack sold on the streets. Plain/sour cream/cheese lángos usually cost 70/90/110Ft.

Eating Out

Types of Eateries An *étterem* is a restaurant with a large selection, including international dishes, and is usually the most expensive type of eatery. A *vendéglő* or *kisvendéglő* is smaller and is supposed to serve regional dishes or 'home cooking', but the name is now 'cute' enough for a lot of large places to use it. An *étkezde* is something like a vendéglő but cheaper, smaller and often with counter seating. The overused term *csárda* originally signified a country inn with a rustic atmosphere, Gypsy music and hearty local dishes. Now any place that

strings dry paprikas on the wall is a csárda. Most restaurants offer a good-value set menu (*menü*) of two or three courses at lunch.

A *bisztró* is a much less expensive sit-down place that is usually *önkiszolgáló* (self-service). A *büfé* is cheaper still with a very limited menu. Here you eat while standing at counters.

Most butcher shops (*hentesáru bolt*) have a büfé on the side selling boiled or fried *kolbász* (sausage), *wirsli* (frankfurters), roast chicken, bread and pickles. Point to what you want; the staff will weigh it and hand you a slip of paper with the price. You usually pay at the *pénztar* (cashier) and hand the stamped receipt back to the staff for your food. Food stalls, known as *Laci konyha* ('Larry's kitchen') or *pecsenyesütő*, sell the same sorts of things, as well as fish when they're by lakes or rivers. At these last few places you pay for everything, including a dollop of mustard for your kolbász, and eat with your hands.

Budapest has always been as famous as Vienna for its cafes and cake shops; at the start of the 20th century, the city counted more than 300 cafes. But by the time of the political change in 1989, there were scarcely a dozen left. In recent years, a new breed of cafe has developed – all polished chrome, neon lighting and straight lines. But the coffee is as good as ever. An *eszpresszó* is essentially a coffee house, but it usually sells alcoholic drinks and light snacks; a *kávéház* is what we think of as a cafe, a *kávézó* is more like a coffee bar. A *cukrászda* serves cakes, pastries and ice cream. In recent years, teahouses (*teaház*) have made a big splash in Budapest.

Costs Very roughly, a two-course meal for one person with a glass of wine or beer for between 900Ft and 1100Ft in Budapest is 'cheap', while a 'moderate' meal hovers around 1500Ft (or slightly more). There's a pretty big jump to an 'expensive' meal (from 2500Ft to 3000Ft per head), and 'very expensive' is anything over that – from 5000Ft to as much as 7000Ft per person.

[Continued on page 134]

The Wines of Hungary

DAVID GREEDY

DAVID GREEDY

Previous page: Fine new Hungarian wine. (Photo by David Greedy.)

Top: Wines from the Tokaj region are probably the most famous in Hungary and are readily available in Budapest.

Bottom: An owner of one of the wine cellars in Eger's 'Valley of the Beautiful Women' pours Egri Bikavér (Bull's Blood) from a flute.

Wine has been produced in Hungary for thousands of years, and it remains very important both economically and socially. You'll find it available by the glass or bottle everywhere in Budapest – at *borozó* (wine bars, but very basic affairs by international standards), food stalls, restaurants, supermarkets and 24-hour grocery stores – at very reasonable prices. In summer, spritzers (wine coolers) of red or white wine and mineral water are consumed in large quantities.

Before WWII Hungarian wine was much in demand throughout Europe, but with the advent of socialism and mass production, foreign wine enthusiasts were generally disappointed by the Hungarian product. Most of what wasn't consumed at home went to the Soviet Union where, frankly, they were happy to drink anything. This and state control offered little incentive to upgrade antiquated standards of wine-making and to apply modern methods to traditional grape varieties.

All of that is changing – and fast. Small to medium-sized upscale family-owned wineries such as Tiffán, Bock, Szeremley, Thummerer and others are now producing very good wines indeed. Joint ventures with foreign vintners (eg, GIA in Eger partnered with Italians, the Hungarian-Austrian Gere-Weninger winery in Villány, and Disznókő with French vintners in Tokaj) are helping to reshape the industry, arguably the most exciting and fastest-growing in Hungary.

When choosing wine here, look for the words *minőségi bor* (quality wine) or *különleges minőségű bor* (premium quality wine), Hungary's version of *appellation controlée*. Generally speaking, vintage (*évjárat*) is not as important here as it is in France or Germany, and the quality of a label can sometimes vary widely from bottle to bottle.

On a Hungarian wine label, the first word indicates where the wine comes from while the second word is the grape variety (eg, Villányi Kékfrankos) or the type or brand of wine (eg, Tokaji Aszú, Szekszárdi Bikavér etc). To decipher other words on Hungarian wine labels, see Drinks in the Language section at the back of this book.

With the inclusion of two new ones in 1998 (Zala and Tolna), Hungary now counts 22 wine-growing areas in Transdanubia, the Northern Uplands and on the Great Plain. They range in size from tiny Somló (essentially just one hill) in Western Transdanubia to the vast vineyards of the Kiskunság on the Southern Plain, with its sandy soil nurturing more than a third of all the vines growing in the country. The wines from the latter are mass-produced, however, and inferior to those from other parts of Hungary.

Of course it's all a matter of taste, but the most distinctive red wines come from Villány and Szekszárd in Southern Transdanubia and the best whites are produced around Lake Balaton and in Somló. However, the reds from Eger and sweet whites from Tokaj are much better known abroad.

TOKAJ

The volcanic soil, sunny climate and protective mountain barrier of the Tokaj-Hegyalja region in the Northern Uplands make it ideal for wine-making. Tokaj wines were exported to Poland and Russia in the Middle Ages and reached the peak of their popularity in Western Europe in the 17th and 18th centuries, gaining some illustrious fans along the way. King Louis XIV famously called Tokaj 'the wine of kings and the king of wines', while Voltaire wrote that 'this wine could only be given by the boundlessly good God'.

Tokaj dessert wines are rated according to the number – from three to six – of *puttony* (butts, or baskets for picking the grapes) of sweet Aszú essence added to the base wines. This essence comes from a grape infected with 'noble rot', a mould called *botrytis cinera* that almost turns it into a raisin on the vine. But Tokaj also produces less-sweet wines: dry Szamorodni (an excellent aperitif); sweet Szamorodni, which is not unlike an Italian *vin santo*; Furmint; and, the driest of them all, Hárs-levelű (Linden Leaf). Some Hungarian wine connoisseurs believe Furmint to be potentially the best white wine in the country – Hungary's own Chardonnay. It has a flavour vaguely reminiscent of apples.

For Tokaji Aszú *the* name to look out for is István Szepsy, one of Hungary's most innovative winemakers, who concentrates on the

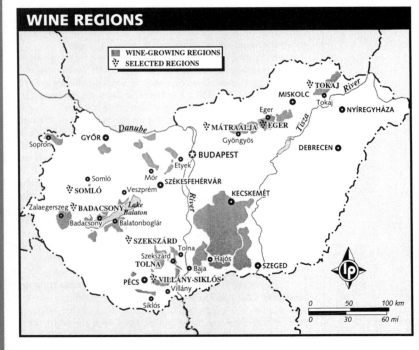

WINE REGIONS

WINE-GROWING REGIONS
SELECTED REGIONS

TOKAJ
MISKOLC
Tokaj
NYÍREGYHÁZA
Eger
Danube
MÁTRAALJA EGER
Gyöngyös
DEBRECEN
GYŐR
Sopron
BUDAPEST
Etyek
Somló
Mór
SZÉKESFEHÉRVÁR
SOMLÓ
Veszprém
KECSKEMÉT
Zalaegerszeg
BADACSONY
Lake Balaton
Badacsony
Balatonboglár
SZEKSZÁRD
Tolna
Szekszárd
Hajós
SZEGED
TOLNA
Baja
PÉCS
VILLÁNY-SIKLÓS
Villány
Siklós

0   50   100 km
0   30   60 mi

upscale six-puttony variety as well as the *Aszúesszencia* itself; his 1995 six-puttony Aszú currently retails for a cool 13,000Ft. Château Pajzos has produced a *natúresszencia*, with such a high concentration of honey-sweet free-run juice that it is almost a syrup. Disznókő produces a six-puttony 1993 Aszú that tastes of apricots (5000Ft to 7000Ft) and a fine sweet Szamorodni. Other good names to watch out for are Oremus and Hétszőlő.

Vintage plays a more important role in Tokaj than elsewhere in Hungary, and it is said that there is only one truly excellent year each decade. The wines produced in 1972, 1988 and 1999 were superb, though 1993 and 1995 were also good years.

EGER

This lovely city flanked by two of the Northern Uplands' most beautiful ranges of hills (the Bükk and the Mátra) is the home of the celebrated Egri Bikavér (Eger Bull's Blood), a wine known the world over. By law, Hungarian winemakers must spell out the blend on the label; the sole exception is Bikavér, though it is usually Kékfrankos (Blaufränkisch) mixed with other reds, sometimes including Kadarka. The only wine-maker's blend of Bikavér known for sure is that of Tibor Gál. His is 50% Kékfrankos and 50% Cabernet and it is excellent.

Eger produces Pinot Noir but it is a far cry from that of Burgundy, its true home. Still, Vilmos Thummerer's 1999 Pinot Noir (6000Ft) promises to be one of the finest produced in Hungary. You'll also find several decent whites in Eger, including Leányka (Little Girl), Olasz-rizling (Italian Riesling) and Hárslevelű from Debrő.

VILLÁNY

Villány is one of Hungary's principal producers of wine, noted especially for its red Oportó, Cabernet Sauvignon, Merlot and Cabernet Franc wines. They are almost always big-bodied Bordeaux-style wines high in tannin. Many are *barrique* wines – those aged in new oak barrels that are then discarded or passed on to other wineries – and remain a favourite of Hungarian yuppies, who like its 'big' flavour and the fact that it is so easy to recognise.

Among the best vintners in Villány is József Bock, whose Cuvée Bar-rique is a smoky, earthy special blend of Kékfrankos (Blaufränkisch), Cabernet and Merlot. Other wines to try include Attila Gere's elegant and complex Cabernet Sauvignon and the austere, tannic Kékoportó (Blue Oporto or Blue Portuguese) and Cabernet Franc produced by Ede Tiffán.

Because of their international exposure, Villány wines tend to be overpriced. At present there is not much competition as the government slaps a 70% duty on all imported wine. But once Hungary joins the European Union and the barriers come down, Villány wine will no doubt be the first to suffer.

THE WINES OF HUNGARY

SZEKSZÁRD

Mild winters and warm, dry summers combined with favourable loess soil help Szekszárd in Southern Transdanubia to produce some of the best red wines in Hungary. They are not like the big-bodied reds of Villány but softer, less complex and easier to drink. And in general they are much better value, with an excellent, premium-quality Szekszárd retailing for 1500Ft to 2000Ft.

The premier grape here is Kadarka, a late-ripening and vulnerable variety that is produced in limited quantities. Franz Schubert is said to have been inspired to write his *Trout Quintet* after a glass or two, and Franz Liszt, a frequent visitor to Szekszárd in the 1840s, preferred to 'drink it until his death' some 40 years later. The best is made by Ferenc Takler (1000Ft).

Kadarka originated in the Balkans and is a traditional ingredient in making Bikavér, a wine that is usually associated with Eger but is also produced in Szekszárd. In fact, many wine aficionados in Hungary prefer the Szekszárd variety of Bull's Blood. The best Merlot and Kékfrankos (1500Ft to 2000Ft) from Szekszárd is produced by Ferenc Vesztergombi, who also makes an excellent Bikavér.

BADACSONY

The Badacsony region is named after the 400m basalt massif that rises like a loaf of bread from the Tapolca Basin along the north-western shore of Lake Balaton. Wine has been produced here for centuries, and the region's Olaszrizling, especially that produced by Huba Szeremley (under 1000Ft), is arguably the best dry white wine for everyday drinking to be had in Hungary.

Olaszrizling, a straw-blond 'Italian Riesling' high in acid that is related to the famous Rhine vintages in name only, is drunk young – in fact, the younger it is, the better.

The area's volcanic soil gives the unique Kéknyelű (Blue Stalk) wine its distinctive mineral taste; it is a blunt, complex and age-worthy tipple wine. Szeremley's version of Kéknyelű (2000Ft) is the only reliably authentic example.

SOMLÓ

The entire region of Somló is a single volcanic dome, and the soil helps to produce wine that is mineral-tasting, almost flinty.

The region can boast two great and indigenous varieties: Hárslevelű and Juhfark (Sheep's Tail); the latter takes its name from the shape of its grape cluster. Firm acids give 'spine' to this wine, and it is best when five years old.

Foremost among the producers of Somló Hárslevelű and Juhfark (under 1000Ft) is Béla Fekete. Another big name in these parts is Imre Györgykovács, whose Olaszrizling (1000Ft to 1500Ft) is a big wine with a taste vaguely reminiscent of burnt almonds.

WINE & FOOD

The pairing of food with wine is as great an obsession in Hungary as it is elsewhere. Everyone agrees that sweets like strudel (*rétes*) go very well indeed with a Tokaji Aszú but what is less appreciated is the wonderful synergy that this wine enjoys with savoury foods like *foie gras*. A bone-dry Olaszrizling from Badacsony is a superb accompaniment to any fish dish, but especially the *fogas* (pike-perch) indigenous to nearby Lake Balaton.

It would be a shame to 'waste' a big wine like a Villány Cabernet on traditional but simple Hungarian dishes like *gulyás* or *pörkölt*; save it for a more complex or sophisticated meat dish. Instead, try Kékfrankos, a wine that never seems to fail. Cheese and cream-based dishes stand up well to late-harvest Furmint, and pork dishes are nice with new Furmint.

For those who would like to learn more about Hungarian wines, the best sources of information are *The Wines and Vines of Hungary* by Stephen Kirkland; the *Wine Guide Hungary*, published annually by the Borkollégium (Wine College) in Budapest; and *Borbarát* (Friends of Wine), a bilingual, fully illustrated quarterly magazine (600Ft) published by Spread Press (✉ borbarat@starkingnet.hu), PO Box 104, 1506 Budapest.

Left: A fine accompaniment to a traditional meal.

Right: Some goulash with your wine, perhaps?

DAVID GREEDY

VERONICA GARBUTT

[Continued from page 128]

Most restaurants are open till midnight, but it's best to arrive by 9 or 10 pm. It is advisable to book tables at medium-priced to expensive restaurants.

DRINKS
Nonalcoholic Drinks
Most international soft drink brands are available in Hungary, but mineral water seems to be the most popular libation for teetotallers in pubs and bars. Fruit juice is usually canned or boxed fruit 'drink' with lots of sugar added.

Hungarians drink a tremendous amount of coffee (*kávé*) – as a single black (*fekete*), a double (*dupla*) or with milk (*tejes kávé*). Most better cafes now serve some variation of cappuccino. Decaffeinated coffee is *koffeinmentes kávé*. Black tea (*tea*, pronounced '**tay**-ah') has never been very popular in Hungary though teahouses seem to be all the rage in Budapest.

Alcoholic Drinks
Wine For details on this most Hungarian of tipples, see the special section in this chapter.

Brandy & Liqueur An alcoholic drink that is as Hungarian as wine is *pálinka*, a strong brandy distilled from a variety of fruits but most commonly from plums or apricots. There are many different types and qualities but the best is Óbarack, the double-distilled 'Old Apricot' and Zwack's Fütyülős Barack.

Hungarian liqueurs are usually unbearably sweet and taste artificial, though the Zwack brand is reliable. Zwack also produces Unicum, a bitter aperitif that has been around since 1790. The Austrian emperor Joseph II christened the liqueur when he tasted it and supposedly exclaimed '*Das ist ein Unikum!*' (This is a unique drink!). It's an acquired taste.

Beer Hungary produces a number of its own beers for national distribution (eg, Dreher and Kőbanyai), though some are usually found only near where they are brewed such as Kanizsai in Nagykanizsa and Szalon in Pécs. Bottled Austrian and German beer like Gösser, Holstein and Zipfer – either imported or brewed in Hungary under licence – are readily available as are Czech imports like Pilsner Urquell, Budweiser and Staropramen.

Beer is available in pubs and shops in half-litre bottles and imported cans, and many licensed pubs and bars now sell their own draught beers in one-half or one-third litre glasses. Locally brewed and imported beer in Hungary is almost always lager, though occasionally you'll find Dreher stout.

PLACES TO EAT – BUDA
Hungarian
The *Fekete Holló* (Black Raven; Map 4; ☎ 356 2367, I Országház utca 10) is the most charming old-style Hungarian eatery of the lot in the Castle District (open 11 am to midnight daily). Not surprisingly this district is full of overpriced, touristy restaurants; if you really want to eat in one of these, try the swish *Alabárdos* (Map 4; ☎ 356 0851, I Országház utca 2) for fish (3500Ft) or *Király* (Map 4; ☎ 212 9891, I Táncsics Mihály utca 25) for game (from 4300Ft).

Aranyszarvas (Golden Stag; Map 4; ☎ 375 6451, I Szarvas tér 1), set in an old 18th-century inn perched above Döbrentei tér, serves – what else? – game dishes and in summer has an lovely outside terrace at the foot of Castle Hill. If your cholesterol is down, the nearby *Tabáni Kakas* (Map 4; ☎ 375 7165, I Attila út 27) will raise it for you – almost everything is cooked in flavour-enhancing goose fat.

Kacsa (Map 3; ☎ 201 9992, II Fő utca 75) is the place for duck, which is what its name means. It's a fairly elegant place with good service and pricey mains (1800Ft to 2900Ft). Open from 6 pm to midnight daily.

Vadrózsa (Map 3; ☎ 326 5817, @ vadrozsa@hungary.com, II Pentelei Molnár út 15), in a beautiful neo-Renaissance villa on Rózsa-domb, remains one the swishest restaurants in Buda and should be one of your first choices if you've got the

Menu Reader

The following is a sample menu as it would appear in many restaurants in Budapest. It's far from complete, but it gives a good idea of what to expect. For more food and ordering words, see the Language section at the back of this book.

Előételek – Appetisers

rántott gombafejek – breaded, fried mushrooms
hortobágyi palacsinta – meat pancakes with paprika sauce
libamáj pástétom – goose-liver paté

Levesek – Soups

gombaleves – mushroom soup
bableves – bean soup
jókai bableves – bean soup with meat
csontleves – consommé
újházi tyúkhúsleves – chicken broth with noodles
meggyleves – cold sour-cherry soup (in summer)

Saláták – Salads

vitamin saláta – seasonal mixed salad
vegyes saláta – mixed salad of pickles
cékla saláta – pickled beetroot
ecetes almapaprika – pickled peppers
paradicsom saláta – tomato salad
uborka saláta – sliced pickled-cucumber salad

Zöldség – Vegetables

gomba – mushrooms
káposzta – cabbage
karfiol – cauliflower
sárgarépa – carrots
spárga – asparagus
spenót – spinach
zöldbab – string (French) beans
zöldborsó – peas

Köretek – Side Dishes

galuska – dumplings
sült hasábburgonya – chips (French fries)
főzelék – Hungarian-style vegetables
rizi-bizi – rice with peas

Készételek – Ready-Made Dishes

gulyás – beef goulash soup
halászlé – spicy fish soup
pörkölt – stew (many types)
csirke paprikás – chicken paprika
töltött paprika/káposzta – stuffed peppers/cabbage

Frissensültek – Dishes Made to Order

hagymás rostélyos – beef sirloin with fried onions
rántott hátszínszelet – breaded, fried rump steak
borjú bécsiszelet – Wiener schnitzel
sült csirkecomb – roast chicken thigh
sült libacomb – roast goose leg
rántott pulykamell – breaded turkey breast
sült libamáj – roast goose liver
sertésborda – pork chop
brassói aprópecsenye – braised pork
cigánypecsenye – roast pork Gypsy-style
csülök – smoked pork knuckle
rántott ponty – fried carp
fogas – Balaton pike-perch

Édességek/Tészták – Desserts

rétes – strudel
somlói galuska – sponge cake with chocolate and whipped cream
gundel palacsinta – flambéed pancake with chocolate and nuts
dobos torta – multilayered chocolate and cream cake with caramelised brown sugar top

Gyümölcs – Fruit

alma – apple
banán – banana
cseresznye – cherries
eper – strawberries
körte – pear
málna – raspberries
meggy – sour cherries
narancs – orange
őszibarack – peach
sárgabarack – apricot
szilva – plum
szőlő – grapes

Cooking Methods

sült or *sütve* – fried
rántva or *rántott* – breaded and fried
párolt – steamed
roston – grilled
főtt or *főve* – boiled
füstölt – smoked
pirított – braised

rich uncle or aunt in tow. It's filled with roses, antiques and soft piano music, and there's no menu – you choose off the cart of raw ingredients and specify the cooking style. Open daily for lunch and dinner to 11 pm. Very expensive.

In the Buda Hills, *Szép Ilona* (☎ 275 1391, II Budakeszi út 1-3) next to Remíz (see International below) is the place to come for heavy, indigenous Hungarian cuisine at very modest prices. More expensive but a perennial favourite with Hungarians and expats alike is *Náncsi Néni (Aunt Nancy;* ☎ 397 2742, II Ördögárok út 80). In autumn and winter go for the game; in summer, it's the seafood and the garden seating that attract.

In Óbuda, try the fish soup at *Új Sípos Halászkert (New Piper Fish Garden; Map 2;* ☎ 388 8745, III Fő tér 6). A popular place for lunch just opposite and next to the town hall is the *Postakocsi (Map 2;* ☎ 250 2286, III Fő tér 2) with an inexpensive *menü*.

Some people think *Kéhli (Map 2;* ☎ 250 4241, III Tanuló Mókus utca 22) in Óbuda has the best traditional Hungarian food. In fact one of Hungary's best-loved writers, the novelist Gyula Krúdy, moonlighted here as a restaurant critic and enjoyed bone marrow on toast (better than it sounds). It's open from 5 pm to midnight weekdays and from noon at the weekend.

My favourite expensive restaurant in this neck of the woods is *Kisbuda Gyöngye (Map 2;* ☎ 368 6402, III Kenyeres utca 34), a cosy place decorated with antiques that manages to create the *fin-de-siècle* atmosphere of Óbuda and serves excellent goose liver dishes (around 1600Ft) and more pedestrian things like *csirke paprikás* (1280Ft). It's open for lunch and dinner till midnight Monday to Saturday.

Garvics (Map 2; ☎ 326 3878, II Ürömi köz 2) remains a favourite with expats – perhaps for its intimate atmosphere, more likely for its volcanic rock cooking *à table*. Mains are 1200Ft to 2900Ft. It's open for dinner till midnight Monday to Saturday.

International
Remíz (☎ 394 1896, II Budakeszi út 5), next to an old tram depot (*remíz*), remains

excellent both for its food (try the grilled dishes, especially the ribs) and prices despite the hype. It has a great atmosphere and is open from 9 am to 1 am daily (the fabulous fresh plum pastries are ready after 9.30 am).

Up in the Buda Hills, *Udvarház (*☎ 388 8780, II Hármashatárhegyi út 2) has the most scenic location in the city, and the outside terrace is a delight in warmer months. The food can be very good. It's open in summer from 11 am to 11 pm Tuesday to Sunday and for dinner only from October to April. Expensive.

French & Belgian
Le Jardin de Paris (Map 4; ☎ 201 0047, II Fő utca 20) is a regular haunt of the staff at the French Institute across the road; it was the first French eatery in the city and remains the favourite of many. Mains are 950Ft to 2500Ft.

If the Belgo chain has got all of London eating mussels, chips with mayonnaise and guzzling *gueuze*, why can't the concept work in Budapest at *Belga (Map 4;* ☎ 201 5082, I Bem rakpart 12). Main courses are 890Ft to 1850Ft.

Greek
One of the better choices for Greek food is *Taverna Ressaikos (Map 4;* ☎ 212 1612, I Apor Péter utca 1), where lunch is 990Ft to 1490Ft and dinner platters range from 1000Ft to 4000Ft.

American
The *Jukebox Diner (Map 3;* ☎ 212 9126, I Bem rakpart 30) is a hip American-style diner below a cardboard-quality housing block adorned with photos of Magyar film stars and serving passable 'continental' food. The terrace offers grand views of Parliament across the Danube. It's open till midnight (to 1 am Friday and Saturday).

Australian
If you really have to have that fix of shark steak and a tinny of Fosters, *Aboriginal* (☎ 388 8749, III Mátyás király út 42) in Óbuda can oblige.

Chinese

Arguably the best Chinese restaurant in the city (and priced accordingly) is the *Hong Kong Pearl Garden* (Map 3; ☎ 212 3131, II Margit körút 2), with dishes for 980Ft to 1400Ft. Try the Peking duck, Sichuan eggplant or the Singapore noodles. If you want to spend half that amount head for *Li Na* (Map 4; ☎ 213 6778, I Fő utca 8), which has a lunch menu for 490Ft.

The *Mongolian Barbecue* (Map 3; ☎ 212 3743, XII Márvány utca 19/a) is another one of those all-you-can-eat pseudo-Asian places found the world over. The big difference here is that for 1490/2590Ft at lunch/dinner you also get to drink as much beer or wine as you like. Open from noon to midnight daily.

Japanese & Korean

Fuji Japán (☎ 325 7111), II Zöldlomb at the corner of Zöldkert, is authentic in every way – from the freshest of fresh sushi (from 450Ft per piece or 2600Ft a mixed plate) and *à table* sukiyaki (3800Ft) to the Japanese-style seating, but it's a long way out at the end of Szépvölgyi út in the Buda Hills.

Seoul House (Map 4; ☎ 201 9607, I Fő utca 8) in Buda serves excellent Korean food from *bulgogi* and *kalbi* grills to *kimchi* and *bibimbop* rice; some would argue that it serves the most authentically Asian dishes in Budapest. Expensive. It is open for lunch and dinner to 11 pm Monday to Saturday.

Indian

Maharaja (Map 2; ☎ 250 7544, III Bécsi út 89-91) in Óbuda specialises in northern Indian dishes (600Ft to 1450Ft) and does takeaway (open noon to 11 pm Tuesday to Sunday).

Nonstop

Hearty Hungarian meals – consider splitting a dish – are served round the clock at *Söröző a Szent Jupáthoz* (Map 3; ☎ 212 2923, II Retek utca 16), a block north of Moszkva tér. Nearby, the *Nagyi Palacsintázója* (Granny's Palacsinta Place; Map 3; ☎ 201 8605, I Hattyú utca 16) serves Hungarian pancakes and *Macbeth* (Map 3; ☎ 224 9004, I Hattyú utca 14) next door serves sandwiches 24 hours a day.

Traditional Cafes

The perfect place for coffee and cake up in the Castle District is the tiny (and crowded) *Ruszwurm* (Map 4; ☎ 375 5284, I Szentháromság utca 7) near Matthias Church. Two more old-style cafes on this side are the atmospheric and service-oriented *Angelika* (Map 3; ☎ 201 4847, I Batthyány tér 5-7) and the untouristy *Déryné* (Map 4; ☎ 212 3824, I Krisztina tér 3).

Modern Cafes

Café Miró (Map 4; ☎ 375 5458, I Úri utca 30) is a favourite in the Castle District, with heavy wrought-iron chairs, light snacks and local artwork on the walls. There's live music here every night (open 9 am to midnight). *Café Gusto* (Map 3; ☎ 316 3970, II Frankel Leó út 12) is a fun little cafe with outside seating along a leafy quiet street loaded with antique shops.

Fast Food & Cheap Eats

As strange as it may seem, the upscale Castle District still has a self-service restaurant – the catering mainstay of both white and blue-collar workers in the old regime – where full meals cost about 400Ft. The *Fortuna Önkiszolgáló* (Map 4; ☎ 375 2401, I Hess András utca 4), above the Fortuna restaurant, is open from 11.30 am to 2.30 pm weekdays.

Gasztró Hús-Hentesáru (Map 3; ☎ 212 4159, II Margit körút 2), opposite the first stop of tram Nos 4 and 6 on the west side of Margaret Bridge, is a butcher shop serving cooked sausages and roast chicken (open from 7 am to 6 pm Monday, 6 am to 7 pm Tuesday to Friday, 6 am to 1 pm Saturday).

Should you be up around Árpád Bridge cooling your heels, say, while waiting for a bus to the Danube Bend or the Pilis Hills, and get hungry, head for *Wraps* (Map 2; ☎ 359 9868, XIII Arbóc utca 6), which serves cheap roll-ups with various fillings (open from 10 am to 8 pm weekdays, from noon Saturday).

Pizza Among the best places in Buda for pizza are *Il Treno (Map 3; ☎ 356 4251, XII Alkotás utca 15)*, with pizzas from 690Ft to 1080Ft and a cheap 750Ft set menu, and *Marcello (Map 6; ☎ 466 6231, XI Bartók Béla út 40)*, popular with students from the nearby university (open from noon to 10 pm and nonsmoking).

Marxim (Map 3; ☎ 316 0231, II Kisrókus utca 23), a short walk from the Mammut shopping mall on Széna tér, is a hang-out for teens who have added a layer of their own graffiti to the communist memorabilia. Okay, we all know Stalin *szuksz*, but it's still a curiosity for those who appreciate the Gulag, Kulák, Lenin and Anarchismo pizzas and the campy Stalinist decor.

Middle Eastern Middle Eastern fast food – especially gyros and kebabs – is now almost as popular as pizza in Budapest. On the Buda side, *Szuper Grill (Map 6; XI Bartók Béla út 52)* has decent gyros as does the nearby *Wikinger (Map 6; ☎ 466 5173, XI Móricz Zsigmond körtér No 4)*, which also does kebabs, falafel and excellent grilled chicken.

Food Markets & Self-Catering

Budapest counts some 20 markets though the lion's share of them are in Pest. The market on II Fény utca (Map 3) is conveniently next to the Mammut shopping mall. Many local people say that the *Kolosy téri sütöde (Map 2; ☎ 368 6571, III Szépvölgyi út 5)*, also called Mozai, is the best takeaway bakery in the city. It's open from 6 am to 8 pm weekdays, to 5 pm Saturday and to 4 pm Sunday. There are 24-hour *nonstop shops* selling everything from cheese and cold cuts to cigarettes and beer all over Buda, including ones at I Attila utca 57 (Map 4), I Alkotás utca 27 (Map 3) and at XI Bartók Béla utca 16 (Map 6).

PLACES TO EAT – PEST
Hungarian

Fatál (Wooden Platter; Map 5; ☎ 266 2607, V Váci utca 67) serves massive Hungarian meals on wooden platters or in iron cauldrons in three rustic rooms daily from 11.30 to 2 am. And don't try to steal the neat wooden box used to deliver the bill; at least a half-dozen people try this every day.

Try to have lunch at the little *Móri Borozó (Map 3; ☎ 349 8390, XIII Pozsonyi út 39)*, a wine bar and restaurant a short walk north of Szent István körút that has arguably the best home-cooked Hungarian food in Budapest. It's cheap (160Ft to 190Ft for soups, 340Ft to 390Ft for *főzelék* and 580Ft to 860Ft for mains) and very popular with local customers, so be prepared to wait for a table. It's open from 10 am to 8 pm weekdays (to 3 pm Friday). Wonderful place.

The *Tüköry (Map 5; ☎ 269 5027, V Hold utca 15)* is a Hungarian pub popular with workers from Magyar Televízió on Szabadság tér. The three-course daily menu – in Hungarian only – is an exceptionally good deal as is the 450Ft one at *Pesti Vendéglő (Map 5; ☎ 266 3227, VI Paulay Ede utca 5)*, a new family-run place conveniently located near the Vista Visitor Centre (see Travel Agencies in the Facts for the Visitor chapter).

Mérleg (Map 5; ☎ 317 5910, V Mérleg utca 6) is how we'd like to see all the old-style Hungarian restaurants go. It's cosy, cheap, welcoming and the food is great (open 10 am to 11 pm Monday to Saturday). A not-dissimilar place is *Kulacs (Map 5; ☎ 322 3611, VII Osvát utca 11)*, which is a popular venue for Hungarian weddings and birthday parties.

For lighter, more up-to-date Hungarian food it's hard to beat the newly renovated *Múzeum* cafe-restaurant *(Map 5; ☎ 338 4221, VIII Múzeum körút 12)*, which is still going strong after more than a century at the same location just up from the National Museum. It has very good fish and duck with fruit (specify this over the usual potatoes and cabbage) and is open from noon to 1 am Monday to Saturday. Expensive. *Club Verne (Map 5; ☎ 318 6274, V Váci utca 60)* is a much cheaper place (especially for the area) serving Hungarian meat with fruit combinations (1100Ft to 1800Ft) amid wacky submarine-meets-the-1970s lounge decor. Open noon to 2 am daily.

One of my favourite 'new' discoveries – I hesitate even to mention it – is *Művész Bohém (Map 5; ☎ 339 8008, XIII Vígszínház utca 5)*, directly behind Gaiety Theatre. With antique furniture, photos of Magyar stars of stage and screen bedecking the walls, and Albert softly tickling the ivories in the background, it's the perfect place for a romantic Hungarian meal. Starters are 350Ft to 700Ft, main courses 900Ft to 1300Ft.

If you're not discouraged by the prospect of spending something like 7000Ft per person for dinner, *Gundel (Map 3; ☎ 321 3550, 🖂 gundel@mail.datanet.hu, XIV Állatkerti út 2)*, next to the zoo and directly behind the Museum of Fine Arts, is the city's fanciest (and most famous) restaurant, with a tradition dating back to 1894. Indeed, it still feeds the Habsburgs when they visit. It's open from noon to 4 pm and 6.30 pm to midnight daily. Very expensive.

Budapest cognoscenti, though, leave this place to the expense-account brigade and head for *Bagolyvár (Owl's Castle; Map 3; ☎ 343 0217, XIV Állatkerti út 2)*, Gundel's little-sister restaurant next door run entirely by women who endeavour to lighten up granny's traditional recipes (open from noon to 10.30 pm daily).

It's a bit of a journey, but if you find yourself in Újpest and want brunch – what Hungarians call 'fork breakfast' – head for the attractive *Külvárosi Kávéház (Map 2; ☎ 379 1568, IV István út 26)*.

International

Café Kör (Map 5; ☎ 311 0053, V Sas utca 17) near St Stephen's Basilica is a great place for a light meal at any time between 10 am and 10 pm Monday to Saturday. Salads, desserts and daily specials (740Ft to 1690Ft) are very good. A great place for breakfast (160Ft to 250Ft), sandwiches (from 200Ft) and salads (around 440Ft) nearby is *Mirákulum (Map 5; ☎ 269 3207, V Hercegprímás utca 19)* open to 1 am weekdays and to 2 am at the weekend.

Gerbeaud's new *Lion Fountain* restaurant *(Map 5; ☎ 429 9021, V Vörösmarty tér 7-8)* next to the Kisgerbeaud takeaway

sparkles and glistens with crystal and china; it's a fabulous place for lunch when the large glass roof lights up the whole restaurant. Try the vegetable-stuffed mushroom caps. It's open 11 am to 11 pm Monday to Saturday, to 3 pm Sunday.

Marquis de Salad (Map 5; ☎ 302 4086, VI Hajós utca 43) is a serious hybrid, with dishes from as far apart as Russia and China, Greece and Azerbaijan (did he say Azerbaijan?). There's lots of quality vegetarian choices too in this beautifully decorated place with a salad bar (650Ft) and cheap lunch menu (750Ft).

If you really want to be in the thick of things hip, head for the upscale *Cosmo (Map 5; ☎ 266 4747, V Kristóf tér 7-8)*, a postmodern, *très artistique* restaurant above the more established *Cyrano* and favourite chichi hang-out of the city's best actors (well, the best paid ones anyway). Very expensive.

The place to secure a table on a warm summer's evening is the lakeside terrace at *Robinson (Map 3; ☎ 343 3776, XIV Városligeti-tó)*, an expensive and touristy but atmospheric eatery in City Park. Starters like sliced goose liver and homemade game paté cost 1200Ft and 1580Ft; mains like *fogas* (Balaton pike-perch), grilled tuna and saddle of venison cost from 2200Ft to 3400Ft.

The food at the *Biarritz* cafe-restaurant *(Map 5; ☎ 311 4413, V Kossuth Lajos tér 18)* ain't nothing to write home about, but the terrace seating is pleasant and the welcome always warm. This is my neighbourhood place.

French

One of the most popular places with expat *français* in Budapest remains *Lou Lou (Map 5; ☎ 312 4505, V Vigyázó Ferenc utca 4)*, a lovely bistro with excellent daily specials; try the *très* garlicky lamb. *La Fontaine (Map 5; ☎ 317 3715, V Mérleg utca 10)* is a Parisian-style brasserie celebrated for its beef and goose liver dishes and *mousse au chocolat*. It's open from 10 am to 11 pm Monday to Saturday.

Chez Daniel (Map 5; ☎ 302 4039, VI Szív utca 32) serves as authentic *cuisine française* as you'll find in Budapest from an overly long and virtually illegible black-board. Service is as cavalier and attitudinal as any you'll find this side of the Right Bank of the Seine. It's open for lunch and dinner to 11 pm Tuesday to Saturday and on Sunday for lunch only to 3 pm. Expensive.

The French-owned ***Bisquine Crêperie*** *(Map 5; ☎ 351 7473, VI Kertész utca 48)* has its flour specially milled for its savoury *galettes* (spinach, egg, cheese, bacon etc; 380Ft to 590Ft) and sweet *crêpes* (chocolate, vanilla, banana, rum etc; 230Ft to 590Ft). Wash it all down with the champagne of ciders, Cidre de Bretagne. It's open from noon to 10 pm weekdays, till midnight at the weekend.

If your taste in French food veers to the east, try ***La Petite France***. *(Map 5; ☎ 302 4078, VI Szobi utca 4)*, an Alsatian (that's *elzászi* in Magyar) restaurant with a large selection of *tartes flambées* (390Ft to 690Ft) near Nyugati train station.

Italian

Arguably the best budget Italian food is from the Italian-owned ***Okay Italia*** chain, with one branch (Map 5; ☎ 349 2991) at XIII Szent István körút 20 and a second one (Map 5; ☎ 332 6960) nearby at V Nyugati tér 6. Pizzas, pastas and Italian main courses range from 800Ft to 1500Ft. The old ***Via Luna*** *(Map 5; ☎ 312 8058, V Nagysándor József utca 1)* has picked up the business clientele of the neighbourhood, but the food (pastas for 650Ft to 890Ft) was better when it was newer. It's open from 11 am to 11 pm weekdays, to 11.30 pm at the weekend. A cheap and cheerful alternative nearby is ***Mastro Geppetto*** *(Map 5; mobile ☎ 06-209 181 039, V Nádor utca 29)* open daily till 11 pm. Pizzas and pasta dishes cost from 750Ft to 1400Ft.

Happy Bank *(Map 5; ☎ none, V Bank utca 3)* is a great place for inexpensive home-made pasta and pizzas (400Ft to 650Ft), but it's only open from 11 am to 9 pm weekdays. The inexpensive ***Sole d'Italia*** *(Map 5; ☎ 337 9638, V Molnár utca 15)* has super-friendly service, good pizzas and pastas and – wait for it – the

cleanest bathrooms around (we check out *everything*). It's open from noon till midnight daily.

Articsóka *(Map 5; ☎ 302 7757, VI Zichy Jenő utca 17)* – more Hungo-Mediterranean than Italian but in that direction – is an impressive arrival, with great decor, an atrium and roof-top terrace (the only one in the city) and a small theatre for post-prandial entertainment. The food (starters 490Ft to 990Ft, pastas 890Ft to 1000Ft), however, is only just above average while the atmosphere wins the trophy.

The less expensive ***Octopus*** *(Map 5; ☎ 331 5920, VI Zichy Jenő utca 47)* takes the reverse tack: minimalist setting, soft music and a few tables, with all the creativity going into the dishes inspired by the cuisines of Italy and southern France.

The most upmarket Italian restaurant in town is still ***Fausto's*** *(Map 5; ☎ 269 6806, VIII Dohány utca 5)* with excellent (though pricey) pasta dishes and daily specials (1700Ft to 3400Ft). There's lots of choices for vegetarians. It's open from noon to 3 pm and 7 pm to midnight. Expensive.

Greek & Middle Eastern

Jorgosz *(Map 5; ☎ 351 7725, VII Csengery utca 24)*, a cellar restaurant just east of Erzsébet körút, has an extensive menu (from 700Ft for mains) but average food. The occasional live bazouki music helps, though. It's open noon till midnight daily and is moderately priced.

Taverna Dionysos *(Map 5; ☎ 318 1222, V Belgrád rakpart 18)* is always crowded but has an excellent view of Gellért Hill; a table on the terrace here should be your first choice in summer. Main courses are 890Ft to 1390Ft. A new place getting some positive reviews is ***Taverna Rembetiko Piraeus*** *(Map 3; ☎ 266 0292, V Fővám tér 2-3)* overlooking a leafy square and the Nagycsarnok (Great Market Hall).

Arguably the most authentic Middle Eastern (in this case, Syrian) place in town and light years from the gyro and falafel places listed under Fast Food & Cheap Eats later in the chapter is ***Al-Amir*** *(Map 5; ☎ 352 1422, VII Király utca 17)*.

Mexican & Latin American

Iguana (Map 5; ☎ 331 4352, Zoltán utca 16) serves decent enough Mexican food (not a difficult task in these parts) but it's hard to say whether the pull is chicken and prawn *fajitas* (1730Ft and 2390Ft), 'whoop ass' enchiladas and burritos (1290Ft and 1490Ft), tortilla chips with salsa (270Ft) or the frenetic, 'we-always-party' atmosphere. It's open daily from 11.30 to 12.30 am. Moderate.

La Bodega (Map 5; ☎ 267 5056, VII Wesselényi utca 35) is a bright and airy place serving Latin American and Spanish specialities (600Ft to 1700Ft). There's Spanish guitar music in the evenings (open noon to 1 am weekdays, from 6 pm at the weekend).

American

The *Tennessee Grill (Map 5; ☎ 338 2429, VIII Rákóczi út 29)* serves decent enough American fare (burgers, steaks, buffalo wings), but the cutesy names of the various 'halls' (Graceland Terem, Nashville Terem, Knox Terem etc) and waiters in plaid flannel shirts despite the weather may put you off your food (burgers from 790Ft, chilli from 605Ft). It's open from 11 am to midnight every day.

For steaks, spare ribs and Caesar salad in upmarket surrounds, the best choice would be *Leroy's Country Pub (Map 3; ☎ 340 3316, XIII Visegrádi utca 50/a)*, a small and very popular place open from noon to 1 am weekdays, till 2 am at the weekend.

Jewish & Kosher

The *Carmel Pince (Map 5; ☎ 322 1834, VII Kazinczy utca 31)* is decidedly not kosher – signs outside proclaim that fact in six living languages – but the Ashkenazic specialities like gefilte fish, matzo-ball soup, cholent and so on are OK and reasonably priced (1200Ft to 2400Ft).

A short distance away is the more atmospheric of Budapest's two kosher restaurants – *Hanna (Map 5; ☎ 342 1072, two entrances: VII Dob utca 35 and VI Kazinczy utca 21)*, housed in an old school behind the Orthodox Synagogue. Be wary

of the hours, though; it opens for lunch only from 11.30 am to 3 pm weekdays and to 2 pm Saturday. *King's (Map 5; ☎ 352 7675, VII Nagy Diófa utca 25-27)*, in King's hotel the next block over, is as soulless a kosher eatery as any though the food is not half bad. It is also a hotel; see the Places to Stay chapter. You'll find a kosher bakery, cake shop (the *Fröhlich*) and delicatessen (the *Kővári*) in this area as well; see Walking Tour 10 in the Things to See & Do chapter for details. The *Rothschild* supermarket chain stocks kosher products (see the Food Markets & Self-Catering section later).

Chinese

Kilenc Sárkány (Nine Dragons; Map 3; ☎ 342 7120, XIV Dózsa György út 56) near City Park is a flashy and relatively authentic Chinese restaurant with dishes from 690Ft to 1200Ft. The smaller and cheaper *Nagy Fal (Great Wall; Map 3; ☎ 343 8895, XIV Ajtósi Dürer sor 1)* almost opposite has dishes for 515Ft to 695Ft. Both are open from 11.30 am to 11 or 11.30 pm. The *Yangtze River (Map 3; ☎ 251 1012, XIV Hungária körút 73)* is convenient to Népstadion and the Station hostel and opens till midnight daily. A decent place closer to the centre is *Xi Hu (West Lake; Map 5; ☎ 337 5697, Nádor utca 5)*, popular with the staff of the nearby Central European University and open from noon to midnight daily.

Japanese & Korean

Sushi An (Map 5; ☎ 317 4239, V Harmincad utca 4) is next to the British embassy and has dishes starting at 800Ft and averaging 1800Ft. Open from noon to 3.30 pm and 5 to 10 pm. *Arigato (Map 5; ☎ 353 3549, VI Teréz körút 23)* has an inexpensive sushi lunch menu (1180Ft) and plenty of other choices but eating alongside a car showroom – a Suzuki one at that – may not be everyone's idea of a Budapest experience. It's open from noon to 11 pm Monday to Saturday.

The *Senara* Korean restaurant *(Map 5; ☎ 269 6549, VII Dohány utca 5)* is a very distant second choice to Seoul House in

Buda. It is open for lunch and dinner to 11 pm daily.

Thai
The standards at ***Chan-Chan*** *(Map 3;* ☎ *318 4266, V Só utca 3)* have fallen considerably over the past few years, but the food does retain something of a Thai/Laotian taste. 'Stick to the spring rolls with peanut sauce,' I've been told by expat residents. Indeed, as Thai a dish as peanut butter is French. Chan-Chan is open from noon to 11 pm daily. Expensive.

A much cheaper alternative is ***Bambusz*** *(Map 5;* ☎ *359 3124, XIII Hollán Ermő utca 3)*, a Thai place by way of Ho Chi Minh City. It's open from noon to 11 pm daily.

Indian
For curries and the like, you might try the flashy ***Bombay Palace*** *(Map 5;* ☎ *332 8363, VI Andrássy út 44)*, with curries and tandoors from 1400Ft, but for the genuine taste of masala dosa, head for ***Lakshmi*** *(Map 5;* ☎ *351 6043, VII Király utca 69)* or ***Govinda*** (see the following Vegetarian section) instead.

Vegetarian
At ***Falafel Faloda*** *(Map 5;* ☎ *267 9567, VI Paulay Ede utca 53)* you pay a fixed price to stuff a piece of pitta bread or fill a plastic container yourself from the great assortment of salad bar options. The bright, modern decor attracts a young crowd (open from 10 am to 8 pm weekdays, to 6 pm Saturday).

Gandhi *(Map 5;* ☎ *269 4944, V Vigyázó Ferenc utca 4)* has a diverse and fresh salad bar where you pay by the weight or choose set menu plates in two sizes: 'moonplate' (660Ft) and 'sunplate' (880Ft). Ugh. Gandhi (nonsmoking) opens from noon till 10.30 pm Monday to Saturday. Even more strictly veg is ***Govinda*** *(Map 5;* ☎ *318 1144, V Belgrád rakpart 18)*, part of the Krishna chain. Why must the children of God make and eat such boring food, though?

Arguably the most upmarket vegetarian (well, near-veg – there are some meat and fish dishes on the menu) is ***Niszrok*** *(Map 3;*

☎ *217 0269, VII Ráday utca 35)*, with main courses for 450Ft to 650Ft. It's open from 11 am to 10 pm Monday to Saturday.

Late Night & Nonstop
The ***Szendvics Bár Center*** *(Map 5;* ☎ *302 5242, VI Teréz körút 46)* has Thai-style dishes and sandwiches: cheap, greasy, and filling for 305Ft to 700Ft. It's open from 9 to 3 am daily and is nonsmoking. The ***Soho Palacsintabár*** *(Map 5;* ☎ *none, VI Nagymező utca 21)* can provide you with a fix of Hungarian pancakes around the clock.

Grill 99 *(Map 5;* ☎ *352 1150, VIII Dohány utca 52)* is a grotty but very popular place for a late, late meal or early, early post-club breakfast. Very cheap. ***Tulipán*** *(Map 5;* ☎ *269 5043, V Nádor utca 34)* is another nonstop also popular with after-club crowds and taxi drivers, which may be a good thing – or a bad thing.

Traditional Cafes
The most famous of the famous traditional cafes in Budapest is ***Gerbeaud*** *(Map 5;* ☎ *429 9000, V Vörösmarty tér 7)*, a fashionable meeting place for the city's elite since 1870, on the west side of Budapest's busiest square. It's still not the place for fast service, a problem even the new German management can't seem to solve.

Művész *(Map 5;* ☎ *322 4606, VI Andrássy út 29)*, almost opposite the Opera House, is a more interesting place to people-watch than Gerbeaud and has a better selection of cakes (try the apple *torta*) at lower prices. It is open from 9 am to midnight daily.

New York Café *(Map 5;* ☎ *322 3849, VII Erzsébet körút 9-11)*, has been a Budapest institution since 1895 (and for other reasons since 1956 when the scaffolding surrounding it first went up). The *belle époque* decor and memories of the cafe's literary associations are fading – but not yet extinguished (open 10 am to midnight daily).

Lukács *(Map 5;* ☎ *302 8747, VI Andrássy út 70)* has reopened its doors after a major renovation and is again dressed up in the finest of divine decadence – all mirrors and gold and soft piano music (with a non-smoking section too). It is open from 9 or 10 am to 8 pm daily.

Although the surrounds lack atmosphere, the *Bécsi Kávéház* (Vienna Café; Map 5; ☎ 327 6333, V Apáczai Csere János utca 12-14) at the Inter-Continental hotel has some of the best cakes in town. For the best cherry strudel in the capital head for *Szalai* (Map 5; ☎ 269 3210, V Balassi Bálint utca 7), a humble little cake shop open from 9 am to 7 pm Wednesday to Sunday.

Modern Cafes

Coquan's Café (Map 5; ☎ 266 9936, V Nádor utca 5) has virtually revolutionised coffee drinking in Budapest by importing (and supplying to others) the best beans from around the world. It's open from 7.30 am to 7.30 pm weekdays, 9 am to 6 pm Saturday and 11 am to 5 pm Sunday. There's another popular branch at VII Ráday utca 15 (Map 3; ☎ 215 2444).

Leafy VI Liszt Ferenc tér is surrounded by hip cafes generally open from 10 or 11 am to 1 or 2 am. If they're not playing music, you can catch strains from musicians practising in the Music Academy at the southern end of the square. Artsy *Café Vian* (Map 5; ☎ 342 8991) at No 9 is the royal court of Budapest 'it' girls and guys though the new *PestiEst* (Map 5; ☎ 344 4381) at No 5 should make an impact with its overall Magyar-ness (read crap service), funky house music and cutting-edge interior. It's a good place to try Unicum (380Ft). *Incognito* (Map 5; ☎ 342 1471) at No 3 was the first on the square and is still going strong; seek out the sofa in back and sip an Irish coffee (open 9.30 am to midnight weekdays and from 11.30 am at the weekend).

Komédiás (Map 5; ☎ 302 0901, VI Nagymező utca 26) has a key location in the reviving theatre district and all the charm of 1920s Paris that a pavement cafe needs. It's an all-ages kind of place and opens from 8 am to midnight daily. Another big favourite is the nearby *Két Szerecsen* (Two Moors; Map 5; ☎ 343 1984, VI Nagymező utca 14) with plum-coloured walls and a

Med-ish menu. Breakfast (from 460Ft) is available from 8 to 11 am.

Café Eklektika (Map 5; ☎ 266 3054, V Semmelweis utca 21) has some of the most comfortable chairs in Budapest and a pleasant clutter of bric-a-brac, with artwork on the walls and low lighting. It's a great place for writing postcards or an early evening rendezvous (open 10 am to midnight). The windows of the *Replay Café* (Map 5; ☎ 266 8333, V Fehér Hajó utca 12-14) – Replay as in the designer jeans – open so wide that inside always feels like outside.

El Greco (Map 3; ☎ 217 6986, IX Ráday utca 11-13) is a wonderful Greek-cum-Spanish (as the name would imply) cafe in the heart of Budapest's liveliest student nightlife district. It's open from 10 am (from noon on Sunday) till 1 am. The *Budapest Blue Café* (Map 5; mobile ☎ 06-309 228 553, VIII Somogyi Béla utca 8) is a bright and friendly oasis in the less-than-salubrious swamp that is the greater Blaha Lujza tér area. It's open till 1 am daily.

Teahouses

1000 Tea (Map 5; ☎ 337 8217, V Váci utca 65) in a small courtyard is the place to go if you want to sip a soothing blend made by tea-serious staff and lounge on pillows in the Japanese-style tearoom (open noon to 9 pm weekdays, from 11 am Saturday). There are several other teahouses around (usually nonsmoking), including the funky *Teaház a Vörös Oroszlánhoz* (Teahouse at the Red Lion; Map 5; ☎ 269 0579, VI Jókai tér 8) north of Liszt Ferenc tér, but my absolute favourite is *CD Fű* (Map 5; ☎ 317 5094, V Szerb utca 15) a popular studenty place in a big old cellar whose name means 'CD Grass' (not the kind you mow). It's open from 11 am to 11 pm weekdays and to 2 pm at the weekend.

Fast Food & Cheap Eats

Fast-food places like McDonald's, Pizza Hut, KFC, Dunkin' Donuts, Wendy's and the local Paprika abound in Pest – Oktogon is full of them, including a McDonald's (Map 5) at Teréz körút 19 open almost 24 hours – but old-style self-service restaurants are few and far between. One of just a few left on this side is the *self-service restaurant* (Map 5) at V Arany János utca 5 open from 11.15 am to 3 pm weekdays only. A bit more upscale is the self-service upstairs at the *Pick Ház* (Map 5) beside the metro entrance on Kossuth Lajos tér (open from 9 am to 6 pm weekdays, from 8 am to 1 pm Saturday). One of the cleanest, most upbeat in this genre is the *Centrál Önkiszolgáló* (Map 5; ☎ 267 4955, VIII Krúdy utca) open from 11 am to 9 pm weekdays, to 8 pm Saturday and Sunday. Also excellent value is the *cafeteria* at the Central European University (Map 5; ☎ 327 3000, V Nádor utca 9) with set meals for around 600Ft and open to the public from 11.30 am to 4 pm weekdays.

Even better value are the wonderful little restaurants called *étkezde* – canteens not unlike British 'cafs' that serve simple dishes. A meal easily costs under 800Ft. Among my favourites is *Kisharang* (Map 5; ☎ 269 3861, V Október 6 utca 17), open from 11 am to 9 pm weekdays, from 11.30 am to 4 pm at the weekend; *Kádár* (Map 5; ☎ 321 3622, X Klauzál tér) in the former Jewish district (open 11.30 am to 3.30 pm weekdays); and *Frici Papa Kifőzdéje* (Papa Frank's Canteen; Map 5; ☎ 351 0197, VI Király utca 55), which is larger than most and opens from 11 am to 9 pm Monday to Saturday. Mains are under 400Ft.

An excellent place for hearty, person-sized sandwiches is the *Marie Kristensen Sandwich Bar* (Map 3; ☎ 218 1673, IX Ráday utca 7). For bite-sized open-face and very cheap sandwiches *Durcin* (Map 5; V Október 6 utca 13-15) is the place to go. It is open from 8 am to 6 pm weekdays, from 9 am to 1 pm Saturday. A branch of Durcin (Map 5; ☎ 266 1144) is at VI Bajcsy-Zsilinszky út 7 near Deák tér.

Pizza There are several pizza places on Nyugati tér, including *Don Pepe* (Map 5; ☎ 322 2954) at No 8, open till the very wee hours. The upbeat *Pink Cadillac* (Map 3; ☎ 216 1412, IX Ráday utca 22), more of a 1950s diner than a pizzeria, still reigns supreme after all this time; not just vegetarians order the spinach and garlic pizza.

Pompeii (Map 5; ☎ 351 8738, VII Liszt Ferenc tér 3) is convenient for a bit of blotter in the heart of publand. Well off the beaten track, *Don Roberto* (Map 2; ☎ 350 8243, XIII, Róbert Károly körút 40) is something of a Pest secret, with great pizza. It's open from 11 am to 11 pm and is smoke-free.

Middle Eastern The *Semiramis* (Map 5; ☎ 311 7627, V Alkotmány utca 20) is the old Middle Eastern stand-by and still has some of the most authentic fare around. Seating is on two levels and it is open from noon to 11 pm Monday to Saturday.

A very inexpensive place for gyros (and reminiscent of a Tom Robbins novel) is the *Török-Kinai Büfé* (Turkish-Chinese Buffet; Map 5; ☎ 269 3128, XIII Szent István körút 13). Husband (the Turk) beats wife (the Chinese) in the culinary contest here, however (open from 11.30 am to 10 pm daily).

Három Testvér (Three Brothers; Map 5; ☎ 329 2951, XIII Szent István körút 22) is great anytime but especially for a late-night snack. There's a branch (☎ 352 1447) at VII Erzsébet körút 35 and another one (☎ 369 1886) at IV Árpád út 67 at the end of the blue metro line. *Gül Baba* (Map 5; ☎ 342 2377, VII Erzsébet körút 17) is a hybrid takeaway/sit-down place with gyros and one-plate meals (500Ft) near Oktogon (open 10 am to 4 am).

Shiraz (Map 3; ☎ 212 0881, IX Mátyás utca 22) is a 'Persian' restaurant with belly dancers, hookahs loaded with apple tobacco, carpets (natch) – the works to lure in the punters. But if you get hungry while waiting for the waiters to arrive, go around the corner to IX Ráday utca 21, where the owners run a *gyros takeaway* window from noon to midnight daily.

Chinese Chinese fast-food places (*gyors kinai büfé*) are all the rage in Budapest these days and you'll find them everywhere. Central ones in Pest include *Arany Folyó* (Gold River; Map 5; ☎ 214 4024, VII Akácfa utca 9) and *Nagy Fal* (Great Wall; Map 5; ☎ 353 4021, V Nádor utca 20). Both have dishes from about 335Ft and stay open till 11 pm daily.

Food Markets & Self-Catering

The *Nagycsarnok (Great Market Hall; Map 3; IX Fővám tér)* is the largest market in the city but has become something of a tourist trap since it was renovated for the millecentenary in 1996. There are some good food stalls on the upper level serving everything from Chinese spring rolls to German sausages, though, and the best and cheapest wine spritzers at a little stall hidden among the tablecloth vendors.

Among other colourful *food markets* in Pest are the ones at VIII Rákóczi tér 34 (Map 3) and at V Hold utca 11 (Map 5) near V Szabadság tér (with a stall selling tasty, inexpensive croissant sandwiches). They are open from 6 or 6.30 am to 6 pm weekdays and till 2 pm Saturday – though Monday is always very quiet.

There are large supermarkets everywhere in Pest, including the *Julius Meinl* on VIII Blaha Lujza tér (Map 5) and at V Ferenciek tere 1 and *Kaiser's* at VI Nyugati tér 1-2 (Map 5) opposite Nyugati train station. *Rothschild* is another large chain with outlets throughout the city including one at XIII Szent István körút 4 (Map 5) and at VI Teréz körút 19. Rothschild has a fair selection of kosher products. Hypermarket chains are a fairly recent development; the UK supermarket chain, *Tesco*, for example, has an enormous outlet on XIV Pillangó utca. Think of the convenience.

The *Nagy Tamás* cheese shop *(Map 5; V Gerlóczy utca 3)* sells over 200 varieties of Hungarian and imported cheeses; ask for the Hungarian goat's cheese made by an eccentric theatre critic. See the Shopping chapter for the best wine shops.

If you've got the urge for something sweet, head for the tiny bakery called *Mézes Kuckó (Honey Nook; Map 5; XIII Jászai Mari tér 4/a)*; its nut and honey cookies are to die for (open from 9 am to 6 pm weekdays, to 1 pm Saturday).

For ice cream, no-one does it better than little *Butterfly* (Map 5) at Teréz körút 20 (*not* the pastry shop next door called Vajassütemények boltja). It's open from 10 am to 6 pm weekdays, to 2 pm Saturday (45Ft per scoop). *Spaghetti Ice (Map 5; VI Andrássy út 14)*, which sells a pasta-like gelato, also has its fans (open 10 am to 11 pm daily).

Nonstop shops in Pest include those at Nyugati train station (next to track No 13; Map 5) and VIII Baross tér 3 near Keleti station (Map 3). You can also find them at VII Rumbach Sebestyén utca 3 (Map 5) and V Apáczai Csere János utca 5 (Map 5) near the Marriott hotel.

PLACES TO EAT

Entertainment

For a city of its size, Budapest has a huge choice of things to do and places to go after dark – from opera and folk dancing to jazz and meat-market clubs. It's almost never difficult getting tickets or getting in; the hard part is deciding what to do.

LISTINGS

Your best sources of general information in the city are the weekly freebies *PestiEst* (in Hungarian but easy to follow) and the English-language *Scene*. The free bilingual publications *Programme in Ungarn/in Hungary* and its scaled-down version for the capital, *Budapest Panorama*. The most thorough listings magazine – from clubs and films to art exhibits and classical music – is the weekly *Pesti Músor* (Budapest Program), also called *PM Magazin*, available at newsstands every Thursday (59Ft). The free *Koncert Kalendárium*, published once a month, lists concerts, opera and dance.

BOOKING AGENCIES

For concerts of all types try the Vigadó Ticket Office (Map 5; ☎ 327 4322), V Vörösmarty tér 1 (metro Vörösmarty tér). It's open from 9 am to 7 pm on weekdays. You can also buy tickets to the philharmonic and other classical concerts at the Nemzeti Filharmónia jegypénztára (Map 5; ☎ 318 0281) at V Mérleg utca 10 (open from 10 am to 6 pm weekdays).

The busiest theatrical ticket agency is the Színházak Központi Jegyiroda (Central Ticket Office; Map 5; ☎ 312 0000), VI Andrássy út 18 (metro Opera), which is open from 10 am to 6 pm weekdays (to 5 pm Friday). It has tickets to numerous theatres and events, although the best are gone a couple of days in advance. If this office is closed as reports suggested at press time, contact the Vista Visitor Centre (see Travel Agencies in the Facts for the Visitor chapter). For opera or ballet tickets, go to the office (☎ 353 0170) two doors down at VI Andrássy út 22. It is open from 11 am to 5 pm weekdays (from 10 am Monday).

Music Mix (Map 5; ☎ 338 2237), V Váci utca 33 (metro Ferenciek tere), has tickets to special events such as rock spectaculars, appearances by foreign superstars etc. It's open from 10 am to 6 pm weekdays and to 1 pm Saturday. Ticket Express (Map 5; ☎ 353 0692), VI Jókai utca 40, is another option with extended hours; it's open from 9.30 am to 9.30 pm daily. The Vista Visitor Centre (see Travel Agencies in Facts for the Visitor) also has a comprehensive booking service, offering tickets to everything from concerts and English-language theatre to sporting events.

PUBS & BARS

Pest is loaded with pubs and bars and there are enough to satisfy all tastes. Inevitably the capital has a number of 'Irish' pubs on offer; if you're into these McDonald's of drinking venues head for *Becketts (Map 5; ☎ 311 1033, V Bajcsy-Zsilinszky út 72)* or the *Irish Cat (Map 5; ☎ 266 4085, V Múzeum körút 41)*, which has Guinness and Kilkenny on tap. The *Columbus (Map 5; ☎ 266 9013)* – and we thought he was Italian – is yet another Irish pub, this time on a boat in the Danube opposite the Inter-Continental hotel.

Cactus Juice (Map 5; ☎ 302 2116, VI Jókai tér 5) is supposed to be 'American rustic' but it's really Wild West out of Central Casting. The Juice is a good place to sip and sup with no distractions. Quite the opposite is *Portside (Map 5; ☎ 351 8405, VII Dohány utca 7)*, which is open till 2 am weekdays, to 4 am at the weekend. This place absolutely packs in a yuppie mingle-and-meat crowd nightly. The *Garage Café (Map 5; ☎ 302 6473, V Arany János utca 9)* is a popular lunch place by day and a watering hole by night with a good wine selection. It's open daily till midnight.

The *Janis Pub (Map 5; ☎ 266 2619, V Királyi Pál utca 8)* near Ferenciek tere, a shrine to the late, great Janis 'Pearl' Joplin, is usually a stop for a quick few on the way to somewhere else, but some people linger here for the choice of imported beer. *Picasso Point (Map 5; ☎ 269 5544, VI Hajós utca 31)* shocked a fair few when it closed and re-emerged *sans* cellar disco and Hungarian pre-teens not too long ago. It's now a laid-back place for a drink and great for meeting people.

Paris, Texas (Map 3; ☎ 218 0570, IX Ráday utca 22) has a coffee-house feel to it and pool tables downstairs; the crowds arrive later in the evenings. *Darshan Udvar (Map 5; ☎ 266 5541, VIII Krúdy utca 7)* is a cavernous new complex of two bars, a restaurant with lots of vegetarian choices (mains 600Ft to 750Ft) and a courtyard terrace cafe with decor that combines cutting-edge Euro-techno with Seattle grunge and Eastern flair. It's open from 10 am to 1 am Sunday to Thursday and to 3 am at the weekend. The much smaller *Darshan Café (Map 5; ☎ 266 7797, VIII Krúdy utca 8)* opposite is open from 10 am to midnight Monday to Saturday and from 4 pm on Sunday.

The *Ball 'n' Bull (Map 5; ☎ 267 0286, VIII Rákóczi út 29)* is in the same building as the Tennessee Grill (see Places to Eat). It's the place where expats (especially American) come to watch sporting events on big-screen TVs, eat American pub grub (nonsense like Hank Aaron chilli for 990Ft, Michael Jordan buffalo wings for 590Ft and 900Ft) and crush beer cans on their foreheads (open noon to 1 am daily).

You won't meet many bikers or smell much engine oil at the *Harley Café (Map 5; ☎ 322 0687, VII Dohány utca 22-24)*, but it just has to be the longest bar in Budapest. It's open till 4 am Wednesday to Saturday.

In Buda, *Oscar's Café & Pub (Map 3; ☎ 212 8017, I Ostrom utca 12)*, with film memorabilia on the wood-panelled walls and leather director's chairs on the floor, serve powerful minty cocktails perfect on a warm summer night; I'd tell you the name of them if I could remember (open from 5 pm to 2 am weekdays, till 4 am at the weekend).

If you're in the mood for something simpler, the *Erzsébet-híd Eszpresszó (Map 4;*

☎ none, I Döbrentei tér 1) is a wonderful old dive with a large terrace and view of the Danube. The *Kisrabló (Map 6; ☎ 209 1588, XI Zenta utca 3)* is an evergreen student pub close to many of the hostels mentioned in the Places to Stay chapter.

In summer the *Ráckert (Map 4; ☎ 356 1322, I Hadnagy utca 8-10)*, in a walled-in garden next to the Rác baths, is the place to sip a cold *korsó* and listen to live music. The *Rolling Rock* pub *(Map 2; ☎ 368 2298, III Bécsi út 53-55)* is where the trendies of Óbuda (not necessarily a contradiction in terms) gather for some of that peculiar American brew in the little green bottles. *Poco Loco (Map 3; ☎ 326 1357, II Frankel Leó út 51)* is a seamier place (and more interesting for that), with live music some nights (open till 2 am daily). There's a flashier branch on the Pest side called *Poco Loco Tropical (Map 5; ☎ 269 3188, VI Lovag utca 3)*.

DISCOS & CLUBS

The top disco in Budapest's ever-changing scene is *Dokk Backstage (Map 2; ☎ 457 1023, II Óbudai hajógyári-sziget 122)*, a club in a converted warehouse on an island in the Danube that attracts the city's *szép ember* (beautiful people). It's at its hottest, grindingest best on a Saturday night. Take a taxi, or it's an easy walk from the HÉV. A hipper, more central place is *Undergrass (Map 5; ☎ 322 0830, VI Liszt Ferenc tér 10)* open from 10 pm to 4 am Tuesday to Saturday.

E-Play Cyber Club (Map 5; ☎ 302 2849, VI Teréz körút 55), in the south wing of Nyugati train station next to McDonald's, has house music – exclusively – a huge dance floor, trippy lights, a glass staircase, lots of youngsters and a go-go dancer to show how it's done. Other cavernous bopping venues are *E-Klub (☎ 263 1614, X Népliget)*, in Népliget (People's Park; Map 6), with three rooms and music styles open from 9 pm to 5 am Friday and Saturday, and *C2 (Map 2; ☎ 343 2641 or mobile ☎ 06-209 626 368, III Szépvölgyi út 15)* in Óbuda.

Discos run by the medical and economics universities – the *SOTE Klub (Map 6; ☎ 459 0351, IX Nagyvárad tér 4)* and the

Közgáz Pince Klub (Map 3; ☎ 218 6855, IX Fővám tér 8) – have fewer frills and charge cheaper covers but there's plenty of room to dance. A rave place for techno heads is *Meduza (Map 6; mobile ☎ 06-209 809 845, XI Fehérvári út 87)* open from 9 pm on Friday and Saturday.

Trocadero (Map 5; ☎ 311 4691, VI Szent István körút 15) attracts one of the most diverse crowds in Budapest with its great canned Latin, salsa Afro, reggae and soul nights.

Less throbbing than the big dance places (or at least with smaller dance floors) are the *Bamboo Club (Map 5; ☎ 312 3619, VI Dessewffy utca 44)* with a floor (dance, that is) you can't avoid and a full house on Wednesday (women allowed in free), and the *Fashion Café (Map 5; ☎ 311 8060, VI Andrássy út 36)*, which attracts a designer-label crowd of party-goers.

Süss Fél Nap (Map 5; ☎ 374 3329), on the corner of V Honvéd utca and Szent István körút, attracts a student crowd and hosts student bands; it's a lot of fun and less expensive than many of the other clubs. Go to *Piaf (Map 5; ☎ 312 3823, VI Nagymező utca 25)* when everything else slows down for dancing and action well into the new day. This place is always a trip and a half.

GAY & LESBIAN VENUES

There are no women-only clubs in Budapest, but gays, lesbians and straights frequent *Capella (Map 5; ☎ 318 6231, V Belgrád rakpart 23)*, which hosts some really bad – in the real sense of the word – nudge-nudge, wink-wink drag shows. *Angel (Map 3; ☎ 351 6490, VII Szövetség utca 33)*, sometimes called by its Hungarian name Angyal, is the largest gay disco with a cavernous dark room in the cellar. It's open from 10 pm to 5 am Thursday to Sunday. The *Mystery Bar (Map 5; ☎ 312 1436, V Nagysándor József utca 3)*, a quiet, neighbourhood-style gay bar, attracts so few clients these days that part of it is now a cybercafe. The name of the *Action Bar (Map 5; ☎ 266 9148, V Magyar utca 42)* says it all; take the usual precautions and have fun. Another gay club called *No Limit*

(Map 5; ☎ 317 0902, V Vitkovics Mihály utca 11-13), on the corner of Semmelweis utca, has a pretty descriptive name, too, but in more of a voyeuristic sense. Full of rent. *Darling (Map 5; ☎ 267 3315, V Szép utca 1)* is a seriously skeezy venue with a big thick black snake at rest in a terrarium in the window.

Like everywhere, gay clubs come and go in Budapest. You can always get the latest information from one of your fellow bathers at the *Király* baths (especially on Friday afternoons), the *Rác* baths on Saturday afternoons or the *Gellért* baths on Sunday mornings. If you prefer to meet friends *en plein air*, the Danube Embankment walkway between Elizabeth and Chain Bridges in Pest is notoriously cruisy after dark (AYOR) and full of hustlers from Romania and Ukraine along with the home-grown variety.

ROCK & POP

Until a December 1999 fire burned it to the ground, the 12,500-seat Budapest Sportcsarnok near Népstadion was the venue for visiting performers like Sting, Michael Jackson, Tina Turner, Jamiroquai and others in recent years. The city has decided to rebuild the stadium, which was not insured, but it will not be ready before 2002.

The *Petőfi Csarnok (Map 3; ☎ 343 4327, XIV Zichy Mihály utca 14, metro Széchenyi fürdő or trolleybus No 72 or 74)*, the city's main youth centre, is in City Park and *the* place for smaller rock concerts in Budapest as the hall is small enough to get really close to the performers. It produces a monthly program available at the information counter and at night spots around Budapest.

The *Almássy téri Szabadidő Központ (Almássy tér Recreation Centre; Map 3; ☎ 352 1572, VII Almássy tér 6)* is a venue for just about anything that's in and/or interesting; the DJs from the very popular Tilos Rádió (Forbidden Radio) often hold events. Visit their Web site (in Hungarian) at w3.datanet.hu/~almassy.

The *Lézerszínház (Laser Theatre; Map 6; ☎ 263 0871, X Népliget, metro Népliget)*, at the Planetarium in Népliget (People's Park), has a mixed bag of video concerts with laser and canned music featuring the likes of Pink Floyd, Queen, U2, Led Zeppelin and Mike Oldfield. There are usually shows at 7.30 pm from Monday to Saturday, which cost 1190/790/500Ft for adults/students/children (Web site: www.laser theater.hu).

Two places in south Buda with live rock bands include the *Park Café (Map 6; ☎ 466 9475, XI Kosztolányi Dezső tér 2)*, on the shores of Buda's 'Bottomless Lake', and the *Wigwam Rock Club (Map 6; ☎ 208 5569, XI Fehérvári utca 202)*. Both are open daily till 5 am.

You simply can't miss a *Cinetrip Vízi-Mozi* (Cinetrip Water-Movie) event at the Rudas bath (see the special section 'Taking the Waters' in the Things to See & Do chapter) if one is taking place during your visit. These events (1500Ft) combine partying and dancing with music, film and bathing and are just short of being all-out orgies. They are held monthly or bimonthly (usually from 8 pm to 2 am Saturday); schedules are available at tourist offices and other venues around town. For information call ☎ 212 2297.

JAZZ & BLUES

Old Man's Music Pub (Map 5; ☎ 322 7645, VII Akácfa utca 13) pulls in the best live blues and jazz acts in town; shows are from 9 to 11 pm. A dinner reservation is usually required to score a table, though the food is pretty good. The dance floor really gets going after midnight.

The *Merlin Club (Map 5; ☎ 317 9338, V Gerlóczy utca 4)*, just around the corner from Károly körút 28, has live music most nights from 10 pm and a good crowd, especially if it's staging something at the adjoining English-language theatre (see the Theatre section later in the chapter).

Hades (Map 5; ☎ 352 1503, VI Vörösmarty utca 31) calls itself (shudder) a 'jazztaurant', but most people go as much for the food as the low-key music. *Fat Mo's (Map 5; ☎ 267 3199, V Nyáry Pál utca 9)* plays the blues early in the evening before the small

bar gets too packed for anything but schmoozin' and cruisin'. Another place for jazz is the *Fél Tíz Jazz Club (Map 5; ☎ 333 7721, VIII Baross utca 30)*, with red velvet and black wrought-iron decor, an eclectic mix of people and dancing later in the evening.

The *Polo Pub (Map 3; ☎ 201 7952, I Batthyány utca 2)* has easygoing live blues nightly in upscale surrounds; it's a great place to finish a long day or start an evening. The *Long Jazz Club (Map 5; ☎ 322 0006, VII Dohány utca 22-24)* has some live acts and house DJs from 6 pm to 2 am daily. A more upscale, sophisticated venue is the new *Jazz Garden (Map 3; ☎ 266 7364, V Veres Pálné 44/a)*, a faux cellar 'garden' with street lamps and a night 'sky' bedecked with some 600 stars.

FOLK & TRADITIONAL MUSIC

Authentic *táncház*, literally 'dance house' but really folk-music workshops, are held at least once a week at several locations around Budapest (350Ft to 500Ft), including three in Buda: the *Fonó Budai Zeneház (Fonó Buda Music House; Map 6; ☎ 206 5300, XI Sztregova utca 3)*; the *Folklór Centrum (Map 6; ☎ 203 3868, XI Fehérvári út 47-51)* at the Municipal Cultural House; and the *Marczibányi téri Művelődési Központ (Marczibányi tér Cultural Centre; Map 3; ☎ 212 4885, II Marczibányi tér 5/a)*, where the popular folk group Muzsikás usually jams at 8 pm Thursday.

In Pest, there's the fabulous *Kalamajka Táncház* at the Belvárosi Ifjúság Ház *(Inner Town Youth House; Map 5; ☎ 317 5928 or 266 3378, V Molnár utca 9)* from 5 pm to midnight Saturday; the *Gyökér Klub (Map 5; ☎ 302 4059, VI Eötvös utca 46)*, which you enter from Szobi utca, with bands and táncház most nights at 8 pm; and the *Láng Művelődési Központ (Láng Cultural Centre; Map 2; ☎ 349 6309, XIII Rozsnyai utca 3)* from 7 pm Saturday. Also, look in any of the listings publications mentioned at the start of this chapter for táncház evenings at the *Petőfi Csarnok* or the *Almássy téri Szabadidő Központ*.

ENTERTAINMENT

Just Folk

It is important to distinguish between 'Gypsy music' and real Hungarian folk music. Gypsy music as it is known and played in Hungarian restaurants from Budapest to Boston is urban schmaltz and based on recruiting tunes called *verbunkos* played during the Rákóczi independence war. At least two fiddles, a bass and a cymbalom (a curious stringed instrument played with sticks) are *de rigueur*; if you want to hear this saccharine csárdás music, almost any hotel restaurant in Budapest can oblige, or you can buy a tape or CD by Sándor Lakatos or his son Déki.

To confuse matters even further, real Roma music does not use instruments but is sung as a cappella (though sometimes it is backed with guitar and percussion); a very good tape of Hungarian Roma folk songs is *Magyarországi Cigány Népdalok*, produced by Hungaroton. The best modern Roma group is Kalyi Jag (Black Fire), which comes from north-eastern Hungary and is led by Gusztáv Várga. The group plays all sorts of unconventional instruments and gives performances from time to time at Budapest *táncházak* (dance houses).

The tánchaz is an excellent place to hear Hungarian folk music and learn to dance. It's all good fun and they're easy to find in Budapest, where the dance house revival began.

CLASSICAL MUSIC

The *Koncert Kalendárium* (see Listings earlier in the chapter) highlights all concerts in Budapest each month, and most nights you'll have several to choose from. Budapest's main concert halls are the stunning **Liszt Ferenc Zeneakadémia** *(Franz Liszt Academy of Music; Map 5;* ☎ *342 0179, VI Liszt Ferenc tér 8)* in Pest and the modern **Budapesti Kongresszusi Központ** *(Budapest Congress Centre; Map 3;* ☎ *209 1990, XII Jagelló út 1-3)* in Buda. The **Pesti Vigadó** *(Map 5;* ☎ *318 9903, V Vigadó tér 2)* has light classical music and touristy musical revues.

There are many places where chamber music is played, but those with the best

atmosphere are the concert halls at the **Liszt Memorial Museum** *(Map 5;* ☎ *322 9804, VI Vörösmarty utca 35)*, the **Béla Bartók Memorial House** *(*☎ *394 2100, II Csalán utca 29)*; and the **Music History Museum** *(Map 4;* ☎ *214 6770, I Táncsics Mihály utca 7)*.

Organ recitals are best heard in the city's churches, including **Matthias Church** *(Map 4; I Szentháromság tér 2)* in the Castle District on various days of the week but always at 8 pm and, in Pest, at **St Stephen's Basilica** *(Map 5; V Szent István tér 1)* at 7 pm Monday from June to mid-October and at **St Michael's Church** *(Map 5; V Váci utca 47)* at 8 pm Friday.

CINEMAS

A couple of dozen movie houses show English-language films with Hungarian subtitles. Consult the listings in *Scene* or *Budapest Sun* newspapers. See anything at the fantastically renovated **Corvin Filmpalota** *(Corvin Film Palace; Map 3;* ☎ *459 5050, VIII Corvin köz 1)*, which saw a lot of action during the 1956 Uprising and led a revolution of a different sort four decades later: the introduction of state-of-the-art sound systems and comfortable seating.

The cinema at the **Örökmozgó Filmmúzeum** *(Map 5;* ☎ *342 2167, VII Erzsébet körút 39)*, part of the Hungarian Film Institute, shows an excellent assortment of foreign and classic films in their original languages. *Művész (Map 5;* ☎ *332 6726, VI Teréz körút 30)* shows artsy and cult films. The *Puskin (Map 5;* ☎ *429 6080, V Kossuth Lajos utca 18)* has a mix of art and popular releases. All three have cafes *in situ*.

THEATRE

In Pest, the **Merlin Theatre** *(Map 5;* ☎ *317 9338, V Gerlóczy utca 4)* stages numerous plays in English, often put on by the local English Theatre Company (ETC). Tickets (around 600Ft to 2000Ft) should always be booked in advance. A more recent arrival, the **International Buda Stage** *(IBS; Map 3;* ☎ *391 2500, II Tárogató út 2-4)* in Buda is another English-language theatre with regular performances (tickets 300Ft to 800Ft).

A Complicated Time

An important note on the complicated way Hungarians tell time: 7.30 is 'half eight' (*fél nyolc óra*) and the 24-hour system is often used in giving times of movies, concerts etc. So a film at 7.30 pm could appear on a listing as 'f8', 'f20', '-½ 8' or '-½ 20'. A quarter to the hour has a -¾ in front ('-¾ 8' means 7.45) while quarter past is -¼ of the next hour ('-¼ 9' means 8.15).

The *Kolibri Pince (Map 5; ☎ 351 3348, VI Andrássy út 77)*, with its entrance facing VI Rózsa utca, has a sporadic schedule of amateur and experimental theatre in English that true theatre-goers would enjoy.

If you want to brave a play in Hungarian, go to the *József Katona Theatre (Map 5; ☎ 318 3725, V Petőfi Sándor utca 6)* for the best acting in the city, the *Új Színház (New Theatre; Map 5; ☎ 351 1406, VI Paulay Ede utca 35)* for the amazing Art Deco decor, or the newly renovated *Thália (Map 5; ☎ 312 4230, VI Nagymező 22-24)*.

You won't have to understand Hungarian to enjoy what's going on at the *Budapest Puppet Theatre (Map 5; VI Andrássy út 69)*; see Budapest for Children in the Facts for the Visitor chapter for details.

OPERA
You should pay at least one visit to the *Opera House (Map 5; ☎ 353 0170 or 331 2550, VI Andrássy út 22)* both to see a production and admire the incredibly rich decoration inside. Tickets range in price from 300Ft to 3000Ft.

Budapest has a second opera house, the modern (and ugly) *Erkel Theatre (Map 3; ☎ 333 0108, VIII Köztársaság tér 30)* southwest of Keleti train station. Tickets are sold just inside the main door (open from 11 am to 7 pm Tuesday to Saturday, from 10 am to 1 pm and 4 to 7 pm on Sunday).

Operettas – always a riot, especially one like the campy *Queen of the Csárdás* by Imre Kálmán – are presented at the *Budapesti Operettszínház (Budapest Operetta Theatre; Map 5; ☎ 269 3870, VI Nagymező*

utca 17). Tickets are sold at the box office at No 19 (☎ 353 2172) of the same street (open 10 am to 6 pm weekdays).

DANCE
Budapest's two so-so ballet companies perform at the Opera House and the Erkel Theatre. If the Győr Ballet from Western Transdanubia is performing in town, however, jump at the chance of a ticket. It's Hungary's best classical dance troupe.

For modern dance fans, Budapest has a few good options. The best stage on which to see it is the *Trafó Kortárs Művészetek Háza (Trafó House of Contemporary Arts; Map 3; ☎ 456 2040, IX Liliom utca 41)*, which has the cream of the crop, including a good pull of international acts, but everyone there got their start at *MU Színház (Map 6; ☎ 209 4014 or 466 4627, XI Kőrösy József utca 17)*. At the *Kamra (Chamber; ☎ 318 2487, V Ferenciek tere 4)*, the studio theatre of the József Katona Theatre (Map 5), watch for performances by contemporary dance darling Yvette Bozsik.

The *Közép-Európai Táncszínház (Central European Dance Theatre; Map 3; ☎ 342 7163, VII Bethlen Gábor tér 3)* celebrates 10 years of folk and contemporary performance in Budapest. The *Thália* (see the Theatre section) usually hosts the Honvéd dancers, one of the city's best folk troupes and now experimenting with modern choreography as well.

As for folk dancing, many people attend táncház evenings (see Folk & Traditional Music earlier) to learn the folk dances that go with the music, and you can become part of the program as well instead of merely watching others perform. At the height of summer many of the main táncházak mentioned earlier may not be taking place and you may have to seek them out in more remote locations. To access the most up-to-date information, check the listings of the Dance Music Guild, a sub-section of just about any Hungarian tourist information Web site under 'Folk'.

At 8.30 pm every Monday and Friday from about May to mid-October the *Folklór Centrum* presents a program of Hungarian dancing accompanied by a Gypsy orchestra at the Municipal Cultural House (see Folk & Traditional Music earlier). This performance is one of the best of its kind in Budapest.

During the same period, the 30 dancers of the Hungarian State Folk Ensemble (Állami Népi Együttes) and two other groups perform at the *Budapest Puppet Theatre* (see the Theatre section), the *Budai Vigadó (Map 4; I Corvin tér 8)* in Buda, and the *Duna Palota (Map 5; V Zrínyi utca 5)* just off Roosevelt tér in Pest on alternative days. The 1½-hour programs begin at 8 pm daily and cost 3900/3500Ft for adults/students. Call Hungaria Koncert (☎ 317 2754 or 201 5928) for information and bookings. The folk ensemble's Gypsy Orchestra performs at the Budai Vigadó at 8 pm on Monday from July to October (5000/4500Ft). Hungaria Koncert also has several opera and classical music evenings at the Duna Palota at 8 pm on Thursday, Friday and Saturday.

SPECTATOR SPORTS
Water Polo
Hungary has dominated the European water polo championships for decades so it's worthwhile catching a professional or amateur match of this exciting seven-a-side sport (if for no other reason to watch a bunch of guys in skimpy bathing suits horse around – if you're so inclined). The Magyar Vízilabda Szövetség (Hungarian Water Polo Association) is based at the *Alfréd Hajós National Sports Pool (Map 3; ☎ 340 4946 or 239 3989)* on Margaret Island and matches take place here and at two other pools – the *Béla Komjádi (Map 3; ☎ 212 2750, II Árpád fejedelem útja)* and the *BUSCH (Map 3; ☎ 251 1670, XIV Szőnyi út)* – during the spring and autumn seasons. Get someone to check the match schedule for you in the *Nemzeti Sport* (National Sport) daily (50Ft).

Football
Like transubstantiation and the allure of British crooner Cliff Richard, Hungary's descent from being on top of the heap of European football to *a bake segue alatt* – 'under the arse of the frog' as the Hungarians describe something *really* low – remains one of life's great mysteries. Hungary's defeat of the England team both at Wembley (6-3) in 1953 and at home (7-1) the following year, is still talked about as if the winning goals were scored yesterday.

There are four premier league football teams in Budapest out of a total 18 nationwide including: Kispest-Honvéd, which plays at *Bozsik* stadium *(☎ 282 9789, XIX Új temető utca 1-3)*; MTK at *Hungária körút* stadium *(☎ 333 6758, VIII Hungária körút 6)*; and Újpesti TE at *UFC* stadium *(☎ 369 7333, IV Megyeri út 13)*. But none dominates Hungarian football like Ferencváros (FTC), the country's loudest and brashest team and its only hope. You either love the boys in white and green from Fradi or you hate them. Watch them play at *FTC* stadium *(☎ 215 1013, IX Üllői út 129)*. The daily sports paper *Nemzeti Sport* has the game schedules.

Horse Racing
The descendants of the nomadic Magyars are keen about horse racing. For trotting, go to the *Ügetőpálya (☎ 334 2958, VIII Kerepesi út 9)*, about 10 minutes south of Keleti train station via bus No 95. About 10 races are held on Saturday from 2 pm and on Wednesday from 4 pm.

The *Lóversenytér (☎ 263 7858, X Albertirsai út 2)*, which is also called the Galopppálya, has flat racing from 2 pm on Thursday and Sunday between April and November. It's in Kincsem Park about a 15-minute walk (follow the signs) south of the Pillangó utca metro station.

Shopping

WHAT TO BUY

Food, alcohol, books and CDs, tapes and records are very affordable in Budapest by international standards, and there is an excellent selection. Traditional products include folk art embroidery and ceramics, wall hangings, painted wooden toys and boxes, dolls, all forms of basketry and porcelain (especially Herend and Zsolnay). Feather or goose-down goods like pillows and duvets (comforters) are of superb quality. Foodstuffs that are expensive or difficult to buy elsewhere – goose liver (both fresh and potted), caviar and some prepared meats like Pick salami – make nice gifts as do the many varieties of paprika (if you're allowed to take them home). Some of Hungary's up-and-coming wines (see the special section 'The Wines of Hungary') make good, relatively inexpensive gifts. A bottle of five or six-*puttonyos* Tokaji Aszú dessert wines always goes down a treat – again and again.

WHERE TO SHOP

Shops in Budapest are well stocked and the quality of the products is generally high. Nowadays traditional markets stand side by side mammoth new shopping malls (see the boxed text 'Magyar Malls' in this chapter), traditional umbrella or button makers next to cutting-edge fashion boutiques. Some streets or areas specialise in certain goods or products. For example, antique shops line V Falk Miksa utca and V Vitkovics Mihály utca in Pest and II Frankel Leó út in Buda.

Antiques & Jewellery Shops

If you don't have time to get to the Ecseri or Petőfi Csarnok flea markets or it's the wrong day of the week (see the later section), check any of the BÁV shops, essentially a chain of pawn and second-hand shops with several branches around town. Try VI Andrássy út 43 for old jewellery and bric-a-brac; V Bécsi utca 3 for knick-knacks, porcelain and glassware; and XIII Szent István körút 3 for chinaware and textiles.

The antique shops along V Falk Miksa utca and V Vitkovics Mihály utca in Pest and II Frankel Leó út in Buda are usually pretty expensive (the Austrians bought all the real bargains years ago) but you never know. Among the best – at least for browsing – are the cavernous Pinter (Map 5; ☎ 311 3030, V Falk Miksa utca 10), Qualitás (Map 5; ☎ 311 8471, V Falk Miksa utca 32) and Belvárosi (Map 5; ☎ 317 6289, V Vitkovics Mihály utca 3-5). Anna Antikvitás (Map 5; ☎ 302 5461, V Falk Miksa utca 18-20) is the place to go if you're in the market for embroidered antique tablecloths, bed linens and pillow cases.

Pless & Fox (Map 5; ☎ 312 1238, XIII Szent István körút 18) has sublime jewellery and *objets d'art* for sale, mostly in the Art Nouveau and Secessionist styles.

Art Galleries

The Polgár Galéria és Aukciósház (Map 5; ☎ 318 6954, V Váci utca 11/b), a 'gallery and auction house' in magnificent 1000-sqmetre premises has antique furnishings and works by reputable Hungarian painters – early and some modern. It's open from 10 am to 6 pm weekdays, to 1 pm on Saturday. The Belvárosi Aukciósház (Inner Town Auction House; Map 5; ☎ 267 3539, V Váci utca 36) has auctions usually with a theme (jewellery, graphics, furniture and carpets etc) at 5 pm on Monday. If there's a piece you want to bid on, speak to the auctioneer beforehand and the prices will be called in English as well. Arten Studio (Map 5; ☎ 266 3127, V Váci utca 25) is physically close by but, with works by modern Hungarian artists, worlds away in what it sells. Rózsa Galéria (Map 4; ☎ 355 6866, I Úri utca 1) features paintings, sculptures and other works by Hungarian naive artists. The lovely Simonyi Galéria (Map 5; ☎ 343 5019, VII Rumbach Sebestyén utca 7) by the Conservative Synagogue exhibits and sells contemporary artworks in every medium imaginable, many of them with a Jewish theme.

Permission Granted

Budapest's antique shops and auction houses are magnets for bargain hunters from Austria and other European countries, and there are numerous outlets around V Váci utca, V Vitkovics Mihály, V Ferenciek tere and V Falk Miksa utca in Pest and II Frankel Leó út in Buda. Those with a trained eye may find the treasures of tomorrow at some of the modern galleries today, but purchases still require you to reach deep into the pocket – at least for the credit card.

Any item over 50 years old requires a permit from the Ministry of Culture; this involves a visit to a museum expert (see the following), photos of the piece and a National Bank form with currency exchange slips or a credit card receipt. Companies that will take care of all this for you and ship the piece(s) include First European Shipping (☎ 06-209 258 400), AES Cargo (☎ 388 0050) or ErDitEx (☎ 226 4670). Be aware that most art shippers won't take a job for under US$300 so if the piece is not really valuable, consider taking it in your suitcase. First European Shipping (www.firsteuropean shipping.com) quotes a price of about US$600 for obtaining export customs clearance, crating and air-freighting a small chest of drawers to JFK Airport in New York.

If you're in a DIY mood, the following are the museums and other offices you must contact for your purchase to be allowed out of the country:

Pictorial works by Hungarian artists
Valuation and permits from the Hungarian National Gallery (Map 4; ☎ 375 7533 ext 460), Wings B, C & D, Royal Palace, I Szent György tér

Books, printed matter, written music, hand-written items from before 1957
Valuation at the Központi Antikvárium (Map 5; ☎ 317 3514), V Múzeum körút 13-15; permits from the Széchenyi National Library (Map 4; ☎ 375 7533 ext 157), Wing F, Royal Palace, I Szent György tér

Foreign paintings, sculptures and other works of art
Valuations and permits from the Fine Arts Museum office (Map 3; ☎ 302 1785), VI Szondi utca 77

Folk art and handicraft items
Valuation and permits from the Museum of Ethnography (Map 5; ☎ 312 4878), V Kossuth Lajos tér

Bookshops

General One of the best English-language-only bookshops in Budapest is Pendragon (Map 3; ☎ 340 4426, XIII Pozsonyi út 21-23), which has an excellent selection of guidebooks (including Lonely Planet titles) and fiction. It's open from 10 am to 6 pm weekdays.

Another bookshop particularly strong in English-language fiction is Bestsellers (Map 5; ☎ 312 1295, V Október 6 utca 11) open from 9 am to 6.30 pm weekdays, 10 am to 6 pm Saturday and 10 am to 4 pm Sunday. Bestsellers also runs the nearby Academic Bookshop (Map 5; ☎ 327 3096, V Nádor utca 9) at the Central European University, which has an excellent selection of serious titles with a regional focus. It's open from 9 am to 6 or 6.30 pm weekdays and from 10 am to 4 pm Saturday.

The new kid on the block is the huge Libri Könyvpalota (Libri Book Palace; Map 5; ☎ 267 4844, VII Rákóczi út 12, metro Astoria) just south-east of the Great Synagogue – Budapest's answer to Waterstones or Borders – with some 6000 foreign-language titles. It is open from 10 am to 8 pm weekdays and to 3 pm Saturday.

Libri Studium (Map 5; ☎ 318 5680, V Váci utca 22) has an excellent selection of English books (including guides) as does Kódex (Map 5; ☎ 331 6350, V Honvéd utca 5), where you'll find Hungarian books on the ground floor and foreign books on the 1st floor as well as a decent selection of classical and jazz CDs. The small bookshop in the Párisi Udvar (see Maps in the Facts for the Visitor chapter) and the Bamako bookshop at the Vista Travel Centre (see Travel Agencies in the Facts for the Visitor chapter) stock both maps and guides. A small foreign-language bookshop called Bookshop (Map 5; ☎ 318 8633, V Gerlóczy utca 7) has Hungarian classics in English and books for teaching English.

Atlantisz (Map 5; ☎ 267 6258, V Piarista köz 1), a tiny alley at the start of 'old' Váci utca, has numerous academic titles in Hungarian and paperback English-language classics for a steal. It is open from 10 am to 6 pm weekdays and from 10 am to 3 pm Saturday. The nearby Orisis (Map 5; ☎ 266 4999, V Veres Pálné utca 4-6) carries a small but quality selection of contemporary English-language works as well as those by up-and-coming Asian writers. It's open from 8 am to 6 pm weekdays only.

For Hungarian authors in translation, try the Írók boltja (Writers' Bookshop; Map 5; ☎ 322 1645, VI Andrássy út 45). With coffee and tables available while browsing, it is one of the most comfortable bookshops in the city and was a popular literary cafe called the Japán for most of the first half of the 20th century. It's open from 10 am to 6 pm weekdays and to 1 pm Saturday.

Antique & Second Hand For antique and second-hand books in Hungarian, German and English try Központi Antikvárium (Map 5; ☎ 317 3514, V Múzeum körút 13-15) near Kálvin tér, established in 1881 and the largest antiquarian bookshop in Budapest. Other good *antikvárium* include Kárpáti és Szőnyi (Map 5; ☎ 311 6431, V Szent István körút 1-3), with an excellent selection of antique prints and maps as well, and Kollin (Map 5; ☎ 311 9023, V Bajcsy-Zsilinszky út 34), which stocks foreign-language titles only.

The gift and bookshop at the Ludwig Museum (Map 4; ☎ 375 9175, I Szent György tér) in Wing A of the Royal Palace has lots of used coffee-table and photography books, some of them in English. Rhythm'n'Books (Map 5; ☎ 266 2226, V Szerb utca 21-23) has an eclectic and rather messy collection of second-hand books and world-music CDs, which you can trade for other titles. It's open from noon to 6 pm weekdays only.

Fashion Salons & Boutiques

Tangó Classic (Map 5; ☎ 318 4394, V Apáczai Csere János utca 3) has well-made women's suits, blazers, jackets and evening attire with a Hungarian twist inspired by folk costumes and military uniforms. Sixvil (Map 5; ☎ 317 4834, V Kecskeméti utca 8) has men's and women's collections by some of Hungary's most talented designers, but they tend to stick to the rules.

For some affordable and downright funky pieces by Hungarian talents, Manier (Map 5; ☎ 318 1292, V Váci utca 53) has wispy, slinky and silvery numbers as well as solid foundation pieces. Monarchia (Map 5; ☎ 318 3146, V Szabadsajtó út 6) stocks funky one-off and made-to-measure items.

Some people travel to Hungary just to have their footwear made by Vass (Map 5; ☎/fax 318 2375, V Haris köz 2), traditional shoemakers that both cobble to order and stock ready-to-wear.

Iguana (Map 5; ☎ 317 1627, VIII Krúdy utca 9) stocks 'younique' leather, suede, velvet and 'madness pieces' from the 1950s, 60s and 70s. For cut-rate new and second-hand fashion, check out the string of shops along XIII Hollán Ernő utca (Map 5) just north of Szent István körút, including Pulóver Centrum, Prima Vera and Raffabello.

Flea Markets

Ecseri (☎ 282 9563, XIX Nagykőrösi út 156), often just called the 'piac' (market), is one of the biggest and best *bolhapiac* (flea markets) in Central Europe, selling everything from antique jewellery and Soviet army watches to old musical instruments and Fred Astaire-style top hats. It's open from 6 am to about 1 pm Tuesday to Saturday (the best day to go). To get there, take

Magyar Malls

In the mid-1990s Budapest began to go mall crazy, and at last count the city had upwards of a dozen, both in the centre of town and on the fringes. 'Mall' may not be the accurate word to describe what the Hungarians call *bevásárló és szorakoztató központ* (shopping and amusement centres), however; here you'll find everything from designer salons, more traditional shops and dry cleaners to food courts, casinos, multiscreen cinemas and live bands. It's a place to spend the entire day, just as you would just about anywhere else in the industrialised world in the third millennium.

Though it's unlikely you've come all the way to Budapest to hang out in a generic, could-be-anywhere shopping centre, it can be fun watching Magyars and malls meet for the first time. The following are the biggest or the most central or the most exclusive or the cheapest of them all:

Duna Plaza (Map 2; ☎ 465 1666, XIII Váci út 178, metro Gyöngyösi utca). Until the advent of the West End City Centre, this was the mother of all Magyar malls, with the requisite Greek taverna and an 11-screen multiplex cinema. Open 10 am to 9 pm daily.

Europark (☎ 282 9266, XIX Üllői út 201, metro Határ út). Conveniently (?) located on the way to/from the airport, Europark is gimmick-free and for serious shoppers only. Open 10 am to 9 pm weekdays and to 6 pm weekends.

Lurdy Ház (Map 6; ☎ 456 1200, IX Könyves Kálmán körút 12-14, bus No 103). This place in Ferencváros is almost a carbon copy of Duna Plaza – right down to the hours and multiscreen cinema complex.

Mammut (Map 3; ☎ 345 8020, II Lövőház utca 2-6, metro Moszkva tér). The most central Magyar mall in Buda, the 'Mammut' is a true 'shopping and amusement centre' with as many fitness centres, billiard parlours and cafes as shops. Open from 10 am to 9 pm weekdays, to 6 pm weekends.

Pólus Centre (☎ 410 2405, XV Szentmihályi út 131). In the far reaches of northern Pest, this mall runs its own bus every half-hour from Keleti train station. There's a big Tesco supermarket here. Open from 10 am to 8 pm daily.

Rózsakert (Map 3; ☎ 275 1846, II Gábor Áron 74-78, bus No 49). In posh Rózsadomb, this mall would have to be the snobbiest and priciest in town. Designer shops big time. Open from 10 am to 8 pm daily (to 7 pm Sunday).

West End City Centre (Map 5; ☎ 238 7777, VI Váci út 1, metro Nyugati pályaudvar). In central Pest, this Goliath has everything you could possibly want or need, with large indoor fountains that may or may not work, a cultural centre and a 260-room Hilton hotel. Open from 10 am to 9 pm daily (to 6 pm on Sunday).

---

bus No 54 from Boráros tér in Pest near the Petőfi Bridge or, better, the red express bus No 54 from the Határ utca stop on the blue metro line and get off at the Fiume utca stop and walk over the pedestrian bridge.

The Petőfi Csarnok Bolhapiac (☎ 251 7266 or 343 4327, XIV Zichy Mihály utca) is a huge outdoor flea market, a Hungarian boot or garage sale if you will. It's held next to the Petőfi Csarnok (Concert Hall; Map 3) in City Park. The usual diamonds-to-rust stuff is on offer – from old records and draperies to candles, honey and herbs. It's open from 7 am to 2 pm on Saturday and Sunday, though the latter is said to be the better day.

A rather unusual place is the so-called Chinese market (Map 2; XIII Fáy utca 60, tram No 14), a series of stalls run by Chinese, Vietnamese and Thais that offer the usual array of knock-off designer clothing and cosmetics, cigarettes and duty-free liquor that seems to have strayed from Ferihegy. There are a lot of good and very authentic eating possibilities here. It's open from 7 am to 6 pm daily.

Folk Art & Souvenir Shops

Before you do any shopping for handicrafts at street markets, have a look in the Folkart Centrum (Map 5; ☎ 318 5840, V Váci utca 14), a large store where everything Magyar-made is available and prices are clearly marked. It's open daily from 9.30 to 4 am (!) for all your chotchky needs. Other good bets are Judit (Map 4; ☎ 212 7050, I Tarnok utca 1) in the Castle District and Babaklinika (Map 5; ☎ 267 2445, V Múzeum körút 5) by the Astoria hotel.

In the far back corner upstairs in the Nagycsarnok (see Markets in the Places to Eat chapter) are a group of stalls where vendors sell Hungarian folk costumes, dolls, painted eggs, embroidered tablecloths etc. Holló Atelier (Map 5; ☎ 317 8103, V Vitkovics Mihály utca 12), near Váci utca, has attractive folk art with a modern look and remains one of my favourite places.

Játékszerek Anno (Map 5; ☎ 302 6234, VI Teréz körút 54) is a wonderful little shop near Nyugati train station selling finely made reproductions of antique toys.

Food & Alcohol Stores

Gourmets will appreciate the Hungarian and other treats – shrink-wrapped and potted foie gras and goose liver paté (1690/ 2800Ft for 100/200g), Astrakhan Malossol caviar (from 3800Ft for 60g), a good selection of dried mushrooms, garlands of dried paprika (350Ft to 450Ft) and souvenir tins of paprika powder (500Ft to 650Ft) – available at the Nagycsarnok (see Markets in the Places to Eat chapter) at a fraction of what you'd pay in the stores on nearby Váci utca.

There's an excellent selection of Hungarian wines at La Boutique des Vins (Map 5; ☎ 317 5919, V József Attila utca 12), which is owned by the former sommelier at Gundel. Ask the staff to recommend a label if you feel lost. A more central (and expensive) place is the Prés Ház (Map 5; ☎ 266 1100, V Váci utca 10), with over 300 wines in an 18th-century courtyard cellar, knowledgeable staff and bottles open for tasting.

Serious oenophiles, however, will travel to the Budapest Wine Society shop (Map 3; ☎ 212 0262, I Batthyány utca 59), southeast of Moszkva tér. No-one but no-one knows Hungarian wines like these guys do. It's open from 10 am to 8 pm weekdays and to 6 pm Saturday; and there are free tastings

Herend Porcelain

Herend porcelain is among the finest of all goods produced in Hungary and makes a wonderful gift or memento. The stuff also has a fascinating history.

A terracotta factory was set up at Herend, north-west of Veszprém, in 1826 and began producing porcelain 13 years later under Mór Farkasházi Fischer of Tata in Western Transdanubia. Initially it specialised in copying and replacing the nobles' broken chinaware settings imported from Asia, and you'll see some pretty kooky 19th-century interpretations of Japanese art and Chinese faces on display in museums or available at some antique shops. But the factory soon began producing its own patterns; many, like the Rothschild bird and *petites roses*, were inspired by Meissen and Sèvres designs from Germany and France. The popular Victoria pattern of butterflies and wild flowers was designed for the eponymous English queen after she admired a display of Herend pieces at the Great Exhibition in London in 1851.

To avoid bankruptcy in the 1870s, the Herend factory began mass production; tastes ran from kitschy pastoral and hunting scenes to the ever-popular animal sculptures with the distinctive scale-like triangle patterns.

In 1992, the factory was purchased from the state by its 1500 workers and became one of the first companies in Hungary privatised through an employee stock-ownership plan.

on Saturday afternoon. The House of Hungarian Wines (Map 4) also has a large selection (see Walking Tour 1 in the Things to See & Do chapter).

For Hungarian spirits (Zwack Unicum, *pálinka* distilled from plums, pears or apricots etc), try Lokomos Csemege (Map 5; ☎ 267 8544, V Váci utca 48) on the corner of Nyáry Pál utca. It's open from 7 am to 8.30 pm weekdays and to 7 pm at the weekend.

If you haven't been able to pick up a jar or two of Hungary's greatest contribution to humanity – traditionally made *lekvár* (fruit jam), especially the apricot variety – at any of the food markets (see the Places to Eat chapter), check out Lekvárium (Map 5;

☎ 321 6543, VII Dohány utca 39), which stocks home-made jam as well as bottled fruit, pickles and honey. For marzipan in all its guises, head for Szamos (Map 5; ☎ 317 3643, V Párizsi utca 3). Its ice cream is also a major magnet.

Glassware & Porcelain Shops

The Ajka crystal shop (Map 5; ☎ 318 3240, VI Teréz körút 50) on the Big Ring Road and away from the touristy areas is significantly cheaper than its counterpart at Váci utca 23 (Map 5) but the choice is narrower.

For fine porcelain, check out the Zsolnay (Map 5; ☎ 318 3712, V Kigyó utca 4) and Herend (Map 5; ☎ 317 2622, V József nádor tér 11) outlets. Haas & Czjzek (Map 5; ☎ 311 4094, VI Bajcsy-Zsilinszky út 23), just up from Deák tér, sells more affordable Hungarian-made Hollóháza and Alföldi porcelain.

Herend Village Pottery (Map 3; ☎ 356 7899, II Bem rakpart 37) is an alternative to prissy, fragile flatware; it stocks ceramic pottery for the kitchen with bold fruit patterns.

Music Shops

The Rózsavölgyi (Map 5; ☎ 318 3500, V Szervita tér 5) is mostly known as a classical music shop but has some pop and folk (eg, the Roma band Kalyi Jag, the Hungarian folk group Muzsikás). Dob (Map 5; ☎ 331 6298, Szent István körút 23) has both Hungarian and international rock, blues, folk, jazz and indie. Another great place for indie and alternative music is Wave (Map 5; ☎ 302 2927, VI Révay köz 2). For locally produced classical records, CDs and tapes, try the Liszt Ferenc Zeneműbolt (Map 5; ☎ 322 4091, VI Andrássy út 45) or the wonderful Concerto Hanglemezbolt (Map 5; ☎ 268 9631, VII Dob utca 33), which is always full of treasures. It's open from noon to 7 pm weekdays and to 4 pm at the weekend.

Other Shops

Feather or goose-down products like pillows or duvets (comforters) are of excellent quality in Hungary and a highly recommended purchase; they last a lifetime. Nádor Tex (Map 5; ☎ 317 0030, V József nádor tér 12) has some of the best prices, with pure down 1000g duvets measuring 135cm x 200cm for just over 20,000Ft. Billerbeck (Map 5; ☎ 321 2082, VII Dob utca 49) has a larger selection but higher prices: from 33,000Ft.

One medium in which the Hungarians have excelled is wrought iron, and Hephaistos Háza (Map 5; ☎ 266 1550, V Molnár utca 27) has a zany collection of furniture, fittings and accessories. There's a branch (☎ 332 6329) at VI Zichy Jenő utca 20.

Selene (Map 5; ☎ 266 0143, V Irányi utca 7) sells everything and anything you might need to kit you and a horse out for riding. The Angler-Horgászüzlet tackle shop (☎ 267 9754, VII Dohány utca 5), in the same building as the Senara Korean restaurant (Map 5), can do the same if you're going fishing.

Excursions

An awful lot in Hungary is within easy striking distance of Budapest, and many of the towns and cities in the Danube Bend, Transdanubia, Northern Uplands and even the Great Plain could be day trips from the capital. You can be in Szentendre (19km) in half an hour, for example, and Eger, a lovely Mediterranean-like town that lies between the Bükk and Mátra Hills, is only 125km to the north-east.

This chapter assumes you'll be returning to Budapest after a day of looking around, though we've included a couple of accommodation options in each section just in case you miss your train or bus or simply decide you like the place. For fuller treatment of these destinations, see Lonely Planet's *Hungary*.

SZENTENDRE
☎ 26 • postcode 2000 • pop 19,350
Just 19km north of Budapest, Szentendre (St Andrew) is the southern gateway to the Danube Bend, the S-shaped curve in the Danube River that begins just below Esztergom, twists for 20km and is the site of the protracted Nagymaros dam controversy (see the boxed text 'Dam Nations'). As an art colony turned lucrative tourist centre, Szentendre strikes many as a little too 'cute', and the town can be crowded and relatively expensive. Still, it's an easy train trip from the capital, and the town's dozens of art museums, galleries and Serbian Orthodox churches are well worth the trip. Just try to avoid it on summer weekends.

For information contact Tourinform (☎ 317 965, fax 317 966, @ szentendre@tourinform.hu), Dumtsa Jenő utca 22, which is open from 9.30 am to 5 pm weekdays and 10 am to 2 pm on weekends from October to April, and from 9.30 am to 4.30 pm weekdays only during the rest of the year.

Things to See
In **Fő tér**, the colourful centre of Szentendre surrounded by 18th and 19th-century

Dam Nations

In 1977 the communist regimes of Hungary and Czechoslovakia agreed – without public or parliamentary debate – to build a canal system and power station along the Danube River. The project would produce cheap electricity and be financed by energy-hungry Austria. It wasn't long before environmentalists foresaw the damage the dam would cause, and the public outcry was loud and unmitigated. In 1989 Hungary's last reform government under communism, including Foreign Minister Gyula Horn, caved in to the pressure and halted all work on its part of the project across from Visegrád at Nagymaros.

Efforts to convince newly democratic Czechoslovakia to do the same with its much larger dam on Gabčikovo Canal upstream near Bratislava dragged on without much success. As Czechoslovakia came closer to dividing, the Czechs turned a blind eye on work continued by the Slovaks, and in October 1992 the river was diverted into the canal. Energy gains were minor as the project depended on the Hungarian dam at Nagymaros, which has now been demolished. Both Hungary and Slovakia put their cases before the International Court in The Hague.

When the court handed down its ruling in 1998, Horn, leader of the reinvented Socialist Party and now prime minister, said his government felt compelled to go ahead with the dam somewhere else along the Danube. This was too much for an electorate tired of old regime-style waffling and untruths. He and the socialists were swept from office in the national elections later that year. The new government has said it will not go ahead with the damn project.

burghers' houses, stands the **Memorial Cross** (1763), an iron cross decorated with icons on a marble base. Across the square to the north-east is the Serbian Orthodox **Blagoveštenska Church**, built in 1754. The church, with fine baroque and rococo elements, hardly looks 'eastern' from the outside (it was designed by the architect András Mayerhoffer), but once you are inside, the ornate iconostasis and elaborate 18th-century furnishings give the game away.

If you descend Görög utca and turn right onto Vastagh György utca, you'll reach the entrance to the **Margit Kovács Ceramic Collection** (Kovács Margit kerámiagyűjtemény) in an 18th-century salt house at No 1. The museum is Szentendre's biggest crowd-pleaser and one of the few open all year. Opening hours are 10 am to 6 pm Tuesday to Sunday and, from June to September, 10 am to 4 pm on Monday too (250/150Ft adults/students and children). Kovács (1902-77) was a ceramicist who combined Hungarian folk, religious and modern themes to create elongated, Gothic-like figures. Some of her works are overly sentimental, but many are very powerful, especially the later ones in which she became obsessed with mortality.

Castle Hill (Vár-domb), which can be reached via the Váralja lépcső, the narrow steps between Fő tér 8 and 9, was the site of a fortress in the Middle Ages, but all that's left of it is the **Parish Church of St John** in Templom tér, from where you can enjoy splendid views of the town. The red tower of **Belgrade Cathedral** (Belgrád székesegyház; 1764) on Alkotmány utca, seat of the Serbian Orthodox bishop in Hungary, rises from within a leafy, walled courtyard to the north. One of the church buildings beside it (entrance at Pátriárka utca 5) contains the **Serbian Ecclesiastical Art Collection** (Szerb egyházművészeti gyűjtemény), a treasure trove of icons, vestments and other sacred objects in precious metals. The collection is open from 10 am to 4 pm Wednesday to Sunday in summer and Tuesday as well in winter (100/50Ft).

The **Hungarian Open-Air Ethnographical Museum** (Magyar szabadtéri néprajzi múzeum), 3km north-west of the centre on Sztaravodai út and accessible by bus, is Hungary's most ambitious open-air museum. While plans ultimately call for some 300 farmhouses, churches, bell towers, mills

and so on to be set up in 10 regional units, so far there are four. The units for the Upper Tisza area of North-East Hungary and the Kisalföld and Őrség regions of Western Transdanubia give full impressions of their regions, while the one representing the Great Plain is still under construction. The museum is open 9 am to 5 pm Tuesday to Sunday from mid-March to October (350/150Ft or 800Ft for a family ticket).

Places to Stay & Eat

Some 2km north of Szentendre on Pap Island is *Pap-sziget Camping* (☎ 310 697, fax 313 777), where two people and a tent pay 1000Ft to 1200Ft and a *bungalow* for four people with bath costs 7000Ft. The 20-room *motel* here has rooms for three/four people with shared bath for 3000/3300Ft. Ibusz (☎ 310 181), Bogdányi utca 11, can organise *private rooms* in town for 1500Ft to 2000Ft per person. The friendly 16-room *Bükkös* hotel (☎ 312 021, fax 310 782, Bükkös part 16) has singles/doubles for 7150/8500Ft.

There are a couple of Italian eateries along the Danube, including *Ristorante da Carlo (Duna korzó 6-8)*, with tables outside in summer, and *Pizza Andreas (Duna korzó 5/a)*. The new kid in town is the posh *Százéves Sólyom (Dumtsa Jenő utca)*, opposite the Marzipan Museum at No 12. The 'Centenary Falcon' serves upmarket Hungarian dishes (800Ft to 1600Ft for main courses).

Getting There & Away

The easiest way to reach Szentendre from Budapest is to catch the HÉV suburban train from Batthyány tér in Buda, which takes just 40 minutes. You'll never wait longer than 20 minutes (half that in rush hour), and the last train leaves Szentendre for Budapest at 11.30 pm. Buses from Budapest's Árpád híd station, which is on the blue metro line, run to Szentendre at least once an hour throughout the day. The HÉV train and bus stations lie side by side south of the town centre; from here walk through the subway and north along Kossuth Lajos utca and Dumtsa Jenő utca to Fő tér.

Potatoes for sale at Lehel tér market.

Craft festival at Buda Castle.

Inside the Nagycsarnok (Great Market Hall).

"Yes, I think I will take it..."

The Danube at Esztergom.

Crafts on display at Szentendre.

Art Nouveau at Szabadság tér, Kecskemét.

GÖDÖLLŐ

☎ 28 • postcode 2100 • pop 28,200

Just 29km to the north-east of Budapest's city centre and easily accessible on the HÉV, Gödöllő (pronounced, very roughly, '**good**-duh-ler') is an easy day trip. The main draw here is the Royal Mansion, which rivalled Esterházy Palace at Fertőd in Western Transdanubia in splendour and size when it was completed in the 1760s. However, the town itself, full of lovely baroque buildings and monuments and home to the seminal Gödöllő Artists' Colony (1901-20), is worth the trip alone.

For information contact Tourinform (☎ 415 402, ✉ godollo@tourinform.hu) at the entrance to the Royal Mansion.

The Royal Mansion

The Royal Mansion (Királyi kastély; ☎ 410 124), Szabadság tér 1, sometimes called the Grassalkovich Mansion after its commissioner, Antal Grassalkovich, count and confidante of Empress Maria Theresa, was designed by Antal Mayerhoffer in 1741. After the formation of the Dual Monarchy, the mansion (or palace) was enlarged as a summer retreat for Emperor Franz Joseph and soon became the favoured residence of his consort, the much beloved Habsburg empress and Hungarian queen, Elizabeth (1837-98), affectionately known as Sissy. Between the two world wars, the regent, Admiral Miklós Horthy, also spent time here regularly, but after the communist takeover, part of the mansion was used as an old people's home and then as temporary housing. The rest was left to decay.

Partial renovation of the mansion began in 1994 and today more than a dozen rooms are open to the public. They have been restored (some would say too heavily) to when the imperial couple were in residence, and Franz Joseph's suites (done up in manly greys and golds) and Sissy's lavender-coloured private apartments are impressive. Check out the Decorative Hall (Díszterem), all gold tracery and chandeliers, where chamber music concerts are held in July; Elizabeth's salon, with a Romantic-style oil painting of Sissy repairing the cloak of

St Stephen with needle and thread; and the study annexe, with a restored ceiling painting and an 18th-century tapestry of the huntress Diana.

The mansion is open from 10 am to 6 pm Tuesday to Sunday from April to October, and to 5 pm the rest of the year. Entry to the reconstructed rooms costs 250/150Ft for adults/students and seniors, and a guide costs 350Ft per hour. A guided tour that also includes rooms and outbuildings not yet reconstructed (the palace chapel, theatre, stables etc) costs 400/250Ft.

Places to Stay & Eat

The *Agricultural University* (☎ 420 591, *Páter Károly utca 1*), a short distance east of the HÉV terminus, has dormitory accommodation available in July and August for 1300Ft. You won't find much other accommodation in central Gödöllő, though the *Silver Club* pension (☎ 420 345, fax 432 410, Isaszegi út 7) is 4.5km to the south and has doubles for 4000Ft and bungalows between 6600Ft and 7500Ft.

Tourinform at the palace has sample menus from restaurants around town and distributes discount vouchers. Two convenient and inexpensive pizzerias are *Carnevale (Dózsa György utca 12)* and *Pizza Joe (Szabadság tér 2)*, both a short distance north of the palace car park. For decent Hungarian dishes, try the nearby *Pelikán (Kossuth Lajos utca 31)*.

Getting There & Away

HÉV trains from Örs vezér tere at the terminus of the red metro line in Budapest link the capital with Gödöllő (45 minutes) about once every half-hour throughout the day. Make sure you get off at the Szabadság tér stop, which is the third one from the last. In addition, buses leave Népstadion about every 30 minutes for Gödöllő. Other destinations served by bus and their daily frequencies include Eger (one to three), Gyöngyös (nine), Hatvan (half-hourly), Jászberény (three to five), Szolnok (one or two) and Vác (six). The bus station is on Szabadság út, some 600m north-east of the palace.

MARTONVÁSÁR

☎ 22 • postcode 2462 • pop 4350

Lying halfway between Budapest and the Central Transdanubian city of Székesfehérvár (33km) and easily accessible by train, Martonvásár is the site of **Brunswick Mansion** (Brunszvik kastély), one of the loveliest summertime concert venues in Hungary. The mansion was built in 1775 for Count Antal Brunswick (Magyarised as Brunszvik), the patriarch of a family of liberal reformers and patrons of the arts. (Teréz Brunszvik established Hungary's first nursery school in Pest in 1828.)

Beethoven was a frequent visitor to the manse, and it is believed that Jozefin, Teréz's sister, was the inspiration behind the *Appassionata* and *Moonlight* sonatas, which the great Ludwig van composed here.

Brunswick Mansion, at Brunszvik út 2 just off Dózsa György utca, was rebuilt in neo-Gothic style in 1875 and restored to its ivory and sky-blue glory a century later. It now houses the Agricultural Research Institute of the Academy of Sciences, but you can see at least part of the mansion by visiting the small **Beethoven Memorial Museum** (Beethoven emlékmúzeum) to the left of the main entrance. It's open from 10 am to noon and 2 to 4 pm Tuesday to Sunday (80/40Ft).

A walk around the grounds – one of Hungary's first 'English parks' to be laid out when these were all the rage in the early 19th century – is a pleasant way to spend a warm summer's afternoon. It's open every day from 8 am to 4 pm (80/40Ft). Concerts are held on the small island in the middle of the lake (reached by a wooden footbridge) during the Martonvásár Summer (Martonvásári Nyár) festival from May to October. The climax is the 10-day Martonvásár Days (Martonvásár Napok) festival in late July. For information contact Tourinform in Székesfehérvár.

The baroque **Catholic church**, attached to the mansion but accessible from outside the grounds, has frescoes by Johannes Cymbal. There's also a small **Nursery Museum** (Óvodamúzeum) in the park, which is open the same hours as the Beethoven museum.

Places to Stay & Eat

The six-room *Macska* (Cat) pension (☎ 460 127, Budai út 21), with doubles for about 6000Ft, is crawling with felines – definitely not the place for hyperallergenics. Instead, you could try the *Tanne* inn (☎ 460 288, Budai út 83), a short distance to the north. The Macska's *restaurant* serves the standard Hungarian *csárda* dishes and has a good wine cellar. In the centre, the *Postakocsi* restaurant (Fehérvári utca 1) is a convenient place for lunch and has courtyard seating.

Getting There & Away

Dozens of daily trains between Budapest-Déli and Székesfehérvár stop at Martonvásár and, if you attend a concert, you can easily make your way back to Budapest on the last train at 11.23 pm. The station is a 10-minute walk along Brunszvik út, northwest of the main entrance to the mansion.

KECSKEMÉT

☎ 76 • postcode 6000 • pop 102,500

Lying halfway between the Danube and the Tisza Rivers in the heart of the Southern Plain some 85km south-east of Budapest, Kecskemét is ringed with vineyards and orchards that don't seem to stop at the limits of this 'garden city'. Colourful architecture, fine museums, apricot groves and the region's excellent *barackpálinka* (apricot brandy) beckon. The Kiskunság National Park, the puszta of the Southern Plain, is right at the back door.

For information contact Tourinform (☎/fax 481 065, ❷ kecskemet@tourinform.hu), which is on the north-eastern side of the town hall at Kossuth tér 1. It's open from 8 am to 6 pm weekdays and from 9 am to 1 pm at the weekend from June to August, and from 8 am to 5 pm weekdays and 9 am to 1 pm on Saturday the rest of the year.

Things to See

On the eastern side of central Kossuth tér is the **Franciscan Church of St Nicholas** (Szent Miklós ferences templom), dating in part from the late 13th century; the **Zoltán Kodály Institute of Music Education**

(Kodály Zoltán Zenepedagógiai Intézet), celebrated for its unique approach to musical education, occupies the baroque monastery behind it to the east at Kéttemplom köz 1. But the main building in the square is the sandy-pink **town hall** (városháza), a lovely late-19th-century building designed by Ödön Lechner, who mixed Art Nouveau/Secessionist with folkloric elements to produce a uniquely Hungarian style. The town hall's carillon chimes out strains of works by Ferenc Erkel, Kodály, Mozart, Handel and Beethoven several times during the day, and groups are allowed into the spectacularly painted and decorated **Council Chamber** (☎ 483 683 for information).

Walking north-east into Szabadság tér, you'll come to two of the city's finest buildings. The Art Nouveau **Ornamental Palace** (Cifrapalota), dating from 1902 and covered in multicoloured majolica tiles, now contains the **Kecskemét Gallery** (Kecskeméti képtár), Rákóczi utca 1. But don't go in so much for the art; climb the steps to the aptly named **Decorative Hall** (Díszterem) to see the amazing stucco peacock, bizarre windows and more tiles. The **House of Technology** (Technika háza; 1871), a Moorish structure across Rákóczi út at No 2, was once a synagogue. Today it is used for conferences and exhibitions.

Kecskemét is chock-a-block with museums costing 150/50Ft and open from 10 am to 5 pm Tuesday to Sunday, but two stand head and shoulders above the rest. The **Hungarian Museum of Naive Artists** (Magyar naiv müvészek múzeuma) is in the Stork House (1730), surrounded by a high white wall at Gáspár András utca 11 just off Petőfi Sándor utca. There are lots of predictable themes here, but the warmth and craft of Rozália Albert Juhászné's work, the drug-like visions of Dezső Mokry-Mészáros and the paintings of András Süli (Hungary's answer to Henri Rousseau) will hold your attention. The granddaddy of all museums here is the **Hungarian Folk Craft Museum** (Magyar népi iparművészeti múzeuma) to the south-west at Serfőző utca 19/a, a block in from

Dózsa György út. Some 10 rooms of this old farm complex are crammed with embroidery, woodcarving, furniture, agricultural tools and textiles, so don't try to see everything.

Places to Stay & Eat

About three blocks from the camping ground, the **GAMF Ságvári College** (☎ 321 916, ✉ koll@gamf.hu, Izsáki út 10) has accommodation in a four-bed room for 1000Ft per person and singles/doubles are available. Officially it's only open from mid-June to August, but you can sometimes get a bed in other months.

Ibusz (☎ 486 955, fax 480 557) in the modern Aranyhomok hotel at Kossuth tér 3 charges from 1500Ft to 2000Ft per person for a *private room*. The friendliest and most charming place to stay in town is the **Három Gúnár** (☎ 483 611, fax 481 253, Batthyány utca 1-7), a small 46-room hotel formed by cobbling four old townhouses together. Singles cost 6900Ft to 7500Ft and doubles 8400Ft to 9400Ft at the 'Three Ganders'.

Labirintus (Kéttemplom köz 2) is a cellar restaurant with pizza and pastas. *Jalta (Batthyány utca 2)*, opposite the Három Gúnár hotel, is a rather homely wine cellar with a menu in English and German. Mains cost 550Ft to 650Ft and specialities include grilled south Slav dishes. If you want to splurge, you couldn't do better than *Liberté (Szabadság tér 2)* in a historical building west of the Great Church. It is one of my favourite places in provincial Hungary.

Getting There & Away

Kecskemét is on the central railway line linking Budapest's Nyugati train station with Szeged and there are frequent departures to and from the capital throughout the day (1¼ hours). Alternatively there are hourly buses to/from Népstadion station in Budapest. Kecskemét's bus and main train stations are opposite one another near József Katona Park. A 10-minute walk south-west along Nagykőrösi utca will bring you to Szabadság tér.

VESZPRÉM

☎ 88 • postcode 8200 • pop 63,800

Spreading over five hills between the northern and southern ranges of the Bakony Hills, Veszprém, 110km south-west of Budapest, has one of the most dramatic locations in Central Transdanubia. The walled castle district atop a plateau, once the favourite residence of Hungary's queens, is now a living museum of baroque art and architecture, and it's a delight to stroll through the Castle Hill district's single street, admiring the embarrassment of fine churches. What's more, Lake Balaton is only 13km to the south.

For information contact Tourinform (☎/fax 404 548, ☻ veszprem@tourinform .hu), Rákóczi utca 3, which is open from 9 am to 6 pm weekdays and to 1 pm on Saturday from June to August, and from 9 am to 5 pm weekdays only the rest of the year.

Things to See

As you ascend Castle Hill (Vár-hegy) and its sole street, Vár utca, you'll pass the **fire-watch tower** (tűztorony), an architectural hybrid of Gothic, baroque and neoclassical styles, that can be climbed. You then go through **Heroes' Gate** (Hősök kapuja), an entrance way built in 1936 from the stones of a 15th-century castle gate.

The U-shaped **Bishop's Palace** (Püspöki palota), Vár utca 16, where the queen's residence stood in the Middle Ages, faces Szentháromság tér, named for the **Trinity Column** (1751) in the centre. The palace, designed by Jakab Fellner of Tata in the mid-18th century, is, sadly, no longer open to the public – its interior is richly decorated with ceiling frescoes, portraits of Veszprém's bishops, carved oak doors and liturgical objects. Next to the Bishop's Palace at Vár utca 18 is the early Gothic **Gizella Chapel** (Gizella-kápolna), named after the wife of King Stephen, who was crowned near here early in the 11th century. Inside the chapel are Byzantine-influenced 13th-century frescoes of the Apostles. The **Queen Gizella Museum** of religious art is opposite at Vár utca 35. Both are open from 9 am to 5 pm daily from May to October and cost 20Ft and 100Ft respectively.

The **cathedral** (székesegyház) is dedicated to St Michael and is the site of the first bishop's palace. Parts of it date from the beginning of the 11th century, but the cathedral has been rebuilt many times since then. The early Gothic crypt is original, though. Beside the cathedral, the octagonal foundation of the 13th-century **Chapel of St George** (Szent György kápolna) sits under a glass dome; it's open from 10 am to 5 pm daily from May to October (20Ft).

From the rampart known as **World's End** at the end of Vár utca, you can gaze north to craggy Benedict Hill (Benedek-hegy) and the Séd Stream and west to the concrete viaduct (now St Stephen's Valley Bridge) over the Betekints Valley. Below you, in Margit tér, are the ruins of the medieval **Dominican Convent of St Catherine** and to the west what little remains of the 11th-century **Veszprém Valley Convent**, whose erstwhile cloistered residents are said to have stitched Stephen's crimson silk coronation robe in 1031. The **statues of King Stephen and Queen Gizella** at World's End were erected in 1938 to mark the 900th anniversary of Stephen's death.

Places to Stay & Eat

Both Balatontourist (☎ 429 630), Kossuth Lajos utca 21, between the bus station and the castle, and Ibusz (☎ 426 492), Kossuth Lajos utca 10, can help with *private rooms* (2000Ft per person).

The *Péter Pál (☎/fax 328 091, Dózsa György utca 3)* is a fine 12-room pension with a lovely garden perched above a busy street. Singles/doubles/triples are 4000/ 5400/6600Ft.

There are very few places to eat on Castle Hill, but the *Tüztorony* Chinese restaurant *(Vár utca 1)* between the firewatch tower and Heroes' Gate is a friendly place open daily to 10.30 pm, and the *Várkert (Vár utca 17)* has a three-course set menu for around 900Ft. There's also *Óváros (Szaadság tér 14)* in a lovely baroque building with outside seating on various levels.

Getting There & Away

Veszprém is on the train line linking Szombathely and Budapest-Déli station via

Székesfehérvár, and there are up to eight trains a day to/from the capital (two hours). In general bus connections are excellent to/from Veszprém, with hourly departures each day to/from Budapest's Erzsébet tér station, including five expresses and many more departures via Székesfehérvár. The bus station is on Piac tér, a few minutes' walk north-east from Kossuth Lajos utca, a pedestrian street of shops and travel agencies. If you turn north at the end of Kossuth Lajos utca at Szabadság tér, you'll soon reach Óváros tér, the entrance to Castle Hill. The train station is 3km north of the bus station at the end of Jutasi út.

EGER
☎ 36 • postcode 3300 • pop 62,000
Everyone loves Eger, 128km north-east of Budapest, and it's immediately apparent why: beautifully preserved baroque architecture gives the town a relaxed, almost Mediterranean feel; it is the home of the celebrated Egri Bikavér (Eger Bull's Blood) wine known the world over; and it is flanked by two of the Northern Uplands' most beautiful ranges of hills.

For information contact Tourinform (☎ 321 807, fax 321 304, ✉ eger@tourinform.hu), next to the Minorite church at Dobó István tér 2. It's open from 9 am to 6 pm weekdays and 10 am to 1 pm on Saturday and Sunday from June to August, and weekdays 9 am to 5 pm and Saturday 10 am to noon the rest of the year. Staff sell a museum card for 500/250Ft, valid for a week, that allows entry to all the exhibitions in the castle area, as well as four city museums.

Eger Castle
The best overview of the city can be had by climbing up the cobblestone lane from Dózsa György tér to the castle, erected in the 13th century following the Mongol invasion. It's open from 9 am to 5, 6 or 7 pm (depending on the season) Tuesday to Sunday, though you can visit the castle casemates from 8 am to 8 pm in summer (earlier in winter) seven days a week. Much of the castle is of modern construction, but you can still see the foundations of 12th-century

St John's Cathedral, which was destroyed by the Turks.

The István Dobó Museum inside the 14th-century Bishop's Palace has models of how the cathedral looked in its prime, as well as furnishings (tapestries, porcelain etc). On the ground floor, a statue of Dobó takes pride of place in Heroes' Hall. The 19th-century building on the north-western side of the courtyard houses the Eger Art Gallery, with portraits of leading contemporary Hungarians and several works by Mihály Munkácsy. Tours to the casemates built after the siege leave from outside the ticket office and are included in the entry fee.

A ticket to see everything in the castle area costs 300/150Ft; if you just want to walk around the grounds without entering anything, it's 100/50Ft. On Monday, when only the casemates are open, the charge is 250/120Ft.

Eszterházy tér
Back in town, you can begin a walking tour of the city at Eger Cathedral (1836), a neoclassical monolith designed by József Hild, the same architect who later worked on the even larger cathedral at Esztergom. Despite the cathedral's size and ornate altars, the interior is surprisingly light and airy.

Directly across Eszterházy tér from the cathedral is the sprawling Zopf-style Lyceum, named after Károly Eszterházy, a bishop of Eger and one of the school's founders. The ceiling fresco (1778) in the library on the 1st floor of the south wing is a trompe l'oeil masterpiece depicting the Counter-Reformation's Council of Trent (1545-63) and a lightning bolt setting 'heretical' manuscripts ablaze. The observatory on the 6th floor of the east wing contains 18th-century astronomical equipment; climb three more floors up to the observation deck for a great view of the city and surrounding vineyards.

The Lyceum is open to the public from 9.30 am to 3 pm Tuesday to Sunday from mid-April to September, and 9.30 am to 1 pm Tuesday to Friday and till noon at the weekend the rest of the year (330/100Ft).

Other Attractions

On the southern side of central Dobó István tér stands the **Minorite church** (1773), one of the most beautiful baroque buildings in the world. The altarpiece of the Virgin Mary and St Anthony (the church's patron) is by Johann Kracker, the Bohemian painter who also created the fire-and-brimstone ceiling fresco in the Lyceum library. Statues of István Dobó and the Hungarians routing the Turks fill the square.

To the north of the square on Knézich Károly utca is the 40m-high **minaret** dating from Turkish times. Non-claustrophobes will brave the 100 narrow spiral steps to reach the top from 10 am to 6 pm daily from April to October. To the south of Dobó István tér is Kossuth Lajos utca, a fine, tree-lined street with dozens of architectural gems. At No 17 stands the former **Orthodox synagogue**, built in 1893 and now backing onto a shopping mall. You'll pass several baroque and Eclectic buildings, including the **county hall** at No 9, with a wrought-iron grid above the main door of Faith, Hope and Charity by Henrik Fazola, a Rhinelander who settled in Eger in the mid-18th century. Walk down the passageway, and you'll see two more of his magnificent works: baroque wrought-iron gates decorated on both sides that have taken over from the minaret as the symbol of Eger. The wrought-iron balcony and window grids of the rococo **Provost's House** (open 10 am to 6 pm weekdays) at No 4 were also done by Fazola.

Wine Tasting

By no means should you miss visiting the wine cellars of the evocatively named **Valley of the Beautiful Women** (Szépasszony-völgy) to the south-west of the centre. From the western end of Eger Cathedral, walk south on Trinitárius utca to Bartók Béla tér and then west along Király utca to Szépasszony-völgy utca. Veer to the left as you descend the hill past the camping ground and into the valley, and you'll see dozens of cellars – some with musicians, some with outside tables, others locked up tight as their owners party elsewhere. This is the place to sample Bull's Blood (one of very few reds produced in Eger) or any of the whites, such as Leányka, Olaszrizling and Hárslevelű from Debrő.

The choice of wine cellars can be a bit daunting and their characters can change, so walk around and have a look yourself. Nos 11, 16 and 17 are always popular; for schmalzy Gypsy music, No 42 is the one. But if you're interested in good wine, visit cellars 5, 13, 18, 23, 31 and/or 32. Be careful though; those 100ml glasses (about 50Ft) go down easily. Hours are erratic, but a few cellars are sure to be open till the early evening.

Places to Stay & Eat

The cheapest place in town is the run-down **Tourist** (☎ 429 014, ✉ egertour@mail .agria.hu, Mekcsey István utca 2), a 'motel' south of the castle with 50 rooms in two buildings. It has singles/doubles with shared bath for 1800/2800Ft and doubles with private bath for 5200Ft. Both Egertourist (☎ 411 724), Bajcsy-Zsilinszky utca 9, and Cooptourist (☎ 311 998, fax 320 333), Dobó István tér 3, can organise **private rooms** for 1300Ft to 2200Ft per person. The **Senator Ház** (☎/fax 320 466, Dobó István tér 11) is a delightful 18th-century inn with 11 rooms in Eger's main square that many people – including me – count among the best small hotels in Hungary. Singles are DM40 to DM70 and doubles are DM60 to DM95, depending on the season.

Two inexpensive places for a decent meal on Széchenyi utca are **Gyros** (Széchenyi utca 10), with Greek salads (385Ft), tsatsiki (350Ft) and moussaka (590Ft), and the **Kondi** salad bar (Széchenyi utca 2). The former is open daily till 10 pm; the latter closes at 7 pm weekdays (5 pm on Saturday, 1 pm on Sunday). The **Pizza Club** (Fazolka Henrik utca 1), south of the castle and open daily till 10 or 11 pm, can be recommended for its pizzas (500Ft to 720Ft). The **HBH Bajor** (Bajcsy-Zsilinszky utca 19) serves reliable Hungarian-Germanic food in a bright, clean environment.

Getting There & Away

Eger is on a minor train line linking Putnok and Füzesabony; you usually have to change at the latter for Budapest, Miskolc or Debrecen. There are up to five direct trains a day to and from Budapest's Keleti station (two hours). Bus services are good, with buses running every hour or so to/from Budapest's Népstadion via route No 3. The bus station on Barkóczy utca is just a few minutes on foot from Dobó István tér. To reach the centre from the main train station on Vasút utca, walk north along Deák Ferenc utca to pedestrian Széchenyi István utca. Dobó István tér is to the east.

Language

Hungarian (Magyar) belongs to the Finno-Ugric language group and is related – only distantly – to Finnish (with five million speakers), Estonian (one million) and about a dozen other minority languages with far fewer speakers in Russia and western Siberia. It's not an Indo-European language, meaning that English is actually closer to French, Russian and Hindi in vocabulary and structure than it is to Hungarian. As a result you'll come across very few familiar words – with the exception of things like *disco* or *hello* (the slangy way young Hungarians say 'goodbye').

There are also a fair number of misleading homophones (words with the same sound but different meanings) in Hungarian: *test* is not a quiz but 'body'; *fog* is 'tooth'; *comb* is 'thigh'; and *part* is 'shore'. *Ifjúság*, pronounced (very roughly) 'if you shag', means 'youth'; *sajt* (pronounced 'shite'), as in every visiting Briton's favourite *sajtburger*, means 'cheese'.

For more Hungarian words and phrases than there is space for here, get a copy of Lonely Planet's *Eastern* or *Central Europe phrasebook*.

Pronunciation

Hungarian is not difficult to pronounce – though it may look strange with all those accents. Unlike English, Hungarian is a 'one-for-one' language: the pronunciation of each vowel and consonant is almost always consistent. Stress falls on the first syllable (no exceptions), making the language sound a bit staccato to untrained ears.

Consonants

Consonants in Hungarian are pronounced more or less as in English; the exceptions are listed below. Double consonants (**ll**, **tt**, **dd**) are not pronounced as one letter as in English, but lengthened so you can almost hear them as separate sounds. Also, what are called consonant clusters (**cs**, **zs**, **gy**, **sz**)

are separate letters in Hungarian and appear that way in the telephone directory and alphabetical listings. For example, the word *cukor* (sugar) appears in the dictionary before *csak* (only).

c	as the 'ts' in 'hats'
cs	as the 'ch' in 'church'
gy	as the 'j' in 'jury' with your tongue pressed against the roof of your mouth
j	as the 'y' in 'yes'
ly	also as the 'y' in 'yes' but with a slight 'l' sound
ny	as the 'ni' in 'onion'
r	pronounced with the tip of your tongue; a slightly trilled 'r' as found in Spanish or Scottish
s	as the 'sh' in 'shop'
sz	as the 's' in 'salt'
ty	as the 'tu' in 'tube' in British English
w	as the 'v' in 'vat' (used in foreign words only)
zs	as the 's' in 'pleasure'

Vowels

Vowels are quite tricky, and the difference between an **a**, **e** or **o** with and without an accent mark is great. *Hát* means 'back' while *hat* means 'six'; *kérek* means 'I want' while *kerek* means 'round'. Try to imagine a Briton with a standard 'TV' accent or an American from Boston pronouncing the following sounds:

a	as the 'o' in hot
á	as the 'a' in 'father' or 'shah'
e	as the 'e' in 'set'
é	as the 'e' as in 'they' (without the 'y' sound)
i	similar to the 'i' in 'hit'
í	as the 'i' in 'police'
o	as the 'o' in 'open'
ó	a longer version of **o** above
ö	as the 'o' in 'worse' (without any 'r' sound)
ő	a longer version of **ö** above

169

u	as the 'u' in 'pull'
ú	as the 'oo' in 'food'
ü	a tough one; similar to the 'u' in 'flute' or as in German *fünf*
ű	even tougher; a longer, breathier version of ü above

Polite & Informal Forms

As in many other languages, verbs in Hungarian have polite and informal form in the singular and plural. The polite address (marked as 'pol' in this guide) is used with strangers, older people, officials and service staff. The informal address (marked as 'inf') is reserved for friends, pets, children and sometimes foreigners, but is used much more frequently and sooner than it is in, say, French. Almost all young people use it among themselves – even with strangers. In the following phrases, the polite 'you' (*Ön* and *Önök*) is given except for situations where you might wish to establish a more personal relationship.

Basics

Yes	*Igen*
No	*Nem*
Maybe	*Talán*
Please	*Kérem.* (asking for something)
	Tessék. (offering/ inviting)
Thank you (very much)	*Köszönöm (szépen)*
	Köszi (inf)
You're welcome	*Szívesen*
Excuse me	*Legyen szíves* (for attention)
	Bocsánat (eg, to get past someone)
I'm sorry	*Sajnálom/Elnézést*

Greetings & Civilities

Hello.	*Jó napot kívánok.* (pol)
Hi.	*Szia* or *szervusz.* (inf)
Goodbye	*Viszontlátásra* (pol)
	Szia/Szervusz (inf)
Good day	*Jó napot* (most common greeting)
Good morning.	*Jó reggelt*
Good evening.	*Jó estét*

Small Talk

How are you?	*Hogy van?* (pol)
	Hogy vagy? (inf)
I'm fine, thanks.	*Köszönöm, jól.*
What's your name?	*Hogy hívják?* (pol)
	Mi a neved? (inf)
My name is ...	*A nevem ...*
I'm a ... tourist/ student.	*Turista/diák.*
Are you married?	*Ön férjezett?* (to a woman)
	Ön nős? (to a man)
Do you like Hungary?	*Tetszik önnek Magyarország?*
I like it very much.	*Nagyon tetszik.*
Where are you from?	*Honnan jön?*

I'm ...	*... vagyok.*
American	*Amerikai*
British	*brit*
Australian	*ausztrál*
Canadian	*kanadai*
a New Zealander	*új-zélandi*

How old are you?	*Hány éves vagy?* (inf)
	Hány éves? (pol)
I'm 25 years old.	*Húszonöt éves vagyok.*
Just a minute.	*Egy pillanat.*
May I?	*Lehet?* (general permission)
	Szabad? (eg, asking for a chair)
It's all right.	*Rendben van.*
No problem.	*Nem baj.*

Language Difficulties

Do you speak...?	*Beszél ...?*
English	*angolul*
French	*franciául*
German	*németül*
Italian	*olaszul*

Does anyone here speak English?	*Van itt valaki, aki angolul beszél?*
I understand.	*Értem.*
I don't understand.	*Nem értem.*
I don't speak Hungarian.	*Nem beszélek magyarul.*
How do you say ... in Hungarian?	*Hogy mondják magyarul ...?*

Please write it down.	*Kérem, írja le.*
Would you please show me (on the map)?	*Meg tudná nekem mutatni (a térképen)?*

Getting Around

What time does ... leave/arrive?	*Mikor indul/ érkezik ...?*
the bus	*az autóbusz*
the tram	*a villamos*
the train	*a vonat*
the boat/ferry	*a hajó/komp*
the plane	*a repülőgép*

The train is ...	*A vonat ...*
delayed	*késik*
on time	*pontosan érkezik*
early	*korábban érkezik*
cancelled	*nem jár*

How long does the trip take?	*Mennyi ideig tart az út?*
Do I need to change trains?	*Át kell szállnom?*
You must change trains.	*Át kell szállni.*
You must change platforms.	*Másik vágányhoz kell menni.*

I want to go to ...	*... akarok menni.*
Esztergom	*Esztergomba*
Debrecen	*Debrecenbe*
Pécs	*Pécsre*

I want to book a seat to Prague.	*Szeretnék helyet foglalni Prágába.*
train station	*vasútállomás/ pályaudvar*
bus station	*autóbuszállomás*
platform	*vágány*
ticket	*jegy*
one-way ticket	*egy útra/csak oda*
return ticket	*oda-vissza/retúrjegy*
ticket office	*jegyiroda/pénztár*
timetable	*menetrend*
left-luggage	*csomagmegőrző*
I'd like to hire a car.	*Autót szeretnék bérelni.*

Signs

Vészkijárat	Emergency Exit
Bejárat	Entrance
Kijárat	Exit
Meleg	Hot
Hideg	Cold
Információ	Information
Tilos Belépni	No Entry
Tilos A Dohányzás	No Smoking
Nyitva	Open
Zárva	Closed
Tilos	Prohibited
Foglalt	Reserved
WC/Toalett	Toilets
Férfiak	Men (toilet)
Nők	Women (toilet)

I'd like to hire a ...	*... szeretnék kölcsönözni.*
bicycle	*kerékpárt*
motorcycle	*motorkerékpárt*
horse	*lovat*

I'd like to hire a guide.	*Szeretnék kérni egy idegenvezetőt.*
I have a visa/ permit.	*Nekem van vízum/ engedélyem.*

Directions

How do I get to ...?	*Hogy jutok ...?*
Where is ...?	*Hol van ...?*
Is it near/far?	*Közel/messze van?*

What ... is this?	*Ez melyik ...?*
street/road	*utca/út*
street number	*házszám*
city district	*kerület*
town	*város*
village	*falu/község*

(Go) straight ahead.	*(Menyen) egyenesen előre.*
(Turn) left.	*(Forduljon) balra.*
(Turn) right.	*(Forduljon) jobbra.*
at the traffic lights	*a közlekedési lámpánál*
next/second/third corner	*következő/második/ harmadik saroknál*
up/down	*fent/lent*
behind/in front	*mögött/előtt*

opposite	*szemben*
here/there	*itt/ott/*
everywhere	*mindenhol*
north	*észak*
south	*dél*
east	*kelet*
west	*nyugat*

Around Town

Where is ...?	*Hol van ...?*
a bank	*bank*
an exchange office	*pénzváltó*
the city centre	*a város központ* or *a centrum*
the ... embassy	*a ... nagykövetség*
the hospital	*a kórház*
the market	*a piac*
the police station	*a rendőrkapitányság*
the post office	*a posta*
a public toilet	*nyilvános WC*
a restaurant	*étterem*
the telephone centre	*a telefonközpont*
tourist information office	*idegenforgalmi iroda*

beach	*strand*
bridge	*híd*
castle	*vár*
cathedral	*székesegyház*
church	*templom*
synagogue	*zsinagóga*
island	*sziget*
lake	*tó*
(main) square	*(fő) tér*
market	*piac*
mosque	*mecset*
palace	*palota*
mansion	*kastély*
ruins	*rom* or *romok*
tower	*torony*

Accommodation

I'm looking for ...	*... keresem.*
a guesthouse	*fogadót*
a campground	*campinget/ kempinget*
the youth hostel	*az ifjúsági szállót*
a hotel	*szállodát*

the manager	*a főnököt*
the owner	*a tulajdonost*
rooms available	*szoba kiadó*
Do you have a ... available?	*Van szabad ...?*
bed	*ágyuk*
cheap room	*olcsó szobájuk*
single room	*egyágyas szobájuk*
double room	*kétágyas szobájuk*

What is the address?	*Mi a cím?*

Do you have ...?	*Van ...?*
a clean sheet	*tiszta lepedő*
hot water	*meleg víz*
a key	*kulcs*
a shower	*zuhany*

for one/two nights	*egy/két éjszakára*
How much is it per night/ per person?	*Mennyibe kerül éjszakánként/ személyenként?*
Is service included?	*A kiszolgálás benne van?*
May I see the room?	*Megnézhetem a szobát?*
Where is the toilet/ bathroom?	*Hol van a WC/ fürdőszoba?*
It is very dirty/ noisy/expensive.	*Ez nagyon piskos/ zajos/drága.*
I'm/We're leaving.	*El megyek/ El megyünk.*

Shopping

How much is it?	*Mennyibe kerül?*
I'd like to buy this.	*Szeretném megvenni ezt.*
It's too expensive for me.	*Ez túl drága nekem.*
Can I look at it?	*Megnézhetem?*
I'm just looking.	*Csak nézegetek.*

I'm looking for...	*Keresem ...*
chemist/pharmacy	*a patikát*
clothing	*ruhát*
souvenirs	*emléktárgyat*

Time & Dates

When?	*Mikor?*
At what time?	*Hány órakor?*
What time is it?	*Hány óra?*

Emergencies

Help!	*Segítség!*
It's an emergency!	*Sürgős!*
There's been an accident!	*Baleset történt!*
Call a doctor!	*Hívjon egy orvost!*
Call an ambulance!	*Hívja a mentőket!*
Call the police!	*Hívja a rendőrséget!*
I've been raped.	*Megerőszakoltak.*
I've been robbed!	*Kiraboltak!*
I'm lost.	*Eltévedtem.*
Go away!	*Menjen el!*
Where are the toilets?	*Hol van a WC?*

It's ... o'clock.	*... óra van.*
1.15	*negyed kettő* ('one-quarter of two')
1.30	*fél kettő* ('half of two')
1.45	*háromnegyed kettő* ('three-quarters of two')

in the morning	*reggel*
in the evening	*este*
noon	*dél*
midnight	*éjfél*
today	*ma*
tonight	*ma este*
tomorrow	*holnap*
day after tomorrow	*holnapután*
yesterday	*tegnap*
all day	*egész nap*
every day	*minden nap*
Monday	*hétfő*
Tuesday	*kedd*
Wednesday	*szerda*
Thursday	*csütörtök*
Friday	*péntek*
Saturday	*szombat*
Sunday	*vasárnap*

January	*január*
February	*február*
March	*március*
April	*április*
May	*május*
June	*június*
July	*július*
August	*augusztus*
September	*szeptember*
October	*október*
November	*november*
December	*december*

Numbers

0	*nulla*
1	*egy*
2	*kettő* (*két* before noun)
3	*három*
4	*négy*
5	*öt*
6	*hat*
7	*hét*
8	*nyolc*
9	*kilenc*
10	*tíz*
11	*tizenegy*
12	*tizenkettő*
13	*tizenhárom*
14	*tizennégy*
15	*tizenöt*
16	*tizenhat*
17	*tizenhét*
18	*tizennyolc*
19	*tizenkilenc*
20	*húsz*
21	*huszonegy*
22	*huszonkettő*
30	*harminc*
40	*negyven*
50	*ötven*
60	*hatvan*
70	*hetven*
80	*nyolcvan*
90	*kilencven*
100	*száz*
101	*százegy*
110	*száztíz*
1000	*ezer*
1 million	*egy millió*

Health

I'm ...	*... vagyok.*
diabetic	*cukorbeteg*
epileptic	*epilepsziás*
asthmatic	*asztmás*
I'm allergic to ...	*... allergiás vagyok*
penicillin	*penicillinre*
antibiotics	*antibiotikumra*

I've got diarrhoea.	*Hasmenésem van.*
I feel nauseous.	*Hányingerem van.*
antiseptic	*fertőzésgátló*
aspirin	*aszpirin*
condoms	*óvszer* or *gumi*
contraceptive	*fogamzásgátló*
medicine	*orvosság*
suntan lotion	*napozókrém*
sunblock cream	*fényvédőkrém*
tampons	*tampon*

FOOD

restaurant	*étterem* or *vendéglő*
food stall	*laci konyha* or *pecsenyesütő*
grocery store/ delicatessen	*élelmiszer csemege*
market	*piac*
breakfast	*reggeli*
lunch	*ebéd*
dinner/supper	*vacsora*
the menu	*az étlap*
set (daily) menu	*napi menü*

At the Restaurant

I'm hungry.	*Éhes vagyok.*
I'm thirsty.	*Szomjas vagyok.*
The menu, please.	*Az étlapot, kérem.*
I'd like the set menu, please.	*Mai menüt kérnék.*
Is service included in the bill?	*Az ár tartalmazza a kiszolgálást?*
I'm a vegetarian.	*Vegetáriánus vagyok.*
I'd like some ...	*Kérnék ...*
Another ... please.	*Még (egy) ... kérek szépen.*
The bill, please.	*A számlát, kérem* or *Fizetek.*
bread	*kenyér*
chicken	*csirke*
coffee	*kávé*
eggs	*tojás*
fish	*hal*
food	*étel*
fruit	*gyümölcs*
fruit juice	*gyümölcslé*
meat	*hús*
milk	*tej*
mineral water	*ásvány víz*
pepper	*bors*

pork	*disznóhús*
salt	*só*
soup	*leves*
sugar	*cukor*
tea	*tea*
vegetables	*zöldség*
water	*víz*
wine	*bor*
hot/cold	*meleg/hideg*
with/without sugar	*cukorral/cukor nélkül*
with/without ice	*jéggel/jég nélkül*

DRINKS
Nonalcoholic Drinks

almalé – apple juice
ásvány víz – mineral water
cappuccino – coffee with whipped cream (see *tejes kávé*)
limonádé – lemonade
narancslé – orange juice
tejes kávé – cappuccino (milky coffee with froth)
üdítő ital – soft drink

Alcoholic Drinks

barackpálinka – apricot brandy
barna sör – dark beer/stout
bor – wine
borozó – wine bar
borpince – wine cellar
csapolt sör – draught beer
édes bor – sweet wine
egészségére! – cheers!
fehér bor – white wine
fél barna sör – dark lager
féledes bor – semisweet wine
félszáraz bor – semidry/medium wine
fröccs – spritzer/wine cooler
itallap – drinks/wine list
korsó sör – mug (half litre) or beer
körtepálinka – pear brandy
őszibarack pálinka – peach brandy
pezsgő – champagne/sparkling wine
pohár bor – glass of wine (size varies)
pohár sör – glass (one-third litre) of beer
sör – beer
söröző – pub/beer hall
szilvapálinka – plum brandy
világos sör – lager
üveg – bottle
vörös bor – red wine

Glossary

If you can't find the word you're looking for here, try the previous Language section.

ÁEV – United Forest Railways
ÁFA – value-added tax (VAT)
Alföld – see *Nagyalföld*
Ausgleich – German for 'reconciliation'; the Compromise of 1867
autóbusz – bus
áutóbuszállomás – bus station
Avars – a people of the Caucasus who invaded Europe in the 6th century
ÁVO – Rákosi's hated secret police; later renamed ÁVH

bal – left
bejárat – entrance
BKV – Budapest's transport company
bolhapiac – flea market
bolt – shop
borozó – wine bar
Bp – abbreviation for Budapest
BTO – Budapest Tourist Office
búcsú – farewell; also a church patronal festival
büfé – snack bar

centrum – town or city centre
Compromise of 1867 – agreement creating the dual monarchy of Austria-Hungary
Copf – a transitional architectural style between late baroque and neoclassicism (see *Zopf*)
csárda – a Hungarian-style inn and/or restaurant
csatorna – canal
csikós – cowboy from the *puszta*
csomagmegőrző – left-luggage office
cukrászda – cake shop or cafe

D – abbreviation for *dél* (south)
Dacia – Roman name for Romania and lands east of the Tisza River
db or **drb** – piece (used in markets, short for *darab*)
de – am (in the morning)
du – pm (in the afternoon)

É – abbreviation for *észak* (north)
Eclectic – an art style popular in Hungary in the Romantic period, drawing from varied sources
élelmiszer – grocery shop, provisions
előszoba – vestibule or anteroom; one of three rooms in a traditional Hungarian cottage
em – abbreviation used in addresses for *emelet* (floor or storey)
erdő – forest
érkezés – arrivals
eszpresszó or **presszó** – coffee shop, often also selling alcoholic drinks and snacks; strong, black coffee
étterem – restaurant

falu – village
fasor – boulevard, avenue
felvilágosítás – information
fogas – pike-perch of Lake Balaton
földszint – ground floor
folyó – river
főpolgármester – lord mayor
főváros – main city or capital
fsz – abbreviation for *földszint*
Ft – forint (see also *HUF*)

gyógyfürdő – bathhouse
gyűjtemény – collection
gyula – chief military commander of the early Magyar

hajdúk – Hungarian for *Heyducks* or Haiduks
hajó – boat
hajóállomás – ferry pier or landing
ház– house
hegy – hill, mountain
helyiautóbusz pályaudvar – local bus station
HÉV – suburban commuter train in Budapest
Heyducks – drovers and outlaws from the *puszta* who fought as mercenaries and artisans against the Habsburgs
híd – bridge

honfoglalás – conquest of the Carpathian Basin by the early Magyars in the late 9th century
HTB – Hungarian Tourist Board (OIH in Hungarian)
HUF – Hungarian forint (international currency code)
Huns – a Mongol tribe that swept across Europe, notably under Attila, in the 5th century AD

Ibusz – Hungarian national network of travel agencies
ifjúsági szálló – youth hostel
illeték – air passenger duty
indulás – departures

jobb – right

K – abbreviation for *kelet* (east)
kamra – workshop or shed; one of three rooms in a traditional Hungarian cottage
kapu – gate
kastély – manor house, mansion (see *vár*)
kb – approximately
kemping – camping ground
KEOKH – foreigners' registration office
képtár – gallery
kerület – district
khas – towns of the Ottoman period under direct rule of the sultan
kijárat – exit
kincstár – treasury
Kiskörút – 'Little Ring Road' in Budapest
kocsma – pub or saloon
kolostor – monastery
komp – ferry
könyvesbolt – bookshop
könyvtára – library
kórház – hospital
körút – ring road
korzó – embankment, promenade
köz – alley, mews, lane
központ – town or city centre
krt – see *körút*
kúria – mansion, country house
kuruc – Hungarian mercenaries/partisans/insurrectionists who resisted the expansion of Habsburg rule in Hungary after the withdrawal of the Turks (late 17th/early 18th centuries)

lángos – deep-fried dough with toppings
lekvár – fruit jam
lépcső – stairs, steps
liget – park

Mahart – Hungarian passenger ferry company
Malév – Hungary's national airline
MÁV – Hungarian State Railways
megye – county
menetrend – timetable
mihrab – Mecca-oriented prayer niche
MNB – National Bank of Hungary
Moorish Romantic – an art style popular in the decoration of 19th-century synagogues
mozi – cinema
műemlék – memorial, monument

Nagyalföld – the Great Plain (also called the *Alföld* or *puszta*)
Nagykörút – 'Big Ring Road' in Budapest
nosztalgiavonat – MÁV vintage steam train
Ny – abbreviation for *nyugat* (west)
nyitva – open

ó – abbreviation for *óra*
önkiszolgáló – self service
óra – hour, o'clock
oszt – abbreviation for *osztály* (department)
OTP – National Savings Bank
Ottoman Empire – the Turkish empire that took over from the Byzantine Empire when it captured Constantinople (Istanbul) in 1453, and expanded into south-eastern Europe right up to the gates of Vienna

pálinka – Hungarian fruit brandy
palota – palace
pályaudvar – train station
Pannonia – Roman name for the lands south and west of the Danube River
panzió – pension, guesthouse (plural *panziók*)
part – embankment
patika, patikaház – pharmacy
patyolat – laundry
pénztár – cashier
pénzváltó – exchange office

piac – market
pince – wine cellar
plébánia – rectory, parish house
presszó – see *eszpresszó*
pu – abbreviation for *pályaudvar*
puli – Hungarian breed of sheepdog with shaggy coat
puszta – common geographical term for wilderness plains, see *Nagyalföld*
puttony – the butt of sweet *aszú* essence added to other base wines in making Tokaj wine

racka – *puszta* sheep with distinctive corkscrew horns
rakpart – quay, embankment
rendőrkapitányság – central police station
repülőtér – airport
Romany – the language and culture of the Roma (Gypsy) people

Secessionism – art and architectural style similar to Art Nouveau
sedile, sedilia – medieval stone niche or niches with seats
sétány – walkway, promenade
skanzen – open-air museum displaying village architecture
söröző – beer bar or pub
stb – abbreviation equivalent to English 'etc'
strand – grassy 'beach' near a river or lake
sugárút – avenue
szálló, szálloda – hotel
székesegyház – cathedral
sziget – island
színház – theatre
szoba kiadó – room for rent

Tanácsköztársaság – the 1919 Communist Republic of Councils under Béla Kun
táncház – an evening of folk music and dance (plural *táncházak*)
tanya – homestead or ranch
távolságiautóbusz pályaudvar – long-distance bus station
temető – cemetery
templom– church
tér – town or market square
tere – genitive form of *tér* as in *Hősök tere* (Square of the Heroes)
tilos – prohibited

tista szoba – parlour; one of three rooms in a traditional Hungarian cottage
tó – lake
toalett – toilet
Trianon Treaty – 1920 treaty imposed on Hungary by the victorious Allies, which reduced the country to one-third of its former size, allowing for the creation of new countries like Yugoslavia and Czechoslovakia
Triple Alliance – 1882-1914 alliance between Germany, Austria-Hungary and Italy – not to be confused with the WWI Allies (members of the *Triple Entente* and their supporters)
Triple Entente – agreement between Britain, France and Russia, intended as a counter-balance to the *Triple Alliance*, lasting until the Russian Revolution of 1917
turul – eagle-like totem of the ancient Magyars and now a national symbol

u – abbreviation for *utca*
udvar – court, courtyards
ünnep – public holiday
úszoda – swimming pool
út – road
utca – street
utcája – genitive form of *utca* as in *Ferencesek utcája* (Street of the Franciscans)
útja – genitive form of *út* as in *Mártíroká útja* (Street of the Martyrs)
üzlet – shop

va – abbreviations for *vasútállomás*
vágány – platform
vár – castle (see *kastély*)
város – city
városház, városháza – town hall
vasútállomás – train station
vendéglő – a type of restaurant
vm – abbreviations for *vasútállomás*
Volán – Hungarian bus company
vonat – train

WC – toilet (see *toalett*)

zárva – closed
Zimmer frei – German for 'room for rent'
Zopf – German and more commonly used word for *Copf*

Alternative Place Names

The following abbreviations are used:
(C) Croatian
(E) English
(G) German
(H) Hungarian
(R) Romanian
(S) Serbian
(Slk) Slovak
(Slo) Slovene
(U) Ukrainian

Alba Iulia (R) – Gyula Fehérvár (H),
Karlsburg/Weissenburg (G)

Baia Mare (R) – Nagybánya (H)
Balaton (H) – Plattensee (G)
Belgrade (E) – Beograd (S),
    Nándorfehérvár (H)
Beregovo (U) – Beregszász (H)
Braşov (R) – Brassó (H), Kronstadt (G)
Bratislava (Slk) – Pozsony (H), Pressburg (G)

Carei (R) – Magykároly (H)
Cluj-Napoca (R) – Kolozsvár (H),
    Klausenburg (G)

Danube (E) – Duna (H), Donau (G)
Danube Bend (E) – Dunakanyar (H),
    Donauknie (G)
Debrecen (H) – Debrezin (G)

Eger (H) – Erlau (G)
Eisenstadt (G) – Kismárton (H)
Esztergom (H) – Gran (G)

Great Plain (E) – Nagyalföld, Alföld or
    Puszta (H)
Győr (H) – Raab (G)

Hungary (E) – Magyarország (H),
    Ungarn (G)

Kisalföld (H) – Little Plain (E)
Komárom (H) – Komárno (Slk)
Košice (Slk) – Kassa (H), Kaschau (G)
Kőszeg (H) – Güns (G)

Lendava (Slo) – Lendva (H)
Lučenec (Slk) – Losonc (H)

Mukačevo (U) – Munkács (H)
Murska Sobota (Slo) – Muraszombat (H)

Northern Uplands (E) – Északi Felföld (H)

Oradea (R) – Nagyvárad (H),
    Grosswardein (G)
Osijek (C) – Eszék (H)

Pécs (H) – Fünfkirchen (G)

Rožnava (Slk) – Rozsnyó (H)

Satu Mare (R) – Szatmárnémeti (H)
Senta (S) – Zenta (H)
Sibiu (R) – Nagyszében (H),
    Hermannstadt (G)
Sic (R) – Szék (H)
Sighişoara (R) – Szegesvár (H),
    Schässburg (G)
Sopron (H) – Ödenburg (G)
Štúrovo (Slk) – Párkány (H)
Subotica (S) – Szabadka (H)
Szeged (H) – Segedin (G)
Székesfehérvár (H) – Stuhlweissenburg (G)
Szombathely (H) – Steinamanger (G)

Tata (H) – Totis (G)
Timişoara (R) – Temesvár (H)
Tirgu Mureş (R) – Marosvásárhely (H)
Transdanubia (E) – Dunántúl (H)
Transylvania (R) – Erdély (H),
    Siebenbürgen (G)
Trnava (Slk) – Nagyszombat (H)

Užgorod (U) – Ungvár (H)

Vác (H) – Wartzen (G)
Vienna (E) – Wien (G), Bécs (H)
Villány (H) – Wieland (G)
Villánykövesd (H) – Growisch (G)

Wiener Neustadt (G) – Bécsújhely (H)

LONELY PLANET

You already know that Lonely Planet produces more than this one guidebook, but you might not be aware of the other products we have on this region. Here is a selection of titles which you may want to check out as well:

Central Europe
ISBN 0 86442 608 9
US$24.95 • UK£14.99 • 180FF

Eastern Europe
ISBN 0 86442 611 9
US$24.95 • UK£14.99 • 180FF

Hungary
ISBN 0 86442 685 2
US$14.95 • UK£8.99 • 99FF

Read this First Europe
ISBN 1 86450 136 7
US$14.99 • UK£8.99 • 99FF

Europe on a shoestring
ISBN 0 86442 648 8
US$24.95 • UK£14.99 • 180FF

Central Europe prasebook
ISBN 1 86450 226 6
US$7.99 • UK£4.50 • 49FF

Budapest city map
ISBN 1 86450 077 8
US$5.95 • UK£3.99 • 39FF

Eastern Europe phrasebook
ISBN 0 86442 260 1
US$6.95 • UK£4.50 • 55FF

Available wherever books are sold.

LONELY PLANET

ON THE ROAD

Travel Guides explore cities, regions and countries and supplies information on transport, restaurant and accommodation, regardless of your budget. They come with reliable, easy-to-use maps, practical advice, cultural and historical facts and a run down on attractions both on and off the beaten track. There are over 200 titles in this classic series covering nearly every country in the world.

 Lonely Planet Upgrades extend the shelf lives of existing travel guides by detailing any changes that may affect travel in a region since the book has been published. Upgrades can be downloaded for free on **www.lonelyplanet.com/upgrades**

For travellers with more time than money, **Shoestring** guides offer dependable, first-hand information with hundreds of detailed maps, plus insider tips for stretching money as far as possible. Covering entire continents in most cases, the six-volume shoestring guides have been known as 'backpackers' bibles' for over 25 years.

For the discerning short-term visitor, **Condensed** guides highlight the best a destination has to offer in a full-colour pocket-sized format designed for quick access. From top sights and walking tours to opinionated reviews of where to eat, stay, shop and have fun.

CitySync lets travellers use their Palm™ or Visor™ handheld computers to guide them through a city's highlights with quick tips on transport, history, cultural life, major sights and shopping and entertainment options. It can also quickly search and sort hundreds of reviews of hotels, restaurants and attractions and pinpoint the place on scrollable street maps. CitySync can be downloaded from www.citysync.com

MAPS & ATLASES

Lonely Planet's **City Maps** feature downtown and metropolitan maps as well as transit routes, and walking tours. The maps come complete with an index of streets, a listing of sights and a plastic coat for extra durability.

Road Atlases are an essential navigation tool for serious travellers. Cross-referenced with the guidebooks, they also feature distance and climate charts and a complete site index.

ESSENTIALS

Read This First books help new travellers to hit the road with confidence. These invaluable pre-departure guides give step-by-step advice on preparing for a trip, budgeting, arranging a visa, planning an itinerary and staying safe while still getting off the beaten track.

Healthy Travel pocket guides offer a regional run down on disease hot spots and practical advice on pre-departure health measures, staying well on the road and what to do in emergency situations. The guides come with a user-friendly design and helpful diagrams and tables.

Lonely Planet's **Phrasebooks** cover the essential words and phrases travellers may need when they're strangers in a strange land. It comes in a pocket-sized format with colour tabs for quick reference, extensive vocabulary lists, easy-to-follow pronunciation keys and two-way dictionaries,

Lonely Planet's **Travel Journal** is a lightweight but sturdy travel diary for jotting down all those on the road observations and significant travel moments. It comes with a handy time zone wheel, world maps and useful travel information.

Lonely Planet's eKno is an all-in-one communication service developed especially for travellers, with low-cost international calls, free email and voicemail so that you can keep in touch while on the road. Check it out on **www.ekno.lonelyplanet.com**

FOOD & RESTAURANT GUIDES

Lonely Planet's **Out to Eat** guides recommend the brightest and best places to eat and drink in the top international cities. These gourmet companions are arranged by neighbourhood, packed with dependable maps, garnished with scene-setting photos and served with quirky features.

For people who live to eat, drink and travel, **World Food** guides are full of lavish photos good enough to eat. They come packed with details on regional cuisine, guides to local markets and produce, sumptious recipes, useful phrases for shopping and dining, and a comprehensive culinary dictionary.

LONELY PLANET

OUTDOOR GUIDES

For those who believe the best way to see the world is on foot, Lonely Planet's **Walking Guides** detail everything from family strolls to difficult treks, with 'when to go and how to do it' advice supplemented by reliable maps and essential travel information .

Cycling Guides map a destination's best bike tours, long and short, in day-by-day detail. They contain all the information a cyclist needs, including advice on bike maintenance, places to eat and stay, innovative maps with detailed cues to the rides and elevation charts.

The **Watching Wildlife** series is perfect for travellers who want authoritative information but don't want to tote a field guide. Packed with advice on where, when and how to view a region's wildlife, each title features photos of over 300 species and contains engaging comments and insights into local flora and fauna.

With underwater colour photos throughout, **Pisces Books** explore the world's best diving and snorkelling areas. Each book contains listings of diving services and dive resorts and detailed information on depth, visibility, difficulty of dives and a round up of the marine life you're likely to see through your mask.

OFF THE ROAD

Journeys, the travel literature series written by renowned travel authors, capture the spirit of a place or illuminate a culture with a journalist's attention to detail and a novelistic flair for words. These are tales to soak up while you're actually on the road or dip into as an at-home armchair indulgence.

The new range of lavishly illustrated **Pictorial** books is just the ticket for both travellers and dreamers. Off-beat tales and vivid photographs bring the adventure of travel to your doorstep long before the journey begins and long after it is over.

The Lonely Planet **Videos** encourage the same independent tough-minded approach as the guidebooks. Currently airing throughout the world, this award-winning series features innovative footage and an all-original soundtrack.

Yes, we know, work is tough, so do a little bit of desk side-dreaming with the spiral bound Lonely Planet **Diary**, the tear away page-a-day **Day to Day Calendar** or any Lonely Planet **Wall Calendar**, filled with great photos from around the world.

TRAVELLERS NETWORK

Lonely Planet online. Lonely Planet's award-winning web site has insider information on hundreds of destinations from Amsterdam to Zimbabwe complete with interactive maps and relevant links. The site also offers the latest travel news, recent reports from travellers on the road, guidebook upgrades, a travel links site, an online book buying option and a lively traveller's bulletin board. It can be viewed at www.lonelyplanet.com or AOL keyword: lp

Planet Talk is the quarterly print newsletter full of gossip, advice, anecdotes and author articles. It provides an antidote to the being-at-home blues and lets you plan and dream for the next trip. Contact the nearest Lonely Planet office for your free copy.

Comet, the free Lonely Planet newsletter, comes via email once a month. It's loaded with travel news, advice, dispatches from authors, travel competitions and letters from readers. To subscribe, click on the Comet subscription link on the front page of the web site.

LONELY PLANET

Guides by Region

Lonely Planet is known worldwide for publishing practical, reliable and no-nonsense travel information in our guides and on our web site. The Lonely Planet list covers just about every accessible part of the world. Currently there are fifteen series: travel guides, Shoestrings, Condensed, Phrasebooks, Read This First, Healthy Travel, Walking guides, Cycling guides, Pisces Diving & Snorkeling guides, City Maps, Travel Atlases, Out to Eat, World Food, Journeys travel literature and Pictorials.

AFRICA Africa on a shoestring • Africa – the South • Arabic (Egyptian) phrasebook • Arabic (Moroccan) phrasebook • Cairo • Cape Town • Cape Town city map • Central Africa • East Africa • Egypt • Egypt travel atlas • Ethiopian (Amharic) phrasebook • The Gambia & Senegal • Healthy Travel Africa • Kenya • Kenya travel atlas • Malawi, Mozambique & Zambia • Morocco • North Africa • Read This First Africa • South Africa, Lesotho & Swaziland • South Africa, Lesotho & Swaziland travel atlas • Swahili phrasebook • Tanzania, Zanzibar & Pemba • Trekking in East Africa • Tunisia • West Africa • Zimbabwe, Botswana & Namibia • Zimbabwe, Botswana & Nambia Travel Atlas • World Food Morocco
Travel Literature: The Rainbird: A Central African Journey • Songs to an African Sunset: A Zimbabwean Story • Mali Blues: Traveling to an African Beat

AUSTRALIA & THE PACIFIC Auckland • Australia • Australian phrasebook • Bushwalking in Australia • Bushwalking in Papua New Guinea • Fiji • Fijian phrasebook • Healthy Travel Australia, NZ and the Pacific • Islands of Australia's Great Barrier Reef • Melbourne • Melbourne city map • Micronesia • New Caledonia • New South Wales & the ACT • New Zealand • Northern Territory • Outback Australia • Out To Eat – Melbourne • Out to Eat – Sydney • Papua New Guinea • Pidgin phrasebook • Queensland • Rarotonga & the Cook Islands • Samoa • Solomon Islands • South Australia • South Pacific • South Pacific Languages phrasebook • Sydney • Sydney city map • Sydney Condensed • Tahiti & French Polynesia • Tasmania • Tonga • Tramping in New Zealand • Vanuatu • Victoria • Western Australia
Travel Literature: Islands in the Clouds • Kiwi Tracks: A New Zealand Journey • Sean & David's Long Drive

CENTRAL AMERICA & THE CARIBBEAN Bahamas, Turks & Caicos • Bermuda • Central America on a shoestring • Costa Rica • Cuba • Dominican Republic & Haiti • Eastern Caribbean • Guatemala, Belize & Yucatán: La Ruta Maya • Jamaica • Mexico • Mexico City • Panama • Puerto Rico • Read This First Central & South America • World Food Mexico
Travel Literature: Green Dreams: Travels in Central America

EUROPE Amsterdam • Amsterdam city map • Andalucía • Austria • Baltic States phrasebook • Barcelona • Berlin • Berlin city map • Britain • British phrasebook • Brussels, Bruges & Antwerp • Budapest city map • Canary Islands • Central Europe • Central Europe phrasebook • Corfu & Ionians • Corsica • Crete • Crete Condensed • Croatia • Cyprus • Czech & Slovak Republics • Denmark • Dublin • Eastern Europe • Eastern Europe phrasebook • Edinburgh • Estonia, Latvia & Lithuania • Europe on a shoestring • Finland • Florence • France • French phrasebook • Germany • German phrasebook • Greece • Greek Islands • Greek phrasebook • Hungary • Iceland, Greenland & the Faroe Islands • Istanbul City Map • Ireland • Italian phrasebook • Italy • Krakow •Lisbon • London • London city map • London Condensed • Mediterranean Europe • Mediterranean Europe phrasebook • Munich • Norway • Paris • Paris city map • Paris Condensed • Poland • Portugal • Portugese phrasebook • Portugal travel atlas • Prague • Prague city map • Provence & the Côte d'Azur • Read This First Europe • Romania & Moldova • Rome • Russia, Ukraine & Belarus • Russian phrasebook • Scandinavian & Baltic Europe • Scandinavian Europe phrasebook • Scotland • Slovenia • Spain • Spanish phrasebook • St Petersburg • Switzerland • Trekking in Spain • Ukrainian phrasebook • Venice • Vienna • Walking in Britain • Walking in Ireland • Walking in Italy • Walking in Spain • Walking in Switzerland • Western Europe • Western Europe phrasebook • World Food Italy • World Food Spain
Travel Literature: The Olive Grove: Travels in Greece

INDIAN SUBCONTINENT Bangladesh • Bengali phrasebook • Bhutan • Delhi • Goa • Hindi & Urdu phrasebook • India • India & Bangladesh travel atlas • Indian Himalaya • Karakoram Highway • Kerala • Mumbai (Bombay) • Nepal • Nepali phrasebook • Pakistan • Rajasthan • Read This First: Asia & India • South India • Sri Lanka • Sri Lanka phrasebook • Trekking in the Indian Himalaya • Trekking in the Karakoram & Hindukush • Trekking in the Nepal Himalaya
Travel Literature: In Rajasthan • Shopping for Buddhas • The Age Of Kali

LONELY PLANET

Mail Order

L onely Planet products are distributed worldwide.They are also available by mail order from Lonely Planet, so if you have difficulty finding a title please write to us. North and South American residents should write to 150 Linden St, Oakland CA 94607, USA; European and African residents should write to 10a Spring Place, London, NW5 3BH; and residents of other countries to PO Box 617, Hawthorn, Victoria 3122, Australia.

ISLANDS OF THE INDIAN OCEAN Madagascar & Comoros • Maldives • Mauritius, Réunion & Seychelles

MIDDLE EAST & CENTRAL ASIA Bahrain, Kuwait & Qatar • Central Asia • Central Asia phrasebook • Dubai • Hebrew phrasebook • Iran • Israel & the Palestinian Territories • Israel & the Palestinian Territories travel atlas • Istanbul • Istanbul to Cairo on a shoestring • Jerusalem • Jerusalem City Map • Jordan • Jordan, Syria & Lebanon travel atlas • Lebanon • Middle East • Oman & the United Arab Emirates • Syria • Turkey • Turkey travel atlas • Turkish phrasebook • Yemen
Travel Literature: The Gates of Damascus • Kingdom of the Film Stars: Journey into Jordan • Black on Black: Iran Revisited

NORTH AMERICA Alaska • Backpacking in Alaska • Baja California • California & Nevada • California Condensed • Canada • Chicago • Chicago city map • Deep South • Florida • Hawaii • Honolulu • Las Vegas • Los Angeles • Miami • New England • New Orleans • New York City • New York city map • New York Condensed • New York, New Jersey & Pennsylvania • Oahu • Pacific Northwest USA • Puerto Rico • Rocky Mountain • San Francisco • San Francisco city map • Seattle • Southwest USA • Texas • USA • USA phrasebook • Vancouver • Washington, DC & the Capital Region • Washington DC city map
Travel Literature: Drive Thru America

NORTH-EAST ASIA Beijing • Cantonese phrasebook • China • Hong Kong • Hong Kong city map • Hong Kong, Macau & Guangzhou • Japan • Japanese phrasebook • Japanese audio pack • Korea • Korean phrasebook • Kyoto • Mandarin phrasebook • Mongolia • Mongolian phrasebook • North-East Asia on a shoestring • Seoul • South-West China • Taiwan • Tibet • Tibetan phrasebook • Tokyo
Travel Literature: Lost Japan • In Xanadu

SOUTH AMERICA Argentina, Uruguay & Paraguay • Bolivia • Brazil • Brazilian phrasebook • Buenos Aires • Chile & Easter Island • Chile & Easter Island travel atlas • Colombia • Ecuador & the Galapagos Islands • Healthy Travel Central & South America • Latin American Spanish phrasebook • Peru • Quechua phrasebook • Rio de Janeiro • Rio de Janeiro city map • South America on a shoestring • Trekking in the Patagonian Andes • Venezuela
Travel Literature: Full Circle: A South American Journey

SOUTH-EAST ASIA Bali & Lombok • Bangkok • Bangkok city map • Burmese phrasebook • Cambodia • Hanoi • Healthy Travel Asia & India • Hill Tribes phrasebook • Ho Chi Minh City • Indonesia • Indonesia's Eastern Islands • Indonesian phrasebook • Indonesian audio pack • Jakarta • Java • Laos • Lao phrasebook • Laos travel atlas • Malay phrasebook • Malaysia, Singapore & Brunei • Myanmar (Burma) • Philippines • Pilipino (Tagalog) phrasebook • Read This First Asia & India • Singapore • South-East Asia on a shoestring • South-East Asia phrasebook • Thailand • Thailand's Islands & Beaches • Thailand travel atlas • Thai phrasebook • Thai audio pack • Vietnam • Vietnamese phrasebook • Vietnam travel atlas • World Food Thailand • World Food Vietnam

ALSO AVAILABLE: Antarctica • The Arctic • Brief Encounters: Stories of Love, Sex & Travel • Chasing Rickshaws • Lonely Planet Unpacked • Not the Only Planet: Travel Stories from Science Fiction • Sacred India • Travel with Children • Traveller's Tales

Index

Text

Boxed Text

MAP 1 – BUDAPEST & ENVIRONS

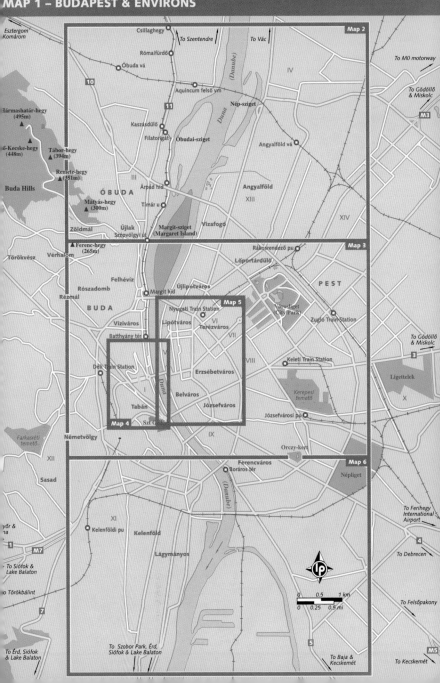

MAP 2

Csillaghegy

To Római Camping,
Touring Hotel &
Aboriginal Restaurant

Rómaifürdő

Óbuda vá

Aquincum
1

Aquincum felső vm

Keled út

Pók u

2

Záhony
3

Aquincum

Kaszásdűlő

Filatorigát

Május park

7

Óbudai-sziget

Bojtár

Kunigunda útja

Bécsi út

Farkastorki út

Huszti út

Hévizi út

8

9

Raktár u

Remetehegyi út

Szépvölgyi út

Remetehegy

Buda Hills

Bécsi út

Szőlő u

ÓBUDA

Vörösvári út

Vöröskereszt utca

10
11
12
13
14
15
16
17

Flórián
tér

Szentlélek
tér

Árpád
híd

Duna
(Danube)

Szabadság
strand

18

To Udvarház
Restaurant

Kiscelli u

42

Serfőző u

38
37

39
40

Árpád híd
(Árpád Bridge)

Mátyás-hegy
(300m)

Kenyeres
41

Dévai Bíró
M tér

San Marco utca

Selmeci u

Tél u

Újlaki rkp

28
29
27

30

31

43

44

Timár u

Viador u

46

45

Nagyszombat u

Újlak

Tinódi u

Elektromos setány

Népfürdő u

32

33
34

Csatárka út

Zöldlomb út

Pusztaszeri út

51

Csemete u

47
49
48

50

Kolosy
tér

Szépvölgyi út

36

Margit-sziget
(Margaret Island)

Zöldmál

Map 3

Cserfa u

MAP 2

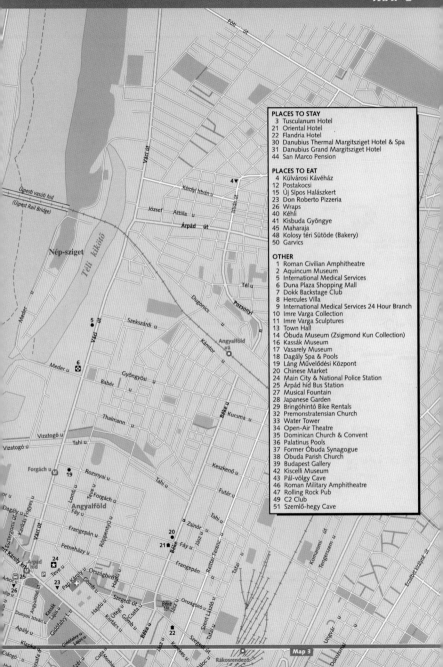

PLACES TO STAY
3 Tusculanum Hotel
21 Oriental Hotel
22 Flandria Hotel
30 Danubius Thermal Margitsziget Hotel & Spa
31 Danubius Grand Margitsziget Hotel
44 San Marco Pension

PLACES TO EAT
4 Külvárosi Kávéház
12 Postakocsi
15 Új Sípos Halászkert
23 Don Roberto Pizzeria
26 Wraps
40 Kéhli
41 Kisbuda Gyöngye
45 Maharaja
48 Kolosy téri Sütöde (Bakery)
50 Garvics

OTHER
1 Roman Civilian Amphitheatre
2 Aquincum Museum
5 International Medical Services
6 Duna Plaza Shopping Mall
7 Dokk Backstage Club
8 Hercules Villa
9 International Medical Services 24 Hour Branch
10 Imre Varga Collection
11 Imre Varga Sculptures
13 Town Hall
14 Óbuda Museum (Zsigmond Kun Collection)
16 Kassák Museum
17 Vasarely Museum
18 Dagály Spa & Pools
19 Láng Művelődési Központ
20 Chinese Market
24 Main City & National Police Station
25 Árpád híd Bus Station
27 Musical Fountain
28 Japanese Garden
29 Bringóhintó Bike Rentals
32 Premonstratensian Church
33 Water Tower
34 Open-Air Theatre
35 Dominican Church & Convent
36 Palatinus Pools
37 Former Óbuda Synagogue
38 Óbuda Parish Church
39 Budapest Gallery
42 Kiscelli Museum
43 Pál-völgy Cave
46 Roman Military Amphitheatre
47 Rolling Rock Pub
49 C2 Club
51 Szemlő-hegy Cave

Map 3

MAP 3

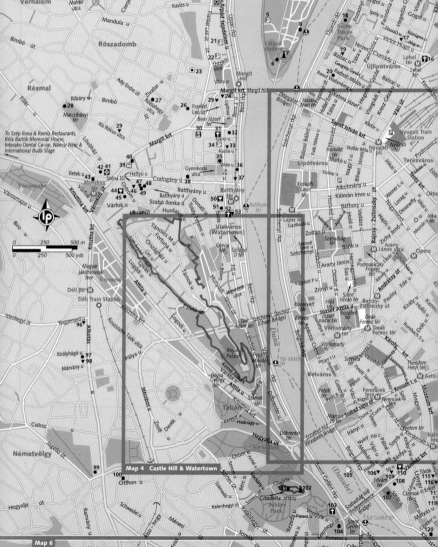

Zöldmál

Map 2

Csemete u
Szépvölgyi út
Kolosy tér

Vizaf

Révész u

Vizaf

Margit-sziget
(Margaret Island)

Vérhalom

Pusztaszeri
Törökvész
Kupeczky u
Pentelei
Molnár
utca

Mandula u

Röszadomb

Rézmal

Ribáry u
28
Marczibányi tér

Bimbó

To Szép Ilona & Remiz Restaurants,
Béla Bartók Memorial House,
Interako Dental Co-op, Náncsi Néni &
International Buda Stage

Városmajor

Déli pu
Déli Train Station

Istenhegyi út

Nagyenyed u
96

Királyhágó u
97
Márvány u
98

Csörsz u

Németvölgy

Hegyalja út

99
100
Otthon

Map 6

Nedec-vár u

Felhévíz

Margit krt

Víziváros
(Watertown)

Tabán

Map 4 Castle Hill & Watertown

Jubilee
Park

Szent Gellért tér

MAP 3

PLACES TO STAY
8 Sirály Hostel
11 California Summer Hostel
12 Diáksport Hostel
14 Góliát Hotel
27 Papillon Pension
38 Buda Center Hotel & Grand Shanghai Restaurant
40 Bakfark Summer Hostel
43 Büro Pension & Söröző a Szent Jupáthoz Restaurant
49 Garzonház Serviced Apartments
56 Liget Hotel
70 Délibáb Hotel
71 Centrál Hotel
75 Radio Inn Hotel
77 Benczúr Hotel
80 Station Guesthouse
82 Dominik Pension
88 Ananda Hostel
91 Park Hotel
95 Royal Guesthouse
100 Kis Gellért Hotel
101 Citadella Hostel & Hotel
104 Gellért Hotel & Baths
111 Selye Hostel
120 Strawberry II Summer Hostel
122 Strawberry I Summer Hostel
123 Thomas Hotel & Trafó Kortárs Művészetek Háza
124 Orient Summer Hostel

PLACES TO EAT
2 Vadrózsa
17 Leroy's Country Pub
19 Móri Borozó
24 Hong Kong Pearl Garden & Gasztró Hús-Hentesáru (Butcher Shop)
25 Café Gusto
29 Marxim Pizzeria
33 Kacsa
37 Jukebox Diner
46 Nagyi Palacsintázója
47 Macbeth
53 Angelika Café
58 Gundel & Bagolyvár
67 Robinson
81 Yangtze River
83 Nagy Fal
84 Kilenc Sárkány
96 Il Treno Pizzeria

98 Mongolian Barbecue
106 Taverna Rembetiko Piraeus
109 Chan Chan Restaurant
115 Marie Kristensen Sandwich Bar
116 El Greco
117 Coquan's Café
118 Shiraz (Takeaway)
119 Shiraz (Restaurant)
121 Niszrok (Vegetarian Restaurant)

MUSEUMS
30 Foundry Museum
57 Museum of Fine Arts
62 Transport Museum
63 Petőfi Csarnok & Aviation Museum
65 Vajdahunyad Castle & Agriculture Museum
69 Műcsarnok (Palace of Art)
72 Ferenc Hopp Museum
73 György Ráth Museum
113 Museum of Applied Arts

OTHER
1 Rózsakert Shopping Mall & Cyber Sushi
3 Újlak Synagogue
4 Poco Loco Pub
5 Alfréd Hajós National Sports Pool
6 Bike Rental & Stadium
7 Centennial Monument
9 Franciscan Church & Monastery Ruins
10 Hélia Thermal Hotel Spa & Pools
13 Ibis Volga Hotel & Americana Rent-a-Car
15 BVSC Swimming Pool
16 Lehel Church
18 Raoul Wallenberg Memorial
20 Pendragon Bookshop
21 Béla Komjádi Swimming Pool
22 Lukács Bath
23 Gül Baba's Tomb
26 Hungarian Automobile Club
28 Marczibányi téri Művelődési Központ
31 St Florian Chapel
32 Foreign Ministry
34 Király Bath

35 Military Court of Justice & Fő utca Prison
36 Herend Village Pottery
39 Széna tér Bus Station
41 Mammut Shopping Mall
42 Fény utca Market
44 Oscar's Café & Pub
45 Budapest Wine Society
48 American Clinic
50 Polo Pub
51 Market Hall & Supermarket
52 St Anne's Church
54 MÁV Hospital
55 MÁV Hospital (Emergency Entrance)
59 City Zoo
60 Fővárosi Nagycirkusz (Grand Circus)
61 Széchenyi Bath
64 George Washington Statue
66 Ják Chapel
68 Millenary Monument
74 Városligeti Calvinist Church
76 British Council
78 KEOKH (Foreign Registration Office)
79 America House Library & ELTE University
85 Közép-Európai Táncszínház
86 Angel (Angyal) Club
87 Almássy tér Reception Centre
89 Erkel Theatre
90 Nonstop Food Shop & Budapest Tourist
92 Budapest Horse Riding Club
93 Népstadion Bus Station
94 Rákóczi tér Market
97 Nonstop Food Shop
99 Budapesti Kongresszusi Központ (Congress Centre)
102 Independence Monument
103 Cliff Chapel
105 International Ferry Landing Stage & Hydrofoil Pier
107 Budapest Economics University & Közgáz Pince Klub
108 Nagycsarnok (Central Market Hall)
110 Jazz Garden
112 Corvin Filmpalota
114 Paris, Texas Club & Pink Cadillac Pizzeria

Central Synagogue, Budapest

MAP 4 – CASTLE HILL & WATERTOWN

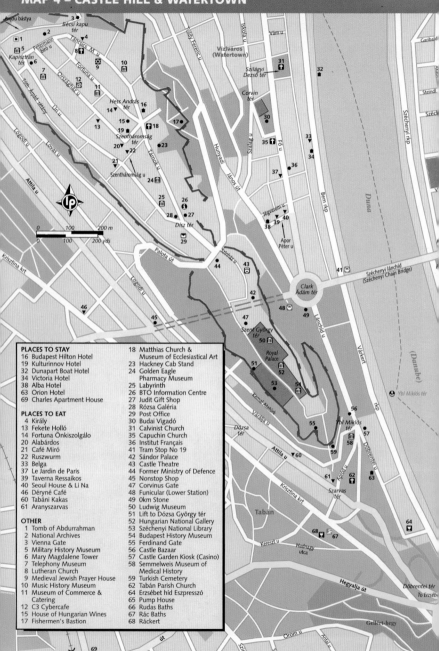

PLACES TO STAY
16 Budapest Hilton Hotel
19 Kulturinnov Hotel
32 Dunapart Boat Hotel
34 Victoria Hotel
38 Alba Hotel
63 Orion Hotel
69 Charles Apartment House

PLACES TO EAT
4 Király
13 Fekete Holló
19 Fortuna Önkiszolgáló
20 Alabárdos
21 Café Miró
22 Ruszwurm
33 Belga
37 Le Jardin de Paris
39 Taverna Ressaikos
40 Seoul House & Li Na
46 Déryné Café
60 Tabáni Kakas
61 Aranyszarvas

OTHER
1 Tomb of Abdurrahman
2 National Archives
3 Vienna Gate
5 Military History Museum
6 Mary Magdalene Tower
7 Telephony Museum
8 Lutheran Church
9 Medieval Jewish Prayer House
10 Music History Museum
11 Museum of Commerce & Catering
12 C3 Cybercafe
15 House of Hungarian Wines
17 Fishermen's Bastion

18 Matthias Church & Museum of Ecclesiastical Art
23 Hackney Cab Stand
24 Golden Eagle Pharmacy Museum
25 Labyrinth
26 BTO Information Centre
27 Judit Gift Shop
28 Rózsa Galéria
29 Post Office
30 Budai Vigadó
31 Calvinist Church
36 Capuchin Church
37 Institut Français
41 Tram Stop No 19
42 Sándor Palace
43 Castle Theatre
44 Former Ministry of Defence
45 Nonstop Shop
47 Corvinus Gate
48 Funicular (Lower Station)
49 0km Stone
50 Ludwig Museum
51 Lift to Dózsa György tér
52 Hungarian National Gallery
53 Széchenyi National Library
54 Budapest History Museum
55 Ferdinand Gate
56 Castle Bazaar
57 Castle Garden Kiosk (Casino)
58 Semmelweis Museum of Medical History
59 Turkish Cemetery
62 Tabán Parish Church
64 Erzsébet híd Eszpresszó
65 Pump House
66 Rudas Baths
67 Rác Baths
68 Ráckert

MAP 5 – CENTRAL PEST

MAP 5

PLACES TO STAY
10 City Ring Pension
11 Metro Hotel
16 Best Hostel
19 Radisson Béke Hotel
24 Yellow Submarine Lotus Hostel
47 Bánki Summer Hostel
66 Caterina Guesthouse
76 Medosz Hotel
122 Club Ambra Hotel
127 K+K Opera Hotel
176 Nemzeti Hotel
177 Emke Hotel
181 Marco Polo Hostel
182 King's Restaurant & Hotel
199 Inter-Continental Hotel
205 Kempinski Corvinus Hotel
215 Budapest Marriott Hotel
236 City Pilvax Pension
245 Millennium Court
271 Museum Guesthouse
276 Ibis Centrum Hotel
280 Apáczai Summer Hostel
284 City Mátyás Pension

PLACES TO EAT
1 Mézes Kuckó Bakery
4 Bambusz
5 Művész Bohém
8 Okay Italia
9 Három Testvér
17 La Petite France
21 Szendvics Bár Center
26 Don Pepe Pizzeria
27 Okay Italia
30 Török-Kínai Büfé
37 Biarritz Cafe-Restaurant
38 Szalai Cafe
45 Semiramis
50 Chez Daniel
54 Lukács Cafe
60 Jorgosz
62 PestiEst Cafe
63 Incognito Cafe & Pompeii Pizza
64 Café Vian & Undergrass Club
68 Teaház a Vörös Oroszlánhoz
70 Butterfly Ice-Cream Shop
71 McDonald's
72 Arigato
75 Octopus
77 Bombay Palace
82 Soho Palacsintabár
87 Marquis de Salade
89 Tüköry & Hold utca Market
92 Pick Ház

93 Tulipán
94 Mastro Geppetto
95 Iguana
101 Via Luna
106 Articsóka
107 Komédiás Cafe
111 Művész Cafe
112 Két Szerecsen Cafe
113 Falafel Faloda
114 Frici Papa Kifőzdéje
115 Bisquine Crêperie
121 Kádár Canteen
126 Spaghetti Ice Gelateria
133 Happy Bank
134 Mirákulum
135 Café Kör
136 Kisharang Canteen
137 Durcin Sandwich Bar
140 Nagy Fal (Fast-Food)
142 Self-Service Restaurant
143 Lou Lou & Gandhi
147 Mérleg
148 Xi Hu & Coquan's Café
149 La Fontaine & National Philharmonic Ticket Office
155 Pesti Vendéglő
156 Durcin Sandwich Bar
159 Lakshmi
160 Al-Amir
161 Kővári Kosher Delicatessen
162 Fröhlich Cake Shop
164 Hanna
165 Carmel Pince
166 Kosher Bakery
168 La Bodega
171 Arany Folyó
172 Gül Baba
173 Kulacs Restaurant
174 New York Café
179 Grill 99
187 Senara & Fausto's
202 Sushi An
210 Gerbeaud & Lion Fountain
213 Replay Café
214 Cyrano & Cosmo
226 Café Eklektika
234 Nagy Tamás Cheese Shop
256 Tennessee Grill & Ball'n' Bull Pub
258 Budapest Blue Café
261 Múzeum Café-Restaurant
275 Centrál Önkiszolgáló
289 CD Fű Teahouse
291 Fatál
293 Club Verne
298 Govinda
299 Taverna Dionysos

300 Sole d'Italia
301 1000 Tea

PUBS, BARS & CLUBS
13 E-Play Cyber Club
29 Trocadero Club
31 Süss Fél Nap
46 Becketts Pub
58 Hades Jazztaurant
67 Cactus Juice
74 Bamboo Club
80 Fashion Café
83 Piaf
84 Poco Loco Tropical
85 Picasso Point
103 Mystery Bar
141 Garage Café
170 Old Man's Music Pub
183 Long Jazz Club
185 Harley Café
186 Portside Pub
198 Columbus Pub
224 Merlin Club & Theatre
227 No Limit Club
252 Darling Bar
266 Action Bar
268 Irish Cat Pub
270 Fél Tíz Jazz Club
272 Darshan Café
273 Darshan Udvar
278 Janis Pub
288 Fat Mo's
297 Capella

TOURIST OFFICES, ACCOMMODATION SERVICES & BOOKING AGENCIES
14 Ibusz
40 Cooptourist
59 Tourinform
65 BTO Information Branch
69 Ticket Express
79 MÁV Ticket Office
96 Express
117 Alfonz Minihotel Room Service
125 Színházak Központi Jegyiroda (Central Theatre Ticket Office)
129 Cooptourist
130 Budatours
145 Budapest Tourist
154 Vista Travel Centre
157 Vista Visitor Centre
191 Ibusz
204 Tourinform (Main Branch)
206 Malév Office

MAP 5

207 Mahart Ticket Office
218 Tribus
228 Express
238 Ibusz (Main Office) & Párisi Udvar
248 Music Mix Ticket Office
250 Charles Tourist Service
281 Pegazus Tours
290 Hotelinfo Travel Agency

MUSEUMS
42 Ethnography Museum
55 Academy of Fine Arts
57 Franz Liszt Memorial Museum
118 Stamp Museum
153 Postal Museum
167 Electrotechnology Museum
190 Great Synagogue & Jewish Museum
264 Hungarian Museum of Literature
267 Hungarian National Museum

SHOPPING
3 Clothing Shops
7 Pless & Fox Jewellers
22 Ajka Crystal
23 Játékszerek Anno
28 Dob Music Shop
32 Anna Antkvitás
33 Qualitás Antiques
34 BÁV Shop
35 Kárpáti és Szőny Antiquarian Bookshop
39 Pinter Antiques
78 Liszt Ferenc Zeneműbolt & Írók Boltja Bookshop
90 Kódex Bookshop
104 Kollin Antiquarian Bookshop
105 Haas & Czjzek Porcelain
119 Billerbeck Duvet Shop
128 Wave Music Shop
138 Bestsellers Bookshop
150 La Boutique des Vins Wine Shop
163 Concerto Hanglemezbolt Bookshop
178 Lekvárium Jam Shop
184 Libri Könyvpalota Bookshop
193 Simonyi Galéria
196 Nádor Tex Duvet Shop
201 Herend Shop
216 Tangó Classic
219 Polgár Galéria és Aukciósház
220 Prés Ház Wine Shop
221 Rózsavölgyi Music Shop

225 Bookshop
232 Belvárosi Antiques
233 Holló Atelier Folk Art
239 Zsolnay
240 Vass Shoemakers
241 Szamos Marzipan Shop
242 Folkart Centrum
243 Ajka Crystal
244 Arten Studio
246 Libri Studium Bookshop
249 Atlantisz Bookshop
251 Monarchia
253 Babaklinika Gift Shop
262 Központi Antikvárium
265 Sixvil
274 Iguana Clothing Shop
279 Rhythm'n' Books
282 Orisis Bookshop
283 Belvárosi Aukciósház
285 Selene Equestrian Shop
294 Manier
302 Hephaistos Háza Furniture

OTHER
2 Rothschild Supermarket
6 Vígszínház (Gaiety Theatre)
12 West End City Centre Shopping Mall
15 Post Office
18 Gyöker Klub
20 Teréz Patika (Pharmacy)
25 Kaiser's Supermarket
36 White House
41 Parliament
43 Economy Ministry
44 Inner Town Police Station
48 Copy General
49 Cityrama Bus Tours
51 Palavicini Palace
52 Former Kodály Residence
53 Kolibri Pince Theatre
56 Bábszínház (Puppet Theatre)
61 Liszt Ferenc Zeneakadémia
73 Művész Cinema
81 Budapesti Operettszínház
86 Cartographia Map Shop
88 Hungária Biztosító
91 Imre Nagy Monument
97 Soviet Army Memorial
98 MTV Building
99 US Embassy
100 National Bank of Hungary
102 British Chamber of Commerce
108 Thália Theatre
109 House of Hungarian Photographers

110 Goethe Institute & Eckermann Cybercafé
116 Örökmozgó Filmmúzeum
120 Ghetto Market
123 Új Színház (New Theatre)
124 Opera House
131 St Stephen's Basilica
132 Top Clean Laundry
139 Central European University & Academic Bookshop
144 Hungarian Academy of Sciences
146 Duna Palota
151 Lira & Lánt Map Shop
152 Inka Car Rental
158 SOS Dental Service
169 BKV Office
175 Julius Meinl Supermarket
180 Libri Map Shop
188 Irisz Szalon Laundry
189 Fotex Photo Shop
192 Nonstop Food Shop
194 Erzsébet tér Bus Station
195 OTP Bank
197 Nádor Szalon Laundry
200 Finance Ministry
203 UK Embassy
208 Pesti Vigadó
209 Vigadó Ticket Office
211 Citibank
212 American Express & American Chamber of Commerce
217 Nonstop Food Shop
222 Belvárosi Telephone Centre & Matáv Internet Café
223 City Hall
229 Puskin Cinema
230 World Press House
231 Pest County Hall
235 Main Post Office & Entrance for Poste Restante
237 József Katona Theatre
247 Inner Town Parish Church
254 DHL
255 Teleport Internet Café
257 Csillag Gyógyszertár (Pharmacy)
259 Kenguru Ride Service
260 Italian Institute of Culture
263 University Library
269 Ervin Szabó Library
277 Budapest Net Cybercafe
286 St Michael's Church
287 Lokomos Csemege
292 Serbian Orthodox Church
295 Kalamajka Táncház
296 Foreign Language Library

MAP 6

Map 3

Szt Gellért tér

Szent
Gellért
tér

Nedec-vár u

Ménesi
Alsó-hegyi
Frosi u
Somlói út

Mínerva u
Kelenhegyi út
Orlay u
Pipacs u
Kelenhegyi út

Csíky
Zenta u
Zenta u

Műegyetem rkp

Petőfi híd

Villányi út
Karolina út
Dioszegi út
Dávid Ferenc u
Tas vezér u

Ménesi
Bartók Béla út
Mányoki út
Mészöly u
Bertalan

Lajos
Lágymányosi
Krusper u
Sztoczek
József u

Fehérkő út
Badacsonyi
Ménesi

Móricz
Zsigmond körtér
Bartók Béla út

Karinthy Frigyes út

Bocskai út
Fehérvári út
Fenceketlen-
tó

Nagyszőlős u
Gárdos M u
Hamzsabégi út

Bártfai

Sárbogárdi út
Kanizsai u
Baranyai u

Körösy József u
Október 23 u
Irinyi József u

Budafoki út
Béközségi u
Budafoki út

Bartók Béla
Bartók
Fraknó
Béla

Budaörsi út
Somorjai út

Kelenföldi
pu

Etele út
Mérnök
Etele út
Bikszádi út

Kelenföld
Galambóc
Fehérvári
Bánát
Lecke u
Hengermalom út

Sopron u
Sztregova u
Nagyboráreviri u

Barazda u

Lágymányos

Major u
Andor u
Csákvár u

Allende
park
Csurgói
Zsombor u
Galvani u

Latinca Sándor
Szabados Sándor
Fehérvári
Temesvár u
Kondorosi
út

Kelenvölgy
Kazinczi u
Hunyadi
Mátyás u
Adács u

Zágrábi u

Építész u

Körmend u

Kunhegyes u
Vegyész u

Szerém u
Hunyadi - János

Duna
(Danube)

Ady Endre út

Rózsavölgy
Ady Endre út
Anna u
Budafok-
Albertfalva
M
Kitérő út
Hunyadi J u

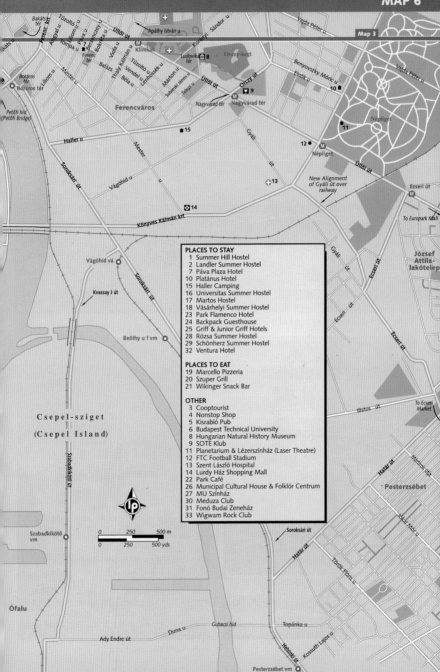

MAP 6

PLACES TO STAY
1 Summer Hill Hostel
2 Landler Summer Hostel
7 Páva Plaza Hotel
10 Platánus Hotel
15 Haller Camping
16 Universitas Summer Hostel
17 Martos Hostel
18 Vásárhelyi Summer Hostel
23 Park Flamenco Hotel
24 Backpack Guesthouse
25 Griff & Junior Griff Hotels
28 Rózsa Summer Hostel
29 Schönherz Summer Hostel
32 Ventura Hotel

PLACES TO EAT
19 Marcello Pizzeria
20 Szuper Grill
21 Wikinger Snack Bar

OTHER
3 Cooptourist
4 Nonstop Shop
5 Kisrabló Pub
6 Budapest Technical University
8 Hungarian Natural History Museum
9 SOTE Klub
11 Planetarium & Lézerszínház (Laser Theatre)
12 FTC Football Stadium
13 Szent László Hospital
14 Lurdy Ház Shopping Mall
22 Park Café
26 Municipal Cultural House & Folklór Centrum
27 MU Színház
30 Meduza Club
31 Fonó Budai Zeneház
33 Wigwam Rock Club

DAVID GREEDY

Parliament on a sweeping bend of the Danube

KIMBERLY GRANT

The old section of Buda

CHRIS MELLOR

Fishermans Bastion, Buda

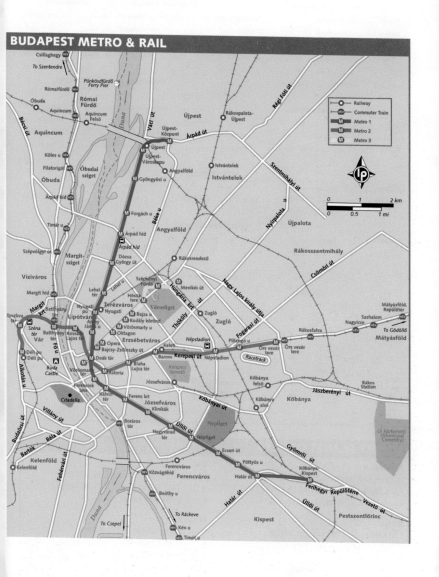

BUDAPEST METRO & RAIL

MAP LEGEND

CITY ROUTES

Freeway .... Freeway	======== Unsealed Road
Highway .... Primary Road	——→—— One Way Street
Road .... Secondary Road	.... Pedestrian Street
Street .... Street	⊓⊓⊓⊓⊓ Stepped Street
Lane .... Lane	)= = = ... Tunnel
.... On/Off Ramp	======== Footbridge

HYDROGRAPHY

.... River, Creek	Dry Lake; Salt Lake
.... Canal	Spring; Rapids
Lake	Waterfalls

REGIONAL ROUTES

========= Tollway, Freeway
========= Primary Road
.... Secondary Road
.... Minor Road

TRANSPORT ROUTES & STATIONS

——○—— Train	─ ─ ─ ─☐ Ferry
─ ─ ─ Underground Train	─ ─ ─ ─ Walking Trail
═══Ⓜ═══ Metro	Walking Tour
═ ═ ═ ═ Tramway	.... Path
──┼─┼─┼── Cable Car, Chairlift	Pier or Jetty

BOUNDARIES

—·—·— .... International
—··—·· .... State
— — — .... Disputed
▬▬▬ .... Fortified Wall

AREA FEATURES

.... Building	.... Market	⌐ .... Beach
❁ .... Park, Gardens	.... Sports Ground	+ + + ... Cemetery

.... Campus
.... Plaza

POPULATION SYMBOLS

✪ CAPITAL .... National Capital	● CITY .... City	● Village .... Village
◉ CAPITAL .... State Capital	● Town .... Town	.... Urban Area

MAP SYMBOLS

● .... Place to Stay	▼ .... Place to Eat	● .... Point of Interest

✈ .... Airport	♆ .... Fountain	▥ .... Museum	▣ .... Swimming Pool
✜ .... Archaeological Site	❶ .... Golf Course	▣ .... Parking	✡ .... Synagogue
❸ .... Bank	✛ .... Hospital	✛ .... Police Station	▣ .... Theatre
▣ .... Bus Terminal	▣ .... Internet Cafe	▭ .... Post Office	▣ .... Tomb
⌂ .... Cave	❊ .... Lookout	▣ .... Pub or Bar	❶ .... Tourist Information
✚ ⊕ .... Church	▲ .... Monument	✛ .... Shopping Centre	▩ .... Winery
▣ .... Cinema	☾ .... Mosque	▥ .... Stately Home	▣ .... Zoo

Note: not all symbols displayed above appear in this book

LONELY PLANET OFFICES

Australia
PO Box 617, Hawthorn, Victoria 3122
☎ 03 9819 1877 fax 03 9819 6459
email: talk2us@lonelyplanet.com.au

USA
150 Linden St, Oakland, CA 94607
☎ 510 893 8555 TOLL FREE: 800 275 8555
fax 510 893 8572
email: info@lonelyplanet.com

UK
10a Spring Place, London NW5 3BH
☎ 020 7428 4800 fax 020 7428 4828
email: go@lonelyplanet.co.uk

France
1 rue du Dahomey, 75011 Paris
☎ 01 55 25 33 00 fax 01 55 25 33 01
email: bip@lonelyplanet.fr
www.lonelyplanet.fr

World Wide Web: www.lonelyplanet.com *or* AOL keyword: lp
Lonely Planet Images: lpi@lonelyplanet.com.au